The Development and Education of the Mind

D0219854

In the World Library of Educationalists, international experts themselves compile career-long collections of what they judge to be their finest pieces – extracts from books, key articles, salient research findings, major theoretical and practical contributions – so the world can read them in a single manageable volume. Readers will be able to follow the themes and strands and see how their work contributes to the development of the field.

In this book American psychologist and educator Howard Gardner has assembled his most important writings about education. Spanning over 30 years, these papers reveal the thinking, the concepts, and the empirical research that have made Gardner one of the most respected and cited educational authorities of our time.

Trained originally as a psychologist at Harvard University, Gardner begins with personal sketches and tributes to his major teachers and mentors. He then presents the work for which he is best known – the theory of multiple intelligences; included is a summary of the original theory as well as accounts of how it has been updated over the years. Also included are seminal papers on the nature of understanding; education in the arts; powerful ways in which to assess learning; broad statements about the educational enterprise; and two accounts of how education is likely to evolve in the globalized world of the twenty-first century.

Following the tradition of John Dewey, Jean Piaget, and Jerome Bruner, Gardner views education as the optimal development of the mind. This volume illustrates how a broad and generous psychological perspective, drawing on other disciplines as well, can bring powerful insights to the processes of education.

Howard Gardner is the John H. and Elisabeth A. Hobbs Professor of Cognition and Education at the Harvard Graduate School of Education. He also holds positions as Adjunct Professor of Psychology at Harvard University and Senior Director of Harvard Project Zero.

Contributors to the series include: Richard Aldrich, Stephen J. Ball, James A. Banks, Jerome S. Bruner, Elliot W. Eisner, John Elliott, Howard Gardner, John K. Gilbert, Ivor F. Goodson, David Labaree, John White, Ted Wragg.

World Library of Educationalists series

Books in the series:

Lessons from History of Education
The selected works of Richard Aldrich
Richard Aldrich

Education Policy and Social Class
The selected works of Stephen J. Ball
Stephen J. Ball

Race, Culture, and Education
The selected works of James A. Banks
James A. Banks

In Search of Pedagogy: Volume I
The Selected Works of Jerome Bruner
1957-1978
Jerome S. Bruner

In Search of Pedagogy: Volume II
The Selected Works of Jerome Bruner
1979-2006
Jerome S. Bruner

Reimagining Schools
The selected works of Elliot W. Eisner
Elliot W. Eisner

Reflecting Where the Action Is
The selected works of John Elliott
John Elliott

The Development and Education of the Mind
The selected works of Howard Gardner
Howard Gardner

Constructing Worlds through Science Education
The selected works of John K. Gilbert
John K. Gilbert

Learning Curriculum and Life Politics
The selected works of Ivor Goodson
Ivor F. Goodson

Education, Markets, and the Public Good
The selected works of David Labaree
David Labaree

The Curriculum and the Child
The selected works of John White
John White

The Art and Science of Teaching and Learning
The selected works of Ted Wragg
E.C. Wragg

The Development and Education of the Mind

The selected works of Howard Gardner

Howard Gardner

Routledge
Taylor & Francis Group

LONDON AND NEW YORK

First published 2006
by Routledge
2 Park Square, Milton Park, Abingdon, Oxon OX14 4RN

Simultaneously published in the USA and Canada
by Routledge
270 Madison Avenue, New York, NY 10016

Routledge is an imprint of the Taylor & Francis Group

© 2006 Howard Gardner

Typeset in Sabon by
Taylor & Francis Books
Printed and bound in Great Britain by
Antony Rowe, Chippenham, Wiltshire

British Library Cataloguing in Publication Data
A catalogue record for this book is available from the British Library

Library of Congress Cataloging in Publication Data
Gardner, Howard.
  The development and education of the mind : the selected works of Howard Gardner
/ Howard Gardner.
     p. cm.
  Includes bibliographical references.
  ISBN 0-415-36728-X (pbk.) -- ISBN 0-415-36729-8 (hardback) 1. Education--
Philosophy. 2. Learning, Psychology of. 3. Multiple intelligences. I. Title.
  LB885.G37D48 2005

  370'.1--dc22

                          2005009320

ISBN10 0–415–36729–8   ISBN13 9-780-415-36729-8 (hbk)
ISBN10 0–415–36728–X   ISBN13 9-780-415-36728-X (pbk)

T&F informa

Taylor & Francis Group is the Academic Division of T&F Informa plc.

To James O. Freedman

Exemplary Leader, Beloved Friend
On the Occasion of his Seventieth Birthday

CONTENTS

ACKNOWLEDGMENTS

The following articles have been reproduced with the kind permission of the respective journals or publications

'Project Zero: Nelson Goodman's legacy in arts education', *Journal of Aesthetics and Art Criticism*, 2000, 58(3), 245–9.

'Developmental psychology after Piaget: an approach in terms of symbolization', *Human Development*, 1979, 22, 73–88.

'Beyond the IQ: Education and human development', *Harvard Education Review*, 1987, 57, 187–93.

'Multimedia and multiple intelligences', *The American Prospect*, November 1st, 1996, 7(29).

'Artistic intelligences', *Art Education*, 1983, 36(2), 47–9.

'Zero-based arts education: an introduction to ARTS PROPEL', *Studies in Art Education*, 30(2), 71–83. Reprinted in *The Journal of Art and Design Education*, 1989, 8, 167–82.

'The unschooled mind: why even the best students in the best schools may not understand', *IB World*, April 1993.

'Teaching for understanding in the disciplines – and beyond', *Teachers College Record*, 1994, 96(2), 198–218.

'Assessment in context: the alternative to standardized testing', Gifford, B.R. and M.C. O'Connor (eds), *Changing assessments: Alternative views of aptitude, achievement, and instruction*, 1991, 77–120.

'The age of innocence reconsidered: preserving the best of the progressive traditions in psychology and education', in Olson, D.R. and N. Torrance (eds.), *The handbook of education and human development: New models of learning, teaching and schooling*, 1996, 28–55.

The following articles have been reproduced with the kind permission of the respective publishers

'Howard Gardner: a biography', in Palmer, J.A and D. E. Cooper (eds), *Fifty Modern Thinkers on Education*, London: Routledge, 2001.

'Jerome S. Bruner as educator', in Palmer, J.A and D.E. Cooper (eds), *Fifty Modern Thinkers on Education*, London: Routledge, 2001.

'Norman Geschwind as a creative scientist', in Schacter, S. and O. Devinsky (eds), *Behavioral Neurology and the Legacy of Norman Geschwind*, Lippincott Williams and Wilkins, 1997.

'The key in the key slot: creativity in a Chinese key', in Gardner, H., *To Open Minds: Chinese Clues to the Dilemma of Contemporary Education*, Basic Books, 1989.

Chapter 1 is a re-edited version of two articles published by *The New York Times*: 'Getting acquainted with Jean Piaget', January 3, 1979; and 'Jean Piaget: The psychologist as Renaissance man', September 21, 1980.

INTRODUCTION

In the middle of the 20th century, young persons whom I knew dreamt about one day becoming astronauts, athletes, or architects. Some thought about becoming writers, a handful considered careers as teachers. I doubt that any contemporaries considered a career as a writer on education. Now, as I introduce a collection of my writings about education, I can spin an autobiography that logically culminates in this volume. And yet, that would be disingenuous.

A scholarly career is anything but a straight line – and that is all to the good. If one could predict a line of work in a discipline with accuracy, it would scarcely be worth carrying out: the surprises are what makes scholarship fun and serious. My own scholarly training has been in psychology. The two great figures in my field – Sigmund Freud and Jean Piaget – both embarked on careers quite different from that originally envisioned. Freud wanted to be a basic scientist in neurology and in fact, before turning to psychoanalysis, constructed a model of how the brain works. (It seems more plausible in 2005 than it did in 1905 or 1955!) Piaget saw himself as a biologist interested in the nature of knowledge. But as he subsequently pointed out, the "detour" that he took to investigate the minds of children lasted a lifetime. While I am under no illusion that my own contributions to psychology rival those of these and other masters, I too followed a career path quite different from that envisioned when I was attracted to psychology by my charismatic undergraduate tutor, Erik H. Erikson (who happened to be a student of Freud's and a colleague of Piaget's).

So, perhaps it is better to spurn autobiographical rationalizations and instead pose four questions about how best to "read" an individual who writes about education.

To begin with, through what disciplinary lens or lenses does the scholar approach educational issues? One approaches Herbert Read, a poet and art critic, quite differently from how one approaches the philosopher John Dewey, the psychologist B.F. Skinner, or the theologian John Henry Cardinal Newman. In my own case, I was trained in developmental psychology, the study of how children evolve in various spheres; cognitive psychology, the effort to model thinking; and neuropsychology, the examination of the effects of brain damage on human cognition and personality. While, among psychologists, I feel a bit of a renegade, I feel very much the psychologist when in the company of those with other disciplinary trainings. When considering human nature, I think almost reflexively in terms of the individual and especially his/her mind; the contributions of biology – neuroscience and genetics – to thought; the equally substantial contributions of parental models, peer examples, teacher input, and the messages that waft thought the culture.

To this scholarly lineage I should add my long-time interest in artistry and artistic cognition. As a child I was a serious pianist, and I have long gained sustenance from involvement with the arts. When I first became a psychologist, I was amazed at the virtual absence in American textbooks of consideration of artistic development and artistic cognition. And so I determined to give as much attention to artistic considerations as most other psychologists direct toward the scientific terrain. As you read my writings, you will discover artistic concerns and leitmotifs throughout.

The second question to raise concerns the personal educational experiences of the writer. It has long been noted that almost everyone has strong opinions about education because all of us have had years of experience in schools. As I reflect on my own education, I note the following chapters.

As a young person in the 1950s, I attended public schools in the small city of Scranton, Pennsylvania. The schools were adequate but certainly undistinguished. I found school unchallenging and learned more through my own wide but haphazard reading and my interaction with a few intellectually oriented peers and a handful of relatives and other adults who took an interest in a talkative and curious young student. More consequential was my own training as a young pianist, training which revealed considerable talent but which I abruptly terminated when but 12 years of age. (I did not want to practice the three hours a day mandated by my teacher.) During my freshman year in public high school I continued to be unchallenged and so decided, with my family, that I should attend an independent school. Nearby Wyoming Seminary was somewhat more intellectually oriented but still insufficiently demanding. Only when I was fortunate enough to attend Harvard College in the early 1960s did I discover what a truly engaging intellectual environment could be like. And that is probably why I have remained at Harvard for 45 years.

Personally, then, my educational experiences ranged from the unremarkable to the privileged. However, other educational experiences have had powerful effects on me. Directly upon completion of college, I had the privilege of working with the psychologist-turned-educator Jerome Bruner on the development of a model elementary school curriculum in the social sciences called "Man: A Course of Study." This curriculum treated fifth graders as active thinkers who could appreciate key insights from the range of the human sciences, from anthropology to linguistics to psychology. While clearly directed toward the "high end" of the market, this curriculum made a deep impression on me. Given that my first wife Judy Gardner and I had both worked for Bruner, it is perhaps not surprising that we decided to send our three children to the Shady Hill School in Cambridge, Massachusetts, at the time one of the outstanding examples of progressive education in the United States. I also became fascinated with the "open classroom" method that had developed in Leicestershire in the 1960s and taught for a semester in an "open classroom" in Newton, Massachusetts. Finally, I must mention my 20-year relationship to the preschools in Reggio Emilia, Italy, to my mind the most impressive demonstration of how even three- and four-year-olds can become intellectually engaged with challenging puzzles and ideas.

Looking back over these personal experiences as a growing child, and the signal exposures during my adult years, it is clear that I reject most of my own formal education as a child, while embracing the more intellectually demanding and personally challenging regime of progressive education. I agree with those educational analysts who assert that the best education is a progressive education; alas, as some also point out, when progressive education is not done well, it can be a disaster, leaving the child with little knowledge, little discipline, and a veiled contempt for what passes as education.

A third question has to do with the general value system of the writer. As already suggested, I am sympathetic to the progressive view of human nature as put forth variously in the writings of Jean-Jacques Rousseau, John Dewey, Jean Piaget, and Jerome Bruner. In contrast to a Lockean view of the child as a blank slate, a Skinnerian view of the child as an actor who must be molded, or a traditionalist view of the child as an inheritor of the best thought of the past and a skepticism vis-à-vis the present and the future, I favor a far more open-ended view of learning. Children have enormous potentials, these potentials should be broadly nurtured, but we should avoid didacticism or excessive guidance. And while there should of course be the transmission of cultural knowledge, I believe that the questions that one learns to ask are ultimately more important than the answers that are passed on from one generation to the other.

At the same time, however, I do not believe that education is easy or natural. In that sense, I depart from the friendlier voices in the progressive tradition. The primary purpose of education should be the inculcation in young minds of the major disciplinary ways of thinking. These turn out to be deeply counterintuitive. And so the educator is challenged to determine how best to counter commonsense views, which are often common nonsense; and how to develop habits of thought – such as those of science, art, mathematics, history – which took centuries to evolve to the current still-tentative form.

This amalgamation of values makes it difficult to pigeonhole me – at least for me! The educational liberals who resonate with my ideas about individual differences are often nonplused or annoyed by my focus on the development of disciplinary thought. And traditionalists who like the focus on disciplines cannot abide my interest in open-ended questions and in the many ways in which a child can be taught or assessed.

A final question to ask of an educational writer concerns his actual writings and the initial reactions to them. Since I have already suggested that most individuals do not hanker to be educational writers, it is important to know what *were* the first writings. In my case, while I had taught both young children and piano and was a researcher at a school of education, I published almost nothing in education until I was 40. My book *Frames of Mind: The Theory of Multiple Intelligences* was a psychological study, aimed primarily at my psychological colleagues. The few educational passages were included primarily because the funder of the study had a strong interest in educational questions.

No one was more surprised than I at the enormous interest elicited by this work, first manifest in the United States, and then, over the next two decades, in many other parts of the world. From being a psychologist who addressed his writings to those in developmental psychology, cognitive psychology, neuropsychology, and – to a limited extent – to the general public, I was instantly converted into a writer – and, indeed, treated as an expert – on educational issues.

Conceivably, I could have ignored this "reaction of the field" and returned to my psychologist's silo. I did not, however. I imagine that my conversion into a writer about education had a number of causes: 1) the fact that I had always had an interest in educational issues, dating back to childhood, and had worked with Jerome Bruner, himself a psychologist who was esteemed by educators; 2) my long-time association with Project Zero, a research group that has always been housed in the Harvard Graduate School of Education; 3) the fact that my book was published in the very year that the famous critique of American education, *A Nation at Risk*, was issued, and that educational issues soon moved to the front burner of policymakers and the public, where it has remained ever since; and 4) not least, the great interest in my work shown by educators. I was showered with attention, asked many good questions, given the support to pursue some of them empirically, and, with little hesitation, I took on these challenges.

On the subject of writing, let me add a reflection on my own writing. I began my scholarly life as an historian and, more than most psychologists, I tend to think of issues in terms of historical determinants and context – perhaps that is why I became a developmental psychologist! I like to read and study widely, and so my writings are more inter-disciplinary than those of most psychologists: you will find here abundant references to the natural sciences, the arts, and the humanities. While it remains for others to critique my writing, from my own perspective my greatest strengths are as a systematizer and a synthesizer. I raise a question – the nature of artistic cognition, the component of intelligence, what it means to understand – read and think widely about the question, and then put forth my own best taxonomy or mosaic or narrative. Much of my early writing put together the work of others; but with the passage of years, I have developed my own strong views and my own (I hope not strident) voice. It will be interesting to see whether readers also discern the shift from Gardner the synthesizer to Gardner the theorizer and occasional provocateur.

While rejecting the presentation of a strict autobiographical account of "how I got here," I have sought to provide information which should help readers understand "where I am coming from." (For those interested in autobiography, I have listed several sources.) In addition, to guide the reader through this collection of papers, I offer a rational account, or at least a rationale, for the selection.

I begin this collection with a set of tributes to the thinkers who had the greatest influence during my intellectual formation. The psychologist Jean Piaget is the giant in my original field of scholarship; like all other cognitive-developmental psychologists, I owe my greatest debt to him. The other three individuals are all persons with whom I had the privilege of working personally. My interests and background are closest to those of Jerome Bruner, and it is probably the case that my career has been more closely modeled after his luminous example than after anyone else's. I was greatly informed – indeed, formed – by the philosophical thinking of Nelson Goodman, the brilliant thinker who started Project Zero; and I was stretched in new and unanticipated ways by my work with Norman Geschwind, an innovative conceptualizer and a keen observer of patients with revealing neurological conditions.

Work with these thinkers led me to pursue two parallel lines of research – one with children, the other with brain-injured adults. This work was rewarding in itself and I believe that I made contributions to the research literatures on children's cognitive development and on the breakdown of cognitive capacities after damage to the brain. Much of this work was carried out with Ellen Winner, whom I had the good fortune to marry in 1982. In the final chapter in this section, written in the late 1970s, I both delineate the reservations that I was developing about the work of Jean Piaget and the synthesis about the nature of human symbolization that I was formulating.

In the next part of the book, I put forth the major claims of the theory of multiple intelligences, the work for which I am best known. The six chapters encompass, respectively, a brief introduction to the theory; a critique of the major misconceptions that I have encountered; a consideration of the political aspects entailed in writing about a topic like intelligence; a proposal of how media can be mobilized to take advantage of our multiple intelligences (MI); my changing views about how best to define intelligence; and a survey of the "MI field" after the first two decades.

My work with Nelson Goodman at Project Zero centered on the nature of artistic cognition and artistic education. Indeed, both my work with children and my work with brain-damaged adults was firmly rooted in artistic cognition. The first three chapters in Part 2 portray, in turn, the relationship between artistry and intelligence; an educational approach to curriculum and assessment called ARTS PROPEL; and a museum exhibit that had remarkable educational power. The final chapter grew out of a series of trips that I made to China in the 1980s in my capacity as an arts educator. My observations and informal experiments (carried out with Ellen Winner) teased out fundamental differences in how our respective cultures think of arts and creativity – and also complexified in instructive ways my own views about the development of creativity.

Upon first learning about multiple intelligences, many individuals see an MI classroom or school as an end in itself. I soon became convinced, however, that MI cannot be a viable educational end. Rather, the goals of education need to arise from our own values, and they need to be stated explicitly and revisited perennially. Once the territory has been staked out, then it becomes possible to determine how a recognition of MI might – or might not – aid in achieving these educational goals.

Once I began to ponder my own educational philosophy, I became convinced of a supravening educational goal: the development of thinking within the major scholarly disciplines. Of course schools can properly pursue more than one goal. But, to my own mind, if education does not inculcate the major disciplinary ways of thinking, then it has failed in a fundamental way. In the fourth part of this book, I delineate my conception of disciplinary understanding; how difficult it is to achieve; and how, once that goal has been set forth, an approach founded on MI can prove productive.

With the passage of time, the accumulation of age, and, one hopes, the achievement of some measure of wisdom, scholars like me are called upon to offer their more general conspectus of education. In the fifth and final part of the book, I put forth my current – though I dare to hope not my final – thoughts about some broad educational issues. I begin by sketching a view of assessment that is far different from the one currently being pursued not only in the United States but in much of the world. Written in the early 1990s, I believe that "assessment in context" is even more timely and more needed now than it was then.

The next three chapters in the book deal, respectively, with the progressive tradition, in whose camp – despite some lapses – I have remained; the ways in which education changes over time, with particular respect to the theme of globalization; and a possible outline of education in the future. The final chapter in the book presents a bridge from my 20 years of writing on education to my current concern with ethics in the professions – a study that my colleagues and I call the "good work project." While the work on professional ethics is not at present rooted in education, we expect that the ultimate result of the study will include educational interventions for young persons, individuals beginning the professions, and veterans who want or need a refresher on the core values of their profession. Just as I have come to believe that all educational issues harbor value components, I also believe that the inculcation of values is fundamentally an educational challenge – one that never ends for the individual or the species.

To the extent possible, I have ordered these chapters so as to convey a coherent, cumulative story. Indeed, one could read the book from beginning to end – though I doubt that many will find that the best way to approach the book. In lieu of my own autobiographical account, which is now available in many places (Gardner 1989b, Chapters 1 to 4; Gardner, in press; Gardner, n.d.; Winner, n.d.), I am pleased to open the volume with a brief biography of me, written by Mindy Kornhaber, a long-time colleague and friend.

I have written a great deal, though I hope that I can escape the dismissive label "no unpublished thought." Indeed, by my calculation, I have authored or co-authored at least 20 books, 400 articles, and 150 topical articles and reviews, about half of them on education. Clearly, with a 130,000 word limit, I have had to be quite selective! I elected not to quote from any of my books, to update passages that were clearly anachronistic, to correct errors, and, to the extent possible, to eliminate passages that are clearly redundant; in such cases, I refer readers to a chapter or chapters that cover essentially the same ground as the eliminated material. That said, I have permitted a limited amount of repetition or paraphrase, so that each chapter can be read as self-standing. In lieu of separate bibliographies, I have amassed all references into a single master bibliography.

It remains for me to thank the colleagues who have explicitly given me permission to reproduce material that we have co-authored: Veronica Boix-Mansilla, Thomas Hatch, Mindy Kornhaber, Shirley Veenema; and several other long-term colleagues, including Mihaly Csikszentmihalyi, William Damon, David Perkins, Ellen Winner, and Edgar Zurif;

my colleagues over the years at the Boston Veterans Administration Medical Center; Harvard Project Zero; and the GoodWork Project; Anna Clarkson, Marianne Bulman and Kerry Maciak from Taylor & Francis, who solicited this volume and aided with its preparation; and, most especially, my assistant Lindsay Pettingill, who cheerfully and expertly handled all of the tasks that I could conceivably give her.

In the current environment, it is impossible for an empirically oriented researcher to proceed without generous funding from public and private sources. At the conclusion of this introduction, I have provided a cumulative list of my funders over the years. But I must single out for special appreciation three foundations – the Atlantic Philanthropies, the Hewlett Foundation, and the Spencer Foundation – for their many years of flexible support. And I must single out six individuals – Jeffrey Epstein, Tom Lee, Ann Tenenbaum, Louise Rosenberg, Claude Rosenberg, and Courtney Ross – for the support of research and their valued friendship.

March 15, 2005

List of funders

The Atlantic Philanthropies
The Bauman Foundation
The Bryant Foundation
The Carnegie Corporation
The Nathan Cummings Foundation
The Fetzer Institute
The Ford Foundation
The W. T. Grant Foundation
The William and Flora Hewlett Foundation
The Christian Johnson Endeavor Foundation
The Lilly Endowment
The John D. and Catherine T. MacArthur Foundation
The Markle Foundation
The James S. McDonnell Foundation
The National Institute of Education
The National Institute of Health
The National Science Foundation
The Pew Charitable Trusts
The Rockefeller Brothers Foundation
The Rockefeller Foundation
The Sloan Foundation
The Spencer Fouindation
The John Templeton Foundation
The Bernard van Leer Foundation
The Veterans Administration

HOWARD GARDNER
A biography

Mindy Kornhaber

Palmer, J.A and D.E. Cooper (eds), *Fifty Modern Thinkers on Education*. London: Routledge, 2001.

> Education must ultimately justify itself in terms of enhancing human understanding.
>
> (Gardner, 1999, p. 178)

Howard Gardner, one of the best-known thinkers in education in the United States at the turn of the millennium, did not seem destined to take up this role. In fact, he published six books and over 100 scholarly articles in cognitive development and neuropsychology prior to gaining much recognition from educators in the field of researchers outside the realm of arts education. His seventh book, Frames of Mind: The Theory of Multiple Intelligences (1983), was not a book that focused on education. In fact, it contained only two pages directly bearing on the application of his MI theory to educational practice. Yet, it is this book, now translated into more than a dozen languages, that has placed Gardner at the center of educational theory and practice in the United States and established for him a prominent role worldwide.

An exploration of Gardner's life and work prior to Frames of Mind, and his intellectual pursuits thereafter, helps to explain Gardner's enormous impact.

Gardner was born in Scranton, Pennsylvania in 1943 to parents who had fled, penniless, from Nazi Germany. His parents had lost a talented first son in a childhood sledding accident at age eight, just prior to Gardner's birth. This fact, along with the horrors of the Holocaust, went undiscussed in Gardner's childhood. Nevertheless, these events "were to exert long-lasting effects on my development and my thinking" (Gardner, 1989b, p. 22). Young Gardner's exposure to activities that might engender physical harm – bicycling and rough sports – were reigned in, even as his early proclivities in music, reading, and writing were eagerly nurtured. As Gardner gradually became aware of these unspoken influences, he recognized that, as the eldest surviving son in his extended family, he was expected to make his mark in this new country. And yet, even before adolescence, Gardner recognized the obstacles to doing so. He knew that other Jewish thinkers of German and Austrian origins – Einstein, Freud, Marx, Mahler – "had lived in the intellectual centers of Europe, and had studied and competed with the leading figures of their generation [while] I had been cast into an uninteresting, intellectually stagnant, and economically depressed Pennsylvania valley" (1989b, p. 23).

Gardner's time in the outpost of Scranton did not last terribly long. He was sent to board at a nearby prep school, at which nurturing teachers showed him great attention. From there it was off to Harvard University in 1961, where he has thus far spent all but two of his ensuing years.

Gardner entered Harvard planning to study history in preparation for a law career. His undergraduate years saw encounters with several of the leading thinkers of the day, but it was his tutor, Erik Erikson, the charismatic psychoanalyst and scholar of development over the lifespan, who "probably sealed my ambition to be a scholar" (Gardner, 1989b, p. 47).

Immediately after graduation, Gardner began working for Jerome Bruner, a cognitive and educational psychologist. Bruner's influence was marked. He was "the perfect career model" (Gardner, 1989b, p. 56). Gardner, in this volume, traces his ultimate attraction to education to Bruner's 1960 book The Process of Education and also to his work on Bruner's curriculum development project "Man: A Course of Study." The curriculum addressed three "mind-opening questions" (Gardner, 1989b, p. 50): "What makes human beings human? How did they get that way? How could they be made more so?" These questions echo in Gardner's own work. Gardner's investigations of human cognition address in part the first of Bruner's questions. Gardner's research on the development of symbol systems may be seen as a response to the second. And his most recent research, which seeks to examine how people operate both brilliantly and humanely, can be seen as inspired by the last.

Gardner's experimental work in human cognition was inspired by his exposure to the work of Jean Piaget during the Bruner project. Piaget's elegant experiments appealed to Gardner's keenly logical mind. At the same time, Gardner recognized that Piaget's stage theory of human development was inadequate. Central to Piaget's work was a conception of the child as an incipient scientist. But Gardner's early musical education, as well as his fascination with all other art forms, indicated that the scientist did not necessarily exemplify the highest form of human cognition. What it meant to be "developed" needed to be informed by attention to the skills and capacities of painters, writers, musicians, dancers, and other artists: "Stimulated (rather than intimidated) by the prospect of broadening the definition of cognition, I found it comfortable to deem the capacities of those in the arts as fully cognitive – no less cognitive than the skills of mathematicians and scientists, as viewed by my fellow developmentalists" (Gardner, 1999, p. 28).

Gardner entered graduate school with an interest in creativity and cognition in the arts, a line of research for which there were no real mentors within the psychology department faculty. His opportunity to pursue this work came in 1967 when the philosopher Nelson Goodman formed Harvard Project Zero, a research group that was intended to strengthen arts education. Through the remainder of his graduate education to the present day, Project Zero has been at the center of Gardner's intellectual life. It has "been the site where my own ideas have developed and the intellectual community in which I have felt especially at home" (Gardner, 1989b, p. 65). Since 1971, when Goodman retired, Project Zero has been under the stewardship of Gardner and his long-time colleague, David Perkins. The organization has grown into one of the leading centers for educational research in the United States. During these years Gardner has mentored scores of young researchers, and the organization has grown from examining cognition in the arts to investigating learning, thinking, and creativity across the range of disciplines, age groups, and educational settings.

At Project Zero Gardner initially pursued studies of children's development in the visual arts, music, and figurative language. Although he also explored the creative processes of adult artists, he was especially concerned with children's development of symbol systems as they are used in the arts. He studied these topics empirically by adapting Piagetian methods to explore the development of children's reasoning with artistic symbol systems. During the 1970s and early 1980s this line of research yielded some forty articles and book chapters. These addressed such issues as children's sensitivity to style in drawings (e.g., Gardner, 1970, 1971, 1972; Gardner and Gardner, 1970; Gardner and Gardner, 1973); their use of figurative language (e.g., Gardner, 1974a; Gardner, Kircher, Winner, and Perkins, 1975; Gardner, Winner, Bechhofer, and Wolf, 1978); and the development of artistry (e.g., Gardner, 1976, 1979; Gardner, Wolf, and Smith, 1975; Wolf and Gardner, 1980).

In an effort to understand how the brain processed different symbol systems, in 1969 Project Zero invited Norman Geschwind, an eminent neurologist, to speak about his work. Geschwind's studies of symbol use and breakdown in brain-damaged patients was "riveting" (Gardner, 1989b, p. 83). Very shortly thereafter, Gardner began conducting empirical work in neuropsychology at the Boston Veterans' Administration Hospital. Over the next two decades he published more than sixty articles and book chapters focused largely on symbol processing in individuals, often-times artists, who have suffered brain injury (e.g., Gardner, 1982b; Gardner, Silverman, Denes, Semenza, and Rosenstiel, 1977; Gardner and Winner, 1981).

These dual lines of empirical research converged on a single compelling point. As Gardner wrote, "the daily opportunity to work with children and with brain-damaged adults impressed me with one brute fact of human nature: people have a wide range of capacities. A person's strength in one area of performance simply does not predict any comparable strengths in other areas" (Gardner, 1999, p. 30).

By the mid-1970s Gardner began to construct a theory of human cognition that ran counter both to Piagetian theory, with its pre-eminent scientist, and to psycho-metric theory, with its keystone of general intelligence or "g." In Gardner's model, the full possibilities of human thinking and accomplishment might be explained. The opportunity to develop this theory was realized during the early 1980s, while Gardner was a leading member in the Project on Human Potential. This project was devised and funded by the Bernard van Leer Foundation "to assess the state of scientific knowledge concerning human potential and its realization" (Gardner, 1985b, p. xix). Gardner's product for the project was his groundbreaking book Frames of Mind, in which he spelled out his theory of MI.

Gardner's theory, unlike those generated by traditional psychometric methods, was not a response to the implicit question: What are the cognitive abilities underlying a good IQ test score? Instead, MI was Gardner's response to the explicit question: What are the cognitive abilities that ultimately enable human beings to perform the range of adult roles (or "end states") found across cultures? (Gardner, 1983).

To get at this question, Gardner scoured a wide range of scientific and social-science literatures for candidate intelligences. He maintained that candidate intelligences should meet most, if not all, of eight criteria that he had developed. An intelligence should be found in isolation among brain-damaged individuals. It should also be seen in relative isolation in prodigies, autistic savants, or other exceptional populations. An intelligence ought to have a distinct developmental trajectory. (For instance, the rate of development from infancy to adult expert is not identical for music, language, or interpersonal abilities.) Gardner also claimed that an intelligence should be plausible from the perspective of evolutionary biology. That is, it would be needed for survival in human ancestors and evident in other mammals. In addition, an intelligence should be encodable in symbol systems. Two additional criteria are that an intelligence should be supported not only by psychometric tests but also by evidence from experimental psychological tasks.

Finally, an intelligence should demonstrate a core set of processing operations, such as pitch detection in music or syntax in language, which are stimulated by information relevant to that intelligence.

Using these criteria, Gardner ultimately identified eight relatively autonomous intelligences: linguistic, logical-mathematical, spatial, musical, bodily-kinesthetic, interpersonal, intrapersonal, and naturalist (Gardner, 1983, 1995b). The latter enables human beings to recognize, categorize, and draw upon features of the environment. Gardner has also noted that additional intelligences may be added, if they meet most of his criteria. The number of intelligences is less important than that there is a multiplicity of them and that each human being has a unique mix (or "profile") of strengths and weaknesses in the intelligences.

While academic psychology has remained lukewarm to the theory (e.g., Herrnstein and Murray, 1994; Scarr, 1985), for educators MI holds enormous appeal. The theory has been widely embraced by teachers throughout North America, South America, and Australia, and in parts of Europe and Asia. It has been applied at all levels of education, from preschool through adult education. It has been used across academic disciplines and in vocational education, and it has found a home in classrooms serving largely typical students as well as those serving the learning disabled or gifted.

There are several reasons why MI has taken hold in education. Among these are that the theory validates educators' everyday experience; students think and learn in many different ways. It also provides educators with a conceptual framework for organizing and reflecting on curriculum, assessment, and pedagogical practices. In turn, this reflection has led many educators to develop new approaches that might better meet the needs of the range of learners in their classrooms (Kornhaber, 1999).

While the educational applications of Gardner's theory are widespread, the quality of these applications has ranged wildly. Because Frames of Mind did not spell out how to apply the theory, teachers, administrators, and numerous independent consultants brought their own ideas to this problem. While some of these appear to enable children's development and understanding of the disciplines, many others simply require that every topic be addressed in seven or eight – oftentimes superficial – ways. The unevenness of the theory's application has led simultaneously to the theory's praise (Knox, 1995; Woo, 1995) and damnation (Collins, 1998; Traub, 1998).

While Gardner recognized the variability in MI applications, he initially felt that it was beyond his sphere, as a theorist and psychologist, to right this situation. Instead, he focused on generating compelling new ideas in the areas of educational assessment (e.g., Gardner, 1991a; Krechevsky and Gardner, 1990; Wexler-Sherman, Gardner, and Feldman, 1988), the development of disciplinary understanding (e.g., Gardner and Boix-Mansilla, 1994a, 1994b; Gardner, 1993a), and creativity (e.g., Gardner, 1993b, 1994; Li and Gardner, 1993). However, he began to take on the task of guiding educational applications of MI in his book The Unschooled Mind (Gardner, 1991c), and more explicitly in Intelligence Reframed (Gardner, 1999) and The Disciplined Mind (Gardner, 2000).

Each of these books underscores Gardner's belief that education's central mission should be the development of understanding. Such understanding is marked by performances in which students take knowledge gleaned in a particular setting and apply it to an unfamiliar problem or setting (Gardner, 1991c). For this to happen, educators must opt for depth over breadth (Gardner, 2000); students must have extended opportunities to work on a topic. Gardner asserts that having opportunities to represent and explore a given topic in many ways, in part by engaging a range of intelligences, makes it more likely that students will be able to apply what they learn in new settings. Recent research undertaken at Project Zero provides some evidence for this (Kornhaber, 1999; Kornhaber, Fierros, and Veenema, 2004).

"[M]y educational vision should be clear. Deep understanding should be our central goal; we should strive to inculcate understanding of what, within a cultural context, is considered true or false, beautiful or unpalatable, good or evil" (Gardner, 2000, p. 186). These themes "motivate individuals to learn about and understand their world" (2000, p. 24). Gardner's views about understanding stand at odds with the contemporary American trend to harness classroom instruction to broad, excessively detailed, and state-mandated curriculum frameworks. It is nevertheless a vision that is well grounded in the traditions of Socrates, John Dewey, and John Henry Cardinal Newman. It is also shaped by empirical understanding of cognition, as well as the reality that modern educational systems reside within increasingly multi-ethnic and technologically driven societies.

For at least a decade Gardner has emphasized that educators must inculcate understanding in the disciplines, which he regards as among the key inventions of humankind. However, crucial as disciplinary understanding is, it has become clear to Gardner that education must aim for something more than this. The "task for the new millennium" is to "figure out how intelligence and morality can work together to create a world in which a great variety of people will want to live. After all, a society led by 'smart' people still might blow up itself or the rest of the world" (Gardner, 1999, p. 4). In line with this task, in 1994 Gardner and his colleagues Mihaly Csikszentmihalyi and William Damon established the "Good Work Project." The ultimate goal of the project is to identify how individuals at the cutting edge of their professions can carry out work that is exemplary, according to professional standards, and yet also contributes to the good of the wider society. By infusing the findings from this project into educational settings, it may be possible to enhance the disciplinary as well as the humanitarian performances of ensuing generations. It is a hope, and a research project, which Gardner plans to pursue for many years to come.

Acknowledgment

Reprinted with permission of the author. Copyright © 2001.

PART 1

INFLUENCES

THE PATHBREAKING WORK OF JEAN PIAGET

This chapter is a re-edited version of two articles published by *The New York Times*: 'Getting acquainted with Jean Piaget', January 3, 1979; and 'Jean Piaget: The psychologist as Renaissance man', September 21, 1980.

At the age of 21, Jean Piaget, the renowned student of human development, wrote a prescient work entitled *Recherche* (Exploration). In this personal journal, presented in the form of a novel, the hero Sebastian resolves an adolescent religious crisis by adopting an "unshakable faith" in science. Inspired by his studies in biology, Sebastian dreams of "a course synthesizing the sciences of life" with a privileged niche for psychology and the theory of knowledge. Through his fictional shadow, Piaget explored for the first time the possibilities of a biological explanation of mental processes, even introducing equilibration – his fundamental mechanism for explaining cognitive changes.

When *Recherche* was published the following year in 1918, Piaget was a precocious young biologist who had already made a name for himself as an investigator of terrestrial and aquatic mollusks. But shortly thereafter, inspired by the dream of a biological account of human knowledge, Piaget made an epochal career shift from malacology to the still fledgling field of psychology. Using the simple technique of asking children questions and analyzing their errors, Piaget launched the research on children's thought processes which made him famous while still in his twenties and the pre-eminent psychologist at the time of his death.

In charting the minds of children, Piaget invented the field of cognitive development. Those who wish to understand Piaget's contributions must therefore engage the problems that he set for himself in the early 1920s. What do children know at birth? What mechanisms are at their disposal to acquire new knowledge? What forms of knowledge do they possess at various stages in childhood? And how can one describe the knowledge of the mature adult?

Spurning the once widespread notion that the child's mind is simply a miniature version of the adult's, Piaget's major contribution was to describe the forms of knowledge characteristic at each stage of development. Over many years, he carried out hundreds of clever experiments with youngsters in Geneva, Switzerland; he reported them in an imposing series of monographs, several featuring his own three children. Many of the studies probed specific forms of knowledge – the child's conception of number, of space, of causality – but, taken together, they yield a general picture of the child's mind at key points during childhood.

The general public thought of Piaget solely as a child psychologist who illuminated the ways in which children's thinking differs from that of adults. With Sigmund Freud and B.F. Skinner, he stood among the most influential figures in twentieth-century psychology. If his difficult writing style and lack of concern with the emotional side of human nature made him less of a household name than the other two scholars, his position within the mainstream of contemporary psychology is perhaps more secure. And his focus on cognition seems more attuned to the future course of psychology than Skinner's concern with overt behavior or Freud's preoccupations with motivation, personality, and the unconscious.

But Piaget did not consider himself a psychologist. A biologist by training and a synthetic thinker by inclination, Piaget viewed himself as founder of a new field of knowledge – that of genetic epistemology. The goal of this field was to illuminate the nature of the basic categories of scientific thought, through study of the origins (or genesis) of this knowledge. The task was inherently inter-disciplinary and Piaget labored for decades, first alone and later with colleagues, in an effort to lay out the core aspects of our conceptions of number, logic, space, time, causality, and other building blocks of knowledge. Key to this effort were experts from each field of science as well as genetic psychologists: experimental researchers trained by Piaget to uncover the origins and developments of basic scientific concepts in the young child. Also part of the research team were philosophers, who defined the concepts, and historians of science, who chronicled the growth of knowledge over the centuries within each scientific field. When the insights from this team of scholars were put together, they would yield the fullest possible account of the particular scientific concept in question.

No one can question the grandeur – or the hubris – of this undertaking. Piaget sought no less than a great chain of mental being, which proceeded from the elementary functioning of genes and nerve cells, through the actions of young children upon the physical objects of the world, to the internal operations of thought in the minds of normal adults and innovative scientists, a chain which culminated in fundamental changes in the structure of science. How matter could give rise to new – and valid – ideas: this was Piaget's guiding passion, one as synoptic as those of Freud and Skinner and, indeed, reminiscent of the vision of the greatest thinkers of the past.

While many others might have doubted the feasibility of this enterprise, both from a scientific and philosophical point of view, Piaget kept any misgivings under control, set up his experiments, and forged ahead. Displaying the discipline, energy, and organizational capacity associated with genius, he produced dozens of books and countless papers, revisiting the same core patterns in the light of his most recent findings. In the middle 1950s he founded an International Center of Genetic Epistemology, and, aided by an energetic group of students and collaborators, raced until the end against time to sketch out the principal lines of his vision. And it seems to me that it is in the light of this vision – first fathomed as a teenager and never deviated from thereafter – that Jean Piaget would wish to be assessed.

But such an undertaking is far too vast for most contemporary scientists and so the bulk of commentary on Piaget has focused on his work in developmental psychology. In assessing how the program of 1920 stands up in the purview of 1980, psychologists have focused on three dimensions: the robustness of the empirical phenomena first described by Piaget; the cogency of the key theoretical concepts by which he explained these phenomena; and the viability of his overall image of the mind of the child.

In his capacity to perceive new and important phenomena through the observation of children (including his own), Piaget remains without peer. Essentially working without technical apparatus, he exhibited a respect for his subject, and an empathy for his subjects, which permitted him to enter totally into children's own views of the world. Many initially skeptical scientists have eventually attested to the existence of the phenomena of non-conservation, where preschool children refuse to believe that matter can change its form and still remain the same quantity; childhood egocentrism, where youngsters are unable to conceive how the world looks to other observers; the impermanence of objects, where infants act as if objects fail to exist when they are no longer in sight. These and dozens of other equally intriguing phenomena now form the mainstay of research in cognitive development. To be sure, it is often possible to discover the roots of these behaviors at an earlier time than Piaget claimed, particularly if the tasks are "stripped down" to their essentials. But, surviving the acid test of scientific validity, the fundamental phenomena continue to be confirmed.

Piaget's terminology and concepts have survived less intact. Many suffer from imprecise or shifting definitions. The stages and structures in which he so firmly believed have been consistently attacked and, while they retain their suggestive quality, cognitive development is now seen as smoother, less stage-like, and less structurally integrated than Piaget had indicated. Piaget's lifelong attempt to explain the causes of intellectual change through the mechanism of equilibration has had comparatively little influence and, though Piaget would have winced at the thought, his embracing of biological terminology has had for others a Lamarckian and even, at times, a Bergsonian air about it.

If Piaget's "middle-level" concepts have not fared well, his overall model of the child as an active problem-solver – a hypothesis-testing scientist in his knickers – has carried the day. Piaget not only put the serious study of the child on the scientific map, but also moved the child's cognitive powers to the forefront, where they have firmly remained. His sense of what the child is like suffuses the writings of even his harshest critics. In the manner permitted only to the most revolutionary scientists, he changed the way in which future researchers will undertake their studies.

To be sure, there have been shifts in the temper of child study, shifts which left Piaget at the end as a bit of an anachronistic figure. The biological metaphor which he cultivated was increasingly replaced by the metaphor of the computer; his careful descriptions of behaviors were supplanted by series of boxes which detail hypothetical "stages of information processing." And the areas of the child's life which he underplayed – the child's personality, his social and affective life, his artistic gifts – have become, mostly by virtue of the fact that Piaget had not already addressed the major issues, rallying grounds for contemporary students of child development. By what he ignored, as much as by what he illuminated, Piaget set the research agenda for the field which he brought to life. His contribution continues to dominate the texts of child study and, in more than a few cases, Piaget *is* the text.

But what had kept thousands of psychologists throughout the world busy for over a generation was still but a chapter in the book of science that Piaget was writing since the time of *Recherche*. As has happened with other lifelong efforts in the behavioral sciences – and particularly ones as self-avowedly inter-disciplinary – few individuals can even read the entire corpus, let alone evaluate it. In an age of fragmented specialization, Piaget was indubitably a Renaissance man. Nowhere is this more poignantly evident than in *Logic and Scientific Knowledge*, an encyclopedic tome that he planned, edited, and largely wrote, and which surveyed all of the sciences from the perspective of genetic epistemology. To prepare for this massive work, Piaget held seminars with experts from every field of knowledge, often collaborating with them for upwards of a year, rose early each morning and stayed awake evenings tutoring himself in the disciplines of that year, and ultimately mastered at least the basic conceptual issues in each. Undertaking such assignments of synthesis was Piaget's method of bridging his own science with every other one.

Indeed, it was his way of pursuing his own religion – the passion for truth, the search for the totality of knowledge.

But this Herculean effort has as yet had little impact. An encyclopedia largely from the hand of one man, no matter how brilliant, seems a throwback to a Johnsonian age. The flaws are too evident. Piaget did not have the necessary first-hand familiarity with the phenomena of other sciences, nor the sympathy with the history and cultural background of other disciplines, nor the sophistication in the philosophical analysis of concepts, which he had for the snails and children of Geneva. Yet what slips through in the 1,250 odd pages is the sense of wonder and exploration which gives rise to knowledge. Till the end, the child – and the adolescent – in Piaget were never stilled. Like Sigmund Freud, he was by temperament a passionate speculator and integrator, who sought ruthlessly to suppress his speculative nature, but – fortunately – never wholly succeeded in doing so.

As with Freud, portions of Piaget's research program and many of his particular concepts will be – and in cases already have been – supplanted by less problematic formulations. Yet the central core of the program – Piaget's portrait of the mind of the child – is as likely to last as Freud's insights into the human personality. Just as Freud extended our knowledge of human nature as it had previously inhered in literature and in clinical medicine, Piaget advanced our understanding of the mind, not only as it had been set forth by his psychological predecessors, but also, and perhaps especially, as it had been elucidated by Descartes and Kant. Though not by contemporary standards a philosopher, he was a philosopher in the traditional sense of the term, and far more than any contemporary psychologist, he wrote works which philosophers of the future will have to examine carefully. Alone among his contemporaries, he took the great epistemological issues seriously and contrived new ways of approaching them. The vision of youthful Sebastian will endure.

Acknowledgment

Copyright © 2005 by the New York Times Co. Reprinted with Permission.

CHAPTER 2

JEROME S. BRUNER AS EDUCATOR

Palmer, J.A and D.E. Cooper (eds), *Fifty Modern Thinkers on Education*. London: Routledge, 2001.

In the late 1980s I attended an international conference on education in Paris. One evening I found myself having dinner with half a dozen persons, none of whom I had met before, representing half a dozen different nations. As we spoke, a remarkable fact emerged. All of us had been drawn to a life in education because of our reading, years before, of psychologist Jerome Bruner's remarkable volume *The Process of Education* (1960).

At some point in their professional lives, many psychologists become involved in educational issues. Such engagement is especially likely in the United States, where educational theory and practice have been heavily influenced by contemporary work in psychology. It is possible that psychologists like B.F. Skinner or E.L. Thorndike have had more influence on specific educational policies, such as testing, but when it comes to enlarging our sense of how children learn and what educators could aspire to, Jerome Bruner has no peers.

Born in New York City in 1915, Jerome Bruner's professional life has been that of a prolific and versatile psychologist. Trained at Duke and Harvard universities, his first paper, published in 1939, was on "the effect of thymus extract on the sexual behavior of the female rat." During the Second World War, Bruner participated as a social psychologist, investigating public opinion, propaganda, and social attitudes. Thereafter, as one of the leaders of the post-war "cognitive revolution," his focus has been chiefly on human perception and cognition.

During the half century since the war, Bruner investigated in turn a series of loosely related topic areas. In his work on the "new look" in perception, he emphasized the role of expectation and interpretation on our perceptual experiences. Maintaining this focus on the active role of the subject, he turned next to the role of strategies in the processes of human categorization. Becoming increasingly concerned with the development of human cognition, Bruner and colleagues at Harvard's newly formed Center of Cognitive Studies undertook a series of studies of the modes of representation used by children.

In 1970 Bruner moved from Harvard to Oxford University. There he continued his developmental studies of infant agency and began a series of investigations of children's language. Following his return to the United States a decade later, he showed a heightened concern with social and cultural phenomena. Rejecting the excessive computationalism of the cognitive perspective that he helped to found, he directed attention to human narrative and interpretive capacities – most recently in the law. And he helped to launch yet a third revolution in psychology – one centered around the practice of cultural psychology.

It is important to sketch Bruner's contributions as a psychologist because they frame his involvement in educational issues. Reflecting his catholic research interests and his own wide learning, Bruner has approached education as a broad thinker rather than as a technician. He has considered the full range of human capacities that are involved in teaching and learning – perception, thought, language, other symbol systems, creativity, intuition, personality, and motivation. He construes education as beginning in infancy, and, especially in recent writings, has emphasized the role assumed in education by the gamut of cultural institutions. He has drawn on our knowledge of early hominids and has consistently viewed education from a cross-cultural perspective. (In the 1990s he began to work regularly with the preschools of Reggio Emilia and other Italian communities.) Indeed, in his most recent writings on cultural psychology, Bruner has proposed education as the proper "test frame" for constructing a full-fledged cultural psychology.

In the late 1950s Jerome Bruner became explicitly involved in precollegiate education in the United States. At that time, following the Russian launching of the satellite Sputnik, many Americans felt that a greater proportion of national resources must be devoted to education, particularly in science, mathematics, and technology. This interest occurred at the very time that the cognitive revolution, partly under the charismatic leadership of Bruner, had been launched. The influential National Academy of Sciences and the National Science Foundation called a meeting of scientists, other scholars, psychologists, and educators at Wood's Hole, Massachusetts, in September 1959. Bruner was the obvious chair for this meeting.

In his landmark book *The Process of Education* (1960) Bruner eloquently sketched the chief themes that had emerged at the conference. Against the widespread notion that youngsters should be learning facts and procedures, the conferees argued for the importance of the structure of scientific (and other) disciplines. If a student understood the principal moves in a subject area, he or she could go on to think generatively about new issues. ("Knowing how something is put together is worth a thousand facts about it" (Bruner, 1983, p. 183).) Against the view of the child as an assimilator of information, and as a little adult, the conferees (inspired by the work of Jean Piaget and Bärbel Inhelder) put forth a still unfamiliar view of the child: the child as an active problem-solver, who had his or her own ways of making sense of the world. Against the notion that certain subjects should be avoided until secondary school or later, the conferees argued for a spiral curriculum, in which topics were introduced in appropriate ways early in school and then revisited, with added depth and complexity, at later points in schooling. This argument inspired the most quoted (and most controversial) line in the book: "We begin with the hypothesis that any subject can be taught effectively in some intellectually honest form to any child at any stage of development" (1960, p. 33).

The response to the Bruner report was swift and electrifying. The book was praised as "seminal," "revolutionary," and "a classic" by a range of scholars and policy leaders. It was translated into nineteen languages and was for many years the bestselling paperback issued by the Harvard University Press. Perhaps most important, *The Process of Education* catalyzed a range of important educational programs and experiments, both in the United States and abroad. As Bruner speculated some years later, "I think the book's 'success' grew from a worldwide need to reassess the functions of education in the light of the knowledge explosion and the new post-industrial technology" (1983, p. 185).

While he might have chosen to return to the psychological laboratory, Bruner instead became directly involved in educational efforts, first in the United States and later in Great Britain. He joined a number of committees and commissions, serving for a while as a member of the Education Panel of the President's Science Advisory Committee under Presidents Kennedy and Johnson. By far his deepest involvement was as chair and architect of a new curriculum for social studies to be used in the middle grades.

In 1964–6, under the auspices of a government research-and-development laboratory called Educational Services Inc., Bruner led the effort to design and implement "Man: A Course of Study." This ambitious effort to produce a full-fledged curriculum drew on the most current thinking in the newly emerging behavioral sciences. As conceptualized by Bruner, the curriculum sought to address three fundamental issues: "What is uniquely human about human beings? How did they get that way? How could they be made more so?"

Reflecting Bruner's belief that even young children could tackle difficult issues, the curriculum presented themes that were "alive" in the behavioral sciences of the era. In the light of linguistic analyses of Charles Hockett and Noam Chomsky, youngsters explored the nature of communication systems. Taking into account Sherwood Washburn's discoveries about the tool use of early man, students investigated ancient and modern tools and media. Inspired by discoveries about the social relations of primates (Irven DeVore) and humans (Claude Lévi-Strauss), students explored kin relations and social organizations of cultures. There was ample material on the art, myths, and childrearing practices of diverse groups. The ideas and themes were presented through rich ethnographic and filmic case studies, drawing in particular on the Netsilik Eskimos of Pelly Bay and the !Kung bushmen of the Kalahari Desert.

Years later Bruner wistfully recalled: "In the heady days of 1962, anything seemed possible" (1983, p. 190). As a young member (age 21–2) of the research team, I can attest to the excitement that permeated this curriculum effort. Scholars, psychological researchers, curriculum planners, master teachers, and eager fifth graders worked shoulder-to-shoulder each day to create and revise curricula that would engage and instruct. The resulting materials were made widely available and circulated through much of the United States and abroad in the late 1960s and early 1970s.

However, the euphoria surrounding such educational experimentation did not last. Within the United States, issues of poverty and racism erupted on the domestic front, and the increasingly frustrating and divisive war in Vietnam sapped the energies of reform. The Bruner curriculum was directly attacked by conservative political and social groups, which took objection to the intellectual aspirations (read: "elitist") and cross-cultural (read: "relativistic") sweep of the materials. Eventually, the National Science Foundation withdrew its support for the curriculum. Bruner conceded that the fault did not lie entirely with external critics. The curriculum worked best with well-prepared teachers working in schools with advantaged students. Bruner was fond of remarking: "We never quite solved the problem of getting the materials from Widener [the main library at Harvard University] to Wichita [largest city in Kansas, the heartland of America]."

Bruner's involvement in education yielded a set of thoughtful essays on learning and instruction, which were gathered together in *Towards a Theory of Instruction* (1966) and *The Relevance of Education* (1971). In these writings, Bruner put forth his evolving ideas about the ways in which instruction actually affects the mental models of the world that students construct, elaborate on, and transform. Drawing on his collaborative developmental studies, he highlighted three ordered ways in which children transform experiences into knowledge: through action, through imagery, and, eventually, through a range of symbolic systems. Much of education involves a negotiation, and sometimes conflict, among these modes of representation. Increasingly influenced by the writings of the Soviet psychologist Lev Vygotsky, Bruner stressed the ways in which much of learning involves the internalization of tools and media that have been constructed over the years by other human individuals and groups. And he continued to reveal an interest in underexplored issues, such as motivation, affect, creativity, and intuition.

Looking back on his educational work of the 1960s and early 1970s, Bruner has come to recognize certain limitations. Part of the limitation represented the psychology of the era: an excessive focus on solo, intrapsychic processes of knowing. A complementary limitation came from a failure to recognize the depth and pervasiveness of societal problems, including poverty, racism, and widespread alienation. As Bruner commented, "it was taken for granted [at that time] that students lived in some sort of educational vacuum, untroubled by the ills and problems of the culture at large" (1996, p. xiii).

By the 1970s and 1980s Jerome Bruner had emerged as a chief critic of the cognitive revolution. He saw it as an unwarranted reduction of human thought to a set of computational routines. With other colleagues, he called for the construction of a cultural psychology in which the historical background and current forces of a culture were given weight. In Bruner's view, such a rejuvenated psychology should discover what is meaningful to individuals and groups – and why it is meaningful.

In light of this framework Bruner revisited educational issues in his 1996 book *The Culture of Education*. He proposed that education is not properly viewed simply as a function of the school, directed at the mind of individual students: "schools as now constituted are not so much the solution to the problem of education as they are part of the problem" (p. 198). One is more likely to achieve educational progress if one sees education as the function of the culture-at-large, and if one looks for learning midst the interactions and joint constructions of students attempting to construct knowledge. No longer should educational theorists ponder the individual child (Piaget's "epistemic subject"), puzzling about conservation of liquid or the subtlety of kinship relations. Rather, educationalists should direct their attention to groups of children attempting together – often with the aid of computer networks and remote experts – to understand the processes of biology, the nature of law, and even the ways in which they themselves learn. Successful students should tell one another what they have learned about the world and about the operations of their individual and collective minds.

As this necessarily rough sketch should suggest, Jerome Bruner has served a vital role in the educational discourse of our time: bringing to bear the latest thinking in psychology on the contemporary problems of the society; always on the lookout for the nagging problems and the most promising paths to their solution; zestfully open to new currents of thought. At the same time, students of Bruner call attention to the powerful themes that permeate a career in psychology that is entering its seventh decade: a belief in the active agency of the human being, a conviction about the construction of knowledge, a perennial concern with purpose, goals, and means, a virtually unerring taste for which issues are important and how best to tackle them, and an unflinching optimism that withstands personal and societal setbacks.

It remains to say that Jerome Bruner is not merely one of the foremost educational thinkers of the era; he is also an inspired learner and teacher. His infectious curiosity inspires all who are not completely jaded. Individuals of every age and background are invited to join in. Logical analyses, technical distinctions, rich and wide knowledge of diverse subject matters, asides to an ever wider orbit of information, intuitive leaps, pregnant enigmas pour forth from his indefatigable mouth and pen. In his own words: "Intellectual activity is anywhere and everywhere, whether at the frontier of knowledge or in a third-grade classroom" (1960, p. 14). To those who know him, Bruner remains the Compleat Educator in the flesh: "Communicator, model, and identification figure" (1960, p. 41).

CHAPTER 3

PROJECT ZERO
Nelson Goodman's legacy in arts education

Journal of Aesthetics and Art Criticism, Blackwell, 2000, 58(3): 245–9

In the late 1960s and early 1970s the eminent philosopher Nelson Goodman founded and directed Project Zero, a research group housed at the Harvard Graduate School of Education. Under Goodman's leadership, Project Zero focused on the nature of artistic knowledge and the ways in which artistic skills and understanding can be enhanced through well-designed programs in schools and museums. Decades later, Project Zero remains an active research center; its current brief is broader, extending well beyond the arts, and involving affiliations with a range of educational institutions. Still, Goodman's original mission – basic research on artistic knowledge and practice – remains a defining feature of Project Zero.

From one point of view, Nelson Goodman was a most unlikely head of an empirically oriented research project in the area of arts education. Until the middle 1960s he was a philosopher's philosopher, carrying out fundamental, theoretically oriented investigations of basic issues in epistemology. He had rarely written about the arts. He had had essentially no contact with education below the collegiate level, let alone the men and women who teach music, visual arts, or drama to the nation's children. And to be honest about it, Nelson Goodman did not have much interest in children or in developmental psychology. He teased me by declaring that developmental psychology reduced to the banality that "kids get smarter as they get older." Most of his attention and affection was lavished on his closest colleagues and students, his pets, and the works of art that he owned.

As this last clause intimates, from another point of view Nelson Goodman was a likely head of a project that investigated the basis of artistry. During his undergraduate years at Harvard College, Nelson Goodman had studied with, and been deeply influenced by, Paul Sachs, then the Associate Director of the Fogg Art Museum. Directly following his graduation in 1928, Goodman had for 15 years run an art gallery in Boston. At that time, he had begun to collect art objects, ultimately accumulating collections of such diversity that few appreciated the full ambit of his taste. During the Second World War Goodman had served as a psychologist in the armed forces and had become fascinated by questions of intelligence, perception, and cognition. Goodman was an inveterate attender of performances across the range of art forms, showing both a discerning eye and ear and a distinct taste for the unusual and the exotic. His wife Katharine Sturgis was a visual artist of some renown; separately and together, they provided material and psychological support for artists and arts projects that captured their fancy.

Still, it is probable that Project Zero would never have been launched had it not been for the concatenation of three factors. First of all, in the 1960s Nelson Goodman completed a lengthy labor of love: his book *Languages of Art*, in which he put forth an approach to the arts grounded in the study of different symbols, symbol systems, and modes of symbolic functioning. While the book was heavily theoretical, Goodman also drew on the findings of psychology, linguistics, and other empirically oriented disciplines. And in a pregnant final passage he speculated:

> We hear a good deal about how the aptitudes and training needed for the arts and for the sciences contrast or even conflict with one another. Earnest and elaborate efforts to devise and test means of finding and fostering aesthetic abilities are always being initiated. But none of this talk or these trials can come to much without an adequate conceptual framework for designing crucial experiments and interpreting their results. Once the arts and sciences are seen to involve working with – inventing, applying, reading, transforming, manipulating – symbol systems that agree and differ in certain specific ways, we can perhaps undertake pointed psychological investigation of how the pertinent skills inhibit or enhance one another, and the outcome might well call for changes in educational technology. The time has come in this field for the false truism and the plangent platitude to give way to the elementary experiment and the hesitant hypothesis.
>
> (Goodman, 1968, p. 265)

A second factor that made possible the creation of Project Zero was the educational atmosphere of the 1960s. Following the launch of the Sputnik satellite by the Soviet Union in 1957, the United States government devoted unprecedented sums of money to the improvement of science, mathematical, and technological education, particularly at the elementary and secondary levels. Little or no attention was directed to education in the arts and humanities. By the middle 1960s both private and public granting agencies were struck by this asymmetry and determined to correct it, at least a bit. And indeed, the first funds for Project Zero were to come from a private foundation, the Old Dominion Foundation, and a branch of the United States Office of Education called the Committee on Basic Research.

The final spur to Project Zero was a particular cast of characters located in a specific geographic and temporal region. After many years at the University of Pennsylvania, Nelson Goodman had moved in the early 1960s to Brandeis University but found his experience there disappointing. At the nearby Harvard Graduate School of Education, Dean Theodore Sizer (himself the son of an eminent professor of art) was looking for ways to foster research and pedagogy in the arts. A key member of the Education School faculty was Israel Scheffler, a distinguished philosopher with an interest in the arts and symbolization, and, not coincidentally, Nelson Goodman's student and friend.

Historians differ on the exact date, but some time between the winter of 1966–7 and the fall of 1967 Project Zero was christened and launched. The name reflected the founder's estimate of the state of firm knowledge about arts education. Nelson Goodman moved his office (and his concept) from the Waltham Campus to Harvard Square. Equipped with a little budget and a lot of lively ideas, Goodman launched an unprecedented research project that has lasted, indeed prospered. In a 1988 essay Goodman recalled:

When Project Zero started twenty years ago with a staff consisting of one philosopher, two psychologists part time, and some volunteer associates, it had no fixed program and no firm doctrines but only a profound conviction of the importance of the arts, and a loose collection of attitudes, hunches, problems, objectives, and ideas for exploration. We viewed the arts not as mere entertainment, but like the sciences, as ways of understanding and even of constructing our environments, and thus looked upon arts education as a requisite and integrated component of the entire educational process. We found at once that we had to begin almost at zero, with basic theoretical studies into the nature of art and of education and a critical scrutiny of elementary concepts and prevalent assumptions and questions.

(1988, p. 1)

As one of the two part-time (and largely uncompensated!) psychologists to whom Goodman refers, I had the privilege of being associated with Project Zero since its inception. The early years of the project were very exciting. Goodman was intellectually charismatic. He had developed a rigorous approach to the analysis of artistic work and process, and he was eager to see it applied: to the analysis of aesthetic concepts (like style, rhythm, metaphor); to the launching of psychological experiments (on how we perceive perspective; how we group patterns rhythmically; whether children can perceive artistic style); and to the education of teachers (through the staging of lecture-performances by well-known artists representing different media and genres).

And so, at least once a week, the aforementioned motley crew would gather around a lengthy table, discuss these issues on a theoretical level, design and critique psychological experiments, listen to (and respectfully challenge) learned speakers, and make sure that the plans were in place for the forthcoming lecture-performances. The table is easier to recall than the building, because Project Zero was like an orphan during its first years. Not really being part of the school's "line item" educational program, we were tossed about annually from one building and from one part of the campus to another. Nelson Goodman locked horns with changing administrations, and did so with tenacity and gusto. I recall one particularly dreary moment when, after months of bickering, it was still not clear whether we had secured a rug for the office. Asked by his friend Paul Kolers whether this experience had tested Nelson's faith in human nature, Goodman growled, "No, it confirms it."

Project Zero accomplished a great deal during the five years that Nelson Goodman stood at the helm. The Goodman era showed that a dogged group of scholars and researchers could bury (or at least bracket) their disciplinary differences and carry forward solid philosophical, psychological, and educational work in the area of arts education. Since we were scholars, the products were mostly ideas and writings.

These writings by early Project Zero personnel are scattered in many places, but one spot where their cumulative effect can be gleaned is the 1977 book *The Arts and Cognition* edited by long-term Project Zero members David Perkins and Barbara Leondar. Included in this collection are essays by Goodman on "When is Art?", philosopher Graham Roupas on pictorial representation, philosopher Vernon Howard on artistic practices and skills, aesthetician Soren Kjorup on the semiotics of film, psychologist Paul Kolers on reading text, psychologist John Kennedy on pictorial perception by the blind, musicologist Jeanne Bamberger on the construction of tunes, visual arts educator Diana Korzenik on children's cognition of pictures, literary scholar Barbara Leondar on the genesis of story making, educator Frank Dent on the vehicle of the lecture-performance, Project Zero co-director David Perkins on poetry editing, and co-director Howard Gardner on the cognitive components of artistry. Subsequent collections include a 1988 issue of *The Journal of Aesthetic Education*, published as the book *Art, Mind, and Education* (Gardner and Perkins, 1989) and a 1994 issue of the *Harvard Graduate School of Education Alumni Bulletin* entitled "The Mark of Zero". Among the distinguished Project Zero contributors to these special issues are philosopher Israel Scheffler and two psychologists who joined Project Zero in 1973: Ellen Winner and Dennie Wolf.

But probably the most precious legacy of the Goodman era is a 100-page unpublished "Final Report" for the Office of Education, supervised in 1972 by Nelson Goodman. Entitled "Basic Abilities Required for Understanding and Creation in the Arts," this monograph sets forth the basic assumptions of the project, surveys the major studies carried out and results achieved to that point, and attempts to evaluate whether "Project Zero has moved toward one."

The report begins with a simple assertion of the purpose of the project: "the advancement of the arts through improved education of artists, audiences, and management." It laments the primitive nature of work in the area of arts education; it chronicles the many obstacles of funding and attitudes that lie in the way of a cognitive approach to the arts; but it declares, with a touch of pride, "in the course of our study to date some promising hypotheses have gained support." Contents of the monograph included:

1   the arguments advanced in *Languages of Art* and how they have been further explored and amplified through systematic philosophical inquiry;
2   exposition of the constructive nature of perception and creation;
3   studies of the difference between linguistic and non-linguistic symbolic systems, with possible correlations in human neurological functioning;
4   studies of perception of pictures, ranging from line drawings to caricatures to tactile-perceived pictures;
5   developmental studies of children's perception of artistic styles;
6   investigations of the nature of problem-solving and problem-finding in different aesthetic media;
7   clarification of concepts in the area of education in the arts and a taxonomy of learning modes;
8   discussion of the issues in evaluation of artistic programs;
9   report on various "field" initiatives, including site visits to institutions of arts education, sponsoring of lecture performances, the initiation of a training program in arts management, and the launching and evaluation of a course on Project Zero.

An examination of this list, decades after the studies were carried out, might erroneously suggest that Project Zero was situated in the mainstream of research in the late 1960s. Nothing could be further from the truth. The ideas of cognitive psychology and psychologically informed philosophy were still relatively new in the academy. They were newer still in the area of education. And they were considered virtual blasphemy in arts education.

Whatever artists and arts educators may have believed in their souls (an entity that Nelson Goodman would not have endorsed!), talk of arts focused very much on emotions, spirit, mystery, the ineffable and unanalyzable. An effort to demystify the arts, to construe them as involving the same kinds of skills and capacities as are involved in other domains and other disciplines, was incendiary. And an effort headed by an epistemologist and staffed by social scientists was deeply suspect. As Goodman later recalled: "In the early years of the Project, the very idea of the arts as cognitive and systematic research into arts education met with widespread and virulent hostility" (1988, p. 2). We once received a rejection of a grant application containing the admonition: "If this research were carried out, the arts would be destroyed." (So much for *ars longa*!) And shortly after Nelson Goodman and Ted Sizer retired (both in 1972), the administration of the Harvard Graduate School of Education literally tried to kill Project Zero by forbidding us to apply for further funding. Only a heroic act of diplomacy by founding member Israel Scheffler saved our still fledgling organization.

It remains for another day to detail the history of Project Zero in the post-Goodman era. Suffice it to say that Project Zero has survived and (dare I say it?) prospered for the succeeding years – and has done so almost entirely through the support of government grants, foundation funding, and generous private donors. Under the direction of David Perkins and Howard Gardner, it has investigated an ever-expanding set of topics, going well beyond the arts to encompass the entire precollegiate curriculum, collaborating with institutions as diverse as museums and testing services, working around the globe, mounting significant collaborations with China, South Africa, and many countries in Europe and Latin America. Dozens of books and many hundreds of articles have been written; dozens of educational programs in the United States and abroad are loosely affiliated with, or have been inspired by, the work of Project Zero. Well over 100 projects have been seen through to completion; and at one time there are between 50 and 100 active researchers involved with the Project, working on 20–30 different projects and offshoots thereof. Information about Project Zero is available at <http://pzweb.harvard.edu.>

It is fair to ask what Nelson Goodman thought of the Project Zero of the 1970s, 1980s, and 1990s, and what his legacy has been to individuals who were not even born when he retired from active participation. Goodman was a man of strong opinions and he did not hesitate to announce them – most memorably at a Fogg Art Museum gala celebrating the 25th anniversary of Project Zero. Goodman very much wanted Project Zero to continue to conduct basic inquiries and to maintain its focus on the arts. And so he approved of new, well-conceived conceptual distinctions and generative collaboration in the arts, such as the Arts in Education concentration that was launched by project investigator Jessica Davis at the Harvard Graduate School of Education. He also liked lines of research that confounded common sense (e.g., developmental studies where children's performances actually declined with age), and was particularly enamored of work on brain damage that provided unexpected support for his theory-based distinction between notational and non-notational work.

On the other hand, Goodman deplored Project Zero's ever-expanding scope of inquiry, particularly when it deviated from the arts. As this highly disciplined, almost ascetic man once quipped, "Ask not what the arts can do for you, ask what you can do for the arts." He never liked my theory of MI, for its conceptual basis eluded him. (He once threatened to send the *New Yorker* a satire called "The Seven Stupidities.") He was suspicious of Project Zero's efforts to improve education directly. As he wrote, seemingly in warning:

Our task is to provide analysis and information that may help in clarifying objectives and concepts and questions, in avoiding some pitfalls, in recognizing obstacles and perceiving opportunities. When Project Zero turns to writing prescriptions and instruction books, when it becomes Project-How-To, it will have passed on to an unjust reward.

(1988, p. 1)

As one of the two individuals who worked with Nelson Goodman from the beginning, as one of dozens of Project Zero members who had the privilege of knowing Nelson Goodman, face to face, let me say a few words about the legacy that he has left to the generations.

To begin with, Nelson Goodman provided us with a bountiful set of concepts and issues, whose exploration can continue to occupy generations of students and scholars across a range of disciplines. Second, we were inspired by an impressively high set of standards of thinking, critiquing, and writing; one did not submit shoddy work to Goodman, and his own stern superego has been internalized by many of us, though, no doubt, insufficiently, he would have reminded us. We absorbed a fascination with non-obvious problems and with seemingly oxymoronic notions: how can a Project be Zero? How can intelligence be multiple? What can the brain possibly tell us about the classification of symbol systems? How can understanding be a performance? We received a respect for ivory-tower analysis, but at the same time were impressed by the need for grounding in real works of art and in direct contact with artists, those who manage arts programs, and the audiences without which no artistic genre can survive. Indeed, one of Nelson Goodman's chief (though largely unsung) contributions to Harvard and the Boston community was his willingness throughout his last years to sponsor innovative arts programs that exemplified his faith in the cognitive aspects of the arts.

Speaking personally and on a first-name basis, I took from Nelson an irreverent but not unhopeful view of the human condition. As I've noted, Nelson could be tough on himself and on others (I think that he saw himself as a "man of the world"), but he had a wonderful, and touchingly naive, faith that the cause of the arts and cognition will advance. Once we were sitting around trying to figure out how to help someone become more creative. One person suggested the provision of interesting problems, the other suggested the technique of brainstorming. Nelson shook his head and said, "Create obstacles, and make sure that they are productive ones." I am reminded of Freud's words at the end of *The Future of an Illusion*: "The voice of the intellect is a soft one, but it does not rest until it has gained a hearing" (1950, pp. 96–7). Nelson Goodman's work has advanced this cause in those spheres of knowledge which had proved most resistant: Nelson's restless voice, words, and example represent his enduring contribution to understanding and to practice in the arts.

CHAPTER 4

NORMAN GESCHWIND AS A CREATIVE SCIENTIST

Schacter, S and O. Devinsky (eds), *Behavioral Neurology and the Legacy of Norman Geschwind*, Lippincott Williams and Wilkins, 1997

Many individuals today have become quite interested in the phenomena of creativity – creative scientists, creative artists, persons who exhibit creativity in finance, advertising, or even the political sphere. As one who monitors the area of creativity, I note as well the accumulation of books, articles, television programs, workshops, and other symptoms of growing interest in the topic. Yet, despite this almost prurient curiosity about the topic, most of us have not had the opportunity to observe a highly creative individual first hand. We read about Freud or Einstein, we watch films of Woody Allen or Martha Graham, and we listen assiduously to interviews with Francis Crick or Barbara McClintock. From these scattered hints, we try to understand the intriguing phenomenon of a single individual who changes the way in which others think about or experience the world.

I was fortunate to have been a colleague and friend of Norman Geschwind, one of the indisputably creative scientists of our era. I learned much about creativity from observing Norman; and some of what I have learned has been useful to me as I have thought more broadly about the parameters of creativity (see Gardner, 1993a). In these notes, I attempt to capture this interplay in my own thinking about Norman Geschwind as a creative scientist and the more general phenomena of creativity.

To introduce the discussion, it is helpful to consider three general points. First of all, there are many different kinds of creativity, ranging from the creativity involved in leading a political revolution, *à la* Mao or Lenin, to the creativity entailed in producing an effective work in a genre, the way that Keats and Rembrandt repeatedly did. Even within the sciences, there are multiple forms of creativity. Darwin and Piaget were masterful observers who were able to draw powerful generalizations from their initial observations. Einstein could conceive of thought experiments and then design crucial empirical and theoretical tests of what he had envisioned. Albert Michelson and Roger Sperry were brilliant experimentalists. Even when one thinks about Nobel laureates in the area of brain and behavior, it is clear that Roger Sperry, Konrad Lorenz, Herbert Simon, and David Hubel are distinctly different from one another. Norman Geschwind's own creative genius spanned observation and theorizing; he was not primarily an experimentalist. As neurologist Antonio Damasio once pointed out, Norman Geschwind's laboratory was located in his head.

A second point recognizes that many different factors contribute to individual and to group creativity. In addition to possible genetic predispositions, one must take into account developmental, family, school, cultural, social class, and motivational factors, among others. For this reason, creativity can never be understood simply from the point of view of a single discipline, be it neurology or genetics or sociology. Clearly Norman Geschwind's accomplishments reflect this range of factors; and it is perhaps appropriate that he himself was superlatively gifted in the way that he could range across disciplines and families of disciplines.

A third point is that creativity should not be confused with other virtues. Individuals can be highly intelligent without being creative; they can be highly successful without being creative; and they can be creative without being "right" in the long run. It is heuristic to think of creativity as the capacity to come up with ideas, problems, solutions and the like that are initially novel but that are ultimately acceptable in at least one domain or discipline or culture. Creative ideas or products change domains; that is the acid test. One can immediately see that individuals with superbly high IQs may have neither inclination nor capacity to change domains; that individuals who are widely acclaimed may exert no appreciable effect on domains; or that individuals may affect domains in the short term but in ways that are ultimately seen as wrong-headed or unproductive. Because Norman Geschwind's ideas have already affected several domains, we know that he was creative, rather than "merely" successful or "merely" intelligent; only time will tell whether he discovered basic truths, in the manner of a genius.

In light of these preliminary considerations, I have isolated four variables which figure importantly in the area of scientific creativity. Perhaps no one of them is critical in itself, but the combination of them surely signals that the individual is "at promise" for leading a creative life. Norman Geschwind illustrates well these factors, in consort as well as in isolation.

To begin with, Norman Geschwind was a man of great raw *intellectual power*. No matter what one's definition of intelligence, or intelligences, it was clear that Norman (as I was privileged to call him) stood out in terms of the power and penetration of his mind. His verbal skills were legendary – speaking, writing, readily mastering languages, reading at a prodigious rate, exhibiting impressive sensitivity to how language works and how it breaks down. Norman had equally powerful gifts in the area of logical-mathematical thinking; he began as a mathematics major in college and never lost the habit of thinking about issues in a rational, logical, and often mathematical way.

Norman was less outstanding in the realms of spatial thinking or in the use of his hands – in this way, he did not resemble many benchtop scientists. But his interests swept across all domains. He confessed to very little competence in music. It is therefore especially notable that he encouraged people like me to study music; that he collaborated with Tedd Judd and me in a study of a composer who became verbally alexic (Judd, Gardner, and Geschwind, 1983); and that he frequently attended concerts, including one just hours before his untimely death at the age of 58 in November 1984. Until the very end of his life, clearly Norman wanted to learn about most everything.

In addition to his polymathic intellect, Norman also had a kaleidoscopic capacity to draw on his knowledge. Virtually everything that he knew – and he knew more about more topics than just about anyone else that I have ever met – was available at his cerebral fingertips. Any new observation or fact could kindle a startling chain of associations, a new pattern, as that kaleidoscope went famously to work and to play. I suspect that if one had been able to perform a scan on Geschwind's brain in operation, one would have beheld a uniquely beautiful series of pictures.

Working hand-in-glove with intellect are the *personality structures* of the individual. Norman Geschwind displayed in abundance all the personality traits that are concomitants of great creativity: a driving personality, prodigious energy, focused attention, perseverance, a willingness to take risks, and a reassuring amount of self-confidence. Those in search of creative role models had no better option than to spend time in the presence of Norman Geschwind. Moreover, like the creative individuals described by Howard Gruber (1981), Norman had an expansive network of enterprise – a large number of individuals and projects that he helped to sustain and that in turn kept him fully occupied and engaged.

But while Norman resembled the textbook case of the creative personality, he also gave us an ensemble of bonuses. He was wonderfully funny; he was a pleasure, a treat, a perpetual feast to be around. He was without a trace of vanity or self-importance. One could never tell a person's status simply by observing his or her encounters with Norman from afar; Norman would spend hours with a naive undergraduate even as he would put a pretentious senior scientist in his place. He set an enviable standard for collegiality, responding to letters and phone calls promptly, and often at admirable length, almost always answering requests favorably, putting himself out for others in ways that were not necessary and that should have filled more of us – the unbridled requesters – with embarrassment. Perhaps it is best to say that Norman made us feel that he was one of us, though, deep down, we knew that he was one of the immortals.

Contrary to what the language hints at, individuals are not intelligent or creative in general – they exhibit these virtues in *specific domains or disciplines*. Norman Geschwind was a true scholar and could probably have made contributions in an ensemble of domains, ranging from mathematics to history to linguistics. But his chosen domain was behavioral neurology, and it was there – and in neighboring disciplines – that he was to make his enduring contributions.

Norman's relation to the domain of behavioral neurology was peculiar. He did not invent the field and he did not for the most part pull it in wholly original directions. Rather, he rediscovered a tradition that had existed a century earlier but had mistakenly been allowed to become dormant. Geschwind revivified the discredited works of scholarly giants like Wernicke, Lichtheim, Liepmann, and the "diagram makers" who attempted to locate specific cognitive facilities in specific brain regions or the connection among them. In the days when doctrines of holism and equipotentiality reigned supreme, this was an act of scholarly courage.

Of course, Norman Geschwind did not just direct his undereducated contemporaries to consult the dusty journals on the shelves of the medical libraries. He described new cases which either confirmed the traditional descriptions or that modified them in fresh and illuminating ways. His work on the disconnection syndromes had become classic within a decade of its original publication. His papers on the aphasias, the apraxias, the alexias, temporal lobe epilepsy and many other neuropsychological syndromes and conditions brought classical typologies in touch with newly observed phenomena and contemporary modes of analysis. He himself was in contact with the outstanding scientists in Russia, Europe, Asia, and the Americas; and he brought the rest of the community of brain and behavior in touch with these same authorities. Under his founding leadership, the Aphasia Research Center at Boston University and the Boston Veterans Administration Medical Center and then the Neurology Units at Boston City and Beth Israel Hospitals became international centers. For years, there was but a tiny minority of behavorial neurologists and neuropsychologists who had not been trained by

Norman Geschwind; and even those who had not been trained at his scintillating rounds flocked to his lectures and combed over the new journals for his writings – and, eventually, for the writings of his students.

Toward the end of his life, Norman Geschwind embarked on what may well have been his most important work – a pioneering effort, undertaken in conjunction with Peter Behan and Albert Galaburda, to tie together information on genetics, laterality, fetal development, sex differences, hormonal systems, immune disorders, and an array of cognitive skills and disabilities. Even to list these domains is to be daunted; only someone of Geschwind's intellectual courage and kaleidoscopic thinking could have undertaken this effort, let alone brought it to an amazing degree of readiness in a tragically short period of time (Geschwind and Galaburda, 1987). In light of subsequent discoveries, the details of this ambitious synthesis will need to be revised; but as is so often the case in science, the set of issues raised by Geschwind and his colleagues will endure. I regard this synoptic effort as one of the first, and one of the most important, instances of what has since come to be called cognitive neuroscience.

A final dimension entailed in the phenomenon of creativity is often overlooked – the dimension called the *"field"* (Csikszentmihalyi, 1988). Whatever the talent of the individual, and the state of readiness of the domain, a creative effort cannot come to be seen as such without the collaboration of those individuals, institutions, award panels, and the like that render judgments of quality.

The field recognized Norman Geschwind's talents at an early age. He was appreciated as a student at Harvard College and the Harvard Medical School; he won more than his share of fellowships, residencies, grants, and prizes; he was appointed the James Jackson Putnam Professor of Neurology at the Harvard Medical School in his early 40s; he was widely honored across the globe at the time of his death. Part of this success has to do with Norman's choice of fields; he was wise enough to be born in New York City at a time when it was a unique cauldron of creative vigor and to find himself at Harvard, Queen's Square, Moscow, and on the European continent at times when intellectual breakthroughs were happening. Of course, the field was also fortunate that Norman Geschwind presented himself for its consideration.

But I want to stress another aspect of the field. Even as Norman helped to reorient the domain of behavioral neurology and its neighbors, he was crucially important in helping to shape its concomitant fields. Norman's judgments about work, his taste with respect to issues worthy of study, his ability to shape discussions and standards were remarkable and, to my way of thinking, remarkably beneficent. Norman Geschwind exerted this effect by his writings, his choice and development of students, his engagement at scientific meetings and, perhaps especially, by his lectures. Nearly everyone who heard Norman Geschwind concurred that he was one of the great scientific lecturers of the age. He could discuss complex issues in a straightforward way, bring new excitement to a discussion, and respond to even the most vexing questions with insight, appropriateness, and timely wit. By his effect on others, directly and indirectly, he almost single-handedly and single-mindedly redirected the standards of what lines of work were important and how such issues could be addressed in an intellectually rigorous way. Indeed, as happens in such cases, Norman exerted a powerful influence even on those who staunchly disagreed with his claims.

Norman Geschwind stood at the center of what Margaret Mead once called a cultural cluster:

whose defining characteristic is at least one irreplaceable individual, someone with such special gifts of imagination and thought that without him the cluster would assume an entirely different character – a genius who makes a contribution to evolution not by biological propagation but by the special turn that he is able to give to the course of cultural evolution.

(Mead, 1964)

I trust that, in terms of the criteria that I have defined, Norman Geschwind emerges as an exceptional individual, one who embodies creativity of a very high order. His combination of probing intellect, driving yet generous personality, substantive reorientation of behavioral neurology, and shaping of the field of judges places him centrally in that privileged group of scientists who have made a difference in our time.

For those who knew him, Norman exceeded these criteria, for he is irreplaceable in two respects: as a scientist with whom one craves further interaction on a myriad of rich issues; and as a marvelously warm, empathic and humane human being – the kind of person who is rare in any domain and virtually without peer in the hard driving and often cut-throat domain of scientific research.

We have but one consolation. Great minds endure not through their genes but through their ideas and their personal examples. Norman Geschwind's ideas fueled a generation of talented researchers in several disciplines spanning the brain and behavior; and his personal example has sustained, and will continue to sustain, all those who were privileged to know him directly, and perhaps even some who only knew him through his reputation. As one who has since studied many creative individuals drawn from a galaxy of domains, I have encountered no one who so well combined intellectual brilliance and personal decency.

CHAPTER 5

DEVELOPMENTAL PSYCHOLOGY AFTER PIAGET

An approach in terms of symbolization

Human Development, S. Karger AG, Basel, 1979, 22, 73–88

Abstract

While many of Piaget's *contributions* have already been assimilated into developmental psychology, certain limitations in his approach have become evident. Piaget's emphasis on logical-rational thought and his correlative neglect of the vehicles by which knowledge is carried point up the need for a new, post-Piagetian perspective. An approach to cognitive development which builds upon certain of Piaget's assumptions and methods but which takes into account the specific characteristics of diverse symbol systems and media is outlined here. Such an approach may account for a number of phenomena left unexplained by Piaget, integrate diverse strands of research, and suggest certain promising new lines of investigation.

Introduction: the Piagetian enterprise

Whatever its ultimate scientific fate, Piaget's contribution has over the past few decades provided a major impetus for research in developmental psychology. Before Piaget began research and publication in the early 1920s, there was relatively little interest in the child's special cognitive and conceptual powers. Most work consisted either of sheer descriptions of objective features of the child's existence (physical milestones, preferred activities, motor capacities), anecdotal accounts of individual children, including ones displaying unusual abilities or difficulties, or broadly speculative interpretations of the course of growth. Moreover, when researchers investigated the child's mental capacities, these scholars generally proceeded on the assumption that the child was simply an immature (or less skilled) adult (or, alternatively a somewhat brighter animal). Even after Piaget had begun publication, there were few who embraced his genetic epistemology. Instead of exploring the origins of such fundamental categories of knowledge as space, time, or causality, and the relations among these domains, researchers continued to examine the manifestations in children of the classic topics of psychological analysis: memory, attention, perception, and problem-solving.

Piaget's major contributions – his stage sequence, his clinical approach, the fascinating phenomena he has uncovered – are well known and widely respected (for reviews, see Piaget, 1983). His enterprise seems more likely to survive than any competing approach in developmental psychology. But precisely because the broad outlines of Piaget's approach are well known and because they are unlikely to change, the time has come to take stock of his bequest to the field and to consider its eventual fate. In what follows I will specify certain methodological guideposts which are central to the Piagetian enterprise; indicate a number of substantive problems in the Piagetian approach which have become increasingly apparent even to sympathetic observers; and then outline a new perspective which has recently emerged among some researchers who wish to carry forward the program launched by Piaget.

Piagetian studies of a domain of knowledge (e.g., time, space, causality) characteristically begin with a delineation of the "end state," or principal features of an adult competence. Tasks are so devised as to elicit the full-blown competence of the mature organism; at the same time, they are designed to draw out qualitative features displayed by "less developed" organisms as they confront the domain in question. The researcher administers the task to subjects possessing a wide range of assumed skills and competences, with the hope (and expectation) that a sequence of stages, ranging from total failure to total success, will emerge.

These "stage descriptions" form the core of Piaget's account of cognitive development. They differ from earlier descriptions in their assertion that the immature organism exhibits a qualitatively different (and inferior) grasp of the domain in question; in the marshaling of a wealth of tasks, protocols, and interpretive materials in support of the stage sequence; and in the collation of both linguistic and non-linguistic response measures.

A number of other features also mark the Piagetian approach. Among them are the "inter-actionist" viewing of cognition as the product of the subject's actions upon the world of objects; the notion that the stages are "structured wholes," with logical underpinnings which tie their components together and which link them to comparable milestones across a slew of conceptual domains; the assertion that higher stages incorporate within their structure the components of earlier stages, which are in turn integrated (and absorbed) into the structure of yet later stages; the acknowledgement of processes of décalage, in which the characteristics of a stage may be manifest somewhat earlier with certain (perhaps more familiar) materials, later with certain other (less familiar) materials; the citation of behaviors which signal that the child may soon effect a transition to a "higher stage" of development.

Critiques of the Piagetian enterprise

As befits an important but novel paradigm, Piaget's approach has been criticized from a variety of perspectives. At the extremes, certain investigators wish to return, wholly or in large part, to the epistemological positions which Piaget has explicitly rejected. One cadre of researchers embraces an empiricist position, placing its reliance on the principles of learning theory. This group argues that the demonstrations made by Piaget can be adequately accounted for – and trained or extinguished – in terms of traditional principles of learning (cf. Brainerd, 1978; Gelman, 1969; Kohnstamm, 1963; Watson, 1968). A rival set of investigators asserts that Piaget has, if anything, overplayed the role of interaction with the world in the development of mental capacities. Embracing a nativist account, such observers prefer to attribute to the child a rich initial mental structure which in itself contains the concepts, and the requisite representational machinery, needed for eventual achievement of the Piagetian end states (Bower, 1974; Chomsky, 1975; Fodor, 1975; Lorenz, 1977). A somewhat related point of view has recently been articulated by Kagan *et al.* (1978), who, while spurning the seductive powers of innate ideas, deem much of development as a regular unfolding at key maturational points of cognitive and social milestones.

It is possible that these harsh critiques will prevail and that the Piagetian enterprise will be wholly abandoned, but I find this outcome very unlikely. Put briefly, the Piagetian enterprise has proved too fruitful, the competing stances too problematic, to make its demise probable. On the other hand, a number of deficiencies in the Piaget position have been so often noted that their eventual rectification has become a virtual certitude in post-Piagetian psychology. Among these gaps are Piaget's indifference to individual differences; his reluctance to deal substantively with issues of learning and pedagogy; his inattention to the role of specific sensory systems; his minimization of cultural and social factors in the child's mental development; his neglect of affective and motivational factors; his difficulty in explaining novelties in development (e.g., transitions); and his failure to develop an adequate conception of language, and of language's role in thought.

These omissions are serious ones. They amount, in effect, to a verdict that large areas of psychology, ones which any comprehensive developmental theory must confront, have been ignored by Piaget. Yet, precisely because they deal with domains somewhat outside the assignment Piaget has posed for himself, domains which he has often explicitly declared "out-of-bounds," their listing does not in itself indicate just which directions the mainstream of cognitive developmental psychology is likely to follow in the next several years.

In my mind, there are two defects in Piaget's account which are critical, precisely because they lie much closer to the mission which he has explicitly pursued. First of all, even though Piaget has claimed to study the development of the mind, he has embraced a surprisingly narrow end state for cognition. In Piaget's view, mature cognition is no less, and no more, than the domain of logical-rational thought; accordingly, his end state is the competent scientist (cf. Gardner, 1973a, 1973c). Piaget has consequently paid little heed to adult forms of cognition removed from the logic of science. There is scant consideration of the thought processes used by artists, writers, musicians, athletes, and equally little information about processes of intuition, creativity, or novel thinking.

The second central deficiency derives from Piaget's disregard of the particular materials, media of presentation, or symbol systems in which a task is posed, and a response secured. As far as one can ascertain, Piaget seems to believe that the topics he investigates can be approached with equal vigor and accuracy irrespective of the physical materials used (beakers of water, balls of clay, building blocks or billiard balls), symbol systems employed (language, pictures, gestures, or numbers), media of transmission (human voice, picture book, three-dimensional models), and mode of response tapped (verbal, pointing, sensori-motor actions, or some combination thereof). At most Piaget is willing to concede a certain décalage across materials; still, this "noise factor" is thought to be of minor significance in determining the developmental sequence in the domain under inquiry.

In the aftermath of Piaget's contribution, cognitive developmental psychology is likely to focus on these two areas. Where Piaget has concentrated exclusively on the logical, rational thought of the scientist, future investigators are likely to probe the skills needed by radically different kinds of thinkers. And where Piaget has rather cavalierly ignored the differences among media, materials, modes of response, and symbol systems, researchers are likely to attempt to unravel the specific effects of each of these elements. Whether significant new insights are likely to flow from these studies will depend in large measure on whether such research efforts merely "tinker" with Piaget's basic demonstrations or whether they are informed by a fresh point of view. Because in my view such a point of view can be discerned in recent studies of human symbolic functioning, it is appropriate to turn to this area of study.

Symbolization: a starting point

Among developmental psychologists there is virtually universal agreement about a major transition in early childhood: in the second, third, and fourth years of life, the child moves from dealing directly (and exclusively) with the physical world of objects (animate and inanimate) to gaining, rendering, and communicating meanings through a range of symbolic vehicles. The one-year-old knows a rattle, a mother, the sun, only through direct sensori-motor experience; a five-year-old can draw a picture, tell a story, and perhaps even offer gestural, numerical, or musical accounts of these topics. Theorists have used a variety of terms to characterize these capacities – symbolic, representational, semiotic, mediational, second signal systems – but these authorities generally concur that the ability to refer to tidings and events at one (or more) symbolic steps removed is a hallmark of human cognition (see Bruner, 1966; Fischer, 1980; Kendler and Kendler, 1962; Luria and Yudovich, 1971; Piaget, 1962; Werner and Kaplan, 1963).

Offering a definition of symbolism is a difficult matter, one intermeshed with a host of sensitive and as yet unresolved philosophical and psychological issues. For present purposes, it may suffice to speak of a symbol as an element – usually a physical mark but one which (like a word) can also denote an (abstract) conception. For individuals within a given culture, symbols carry meanings of one or another sort, and can generally enter into meaningful relationships with other elements from the same class, thereby constituting a symbol system. The meaning relations are of two broad types: denotational meaning, in which the symbolic element designates an item which exists (or could potentially exist) in the world of experience; and expressive or exemplificatory meaning, in which the symbol captures a property (usually expressive, qualitative, or affective) of human experience without, however, designating a specific object or field of reference (cf. Gardner *et al.*, 1974, and Goodman, 1968, for elaboration of these points).

Though the number of symbol systems universally employed is sharply restricted, there is in principle no reason why one cannot have an indefinite number of symbols, and an indefinite number of symbol systems. All that is needed are some elements, marks, or vehicles, a field of reference, and some rules for mapping the symbolic onto the referential. Where symbol systems differ instructively from one another is in the extent to which they embody the two principal forms of symbolic reference. Some symbol systems, like numerical notation, highlight denotational elements, while having little or no expressive potential; other systems, like improvised jazz, have only minimal denotational power but exhibit a wide range of expressive reference; still other systems, like language, dance, or pictorial depiction, can vary from instances where denotation is key (e.g., scientific papers, mime, representational drawings and diagrams) to instances where expressive properties are foregrounded (poetry, modern dance, abstract art).

Study of the "operation" of symbol systems is still at an early stage, but insights from a number of philosophical and psychological perspectives suggest the following picture (cf. Cassirer, 1957; Goodman, 1968; Langer, 1942; McLuhan, 1964;

Peirce, 1933). Rather than being essentially equivalent, symbol systems differ widely from one another in what they can encode (contrast language with music), what they typically express (contrast line drawings with dance), and which features they highlight (contrast the way in which volume is presented in number, music, or sculpture). Symbol systems also differ dramatically in their notationality: some allow a faithful mapping back and forth between notations and a field of reference (e.g., musical scores, Morse code); others, infinitely replete, permit an indefinite number of readings, which thereby preclude any exhaustive mapping back and forth between elements and referents (consider a portrait or a dance performance).

The psychological significance of these logical distinctions remains a matter of some controversy. Despite the feeling among some researchers that certain symbol systems (e.g., pictorial representations) are "less symbolic" or "more iconic," there seems to be little question that considerable skill is needed to make sense of, and achieve fluency in, any symbol system. Indeed, every symbol system can be analogized to written language in the sense that one needs time and experience (and, if possible, instruction) before one can "read" products in that symbol system, and before one is able oneself to create (or "write") products in that system. Across the range of symbol systems, there exist numerous features which take considerable expertise to appreciate, ranging from embedded sentences in language, to retrograde inversions in music, to differential equations in mathematics. Nor are most systems ever mastered in their entirety: if one can learn readily to read photographic-like drawings, it still takes years to gain familiarity with the expressive, stylistic, and compositional facets of paintings, and skill in "reading" and "writing" such symbolic entities continues to accrue across one's lifetime. And because symbols come from one's community, they reflect the continually changing norms, values, and attitudes of one's community, even as they eventually contribute to and ultimately determine these communal elements.

Clearly, then, mastery of diverse symbol systems is a lengthy and complex process. One needs skills to read or decode symbol systems, to perform credibly within them, to relate the products of one symbol system (say, a diagram of a physical process) to those in another (a linguistic or numerical account of that process). Nor can we assume that information can ever be captured in exactly equivalent form across symbol systems; it may well be that each symbol system has its properties and limitations which preclude preservation of identity of meaning across an "intersymbolic" translation.

If the above account of the nature and importance of symbolization is cogent, if symbol use and the processes of symbolization are indeed central to human cognitive enterprise, then a program of research in developmental psychology suggests itself. The nature of competences in specific symbol systems needs to be defined; the steps *en route* to these achievements need to be delineated; the role of various symbolic competences in a wide range of adult end states needs to be specified; and, perhaps most crucially, the relationships among these various trajectories of symbolic development and their connection to earlier accounts of cognitive development need to be articulated.

Clearly such a task will call for efforts of the range and perspective of those undertaken by Piaget in the logical-scientific domain. Of particular importance will be the delineation of the optimal means for the study of symbolism; it will be necessary to avoid the Scylla of equating all symbol systems (thereby returning in effect to an uncritically Piagetian position) as well as the Charybdis of spawning countless systems (and thus embracing a mindless "task" position with every use of symbols entails its own stage sequence). The aim, in other words, must be to slice Nature at its crucial "symbolic" joints.

Having suggested the broad outlines of an approach in terms of symbol systems, we must now consider how such an approach might address those areas of study which have been largely ignored by the Piagetian enterprise. To begin with, recognition of a range of symbols, and symbol systems, underscores the parochiality of Piaget's end state of cognition. For while numerical and, to a lesser extent, linguistic symbols dominate the everyday practice of the scientist, quite other symbol systems, and combinations of symbol systems, occupy center stage in other kinds of minds. A focus on musical cognition would highlight musical and numerical symbols; an interest in graphic cognition would stress pictorial symbol systems; an investigation of legal reasoning would highlight linguistic systems, and so on. Study of these diverse cognitive end states would likely yield different developmental trajectories, and thereby call into severe question Piaget's univocal scheme of cognitive development, his belief in "structures of the whole."

An approach in terms of symbol systems raises equally serious problems for Piaget's assumption that all vehicles of meaning are essentially equivalent. Indeed, the basic thrust of the symbol system position outlined here suggests that both the knowledge obtained, and the manner in which it is attained, may differ fundamentally, depending upon the specific materials, symbols, or media which serve as the vehicles of knowledge. Piaget would contend that an individual's basic conception of time, space, or causality should be equally evident and comparably advanced, whether it be probed in words, pictures, or numbers; in contrast, the "symbol system" position holds that one's understanding of these domains will be fundamentally colored by the particular symbolic vehicles with which one has come into contact, and the particular materials and modalities with which this knowledge is tested. So, for example, one group of subjects might be expected to exhibit relatively advanced rhetorical causality (in the manner of a lawyer), while another group might excel in physical causality (in the manner of a scientist or engineer). By the same token, conceptions of time, as embodied in music, might turn out to be fundamentally different from the temporal concepts captured in numerical or gestural systems.

It should be emphasized that, while an undeniable tension exists between Piaget's central system of mental operations and an approach in terms of symbol systems, this latter position is in no way intended as a replacement for Piaget's contributions. Indeed, as currently practiced by a number of researchers, basic tenets of Piaget's contribution are assumed: characteristically, an end state will be defined, developmental stages will be sought, and underlying structural relations among specific behaviors and components will be anticipated. Where these investigators deviate from traditional cognitive-developmental theory is primarily in their willingness to treat as an empirical issue Piaget's assumption that a concept will be manifest in essentially equivalent form, independent of the specific symbol system employed.

Relatively little research has yet been framed in such a way as to permit a direct comparison of these competing views. In my own laboratory we have approached this set of issues from two complementary perspectives. In a longitudinal study of a small group of preschool subjects, we have been examining the rate, and the manner, in which referential and expressive competences unfold in seven different symbolic media (cf. Shotwell *et al.*, 1979; Wolf and Gardner, 1979). A strictly Piagetian "semiotic approach" predicts that mastery of symbolic reference should unfold in closely parallel form across the range of systems; the rival "autonomy of symbol systems" perspective predicts little regularity across subjects and symbol systems. We have in fact found evidence for an intermediate position: close links exist among certain families of symbols (e.g., language is yoked to symbolic play, two-dimensional and three-dimensional depiction are closely allied), more distant links may obtain among certain other symbol systems (e.g., music and number), while little integral relation exists among these three separate families. In a separate but parallel line of study, we have been investigating the breakdown after brain damage of the full range of symbol-using skills (Gardner, 1974b; Wapner and Gardner, 1978). These studies indicate that linguistic and pictorial symbolization occur in virtual independence of one another; that definite and unanticipated links exist among other more specific sets of symbol systems (e.g., ideographic scripts and pictorial representation; logical reasoning and comprehension of syntax); certain other symbolic skills – e.g., musical and numerical competence – seem organized in quite different ways across a range of subjects (cf. Gardner, 1975). Taken together, these avenues of study suggest that competences likely to be equated (or ignored) in a Piagetian position display their own characteristic pattern of development and dissolution.

Related studies by other investigators have focused on the role of specific vehicles or media in the child's acquisition of specific concepts. Olson (1970), for example, has shown that the child's grasp of diagonality must be worked out over a considerable period of time through a wide range of physical materials and performatory modes; a child will "have" the diagonal in certain tasks and responses long before he has elaborated this concept in a more demanding guise. Similarly, Golomb (1973) investigated the child's concept of the human figure, documenting that far greater knowledge of the figure is available when the child is given dictation tasks, or asked to assemble components, than when he must produce the figure "from scratch." And Goodnow (1972) has examined "tricks of the trade" where a child's level of competence can be significantly bolstered by a demonstration (to the child) of the way in which specific media or materials are characteristically employed.

Adoption of this perspective, it should be pointed out, often yields a focus on a set of issues different from those normally featured in Piagetian studies. A tension is created between the concept at issue – which can still be thought of as potentially representable in a highly general (logical) form – and the numerous possible presentations, manifestations, and degrees of mastery of this concept. Attention comes to fall on the nature of specific materials and media, the skills needed to "read messages" with each of these media and to so employ materials that they embody messages which suit one's own purpose while also communicating effectively with others. The point emerges that the "disembodied" knowledge proved by Piagetians may be a fiction. Any concept, any domain, must be encountered in a specific medium, and in a particular task; understanding of competence inheres in a description of various "occasions for mastery" and a delineation of the kinds of transfer which can ultimately be expected. Indeed, it may well be that each material, or medium, has by its very nature a certain "symbolic" bias (cf. Salomon, 1978); there may be no way in which one can present absolutely equivalent stories in two media (say, television and book form) because each medium ineluctably favors certain symbol systems and highlights certain meanings at the expense of others. Such a state of affairs in no way lessens the interesting results which emerge when attempts are made to compare presentations across media (cf. Meringoff,

1978); indeed, these findings merely reinforce the importance of attending not only to the symbol systems involved, but also to the particular media in which they are presented.

Relation to other lines of inquiry

Awareness of the centrality of symbol use, and the importance of detailing its development, is by no means a new phenomenon; in fact Werner and Kaplan (1963) devoted a seminal book to this topic several years ago. There have also been numerous examinations of development in specific domains, including language (Brown, 1973), drawing (Lowenfeld, 1947), gesture (Kaplan, 1968), and number (Gelman, 1969). Moreover, many studies of the range of human abilities, conducted in the testing and factor-analytic tradition, also contain information relevant to this inquiry.

Yet, these previous efforts are at least partially flawed. Broad treatments of the range of symbolic development have paid insufficient attention to the peculiarities of specific symbol systems; there has been an unfortunate tendency to lump together all manner of symbol systems, thus falling prey to the Scyllian alternative sketched above. Studies of specific systems or media, on the other hand, are admirably detailed but leave unexamined the issue of how progress in one domain relates to events in other putatively neighboring (or remote) domains. Finally, while there are considerable data already collected in the factor-analytic and testing traditions, these findings were rarely obtained within the developmental framework. Accordingly, they lack precisely that information about "level of conceptualization" and "stage of understanding" crucial to an integration within cognitive-developmental theory. And, because of a typically atheoretical orientation guiding task selection, they threaten us with either a plethora of symbolic families or, equally perniciously, a set which fails to respect Nature's proper joints.

Thus far, symbols and symbol systems have been portrayed as sets of meaning-bearing vehicles which can enter into relations with one another, and can be mapped onto a field of reference. In practice, however, this description bypasses a host of crucial psychological distinctions. As suggested above, one needs to distinguish among symbol systems and (a) the *media* – the physical materials, like a television set or a book, in which a range of symbol systems can be conveyed; (b) the *sensory and motor systems*, which can likewise perceive and deliver instances from numerous symbol systems; (c) the *developmental domains*, like map-making or chess-playing, which may be peculiar to a specific culture and which, too, can invoke a number of symbol systems (Feldman, 1980). Though such a classificatory effort will be time consuming, it should ultimately indicate the extent to which a treatment in terms of symbol systems reinforces, or contradicts, alternative accounts rooted in media, sensory systems, or cultural-developmental domains. It is my own view that symbol systems, because they can be rigorously defined and described, will prove the most suitable point of departure for post-Piagetian developmental psychology; but certainly a treatment in terms of media, sensory systems, or domains could be envisioned.

A parallel line of inquiry needs to be undertaken with respect to the skills germane for mastery of specific symbol-using domains. It must be determined to what extent the skills required, say, to read a painting, or to perform a piece of music, are identical, or at odds, with the kinds of central skills described by researchers unconcerned with symbolization. For example, one needs to determine whether the mental operations described by Piaget, the notions of computing space proposed by Pascual-Leone (1970), or the mediational processes delineated by Kendler and Kendler (1962) are equally valid across diverse symbol systems, whether they prove particularly relevant to certain symbol systems (e.g., notational ones), or whether they seem relatively orthogonal to an analysis in terms of key symbol systems.

A final, and particularly daunting, challenge concerns the relations between mental representations and the family of symbol systems. It may be that each symbol system has a specific, even unique, mental presentation, but, given the potential infinitude of symbol systems, it seems far more likely that families of symbol systems may be represented by related or even identical mental structures. It will therefore become important to build a model of the relations among these symbol systems; one will then have the opportunity to test predictions about which systems might complement or even enhance one another, and which would be more likely to interfere with the operation (or development) of other systems (cf. Brooks, 1968; Gardner, 1977; Kinsbourne, 1973). Such an inquiry may provide powerful evidence about the "natural joints" undergirding human symbolic capacities.

Conclusion

A principal task of developmental psychology after Piaget, then, is to identify and map the major domains of symbolic development; to trace the developmental milestones within each of these domains; to explore the relation which may obtain among these domains; to relate the emerging portrait of symbolic development to other traditions in developmental psychology; and, perhaps foremost, to ascertain the relation of the resulting portrait to the "central cognition" position outlined by Piaget. It is futile to anticipate in any detail the result of this enterprise; but it seems possible that there will emerge a number of domains with but a loose relation to one another. Among them could be a domain of logical-rational thought (along the lines outlined by Piaget); a domain of visual representation (along the lines outlined, say, by Arnheim, 1969); a sphere of language competence (combining syntactic, semantic, pragmatic, and figurative facets); and a separate avenue for musical growth. A remaining task, then, will be to tease out in each of these domains the role of logical processes and operational structures, the place (if any) occupied by linguistic abilities, and the contributions (if any) made by some of the general developmental phenomena outlined by Piaget, including egocentrism, animism, décalage, and the like. Also desirable will be efforts which trace the use of symbols in such developmental processes as Kohlberg's (1969) portrait of moral development, Selman's (1974) account of social development, and Tompkins' (1963) account of affective development. Of considerable interest, too, will be the contributions of symbolic development to various individual differences, both those of a characterological or personality sort, and those with a significant cognitive component. After all, while individual proclivities may not be of great moment in those general cognitive spheres sketched by Piaget, there is every reason to expect that progress made in more specific symbolic realms (e.g., music) may reflect individual genetic factors, specific parental styles, and idiosyncratic personal experiences, and that the dependence upon particular symbolic forms will produce at least some of the distinctive patterns of human cognition.

Despite my suggestions to the contrary, research on symbolic development may ultimately reinforce Piaget's overall picture, highlighting the principal operational structures and revealing only marginal modifications in terms of specific symbol systems. It may also emerge that we possess but a single language of mental representation (cf. Fodor, 1975; Pylyshyn, 1973) and that, whatever the vagaries of individual development, all symbolic materials (which may include all cognitive materials) are eventually represented in a single computational *lingua franca*. Indeed, whether one chooses to highlight the degree of interconnectedness, or even identity, among the mental representations of particular symbol systems, or whether one elects instead to highlight the importance of the discreteness of each symbol system, is at least to some extent a matter of definition and scientific strategy. Nonetheless, the time for a treatment in terms of symbolism seems at hand. As White (1976) has commented: "In my considered judgment, the area that we now speak of as cognitive development, we will some day speak of as the development of symbolic forms."

Ultimately, the role attributed to symbol use in cognition should not be entirely an accidental matter. It seems parsimonious to assume that we have been prepared by our evolutionary heritage to achieve competence in a range of symbol systems; in some systems, such as language, nearly everyone proves highly skilled, in others, like music, the distribution of gifts seems much less egalitarian. We cannot roll back the calendar of prehistory to discover whether the courses of individual symbol competences closely parallel one another, or whether each system has its own peculiar ontogenesis and genius. Yet by examining patterns of breakdown of symbolic functioning after damage to the competent adult brain, one can receive intriguing cues regarding the normal organization of symbol-using capacities. Such studies lend a measure of credence to the view that there exist overall levels of symbolic competence (Head, 1926; Jackson, 1932; Kaplan, 1968); but at present they offer much more sustenance to the rival position that human beings have available a range of symbol-using faculties, which draw upon a relatively independent set of cognitive skills. Indeed, the evidence emerging from neuropsychology may be the strongest ground on which to base a belief that a study of the development of individual symbol-using capacities can significantly enhance our understanding of human cognition.

PART 2

MI THEORY

███████████

CHAPTER 6

BEYOND THE IQ
Education and human development

This chapter is based on an informal talk given on the 350th anniversary of Harvard University on September 5, 1986. *Harvard Education Review*, Harvard Education Publishing Group, 1987, 57, 187–93.

Allow me to transport all of us to the Paris of 1900 – La Belle Époque. Around 1900 the city fathers of Paris approached a psychologist named Alfred Binet with an unusual request: could he devise some kind of measure which would predict which youngsters would succeed and which would fail in the primary grades of Paris schools? As almost everybody knows, Binet succeeded. He produced a set of test items that could predict a child's success or failure in school. In short order, his discovery came to be called the "intelligence test," his measure the "IQ." Like other Parisian fashions, the IQ soon made its way to the United States, where it enjoyed a modest success until the First World War. Then it was used to test over one million American recruits, and it had truly arrived. From that day on, the IQ test has looked like psychology's biggest success – a genuinely useful scientific tool.

What is the vision that led to the excitement about IQ? At least in the West, people had always relied on intuitive assessments of how smart other people were. Now intelligence seemed to be quantifiable. You could measure someone's actual or potential height, and now, it seemed, you could also measure someone's actual or potential intelligence. We had one dimension of mental ability along which we could array everyone.

The search for the perfect measure of intelligence has proceeded apace. Here, for example, are some quotations from an ad for a widely used test:

> Need an individual test which quickly provides a stable and reliable estimate of intelligence in four or five minutes per form? Has three forms. Doesn't depend upon verbal production or subjective scoring. Can be used with the severely physically handicapped (even paralyzed) if they can signal yes or no, handles two-year-olds and superior adults with the same short series of items and the same format. Only $16.00 complete.

Now, that's quite a claim. Psychologist Arthur Jensen suggests that we could look at reaction time to assess intelligence: a set of lights go on, how quickly can the subject react? Psychologist Hans Eysenck suggests that investigators of intelligence should look directly at brain waves.

There are also, of course, more sophisticated versions of the IQ test. One of them is called the Scholastic Aptitude Test (SAT). It purports to be a similar kind of measure, and if you add up a person's verbal and math scores, as is often done, you can rate him or her along that dimension. Programs for the gifted, for example, often use that kind of measure.

I want to suggest that along with this one-dimensional view of how to assess people's minds comes a corresponding view of school, which I will call the "uniform view." In the uniform school there is a core curriculum, a set of facts that everybody should know, and very few electives. The better students, perhaps those with higher IQs, are allowed to take courses that call upon critical reading, calculation, and thinking skills. In the "uniform school" there are regular assessments, using paper and pencil instruments, of the IQ or SAT variety. They yield reliable rankings of people; the best and the brightest get into the better colleges, and perhaps – but only perhaps – they will also get better rankings in life. There is no question that this approach works well for certain people – a university like Harvard is eloquent testimony to that. Since this measurement and selection system is clearly meritocratic in certain respects, it has something to recommend it.

But there is an alternative vision that I would like to present – one based on a radically different view of the mind and one that yields a very different view of school. It is a pluralistic view of mind, recognizing many different and discrete facets of cognition, acknowledging that people have different cognitive strengths and contrasting cognitive styles. I would also like to introduce the concept of an individual-centered school that takes this multifaceted view of intelligence seriously. This model for a school is based in part on findings from sciences that did not even exist in Binet's time: cognitive science (the study of the mind) and neuroscience (the study of the brain). One such approach I have called my "theory of multiple intelligences." In brief form, I will now tell you something about its sources, its claims, and its educational implications for a possible school of the future.

Dissatisfaction with the concept of IQ and with unitary views of intelligence is fairly widespread – one thinks, for instance, of the work of L.L. Thurstone, J.P. Guilford, and other psychologist-critics. From my point of view, however, these criticisms do not suffice. The whole concept has to be challenged; in fact, it has to be replaced. I believe that we should get away altogether from tests and correlations among tests and look instead at more naturalistic sources of information about how peoples around the world develop skills important to their ways of life. Think, for example, of sailors in the South Seas, who find their way around hundreds, or even thousands, of islands by looking at the constellations of stars in the sky, feeling the way a boat passes over the water, and noticing a few scattered landmarks. A word for intelligence in a society of these sailors would probably refer to that kind of navigational ability. Think of surgeons and engineers, hunters and fishermen, dancers and choreographers, athletes and athletic coaches, tribal chiefs and sorcerers. All of these different roles need to be taken into account if we accept the way I define intelligence – that is, as the ability to solve problems or to fashion products that are valued in one or more cultural settings. For the moment I am saying nothing about whether there is one dimension, or more than one dimension, of intelligence; nothing about whether intelligence is inborn or developed. Instead I emphasize the ability to solve problems and to fashion products. In my work I seek the building blocks of the intelligences used by the aforementioned sailors and surgeons and sorcerers.

The science in this enterprise, to the extent that it exists, involves trying to discover the right description of the intelligences. What is an intelligence? To try to answer this question, I have, with my colleagues, surveyed a wide set of sources which, to my knowledge, have never been considered together before. One source is what we already know of the development of different kinds of skills in normal children. Another source, and a very important one, is information on the ways that these abilities break down under conditions of brain damage. When one suffers a stroke or some other kind of brain damage, various abilities can be destroyed, or spared, in isolation from other abilities. This research with brain-damaged patients yields a very powerful kind of evidence, because it seems to reflect the way the nervous system has evolved over the millennia to yield certain discrete kinds of intelligence.

My research group looks at other special populations as well: prodigies, idiot savants, autistic children, children with learning disabilities, all of whom exhibit very jagged cognitive profiles – profiles that are extremely difficult to explain in terms of a unitary view of intelligence. We examine cognition in diverse animal species and in dramatically different cultures. Finally, we consider two kinds of psychological evidence: correlations among psychological tests of the sort yielded by a factor analysis of a test battery and the results of efforts of skill training. When you train a person in skill A, for example, does that training transfer to skill B? So, for example, does training in mathematics enhance one's musical abilities, or vice versa?

Obviously, through looking at all these sources – information on development, on breakdowns, on special populations and the like – we end up with a cornucopia of information. Optimally, we would perform a factor analysis, feeding all the data into a computer and noting the kinds of factors or intelligences that are extracted. Alas, this kind of material did not exist in a form that is susceptible to computation, and so we had to perform a more subjective factor analysis. In truth, we simply studied the results as best we could and tried to organize them in a way that made sense to us and, hopefully, to critical readers as well. My resulting list of intelligences is a preliminary attempt to organize this mass of information.

I want now to mention briefly the intelligences we have located and to cite one or two examples of each intelligence. Linguistic intelligence is the kind of ability exhibited in its fullest form, perhaps, by poets. Logical-mathematical intelligence, as the name implies, is logical and mathematical ability, as well as scientific ability. Jean Piaget, the great developmental psychologist, thought he was basically studying *all* intelligence, but I believe he was studying the development of logical-mathematical intelligence. Although I name the linguistic and logical-mathematical intelligences first, it is not because I think they are the most important – in fact, I think all seven of the intelligences have equal claim to priority (for an update see Chapters 8, 10, and 11). In our society, however, we have put linguistic and logical-mathematical intelligences, figuratively speaking, on a pedestal. Much of our testing is based on this high valuation of verbal and mathematical skills. If you do well in language and logic, you will do well in IQ tests and SATs, and you may well get into a prestigious college; but whether you do well once you leave is probably going to depend as much on the extent to which you possess and use the other intelligences, and it is to those that I want to give equal attention.

Spatial intelligence is the ability to form a mental model of a spatial world and to be able to maneuver and operate using that model. Sailors, engineers, surgeons, sculptors, and painters, to name a few examples, all have highly developed spatial intelligence. Musical intelligence is the fourth category of ability we have identified: Leonard Bernstein has lots of it; Mozart, presumably, had even more. Bodily-kinesthetic intelligence is the ability to solve problems or to fashion products using one's whole body, or parts of the body. Dancers, athletes, surgeons, and craftspeople all exhibit highly developed bodily-kinesthetic intelligence.

Finally, I propose two forms of personal intelligence – not well understood, elusive to study, but immensely important. Interpersonal intelligence is the ability to understand other people: what motivates them, how they work, how to work cooperatively with them. Successful salespeople, politicians, teachers, clinicians, and religious leaders are all likely to be individuals with high degrees of interpersonal intelligence. Intrapersonal intelligence, a seventh kind of intelligence, is a correlative ability, turned inward. It is a capacity to form an accurate, veridical model of oneself and to be able to use that model to operate effectively in life.

These, then, are the intelligences that we have described in our research. (Later I added an eighth – "naturalist" intelligence – and also considered the possibility of a ninth – "existential" intelligence; see Chapters 8, 10, and 11.) This is a preliminary list; as I have said, obviously each form of intelligence can be subdivided, or the list can be rearranged. The real point here is to make the case for the plurality of intellect. Also, we believe that individuals may differ in the particular intelligence profiles with which they are born, and that certainly they differ in the profiles they end up with. I think of the intelligences as raw, biological potentials, which can be seen in pure form only in individuals who are, in the technical sense, freaks. In almost everybody else the intelligences work together to solve problems, to yield various kinds of cultural end states – vocations, avocations, and the like.

This is my theory of multiple intelligences in capsule form. In my view, the purpose of school should be to develop intelligences and to help people reach vocational and avocational goals that are appropriate to their particular spectrum of intelligences. People who are helped to do so, I believe, feel more engaged and competent and therefore more inclined to serve society in a constructive way.

These thoughts, and the critique of a universalistic view of mind with which I began, lead to the notion of an individual-centered school, one geared to optimal understanding and development of each student's cognitive profile. This vision stands in direct contrast to that of the uniform school that I described earlier.

The design of my ideal school of the future is based upon two assumptions. The first is that not all people have the same interests and abilities; not all of us learn in the same way. (And we now have the tools to begin to address these individual differences in school.) The second assumption is one that hurts: it is the assumption that nowadays no one person can learn everything there is to learn. We would all like, as Renaissance men and women, to know everything, or at least to believe in the potential of knowing everything, but that ideal clearly is not possible any more. Choice is therefore inevitable, and one of the things that I want to argue is that the choices that we make for ourselves, and for the people who are under our charge, might as well be informed choices. An individual-centered school would be rich in assessment of individual abilities and proclivities. It would seek to match individuals not only to curricular areas, but also to particular ways of teaching those subjects. And after the first few grades, the school would also seek to match individuals with the various kinds of life and work options that are available in their culture.

I want to propose a new set of roles for educators that might make this vision a reality. First of all, we might have what I will call "assessment specialists." The job of these people would be to try to understand as sensitively as possible the abilities and interests of the students in a school. It would be very important, however, that the assessment specialists use "intelligence-fair" instruments. We want to be able to look specifically and directly at spatial abilities, at personal abilities, and the like, and not through the usual lenses of the linguistic and logical-mathematical intelligences. Up until now nearly all assessment has depended indirectly on measurement of those abilities; if students are not strong in those areas, if, for example, they are not good at solving multiple-choice questions, their abilities in other areas may be obscured. Once we begin to try to assess other kinds of intelligences directly, I am confident that particular students will reveal strengths in quite different areas, and the notion of general brightness will disappear or become greatly attenuated.

In fact, I am involved with colleagues in two collaborations through which we are attempting to determine what assessment might be like in the future. One such effort, undertaken with my colleague David Feldman, is taking place at a local preschool with which we are working closely. We have richly equipped the school with materials that should engage the range of the students' intelligences, and in fact we call our effort "Project SPECTRUM." The children are allowed to gravitate naturally to a wide variety of games, puzzles, and other materials. They can show us, through their play activities, what their particular combinations of interests and strengths are. At the conclusion of the school year we present what we call a "spectrum profile" for each child to his or her parents and teachers. This is a description in plain English of a child's particular cognitive profile, together with some concrete suggestions of what might be done at home, in school, and in the wider community to help that particular child to develop his or her interests and abilities (see Chapter 19 and Gardner, Feldman, and Krechevsky, 1998).

Our second research collaboration involves the teaching of the arts and humanities to preadolescent and adolescent students. We are working with the Educational Testing Service, which does many things other than administer the SAT. In this project, named "ARTS PROPEL," we are trying to develop new ways of figuring out the strengths of students in the junior and senior high school in the arts and humanities. We are agreed that, whatever use paper-and-pencil tests may have in other areas, they are not the optimal way to reveal students' latent abilities in the arts and humanities. In ARTS PROPEL, students are working instead in a much more molar way on large-scale projects, which will then be collected in portfolios for us to assess. It is my hope that a student profile based on such assessments might serve at least as an adjunct to standardized testing, and that perhaps it may eventually even serve as an alternative to testing (see Chapter 13).

In addition to the assessment specialist, the school of the future might have the "student curriculum broker." It would be his or her job to help match students' profiles, goals, and interests to particular curricula and to particular styles of learning. Incidentally, I think that the new interactive technologies offer considerable promise in this area; it will probably be much easier in the future for "brokers" to match individual students to ways of learning that prove comfortable for them.

There should also be, I think, a "school-community broker," who would match students to learning opportunities in the wider community. It would be this person's job to find situations in the community, particularly options not available in the school, for children who exhibit unusual cognitive profiles. I have in mind apprenticeships, mentorships, internships in organizations, "big brothers," "big sisters," individuals and organizations with whom these students might work to secure a feeling for different kinds of vocational and avocational roles in the society. I am not worried about those rare youngsters who are good in everything; they're going to do just fine. I'm concerned about those who don't shine in the standardized tests, and who, therefore, tend to be written off as not having gifts of any kind. It seems to me that the school-community broker could spot these youngsters and find placements in the community that provide chances for them to shine.

There is ample room in this vision for teachers as well, and also for master teachers. In my view, teachers would be freed to do what they are supposed to do, which is to teach their subject matter, in their preferred style of teaching. The job of master teacher would be very demanding. It would involve, first of all, supervising the novice teachers and guiding them, but the master teacher would also seek to ensure that the complex student–assessment–curriculum–community equation is balanced appropriately. If the equation is seriously unbalanced, master teachers would intervene and suggest ways to make things better.

Clearly, what I am describing is a tall order; it might even be called utopian. And there is a major risk to this program, of which I am well aware. That is the risk of premature billeting – of saying, "Well, Johnny is four, he seems to be musical, so we are going to drop everything else and send him to Juilliard." There is, however, nothing inherent in the approach that I have described that demands this early channeling – quite the contrary. It seems to me that early identification of strengths can be very helpful in indicating what kinds of experiences children might profit from, but early identification of weaknesses can be equally important. If a weakness is identified early, there is a chance to attend to it before it is too late and to come up with alternative ways of teaching or of covering an important skill area.

We now have the technological and human resources to implement such an individual-centered school. Achieving it is a question of will, including the will to withstand the current enormous pressures toward uniformity and unidimensional assessments. There are strong pressures now, which you read about every day in the national and local newspapers, to compare students, teachers, states, even entire countries, using one dimension or criterion, a kind of crypto-IQ assessment. Clearly, everything I have described today stands in direct opposition to that particular view of the world. Indeed that is my intent – to provide a ringing indictment of such one-track thinking.

I believe that in our society we suffer from three biases, which I have nicknamed "Westist," "Testist," and "Bestist." "Westist" involves putting certain Western cultural values, which date back to Socrates, on a pedestal. Logical thinking, for example, is important; rationality is important; but they are not the only virtues. "Testist" suggests a bias toward focusing upon those human abilities or approaches that are readily testable. If it can't be tested, it sometimes seems, it is not worth paying attention to. My feeling is that assessment can be much broader, much more humane than it is now, and that psychologists should spend less time ranking people and more time trying to help them.

"Bestist" is a not very veiled reference to a book by David Halberstam called *Best and the Brightest* (1972). Halberstam referred ironically to figures such as Harvard faculty members who were brought to Washington in the early 1960s to help the Kennedy administration and in the process launched the Vietnam war. I think that any belief that all the answers to a given problem lie in one certain approach, such as logical-mathematical thinking, can be very dangerous.

It is of the utmost importance that we recognize and nurture all of the varied human intelligences and all of the combinations of intelligences. We are all different from one another largely because we all have different combinations of intelligences. If we recognize this, I think we will have at least a better chance of dealing appropriately with the many problems that we face in the world. If we can mobilize the spectrum of human abilities, not only will people feel better about themselves and feel more competent; it is even possible that they will also feel more engaged and more readily able to join with the rest of the world community in working for the broader good. Perhaps if we can mobilize the full range of human intelligences and ally them to an ethical sense, we can help to increase the likelihood of our survival on this planet and perhaps even contribute to our thriving.

CHAPTER 7

REFLECTIONS ON MI

Myths and messages

Phi Delta Kappan, 1995, 77 (3), 200–209

A silence of a decade's length is sometimes a good idea. I published *Frames of Mind*, an introduction to the theory of multiple intelligences (MI theory), in 1983. Because I was critical of current views of intelligences within the discipline of psychology, I expected some controversy among my fellow psychologists. This expectation was not disappointed.

I was unprepared for the large and mostly positive reaction to the theory among educators. Naturally I was gratified by this response and was stimulated thereby to undertake some projects in which the implications of MI theory were explored. I also took pleasure from – and was occasionally moved by – the many attempts to institute an MI approach to education in schools and classrooms. By and large, however, except for a few direct responses to criticisms (Gardner, 1987b), I did not speak up about new thoughts concerning the theory itself.

In 1993 my self-imposed silence was broken in two ways. My publisher issued a tenth anniversary edition of *Frames of Mind*, to which I contributed a short, reflective introductory essay. In tandem, the publisher also issued *Multiple Intelligences: The Theory in Practice* (1993c), a set of articles chronicling some of the experiments undertaken in the wake of MI theory – mostly projects undertaken by colleagues at Harvard Project Zero, but also descriptions of other MI initiatives. This collection also gave me the opportunity to answer some other criticisms leveled against MI theory and to respond publicly to some of the most frequently asked questions.

In the years since *Frames of Mind* was published, I have heard, read, and seen several hundred different interpretations of what MI theory is and how it can be applied in schools. Until now, I have been content to let MI theory take on a life of its own. As I saw it, I had issued an "ensemble of ideas" (or "memes") to the outer world, and I was inclined to let those "memes" fend for themselves. Yet, in light of my own readings and observations, I believe that the time has come for me to issue a set of new "memes" of my own.

In the second part of this chapter, I discuss seven myths that have grown up about MI and, by putting forth seven complementary "realities," I attempt to set the record straight. Then, in the third part of the essay, reflecting on my observations of MI experiments in the schools, I describe three primary ways in which education can be enhanced by an MI perspective.

In what follows, I make no attempt to isolate MI theory from MI practice. "Multiple intelligences" began as a theory but was almost immediately put to practical use. The commerce between theory and practice has been ready, continuous, and, for the most part, productive.

Myth #1 Now that seven (or more) intelligences have been identified, one can – and perhaps should – create seven tests and secure seven (or more) scores.

Reality #1 MI theory represents a critique of "psychometrics-as-usual." A battery of MI tests is inconsistent with the major tenets of the theory.

Comment: My concept of intelligences is an outgrowth of accumulating knowledge about the human brain and about human cultures; it is not the result of *a priori* definitions nor of factor analyses of test scores. As such, it becomes crucial that intelligences be assessed in ways that are "intelligent-fair," in ways that examine the intelligence directly rather than through the lens of linguistic or logical intelligence (as ordinary paper-and-pencil tests do).

Thus, if one wants to look at spatial intelligence, one should allow an individual to explore a terrain for a while and see whether they can find their way around it reliably. Or if one wants to examine musical intelligence, one should expose an individual to a new melody in a reasonably familiar idiom and see how readily the person can learn to sing it, recognize it, transform it, and the like.

Assessing multiple intelligences is not a high priority in every setting. But when it is necessary or advisable to assess an individual's intelligences, it is best to do so in a comfortable setting with materials (and with cultural roles) that are familiar to that individual. These conditions are at variance with our general conception of testing, as a decontextualized exercise using materials that are unfamiliar by design; but there is no reason in principle why an "intelligence-fair" set of measures cannot be devised. The production of such useful tools has been our goal in such projects as Spectrum, ARTS PROPEL, and Practical Intelligence for School (PIFS) (see Gardner 1993c and 1999, and Chapters 13 and 19).

Myth #2 An intelligence is the same as a domain or a discipline.

Reality #2 An intelligence is a new kind of construct, and it should not be confused with a domain or a discipline.

Comment: I must shoulder a fair part of the blame for the propagation of this myth. In writing *Frames of Mind*, I was not as careful as I should have been in distinguishing intelligences from other related concepts. As I have now come to understand, largely through my interactions with Mihaly Csikszentmihalyi and David Feldman (Feldman, Csikszentmihalyi, and Gardner 1994), an *intelligence* is a biological and psychological potential; that potential is capable of being realized to a greater or lesser extent as a consequence of the experiential, cultural, and motivational factors that affect a person.

In contrast, a *domain* is an organized set of activities within a culture, one typically characterized by a specific symbol system and its attendant operations. Any cultural activity in which individuals participate on more than a casual basis, and in which degrees of expertise can be identified and nurtured, should be considered as a domain. Thus, physics, chess, gardening, and rap music are all domains in Western culture. Any domain can be realized through the use of several intelligences: thus the domain of musical performance involves bodily-kinesthetic and personal as well as musical intelligences. By the same token, a particular intelligence, such as spatial intelligence, can be put to work in a myriad domains, ranging from sculpture to sailing to neuroanatomical investigations.

Finally, the *field* is the set of individuals and institutions that judge the acceptability and creativity of products, fashioned by individuals (with their characteristic intelligences) within established or new domains. Judgments of quality cannot be made apart from the operation of members of a field, though it is worth noting that both the members of a field and the criteria that they employ can and do change over time.

Myth #3   An intelligence is the same as a "learning style," a "cognitive style," or a "working style."

Reality #3   The concept of *style* designates a general approach that an individual can apply equally to every conceivable content. In contrast, an *intelligence* is a capacity, with its component processes, that is geared to a specific content in the world (like musical sounds or spatial patterns). A person with a high intelligence in my sense of the term is one whose computational capacities are very effective with a particular form of information or content. For instance, Judy's musical intelligence is high because she learns new melodies easily. Her spatial intelligence is weak because she has difficulties assimilating and mastering an unfamiliar terrain.

Comment: To highlight the difference between an intelligence and a style, consider this contrast. If a person is said to have a "reflective" or an "intuitive style," this designation assumes that the individual will be reflective or intuitive with the full gamut of content ranging from language to music to social analysis. However, such an assertion reflects an empirical assumption that actually needs to be investigated. It might well be the case that an individual is reflective with music, but fails to be reflective in a domain that requires mathematical thinking; or that a person is highly intuitive in the social domain but not in the least intuitive when it comes to mathematics or mechanics.

In my view, the relation between my concept of intelligence and the various conceptions of style needs to be worked out empirically, on a style-by-style basis. We cannot assume that style means the same thing to Carl Jung, Jerome Kagan, Tony Gregoric, Bernice McCarthy, and other inventors of stylistic terminology. There is little authority for assuming that an individual who evinces a style in one milieu or with one content will necessarily do so with other diverse contents – even less authority for equating styles with intelligences.

Myth #4   MI theory is not empirical.
(Variant of Myth #4   MI theory is empirical and has been disproved.)

Reality #4   MI theory is based wholly on empirical evidence and can be revised on the basis of new empirical findings.

Comment: Anyone who puts forth Myth #4 cannot have read *Frames of Mind*. Literally hundreds of empirical studies were reviewed in that book, and the actual intelligences were identified and delineated on the basis of empirical findings. The intelligences described in *Frames of Mind* represented my best-faith effort to identify mental abilities of a grain size that could be readily discussed and critiqued.

No empirically based theory is ever established permanently. All claims are at risk in the light of new findings. In the past decade I have collected and reflected upon empirical evidence that is relevant to the claims of MI theory, 1983 version. Thus, work on the development in children of a "theory of mind," as well as the study of pathologies in which an individual loses a sense of social judgment, have provided fresh evidence for the importance and independence of interpersonal intelligence. In contrast, the findings of a possible link between musical and spatial thinking has caused me to reflect on the possible relations between faculties that have previously been thought to be independent. Many other lines of evidence could be mentioned here; the important point is that MI theory is constantly being reconceptualized in terms of new findings from the laboratory and from the field (see also Myth #7).

Myth #5   MI theory is incompatible with "g" (general intelligence), with hereditarian accounts, or with environmental (cultural) contents.

Reality #5   MI theory questions not the existence but the province and explanatory power of "g." By the same token, MI theory is neutral on the question of the heritability of specific intelligences, instead underscoring the centrality of gene–environmental interactions.

Comment: Interest in "g" comes chiefly from those who are probing scholastic intelligence, and those who traffic in the correlations among test scores. (Recently there have been interests in the possible neurophysiological underpinnings of "g"; and, sparked by the publication of *The Bell Curve* (Herrnstein and Murray, 1994), interest in the possible social consequences of "low g.") While I have been critical of much of the research in the "g" tradition, I do not consider the study of "g" to be scientifically improper, and I am willing to accept the utility of "g" for certain theoretical purposes. My interest, obviously, centers on those intelligences and intellectual processes that are not covered by "g."

While a major animating force in psychology has been the study of the heritability of intelligence(s), my inquiries have not oriented in this direction. I do not doubt that human abilities, and human differences, have a genetic base: can any serious scientist question this today? And I believe that behavioral genetic studies, particularly of twins reared apart, can illuminate certain issues. However, along with most biologically informed scientists, I reject the "inherited vs. learned" dichotomy and instead stress the interaction, from the moment of conception, between genetic and environmental factors.

Myth #6   MI theory so broadens the notion of intelligence that it includes all psychological constructs and thus vitiates the usefulness, and the usual connotation, of the term.

Reality #6   This statement is simply wrong. In my view, it is the standard definition of intelligence that narrowly constricts our view, treating a certain form of scholastic performance as if it encompassed the range of human capacities and leading to disdain for those who happen not to be psychometrically bright. Moreover, I reject the distinction between talent and intelligence; in my view, what we call "intelligence" in the vernacular is simply a certain set of "talents" in the linguistic and/or logical-mathematical spheres.

Comment: MI theory is about the intellect, the human mind in its cognitive aspects. I believe that a treatment in terms of a number of semi-independent intelligences presents a more sustainable conception of human thought than one that posits a single "bell curve" of intellect.

Note, however, that MI theory makes no claims whatsoever to deal with issues beyond the intellect. MI theory is not, and does not pretend to be, about personality, will, morality, attention, motivation, and other psychological constructs. Note, as well, that MI theory is not connected to any set of morals or values. An intelligence can be put to an ethical or an anti-social use. Poet and playwright Johann Wolfgang von Goethe and Nazi propagandist Joseph Goebbels were both masters of the German language; but how different were the uses to which they put their respective talents?!

Myth #7   There are additional intelligences, like spiritual or humor intelligence.

Reality #7   I continue to work on this issue.

Comment: For the reasons suggested above, I thought it wise not to attempt to revise the principal claims of MI theory before the 1983 version of the theory had been debated. But recently I have turned my attention to possible additions to the list. If I were to rewrite *Frames of Mind* today, I would add an eighth intelligence: the intelligence of the naturalist. It seems to me that the individual who is able readily to recognize flora and fauna, to make other consequential distinctions in the natural world, and to use this ability productively (in hunting, in farming, in biological science) is exercising an important intelligence, and one that is not adequately encompassed in the current list. Individuals such as Charles Darwin or E.O. Wilson embody the naturalist's intelligence; and in our consuming culture, youngsters (and some others) exploit their naturalist's intelligence as they effect acute discriminations among kinds of cars, sneakers, or hairstyles.

I have read in several secondary sources that there is a spiritual intelligence and, indeed, that I have endorsed a spiritual intelligence. That statement is not true. It is true that I have become interested in understanding better what is meant by "spirituality" and by "spiritual individuals." Whether or not it proves appropriate to add "spirituality" to the list of intelligences, this human capacity certainly deserves discussion and study in non-fringe psychological circles. At present, I prefer to speak about a possible "existential intelligence" – an intelligence that denotes the human capacity to raise and ponder large questions.

If one were to continue adding myths to the list, a promising one would read: "There is a single educational approach based on MI theory."

I trust that I have made it clear that I do not subscribe to this myth. On the contrary, MI theory is in no way an educational prescription. There is always a gulf between psychological claims about how the mind works and educational practices, and such a gulf is especially apparent in a theory that was developed without specific educational goals in mind. Thus, in educational discussions, I have always taken the position that educators are in the best position to determine the uses to which MI theory can and should be put.

Indeed, contrary to much that has been written, MI theory does *not* incorporate a "position" on tracking, gifted education, inter-disciplinary curricula, the layout of the school day, length of the school year, or many other "hot button" educational issues. I have tried to encourage certain "applied MI efforts," but in general my advice has echoed the traditional Chinese adage "Let a hundred flowers bloom." And often I have been surprised and delighted by the fragrance of some of these fledgling plants – for example, the use of an "MI curriculum" in order to facilitate communication among youngsters drawn from different cultures; or the conveying of pivotal principles in biology or social studies through a dramatic performance designed and staged by students.

I have become convinced, however, that while there is no "right way" to conduct an MI education, some current efforts go against the spirit of my formulation and embody one or more of the myths sketched above. Let me mention a few applications that have jarred me:

- The attempt to teach all concepts or subjects using all the intelligences. As I indicate below, most topics can be powerfully approached in a number of ways. But there is no point in assuming that every topic can be effectively approached in at least seven or eight ways, and it is a waste of effort and time to attempt to do this.
- The belief that it suffices, in and of itself, just to go through the motions of exercising a certain intelligence. Thus, I have seen classes in which children are just encouraged to move their arms, or to run around, on the assumption that exercising one's body represents in itself some kind of MI statement. Don't read me as saying that exercise is a bad thing; it is not. But random muscular movements have nothing to do with the cultivation of the mind ... or even of the body! Nor is a youngster who is hyperactive necessarily displaying bodily-kinesthetic intelligence.

- The use of materials associated with an intelligence as background. In some classes, children are encouraged to read or to carry out math exercises while music is playing in the background. Now I myself like to work with music in the background. But unless I focus on the performance (in which case the composition is no longer serving as background), the music's function is unlikely to be different from that of a dripping faucet or a humming fan.

- The use of intelligences primarily as mnemonic devices. It may well be the case that it is easier to remember a list if one sings it, or even if one dances while reciting it. I have nothing against such aids to memory. However, these uses of the materials of an intelligence are essentially trivial. What is not trivial – as I argue below – is to think musically, or to draw on some of the structural aspects of music in order to illuminate concepts such as biological evolution or historical cycles.

- The conflating of intelligences with other desiderata. This practice is particularly notorious when it comes to the personal intelligences. Interpersonal intelligence has to do with understanding other people – but it is often distorted as a license for cooperative learning or applied to individuals who are extroverted. Intrapersonal intelligence has to do with understanding oneself, but it is often distorted as a rationale for self-esteem programs or applied to individuals who are loners or introverted. One receives the strong impression that individuals who use the terms in this promiscuous way have not read my own writings on intelligence.

- The direct evaluation (or even grading) of intelligences, without regard to context or content. Intelligences ought to be seen at work when individuals are carrying out productive activities that are valued in a culture. And that is how reporting of learning and mastery should take place, in general. I see little point in grading individuals in terms of how "linguistic" or how "bodily-kinesthetic" they are; such a practice is likely to introduce a new and unnecessary form of tracking and labeling. As a parent (or as a supporter of education), I am interested in the *uses* to which children's intelligences are put; reporting about specific youngsters should have this focus. Note that it is reasonable, for certain purposes, to indicate that a child seems to have a relative strength in one intelligence and a relative weakness in another. However, these descriptions should be mobilized in order to help students perform better in meaningful activities and perhaps even to show that a label was premature or erroneous.

Having illustrated some problematic applications of MI theory, let me now indicate three more positive ways in which MI can be – and has been – used in schools.

1 *The cultivation of desired end states.* Schools should cultivate those skills and capacities that are valued in the community and in the broader society. Some of these desired roles are likely to highlight specific intelligences, including ones that have usually been given short shrift in the schools. If, say, the community believes that children should be able to perform on a musical instrument, then the cultivation of musical intelligence toward that end becomes a value of the school. Similarly, emphasis on such end states as taking into account the feelings of others, being able to plan one's own life in a reflective manner, or being able to find one's way around an unfamiliar terrain, is likely to result in an emphasis on the cultivation of interpersonal, intrapersonal, and spatial intelligences, respectively.

2   *Approaching a concept, subject matter, or discipline in a variety of ways.*
Along with many other school reformers of the day, I am convinced that
schools attempt to cover way too much material, and that superficial understandings (or non-understandings) are the inevitable result. It makes far more
sense to spend a significant amount of time on key concepts, generative ideas,
essential questions, and to allow students to become thoroughly familiar with
these notions and their implications.

Once the decision has been made to dedicate time to particular items, it
then becomes possible to approach those topics or notions in a variety of ways.
Not necessarily in seven or eight, let alone 1,000 ways, but in a number of ways
that prove pedagogically appropriate for the topic at hand. Here is where MI
comes in. As I argue in *The Unschooled Mind* (1991c), nearly every topic can be
approached in a variety of ways, ranging from the telling of a story, through a
formal argument, to an artistic exploration, to some kind of "hands-on" experiment or simulation. Such pluralistic approaches should be encouraged.

When a topic has been approached from a number of perspectives, three
desirable outcomes ensue. First of all, because children do not all learn in the
same way, more children will be reached – I term this desirable state-of-affairs
"multiple windows leading into the same room." Second, students secure a
sense of what it is like to be an expert when they behold that a teacher can represent knowledge in a number of different ways, and that they themselves are
also capable of more than a single representation of a specified content. Finally,
since understanding can also be demonstrated in more than one way, a pluralistic approach opens up the possibility that students can demonstrate *their* new
understandings – as well as their continuing difficulties – in ways that are comfortable for them and accessible to others. Performance-based examinations
and exhibitions are tailor-made for the foregrounding of a student's MI.

3   *The personalization of education.*   Without a doubt, one of the reasons that
MI theory has attracted attention in the educational community is because of its
ringing endorsement of an ensemble of propositions: we are not all the same; we
do not all have the same kinds of minds; education works most effectively for
most individuals, if these differences in mental processes and strengths are taken
into account rather than denied or ignored. I have always believed that the heart
of the MI perspective – in theory and in practice – inheres in taking extremely
seriously the differences among human beings. At the theoretical level, one
acknowledges that all individuals cannot be profitably arrayed on a single intellectual dimension. At the practical level, one acknowledges that any uniform
educational approach is likely to serve only a minority of children.

When I visit an "MI school," I look for evidence of personalization: evidence that all involved in the educational encounter take such differences
among human beings extremely seriously; evidence that they construct curricula, pedagogy, and assessment insofar as possible in the light of these differences. All the MI posters, indeed all the references to me personally, prove of
little avail if the youngsters continue to be treated in homogenized fashion. By
the same token, whether or not members of the staff have even heard of MI
theory, I would be happy to send my children to a school with the following
characteristics: differences among youngsters are taken seriously; knowledge
about differences is shared with children and parents; children gradually
assume responsibility for their own learning; and materials that are worth

knowing are presented in ways that afford each child the maximum opportunity to master those materials and to show others (and themselves) what they have learned and understood.

I am often asked for my views about schools that are engaged in MI efforts. The implicit question may well be: "Aren't you upset by some of the applications that are carried out in your name?"

In truth, I do not expect that initial efforts to apply any new ideas are going to be stunning. Human experimentation is slow, difficult, and filled with zigs and zags. And so I fully expect the initial applications of any set of innovative ideas will at times be half-hearted, superficial, even wrong-headed.

For me the crucial question concerns what has happened in a school (or class) two, three, or four years after it has made a commitment to an MI approach. Often, the initiative will be long since forgotten – the fate, for better or worse, of most educational experimentation. Sometimes, the school will get stuck in a rut, repeating the same procedures of the first days without having drawn any positive or negative lessons from this exercise. Needless to say, I am not happy with either of these outcomes.

I cherish an educational setting where discussions and applications of MI have catalyzed a more fundamental consideration of schooling: its overarching purposes, its conceptions of what a productive life will be like in the future, its pedagogical methods, and its educational outcomes, particularly in the context of the values of that specific community. Such discussions generally lead to more thoughtful schooling. Visits with other schools, and more extended forms of networking among MI enthusiasts (and critics), constitute important parts of this building process. If, as a result of these discussions and experiments, a more personalized education is the outcome, I feel that the heart of MI theory has been embodied. And if this personalization is fused with a commitment to the achievement of worthwhile (and attainable) educational understandings for all children, then the basis for a powerful education has indeed been laid.

The MI endeavor is a continuing and changing one. There have emerged over the years new thoughts about the theory, new understandings and misunderstandings, and new applications, some very inspired, some less so. Especially gratifying to me has been the demonstration that this process is dynamic and interactive: no one, not even its creator, has a monopoly on MI wisdom or foolishness. Practice is enriched by theory, even as theory is transformed in the light of the fruits and frustrations of practice. The burgeoning of a community that takes MI issues seriously is not only a source of pride to me but also the best guarantor that the theory will continue to live in the years ahead.

CHAPTER 8

WHO OWNS INTELLIGENCE?

The Atlantic Monthly, 1999, 67–76.

As a psychologist, I've always assumed that my fellow psychologists and I owned the concept of intelligence. Of course, I realize that the word "intelligence" is used by those in the diplomatic community, and that it has a proper place in our idle chatter. But when it comes to the scientific study of intelligence, psychologists have had a virtual monopoly on the territory – at least until now.

We can even pinpoint the paternity of the scientific approach to intelligence. It belongs to Alfred Binet, a gifted psychologist, who devised the first intelligence test at the dawn of the twentieth century. Binet is a hero to many psychologists. He was a keen observer, a careful scholar, an inventive technologist. Perhaps even more important for his followers, he devised the instrument which is often considered psychology's greatest success story. Millions of people who have never heard Binet's name have had their fates determined by instrumentation that the French psychologist inspired. And thousands of measurement specialists – called psychometricians – earn their livings courtesy of Binet's invention.

But while successful over the long run, the psychologist's version of intelligence is now facing its biggest threat. Many scholars and observers – and even some iconoclastic psychologists – feel that intelligence is too important to leave to the psychometricians. Experts are extending the breadth of intelligence – proposing many intelligences, including emotional intelligence and moral intelligence. They are experimenting with new methods of ascertaining intelligence, including ones that avoid tests altogether in favor of direct measures of brain activity. They are forcing society to confront a number of questions. What is intelligence? How ought it to be assessed? And how do our notions of intelligence fit with what we value about human beings? In short, as my title suggests, experts are competing for the "ownership" of intelligence in the next century.

The outline of the psychometricians' success story is well known. Binet's colleagues in England and Germany contributed to the conceptualization and instrumentation of intelligence testing – which soon became known as the IQ test. (An Intelligence Quotient designates the ratio between mental age and chronological age. Clearly it is preferable for a child to have an IQ of 120 – where one is smarter than one is old – than an IQ of 80 – where one is older than one is smart.) And, like other Parisian fashions of the period, the intelligence test migrated easily to the United States. First used to determine who was feeble-minded, it was soon used to assess "normal children," to identify the "gifted," and to determine who was fit to serve in the army. By the 1920s the intelligence test had become a fixture in educational practice in the United States and through much of western Europe.

Early intelligence tests were not without their critics. Many enduring concerns were first raised by the influential journalist Walter Lippmann in a series of published debates with Stanford University's Lewis Terman, the "father" of IQ testing in America. Lippmann noted the superficiality of the questions, their possible cultural biases, and the "high-stake" risks of assessing an individual's intellectual potential via a brief oral or paper-and-pencil measure. IQ tests were also the subject of many jokes and cartoons. Still, by sticking to their trade, the psychometricians were able to defend their instruments, even as they made their way back and forth between the halls of academe, their testing cubicles in schools and hospitals, and the ever-expanding vaults in their banks.

Perhaps surprisingly, the conceptualization of intelligence did not advance much in the decades following Binet and Terman's pioneering contributions. Intelligence testing came to be seen, rightly or wrongly, as primarily a technology for selecting individuals to fill academic or vocational niches. In one of the most famous – if irritating – quips about intelligence testing, the influential Harvard psychologist E.G. Boring declared: "Intelligence is what the tests test." So long as these tests did what they were supposed to do – that is, give some indication of school success – it did not seem necessary or prudent to probe too deeply into their meanings or to explore alternative views of the matter.

Psychologists of intelligence have argued chiefly about three questions. The first: is intelligence singular, or are there various more-or-less independent intellectual faculties? Hedgehog purists – ranging from the English psychologist Charles Spearman at the turn of the twentieth century to his latter-day disciples Richard Herrnstein and Charles Murray (of *The Bell Curve* fame) – defend the notion of a single supervening "g" or general intelligence. Fox-like pluralists – ranging from Chicago's L.L. Thurstone, who posited seven vectors of the mind, to California's J.P. Guilford, who discerned 150 factors of the intellect – construe intelligence as composed of some or even many dissociable components. In his much cited *The Mismeasure of Man* (1981), paleontologist Stephen Jay Gould argued that the conflicting conclusions reached on this issue simply reflect alternative assumptions about statistical procedures rather than "*the* way the mind is." Still, psychologists continue to debate this issue, with a majority sympathetic to a single, "general intelligence" perspective.

The lay public is more interested in a second contentious question: is intelligence (or are intelligences) largely inherited? It should be noted that this is by and large a Western question. In the Confucian societies of East Asia, it is assumed that individual differences in endowment are modest and that differences in achievement are due largely to differences in expended effort. In the West, however, there is much sympathy for the view – first defended vocally within psychology by Lewis Terman – that intelligence is inborn and that there is little one can do to alter one's quantitative intellectual birthright.

Studies of identical twins reared apart provide surprisingly strong support for the "heritability" of psychometric intelligence. That is, if one wants to predict someone's score on an intelligence test, it is more relevant to know the identity of the biological parents (even if the child has not had appreciable contact with them) than the identity of the adoptive parents. By the same token, the IQs of identical twins are more similar than the IQs of fraternal twins. And, contrary to common sense (and political correctness), IQs of biologically related individuals grow more similar in the later years of life, rather than more different. Still, because of the limitations of the discipline of behavioral genetics, and the difficulties of conducting valid experiments with human childrearing, one still finds those who defend the proposition that intelligence is largely environmental, as well as those who believe that we cannot answer this question at all.

Most scholars agree that, even if psychometric intelligence is largely inherited, it is not possible to pinpoint the sources of differences in average IQ *between* groups, such as the fifteen-point difference typically observed between African-American and white populations. That is because it is not possible in our society to equate the contemporary (let alone the historical) experiences of these two groups. The conundrum: one could only ferret out the differences (if any) between black and white populations in a society that was literally colorblind.

One other question has intrigued lay individuals and psychologists: are intelligence tests biased? If one looks at early intelligence tests, the whopping cultural assumptions built into certain items are evident. There are obvious class biases – who except the wealthy can, without formal study, answer a question about polo or fine wines? There are also subtler nuances – while ordinarily it makes sense to turn over money found on the street to the police, what happens in the case of a hungry child? Or with respect to a police force that is known to be hostile to members of one's own minority group? Normally, only the canonical response to such a question would be scored as correct.

Psychometricians have striven to remove the obviously biased items from such measures. Yet it is far more difficult to deal with biases that are built into the test situation itself. For example, an individual's background certainly figures into his reactions to being placed in an unfamiliar locus, instructed by an interrogator dressed in a certain way, and having a printed test booklet thrust into his hands. And as psychologist Claude Steele has shown, the biases prove even more acute in cases where an individual knows that her intellect is being measured, and where she belongs to a racial or ethnic group that is widely considered to be less smart than the dominant social group.

Talk of bias touches on the frequently held assumption that tests in general, and intelligence tests in particular, are inherently conservative instruments – Tools of the Establishment. It is therefore worth noting that many test pioneers thought of themselves as progressives in the social sphere. They were devising instruments that could reveal individuals of talent, even if those persons came from "remote and apparently inferior backgrounds." And the tests did discover intellectual "diamonds in the rough." More often, however, the tests picked out individuals of privilege – the correlation between zip code and IQ is high. The still-unresolved question of the casual relation between IQ and social privilege has stimulated many a dissertation across the social sciences.

Paradoxically, one of the clearest signs of the success of intelligence tests is that the tests themselves are not widely administered any more. In the wake of legal cases about the propriety of making consequential decisions about education on the basis of IQ scores, many public-school officials have become test-shy. By and large, testing of IQ in public schools is restricted to cases in which there is a recognized problem (a suspected learning disability) or selection procedure (determining eligibility for a program that serves gifted children).

However, despite this apparent setback, intelligence testing, and the line of thinking that underlies it, have actually won the war. Many widely used scholastic measures, chief among them the Scholastic Aptitude Test (recently renamed the

Scholastic Assessment Test and more recently still simply the SAT), are thinly dis-guised intelligence tests – almost clones thereof – which correlate highly with scores on standard psychometric instruments. Virtually no one raised in the devel-oped world today has gone untouched by Binet's deceptively simple invention of a century ago.

Secure in practice, the concept of intelligence has in recent years undergone its most robust challenge since the days of Walter Lippmann. Individuals informed by psychology but not bound by the assumptions of the psychometricians have invaded this formerly sacrosanct territory. They have put forth their own concep-tions about what intelligence is, how (and whether) it should be measured, and which values should be invoked in considerations of the human intellect. For the first time in many years, the Intelligence Establishment is clearly on the defensive – and it seems likely that the new century will usher in quite different ways of think-ing about intelligence.

The history of science is a tricky business, particularly when one sits in the midst of current scientific debate. One evident factor in the rethinking of intelli-gence is the perspective introduced by those scholars who are not psychologists. Anthropologists have noted the parochialism of the Western view of intelli-gence. Some cultures do not even have a concept called intelligence, and others define intelligence in terms of traits that we in the West might consider irrele-vant – obedience, or good listening skills, or moral fiber, for example. Neuroscientists are skeptical that a single or unitary form of intelligence is con-sistent with the highly differentiated and modularized structure of the brain. Computer scientists have devised programs deemed to be intelligent; these pro-grams often go about problem-solving in ways quite different from those fol-lowed by human beings or other animals.

The insularity of most psychological discussions came home to me recently when I appeared on a panel devoted to the topic of intelligence. I was the only psy-chologist. An ethologist summarized what is known about the intelligence of dif-ferent animals. A mathematical physicist discussed the nature of matter, such that it allows for conscious and intelligent behavior. A computer scientist described the kinds of complex systems that can be built out of simple, nerve-like units, and the point at which these systems begin to exhibit intelligent and perhaps even creative behavior. As I listened intently to these thoughtful scholars, I realized with clarity how psychologists no longer own the term of intelligence – if they ever really did. What it means to be intelligent can turn out to be a profound philosophical ques-tion – one that requires grounding in biological, physical, and mathematical knowledge. Correlations among test scores just do not cut it, once one ventures beyond the campus of the Educational Testing Service.

Even within the field of psychology, the natives have been getting restless. Unquestionably the most restless is Yale psychologist Robert Sternberg (see Sternberg, 1985). A prodigious scholar, Sternberg has written dozens of books and hundreds of articles, a plurality of them focusing on intelligence in one or another way. Sternberg began with the strategic goal of understanding the actual mental processes mobilized on standard test items, such as the solving of analogies. But he soon went beyond the components of standard intelligences testing by insisting on two hitherto neglected forms of intelligence: the "practical" ability to adapt to varying contexts (as we all must in these days of divorcing and downsizing), and the capacity to automate familiar activities so that one can deal effectively with novelty and display "creative" intelligence.

More so than many other critics of standard intelligence testing, Sternberg has gone to some pains to measure these new forms of intelligence through the kinds of paper-and-pencil laboratory methods favored by the profession. And he has found that a person's ability to deal with novel information, or to adapt successfully to diverse contexts, can be differentiated from success at standard IQ test style problems. His efforts to create a new intelligence test have not yet been crowned with easy victory. Most psychometricians are conservative – they like their Wechslers and their Stanford-Binets "straight"; and if new tests are to be marketed, it is thought that they must correlate well with existing instruments! So much for openness to novelty within the psychometric industry.

Others in the psychology orbit, less bound by the strictures of the tribe, are really pushing the envelope in the struggle over the ownership of intelligence. Psychologist-journalist Daniel Goleman has achieved worldwide success with his book *Emotional Intelligence* (1995). Contending that this new concept (sometimes nicknamed EQ) may matter as much as IQ, Goleman draws attention to such pivotal human capacities as the ability to control one's own emotional reactions and to "read" the signals of other individuals. Noted psychiatrist Robert Coles has published *The Moral Intelligence of Children* (1997). In Coles's view (following that earlier sage of "Concord," Ralph Waldo Emerson) "character is higher than intellect." He decries the amorality of our families and, hence, our children; he shows how we might cultivate human beings who develop a sense of right and wrong and who are willing to act on that sense even when it runs counter to self-interest. There are more frankly popular accounts, dealing with Leadership Intelligence (LQ), Executive Intelligence (EQ or ExQ), and even Financial Intelligence (we have avoided abbreviating this term so far ...).

Like Coles's and Goleman's efforts, my own work on "multiple intelligences" also eschews the psychologists' credo of operationalization and test-making. Instead, I began by asking two questions: the Evolutionary Question, "How did the human mind/brain evolve over millions of years?" and the Comparative Question, "How can we account for the diverse skills and capacities that are or have been valued in different communities around the world?"

Armed with those questions, and a set of eight criteria for what "counts" as an intelligence, I have concluded that all human beings possess at least eight intelligences: linguistic and logical-mathematical (the two most prized in school and the ones central to success on intelligence-test-type instruments), musical, spatial, bodily-kinesthetic, naturalist, and two forms focused on human beings (interpersonal and intrapersonal).

I make two complementary claims about intelligence. The first is a universal claim. We all possess these eight intelligences – and possibly more. Indeed, rather than seeing the human as a "rational animal," I offer a new definition of what it means to be a human being, cognitively speaking: *homo sapiens sapiens* is the animal that possesses these eight forms of mental representation.

My second claim concerns individual differences. Due to the accidents of heredity, environment and their interactions, no two of us exhibit the same intelligences in precisely the same proportion and blend. Our "profiles of intelligence" differ from one another. This fact poses intriguing challenges and opportunities for our educational system. We can either ignore these differences and pretend that we are all the same; historically speaking, that is what most educational systems have done. Or we can fashion an educational system that tries to exploit these differences, individualizing instruction and assessment as much as possible.

As the century of Binet and his successors draws to a close, it is apposite to take stock and to anticipate the course of thinking about intelligence. While my crystal ball is no clearer than anyone else's (the species may lack Future Intelligence), it seems safe to predict that interest in intelligence will not go away.

To begin with, the psychometric community has scarcely laid down its arms. New versions of the standard tests continue to be created, and occasional new tests (such as the Kaufman A B C) surface as well. Researchers in the psychometric tradition churn out fresh evidence of the predictive power of their instruments and the correlations between measured intelligence and one's life chances. And, quite intriguingly, some in the psychometric tradition are searching for the biological basis of intelligence: the genes that may "load" for intelligence; the neural structures that are crucial for intelligence; or tell-tale brain wave patterns or neuro-imaging profiles that distinguish the bright from the cognitively-challenged.

Beyond various psychometric twists, interest in intelligence is likely to grow in other ways. It will be fed, on the one hand, by the creation of machines that display intelligence, and, on the other, by the possibility that we can genetically engineer organisms of specific intelligence or intelligences. Moreover, observers as diverse as the authors of *The Bell Curve* (Herrnstein and Murray, 1994) and lawyer and economist Robert Reich have agreed that in coming years, a large, perhaps disproportionate, part of society's rewards will go to those individuals who are skilled symbol analysts – who can sit at a computer screen (or its technological successor), manipulate numbers and other kinds of symbols, and use the results of their operations to suggest plans, tactics, and strategies for an enterprise – ranging from business to science to war games. These individuals may well color how "intelligence" is conceived in decades to come – just as the need to provide good middle-level bureaucrats to man an empire served as a primary molder of intelligence tests in the early years of the century.

Surveying the landscape of intelligence, I discern three sets of struggles between opposing forces. The extent to which, and the manner in which, these various struggles are resolved will influence the lives of millions of individuals. To put my cards on the table, I feel that the three struggles are interrelated; the first struggle provides the key to the others; and there is an optimal way in which to resolve the ensemble of struggles.

The first struggle concerns *the breadth* of our definition of intelligence. One camp consists of *traditionalists* who believe in a single form of intelligence, one that basically predicts success in school and in school-like activities. Arrayed against the traditionalists are the *progressive pluralists*. These individuals believe that there are many forms of intelligence. And some of these pluralists would like to broaden the definition of intelligence considerably, to include the abilities to create, to lead, and to stand out in terms of emotional sensitivity or moral excellence.

The second struggle concerns the *assessment of intelligence*. Again, one readily encounters a traditional position. Once sympathetic to paper-and-pencil tests, the traditionally oriented practitioner now looks to computers to provide the same information more quickly and more accurately.

But other positions abound. "Purists" disdain psychological tasks of any complexity, preferring to look instead at reaction time, brain waves, neuro-imaging profiles, and other "purer" physiological measures of intellect. "Simulators" move in the opposite direction, to more realistic life-sized measures that closely resemble the actual abilities that are prized. And "skeptics" warn against the continuing expansion of testing. They emphasize the damage often done to individual life chances and self-esteem by a regimen of psychological testing. And they call instead for less technocratic, more humane methods. These range from self-assessment, to the examination of portfolios of student work, to selection in the service of social equity.

The final struggle concerns the *relationship between intelligence and what qualities we value in human beings*. While no one would baldly equate intellect and human value, nuanced positions have emerged on this issue. Some (in the *Bell Curve* tradition) see intelligence as closely related to a person's ethical and value system; they anticipate that brighter individuals are more likely to appreciate moral complexity and to behave judiciously. Some call for a sharp distinction between the realm of intellect, on the one hand, and character, morality, or ethics on the other. Society's ambivalence on this issue can be discerned in the figures that become heroes in the media. For every real-life Albert Einstein or Bobby Fischer who is celebrated for his intellect, there is a cinematic Forrest Gump or Chauncey Gardiner who is celebrated precisely for those human (and humane) traits that would never be captured on any kind of an intelligence test.

Reflecting on these struggles, I believe that the most pivotal battlefield is likely to be the one in which the new dimensions and boundaries of intelligence are thrashed out. Thanks to the work of the past decade or two, the stranglehold of the psychometricians has at last been broken. This is a beneficent development. Yet now that the Scylla of the psychometricians has been overcome, we risk succumbing to the Charybdis of "anything goes" – emotions, morality, creativity all become absorbed into the "New Intelligence." The challenge is to chart a concept of intelligence that reflects new insights and discoveries and yet can withstand rigorous scrutiny.

An analogy may help. One can think of the scope of intelligence as represented by an elastic band. For many years, the definition of intelligence went unchallenged and the band seemed to have lost its elasticity. Some of the new definitions expand the band so that it has become quite taut and resilient; and yet earlier work on intelligence is still germane. Other definitions so expand the band that it finally snaps – and the earlier work on intelligence can no longer be drawn upon.

Until now, the term 'intelligence' has been limited largely to certain kinds of problem-solving involving language and logic – the kinds of skills at a premium in the lawyer or law professor. However, humans are able to deal with numerous other contents besides words, numbers, and logical relations – for example, the contents of space, music, the psyches of other human beings. Like the elastic band, conceptions of intelligence need to be expanded to include human skill in dealing with these diverse kinds of contents. And we must not restrict attention to the solving of problems that have been posed by others; we must consider equally the capacities of individuals to *fashion products* (like works of art, scientific experiments, effective organizations) that draw on one or more of several human intelligences. The elastic band can accommodate such broadening as well.

So long as intelligences are restricted to the processing of "contents in the world," we avoid epistemological problems. So it should be. "Intelligence" should not be expanded to include personality, motivation, will, attention, character, creativity, and other important and significant human capacities. Such stretching is likely to snap the band of intelligence altogether.

Let's see what happens when one crosses one of these lines – for example, when one attempts to conflate intelligence with creativity. Beginning with a definition, we extend the descriptor "creative" to those individuals (or works or institutions) that meet two criteria: 1) they are innovative; 2) their novelty is eventually accepted by a relevant community or domain.

No one denies that creativity is important – and, indeed, it may prove even more important in the future, when nearly all standard (algorithmic) procedures are likely to be carried out by computers. Yet creativity should not be equated with intelligence. An expert may be intelligent in one or more domain, but there is no necessity that he or she be inclined toward, or successful in, innovation. Similarly, while the ability to innovate clearly requires a certain degree of intelligence (or intelligences), there is not otherwise a significant correlation between measures of intellect and creativity. Indeed, creativity seems more dependent on a certain kind of temperament and personality (risk-taking, tough-skinned, persevering, above all having a lust to alter the status quo and leave a mark on society) than on efficiency in processing various kinds of informational content. By collapsing these categories together, we risk missing dimensions that are important but separate; and we may think that we are training (or selecting) one, when we are actually training (or selecting) the other.

Consider, next, what happens when one stretches intelligence to include good or evil attitudes and behaviors. By this incursion into morality, we are now confronting human values within a culture. There may be a few values that can be expressed generically enough so that they command universal respect: the Golden Rule is one promising candidate! Almost every other value, however, turns out to be specific to cultures or subcultures – even such seemingly unproblematic ones as the unacceptability of incest, killing, or lying. Once one conflates morality and intelligence, one needs to deal with the widely divergent views of what is good and bad, and why. Moreover, one must deal with the fact that individuals who score highly on tests of moral reasoning often act immorally outside the test situation; and one must acknowledge as well that courageous and self-sacrificing individuals turn out to be unremarkable on formal tests of moral reasoning and on intelligence tests (Moran and Gardner, in press). Far preferable to construe intelligence itself as morally neutral, and then apply a different set of calipers to decide whether a given use of intelligence qualifies as moral, immoral, or amoral in a given context.

As I see it, no intelligence is moral or immoral in itself. One can be gifted in language and use that gift (as did Johann Wolfang von Goethe) to write great verse, or (as did Joseph Goebbels) to foment hatred. Mother Teresa and Lyndon Johnson, Niccolò Machiavelli and Mohandas Gandhi may have had equivalent degrees of interpersonal intelligence, but the uses to which they put their skills could not have been more varied.

One might respond by saying: "Perhaps there is an intelligence that determines whether or not a situation harbors moral considerations or consequences." I have less problem with such a formulation. Note, however, that the term "moral intelligence" loses much of its force. After all, Adolf Hitler or Joseph Stalin may well have had an exquisite sense of which situations were considered moral; however, either they did not care, or they embraced their own peculiar code of what counted as moral ("eliminating Jews is the moral thing to do in quest of a pure Aryan society"; "wiping out a generation is a desirable or at least necessary move if you want to establish a communist state").

Writing as a scholar rather than a layperson, I see two problems with the notion of an emotional intelligence. First of all, unlike language or space, the emotions are not "contents" to be processed; rather, cognition has evolved so that we can make sense of human beings (self and others) that possess and experience emotions.

Emotions are part-and-parcel of *all* cognition, though they may well prove more salient at certain times or under certain circumstances; they accompany our inter-actions with others, our listening to great music, our feelings when we solve – or fail to solve – a difficult mathematical problem. If one calls *some* intelligences emo-tional, this term suggests that other intelligences are not – and that implication flies in the face of experience and empirical data.

The second problem is the conflation of emotional intelligence with a certain preferred pattern of behavior. This is the trap that Daniel Goleman sometimes falls into in his otherwise admirable volume *Emotional Intelligence* (1995). Goleman singles out as emotionally intelligent those individuals who use their understanding of emotions to make individuals feel better, solve conflicts, or cooperate in home or work situations. No one would dispute that such individuals are desirable. However, it is important not to assume that individuals who are emotionally intel-ligent will necessarily use their skills for prosocial ends.

For this reason, I prefer the term "emotional sensitivity" – a term (encompass-ing my two "personal intelligences") that could apply to individuals who are sen-sitive to emotions in themselves and others. Presumably, clinicians and salespersons excel in sensitivity to other persons; poets and mystics to emotions in themselves. And there are other individuals – autistic or psychopathic persons, for example – who seem completely insensitive to the emotional realm. I would insist, however, on a strict distinction between emotional sensitivity and being a "good" or "moral" person. A person may be sensitive to the emotions of others, but use that sensitivity to manipulate, deceive, or create hatred. Just as sadists know well what causes pain for others, masochists know only too well what causes pain in themselves.

I call, then, for a delineation of intelligence that includes the full range of con-tents to which human beings are sensitive; but one which, at the same time, desig-nates as off limits such valued but separate human traits as creativity, morality, or emotional appropriateness. I believe that such a delineation makes scientific and epistemological sense. It reinvigorates the elastic band without stretching it to breaking point, and it helps to resolve the two remaining struggles: how to assess, and what kinds of human beings to admire.

Once we decide to restrict intelligence to human information-processing and product-making capacities, we can make use of the established technology of assessment. That is, we can continue to use paper-and-pencil or computer-adapted testing techniques, while looking at a broader range of capacities, such as musical sensitivity or the understanding of other persons. And we can avoid ticklish and possibly unresolvable questions about the assessment of values and morality that may well be restricted to a particular culture, and that may well change over time.

Still, even with a limited perspective on intelligence, important questions remain about which assessment path to follow – that of the purist, the simulator, or the skeptic. Here I have strong views. I think it is a fool's errand to embrace the search for a "pure" intelligence – be it general intelligence, musical intelligence, or inter-personal intelligence. I do not believe that such alchemical intellectual essences actually exist. They are a product of our penchant for creating terminology and not determinable and measurable entities. Moreover, the correlations that have been found between "pure measures" and the skills that we actually value in the world are too modest to be useful.

What does exist is the use of intelligences, individually and in concert, to carry out tasks that are valued by a society. Accordingly, we should be assessing the extent to which humans succeed in carrying out tasks of consequence that presumably involve certain intelligences. And so, to be concrete, we should not test musical intelligence by looking at the ability to discriminate between two tones or timbres; rather we should be teaching individuals to sing songs or play instruments or transform melodies and see how readily they master such skills. By the same token, we should abjure a search for pure emotional sensitivity – e.g., a test that matches facial expressions or sensitivity to one's own galvanic skin response. Rather, we should place (or observe) individuals in situations where they have to be sensitive to the aspirations and motives of others. For example, we could see how individuals handle a situation where they and colleagues have to break up a fight between two teenagers or convince a boss to change a policy of which they do not approve. These are realistic contexts for assessing a person's mastery of the emotional realm.

Here powerful new simulations can be invoked. We are now in a position to draw on technologies that can not only deliver realistic situations or problems; these simulations also record the success of subjects in dealing with these virtual realities, and even "intelligently" revise next steps in light of what the subjects have (or have not) accomplished. And so, to build on the same examples, one can present a student with an unfamiliar tune on a computer and have the student learn that tune, transpose it, orchestrate it, and the like. Such experiences would reveal much about the student's intelligence in musical matters.

By the same token, one can present simulated human interactions and ask subjects to judge the shifting motivations of each actor. Or one can create an interactive hypermedia production, featuring unfamiliar persons trying to accomplish some sort of goal; the subject can be asked to work with these persons and to respond to their various moves and countermoves. The program can alter responses in light of the "moves" of the subject. While not perhaps identical to a poker game with high stakes, such a measure should reveal much about the interpersonal or emotional sensitivity of a subject.

A significant increase in the breadth – the elasticity – of our concept of intelligence, then, should open the possibility for innovative forms of assessment, ones far more realistic than the classical short-answer examinations. Why settle for an IQ or SAT test, where the items at best are remote "proxies" for the ability to design experiments, write essays, critique musical performances, etc.? Why not instead ask individuals actually (or virtually) to carry out such tasks? And yet, by not opening up the Pandora's box of values and subjectivity, one can continue to make judicious use of the insights and technologies achieved by those who have devoted decades to perfecting mental measurement.

To be sure, one can create a psychometric instrument for any conceivable human virtue, including morality, creativity, and emotional intelligence in its several senses. Indeed, since Daniel Goleman's book was published, there have been dozens, if not hundreds, of efforts to create tests for emotional intelligence. But the resulting instruments are not necessarily meritorious. Such instruments are far more likely to satisfy the testmaker's desire for reliability (the person gets roughly the same score on two separate administrations of an instrument) than the need for validity (the test measures the trait that it purports to measure, such as emotional sensitivity or genuine musicality).

Such instruments-on-demand prove dubious for two reasons. First of all, beyond some platitudes, it is too difficult to secure agreement on what it means to be moral, ethical, a good person; consider the different values of George Washington and George W. Bush, Margaret Thatcher and Margaret Mead. Second of all, individuals' "scores" on such tests are much more likely to reveal their test-taking savvy (skills in language and logic) than their fundamental character.

In speaking about character, I turn to our final concern: the relationship between intelligence and what I will, for short, call virtue, those qualities of the human being that we admire and that we wish to hold up as examples to our own children and to other people's children. No doubt, the desire to expand intelligence to encompass ethics and character represents a direct response to the general feeling that our society is lacking in these dimensions; the expansionist view of intelligence reflects the hope that if we transmit the technology of intelligence to these virtues, we might in the end secure a more virtuous population.

I have already indicated my strong reservations about hijacking the word 'intelligence' so that it becomes all things to all people – the psychometric equivalent of the true, the beautiful, and the good. Yet the problem remains: how, in a post-Aristotelian, post-Confucian era, one in which psychometrics looms large, do we think about the virtuous human being?

My analysis suggests one promising approach. We should recognize that intelligences, creativity, and morality – to mention just three desiderata – are separate. Each may require its own form of measurement or assessment, and some will prove far easier to assess in an objective manner than others. Indeed, with respect to creativity and morality, we are well advised to rely on overall judgments by experts than on any putative test battery. At the same time, there is nothing to prevent us from looking for individuals who combine more than one of these attributes: individuals who have musical and interpersonal intelligence; individuals who are psychometrically intelligent and creative in the arts; individuals who combine emotional sensitivity and a high standard of moral conduct.

Let me introduce another analogy at this point. In college admissions, much attention is paid to scholastic performance, as measured by College Board examinations and grades. However, other features are also weighed, and sometimes a person with lower test scores is admitted in preference to those who "ace" the tests; the former candidate proves exemplary in terms of citizenship or athletics or motivation. Admissions officers do not confound these virtues (indeed they may use different "scales" and issue different "grades"), but they recognize the attractiveness of candidates who exemplify two or more of these desirable traits.

We have left an Eden where various intellectual and ethical values necessarily comingle, and it is unlikely that we will ever recreate one. We should recognize that these virtues can be separate and, empirically speaking, will often prove to be all too remote from one another. When we attempt to aggregate them, through phrases like "emotional intelligence," "creative intelligence," or "moral intelligence," we should realize that we are expressing a wish rather than denoting a necessary or even a likely coupling.

There is one ally in converting this wish to reality. That is the existence of powerful examples – individuals who actually succeed in exemplifying two or more cardinal human virtues. It is always risky to name names – particularly in an era where one generation's heroes become the subject of the next generation's pathographies. And yet, in the recent past, one can without apologies mention scientists like Niels Bohr, statesmen like George Marshall, writers like Rachel Carson, athletes like Arthur Ashe, and musicians like Louis Armstrong or Pablo Casals or Ella Fitzgerald.

In studying the lives of individuals like this, we discover human possibilities. Young human beings learn primarily from the examples of powerful adults around them – ones who are admirable as well as ones who are simply glamorous. It is possible that sustained attention to such estimable examples will increase the incidence of future individuals who actually do yoke capacities that, we now understand, are scientifically and epistemologically separate.

In one of the most important (and oft-quoted) phrases of the century, the British novelist E.M. Forster counseled us "only connect." I believe that, though well motivated, some expansionists in the territory of intelligence have prematurely asserted connections that do not exist. But I also believe that it is within our power as human beings to help forge connections that may be important for our physical and psychic survival.

Just how the precise borders of intelligence are drawn is a question that we can leave to scholars. But the imperative to broaden our definition of intelligence in a responsible way goes well beyond the academy. Who "owns intelligence" promises to be an even more critical issue in the new century than it has been in this era of the IQ test.

CHAPTER 9

MULTIMEDIA AND MULTIPLE INTELLIGENCES

Shirley Veenema and Howard Gardner

The American Prospect, 7 (29), November 1st 1996.

Beyond hype or gloom

Despite enormous advances in technology, schools – and education more broadly – have remained remarkably unchanged over the centuries throughout the world. Recently, however, expectations for an education that exploits the new technologies have reached unprecedented heights – an inevitable reaction, perhaps, in a country where technological fixes have long been the solution of first resort.

Yet it should be evident that media and technologies of themselves are neutral – one can use a pencil to write a superlative essay, to drum away the time, or to poke out someone's eye. Quality television has educated thousands, while the daily network offerings dull the sensibilities of millions. The Internet and the World Wide Web are seen by optimists as creating democratic communities of unusual strength and promise, but pessimistic eyes might anticipate *ad hoc* liaisons of little merit or perhaps, more nefariously, the creation of communities that join forces to support anti-democratic ends.

Avoiding hype or gloom, we seek in this chapter to identify some ways in which one new form of technology might be yoked to the achievement of important educational goals. Specifically, we examine one promising interactive multimedia design to suggest how this new medium might help more students to approach an important historical event and to achieve deeper forms of understanding of that event. We place this example in the context of recent new understandings of mind which, we believe, lay the groundwork for more effective uses of the new technologies.

Half a century ago a new movement in science began to coalesce. Now termed cognitive science, this field seeks to integrate insights from several disciplines (including psychology, linguistics, artificial intelligence, and neuroscience) in order to put forth a better, more comprehensive understanding of the human mind. We believe that the conceptualization of mind fostered by the cognitive revolution has enormous, if not yet widely appreciated, implications for educational practice.

Even in science, one cannot have a revolution without an enemy. In the case of the cognitive revolution, there were two separate, though related, foes. The behaviorist perspective, as epitomized in the work of B.F. Skinner, disdained any concern with the mind and its contents; all that mattered, from the behaviorist perspective, was that an organism perceived a stimulus and responded to it, or that the organism acted in some way and was positively or negatively rewarded for so acting. The apotheosis of the behaviorist perspective, from the point of view of education, was the teaching machine – which, suitably upgraded, remains central in computer-assisted instruction today.

The second antagonist, from the perspective of cognitivists, was a certain view of the mind. In this view, what the mind contained was intelligence – more or less of it. Intelligence was a fixed and unexamined entity. Individuals were born with a certain amount of intelligence and this amount, for better or worse, was essentially fixed. Few asked just what intelligence was or how it could be improved, increased, or transformed – indeed, the not entirely whimsical definition put forth by psychologists was that "intelligence is what the tests test." The IQ test and its descendants, in measures such as the Scholastic Aptitude Test, constitute the contemporary monument to this way of thinking.

In direct response to these entrenched perspectives, the key idea put forth by cognitivists is that there are important entities within the mind/brain – and these are called mental representations. Individuals do not just react to or perform in the world; they possess minds and these minds contain images, schemes, pictures, frames, languages, ideas, and the like. Individuals are born with certain mental representations and some of these prove quite enduring, but many other representations are created, transformed, or dissolved over time as the result of experiences and reflections upon those experiences. Like a digital computer, the mind processes and transforms information, and it is vital to understand the nature of this computing machinery – or, perhaps more aptly, these types of computing machinery.

It is important for the "educationally inclined" to ponder two central ideas in the cognitivist's armamentarium. First of all, the mind does not consist in a single representation, or even a single language of representations. Rather, all individuals harbor numerous internal representations in their mind/brains. Some scholars speak of modules of mind, some of a society of mind; in our own work, we speak of the possession of MI, which span the range from linguistic and logical intelligences (the usual foci of school work) to musical, naturalist, and personal intelligences (see Chapters 6 to 8).

These intelligences constitute the ways in which individuals take in information, retain and manipulate that information, and demonstrate their understandings (and misunderstandings) to themselves and others. So, for example, with reference to understanding the American Civil War, some individuals would favor a linguistic or narrative approach, others can be most easily reached through an artistic depiction, still others might resonate to the personal dimension – how an internecine struggle affects neighbors and relatives, and even generates ambivalence within one's own self. While most individuals can use and appreciate these different perspectives and "intelligences" over time, each of us constructs our own amalgamation of intelligences. Surprisingly (and counter to the claims of classical intelligence theory), strength (or weakness) in one area does not predict strength (or weakness) in other areas. And it is here that we encounter a seminal educational enigma.

Until now, most schools all over the world have been selecting devices. These institutions have honored a certain kind of mind – ideally, one that combines language and logic – and try to select individuals who excel in these forms. Those individuals who favor other mental representations have received little honor in most schools.

The cognitivist's acknowledgment of different kinds of minds opens up enormous educational opportunities. If individuals do differ from one another, and we want to reach as many individuals as possible, it makes little sense to treat all individuals in a "one size fits all" manner. Rather, we need to understand as much as we can about the *specific* minds involved in an educational encounter; and, insofar as possible, we should build our education – and our choices of educational technology – on the basis of this knowledge. And so, whether the course be history or physics or dance, we should try to teach individuals in ways that are consonant with, or that stretch, their current mental representations. Equally, we should give individuals the opportunity to exhibit their understandings by means of media and representations that make sense to them.

A second, and quite surprising, finding that has emerged from cognitive research is this: many early representations are extremely powerful and prove very difficult to change. It is as if, in the first years of life, the mind/brain becomes engraved with a certain scheme or frame by which it apprehends parts of experience. Often this scheme is seen as inadequate, and so educators inside and outside of school seek to transform the initial engraving. They may well feel that they have been successful in bringing about this transformation, because the student has acquired more information, especially more facts. And yet, in a majority of cases, even good students at good schools do not really alter their representations. Indeed, when students are examined outside the scholastic context, they often give just the same answers as students who have not even studied the subject matter or discipline in question. It is as if school consists of layers of powder which obscure rather than alter the initial engraving; and once that powder has blown away, the original representations have changed very little (see Chapters 16 and 18).

If one wants to educate for genuine understanding, then, it is important to identify these early representations, appreciate their power, and confront them directly and repeatedly. Only then is it possible, in a reliable manner, to construct new and more adequate mental representations that themselves become robust and enduring.

As we have already emphasized, technologies alone cannot identify – let alone achieve – central educational goals. That is the task of the community, and it is hardly an easy or idle one. Stimulated by reflections on the cognitive revolution, we propose here two important educational goals: 1) the encouragement of deeper forms of understanding within and across the disciplines; 2) the "opening up" of the educational process to the widest spectrum of children, especially those who do not stand out in the traditionally canonical intelligences of language and logic.

Why study any particular discipline or content?

Regardless of whether technology is involved or not, we need to question why students should spend time doing whatever it is that we propose. Why study history? For that matter, why study anything we teach in school? Some disciplines we readily deem worthy of attention. For example, while we may debate what specifically to include, we generally assume that history is a discipline worthy of study because it offers us a laboratory for the study of past human experience in which to anchor our perceptions of contemporary life and the future.

Similarly, particular content within any discipline bears scrutiny in relation to our goals: Why study the American Civil War; why include extensive study of any particular battle? These are questions we must ask of all schooling, whether technologically enhanced or not. If, for example, we believe that knowledge of the American Civil War helps students to understand many of the tensions in our nation today, then particular battles warrant inclusion insofar as they advance understanding of specific aspects of the war or the study of history in general.

Traditionally, on account of its military and political significance, history curricula include the battle fought at Sharpsburg, Maryland on September 17, 1862. Revealing the still-charged nature of the encounter, even today Northerners call this battle Antietam, while to Southerners it remains the battle of Sharpsburg.

The generally agreed-upon facts are these. The Federal army, under the command of George B. McClellan, stalked Robert E. Lee's Confederate army as it moved to invade the North to get food and supplies. Both armies converged just outside the town of Sharpsburg and fought what turned out to be the worst one day of slaughter in American history. Although neither side could claim a decisive victory, Lee's first invasion of the North had failed, and no longer did it seem possible that England would recognize the Confederacy. Indeed, the very goals of the conflict changed, when Lincoln seized the occasion to announce the Emancipation Proclamation, linking freedom for slaves to the war goals.

Most textbooks present this material in such straightforward form. They may well provide an illustration or two. They generally convey the impression that there is an authoritative view of the battle and, depending upon the authors, often relate the battle from the perspective of the North or the South. Assessments generally ask students to give back this information in factual form. Such a style of presentation and assessment is particularly appropriate for individuals who favor linguistic modes of learning. And such presentations rarely challenge the widespread assumption among students that there is a single objective account of a battle and that the Civil War featured a battle between Right and Wrong.

In what follows, we describe a CD-ROM design, *Antietam/Sharpsburg*, that features this important and well-known battle of the American Civil War. The application transcends the usual textbook portrait of the battle in that, first, it recognizes and allows us to take advantage of the fact that intelligences of one student can differ from intelligences of other students in significant ways; and, second, it strives to inculcate deeper forms of understanding and attempts to deal directly with misconceptions and stereotypical habits of thought.

The example reflects our belief that technology applications should provide ways in which a variety of minds can gain access to knowledge. On the other hand, in no way are we jettisoning the major rationale for including history in a liberal education. Indeed, effective use of the technology reinforces both senses of the word 'discipline': students should apprehend the major focus of thinking involved in a discipline such as history and should do so in a steady, cumulative, and inherently disciplined way. Our example suggests ways in which new media might help students to approach an important historical event and to achieve deeper forms of understanding of that event.

Can technology enhance understanding?

The CD-ROM design *Antietam/Sharpsburg* uses physical representations made by eyewitnesses to tell the story of the American Civil War battle of September 17, 1862 at Sharpsburg, Maryland. It offers a close-up view of important considerations of history via a physical site, artifacts, and guides. Primary source materials in a variety of media highlight the idea that we owe our knowledge of this battle to the explicit physical representations left us by observers who encoded their impressions in specific symbol systems (e.g., written journalism of the time; Alexander Gardner's photos; drawings by the artistic journalist Alfred Waud; telegraph and signal reports from the Federal troops).

On September 17, 1862 each observer saw particular aspects of the battle. George W. Smalley, correspondent for the *New York Tribune*, began the day near the cornfield where the fighting started, and then moved on to several other sites, including General McClellan's headquarters; Felix Gregory de Fountaine, the correspondent for the *Charleston Courier*, specifies his position as "upon the centre," where he could see little or nothing of the fight upon the left. Our contemporary narrative is constructed from the physical representations left us by observers like these. Not only was there no single observer able to see the whole battle and tell us the comprehensive story, but there was also no authoritative interpretation.

The idea that there exists a singular perspective is surprisingly hard to change. In fact, too often the seductive idea that there is a "right" view leads students to embrace the perspective of *any* perceived authority – teacher, textbook, or "expert" – instead of realizing that students themselves need to weigh the evidence, evaluate sources, and come up with interpretations and their justifications. The idea that there is no single observer who can tell us the whole story lies at the heart of *Antietam/Sharpsburg*. An emphasis on multiple observers counters head on the idea that there is a singular interpretation and one "right" dramatic narrative.

Technologies like CD-ROM that are capable of presenting both pictorial and textual renderings of a battle from several perspectives can help to dissolve single-dimensional perspectives; they counter the bias toward a single narrative for history and good-guy vs. bad-guy roles in a conflict. As we noted earlier in our discussion of cognitive representations, such stereotypical ways of thought impede deeper understandings and prove very hard to change. Consequently, they need to be addressed directly. The variety of approaches and media available to new technologies may in fact provide fertile opportunities to eradicate these and other common misconceptions that are formed early in a student's life.

The reality of a battle is also far more complex than what we typically see in the movies today. However, we are not alone in perpetuating simple dramas. For nineteenth-century audiences, these dramas were played out in paintings and prints in which orderly ranks of soldiers responded to the directions of their leader. Often on horseback, the leader gallantly led his obedient and patriotic forces forward. In reality, battles are typically chaotic, life-and-death situations, fought by individuals pumped high with adrenaline. It is a rare post-battle account that can capture the complex nature of an armed struggle.

As in any battle, geography played a role at Sharpsburg. Cornfields offered no cover for troops battling back and forth; hills offered advantageous positions for Southern troops holding off Northern troops attempting to cross a stream, and an old roadway sunken by erosion and the weight of wagons provided a natural trench from which Confederates could train their rifles on Federal troops. Moreover, troops on both sides had yet to accommodate their maneuvers to opponents' newly advanced weaponry. With little available communications technology, strategic information was communicated by word of mouth or by notes. In addition, signal flags and the telegraph carried news of the smoke-enshrouded conflict to George McClellan and the Federal troops.

The multiple media of a technology like CD-ROM make possible complex renderings of an event, but particular understandings need to be a design priority. For example, photographic sequences and text that "walk" the battlefield in *Antietam/Sharpsburg* are designed to help students understand relationships among the geographic terrain, strategies of the battle, and the course of the fighting (e.g., battle positions in relation to rivers, ridges, fields). In decoding telegraph reports that convey a sense of just how hard it was to know what was going on during the battle, students may realize how difficult it was to communicate under fire, and why there were so many missteps and conflicting messages.

What observers reported at Sharpsburg had more to do with just physical location. While we cannot know what any observer actually thought, we can say that the form of representation and symbol system used by each witness profiles a characteristic way of thinking. Reporters from the *New York Tribune* and *Charleston Courier* used words to fashion strikingly different descriptions of events, actions, and personalities. Alfred Waud, the artist who did pencil-and-chalk sketches for *Harper's Weekly*, drew aspects of the conflict in which he paid careful attention to the nuances of soldiers' positions and facial expressions. The signal officers did more than just wave flags to encode messages; by the force and speed of their motions, they conveyed to those far away the pace and tension of the battle.

If we believe that mind is neither singular nor revealed in a single language of representation, then our use of technologies should reflect the fact that individuals construct their understandings in different ways. Technologies like CD-ROM that include a variety of media and ways to make meaning may well be able to help more students form rich representations of an event and cultivate deeper understandings. However, it is unrealistic to expect this educational outcome to be achieved as a simple consequence of adding more information and more media. Instead, our authoring has to have the explicit goal of greater access for more students, and we need ways to assess whether and how the information has been apprehended.

The guided paths in *Antietam/Sharpsburg* provide one example of what such authoring might be like. The four paths that present the battle of September 17, 1862 – map, observers, battlefield walk, archives and activities – provide a mode of interacting with the material that ranges from structured to exploratory. None rely exclusively on language, and each instead provides several means of representing the battle. The map path uses a collage presentation of photographs, historical images, text and audio to present an overarching narrative of the battle, and suggests some of the reasons why this battle is important to the war.

The observers' path uses physical representations left us by the eyewitness observers to convey details of events from the perspective of each. At any point it is possible to leave both the map and observers' paths in order to browse additional related material and then return to the presentation.

To some people the ebb and flow of the various battle stages doesn't make sense without a walk through the landscape to trace out the movements of troops at each site. By means of virtual reality movies, the battlefield walk path in *Antietam/Sharpsburg* allows one to "walk" the sites and learn things about the battle that can only be understood by experiencing the landscape and feeling its impact on what happened during the battle. Through sequential photographs assembled as motion sequences, it is possible to feel what it was like to fight in the dense tangle of trees in the North Woods or what it was like to look over the hill at the approaching enemy from the sunken road.

The archive and activities path provides different modes of interacting with the material – this time with only one's own direction. There are options to browse the image, text or reference archives. Activities like moving signal flags to send a message and decoding a message sent by these signals are also an option. Here, too, the goal is to help more students know an event in its complexity and in ways that encourage richer mental representations and forms of understanding. For unless students have opportunities to learn in ways compatible with their variety of minds, school will continue to benefit only students who are strong in traditional linguistic and logical ways of thinking.

Students who understand the battle at Sharpsburg on September 17, 1862 should be able to exhibit this understanding in several ways. Some students might use language to argue, question, make connections to their own lives, to other units, other battles, etc. Others might explain the course of the battle and thereby show that they have processed information in a narrative form. Students might also present understandings by means other than words. They might put on a play, make a series of sketches or a short video, compose martial or funereal music, or even master unfamiliar sets of symbols so that they could portray the battle in signal or Morse code. In fact, students could even use several media to publish a page on the World Wide Web.

As more students use virtual environments like CD-ROM, educators must be resourceful in providing ways by which students can demonstrate their understandings. We cannot assume that these new media are better – or, for that matter, worse – than more traditional modes. Rather, we must search for direct evidence that students more fully appreciate the need to take into account multiple perspectives, the partially subjective nature of interpretation, the risks of a simplistic "good/bad" interpretation of complex events. New technologies provide avenues for demonstrating these understandings, but producing assessments that differentiate genuine from surface understanding constitutes a non-trivial challenge.

We also need to think critically about the risks and benefits of products like *Antietam/Sharpsburg*. For example, students might seem really engaged but understand little because the facility of their connections relates more to the medium than to an understanding of the battle per se. Interpretation may become overly subjective and relativistic in the absence of canonical text. Additionally, working extensively with one battle requires time, which means sacrificing coverage of other relevant aspects of the war.

On the other hand, as a result of such mediated experiences, students may be able to engage rich, textured material in ways that yield a more rounded understanding. They may also be encouraged to think more creatively and critically by encountering material that goes beyond summary text. Structures like guided walks can minimize media meanderings or cul-de-sacs. In fact, an experience that encourages understanding in a closed environment like a CD-ROM may ultimately benefit students more than unlimited access to quantities of information via the Internet. The CD-ROM might help students to develop a search strategy for the Internet, one based on information needed to further their understanding of some particular aspect. One student might use the American Memory Project at the Library of Congress to see how Alexander Gardner's images of the battlefield at Sharpsburg compared with his earlier work; another might want to read soldiers' letters from the battlefield.

But beyond a specific technology like CD-ROM, we need to think about any technology in relationship to our educational goals. For example, how we use an application like *Antietam/Sharpsburg* will depend on whether our goals are to teach historical reasoning, to allow individuals to make sense of original sources, to sensitize students to the radically different perspectives of various observers and various participants, to appreciate analogies for the battle of Antietam (for example, contemporary Balkan or Middle Eastern battlefields), and to explore the relationship among traditional historical texts, television series like *The Civil War* by

Ken Burns, and fictional works like *Gone with the Wind*. Unless educators are clear about these goals and their own priorities, students will be confused rather than enlightened, the technology becoming a tool of obfuscation rather than a tool of clarification.

Few ideas in education are wholly new. There have always been educators who have sought to enhance student understanding; educators who have tried to understand the minds of all of their students; educators who have exploited the latest technology toward such ends. By the same token, none of the aims outlined in this chapter depend specifically on the CD-ROM technology. The ingenious teacher of times past could make available different perspectives of an event, use various media of representation, and even lead students through a real or imagined trek across the battlefield.

Yet sometimes a series of quantitative differences can yield a qualitative difference. We are convinced that technologies like the CD-ROM make it possible for ordinary students to gain an understanding of an American Civil War battle – and numerous other rich curricula units – that may have been accessible only to the extraordinary classroom in years past. Moreover, the actual procedures used in such a mediated presentation – for example, the guided walk, the ready shift across perspectives – may stimulate the development of new mental representations that can be used in the study of other topics, even when a CD-ROM is not available.

To be sure, the technology in itself cannot spawn a revolution in educational approaches or results. Even as it was possible in earlier days to have a rounded understanding of the Sharpsburg battle, it would be possible tomorrow to use the CD-ROM to pursue quite banal goals, such as a comparison of the facts that are provided in the different written reports, or a purely descriptive account of what one observes in the virtual movie. Here teachers' favored forms of assessment give away the game; it matters enormously whether a well-crafted unit on the battle of Antietam culminates in an objective multiple-choice text, a straightforward request to recite or narrate the principal events of the battle, the posing of a provocative comparison to be discussed in essay form. One can also envision more ambitious and adventurous forms of assessment, such as the assignment of creating a multi-medium work of art that captures the response to Alexander Gardner's photographs or the actual creation by a student of a teaching lesson involving the use of the *Antietam/Sharpsburg* CD-ROM. Not incidentally, these more adventurous forms give maximum opportunities for students to draw on their own distinctive blend of intelligences, thereby both giving them new venues for demonstrating their understandings and broadening the ensemble of possibilities for their peers and their teachers.

Nearly every serious student of contemporary education – whether conservative or progressive – agrees that we need to move beyond banal educational goals; to proceed from the mastery of factual or informational knowledge to the capacity to understand and to interpret; and to make serious efforts to reach a greater proportion of youngsters, with a variety of intellectual strengths and styles. These more ambitious goals do not themselves depend upon the cognitive revolution, but the cognitive revolution has stimulated both a better understanding of the ways that students learn and the production of educational materials that hold promise for attaining such precious educational goals.

In the last analysis, effective education requires firm steering toward highly valued goals. European and Asian countries routinely surpass the United States in educational accomplishments not because their technology is more glitzy, but because the educational enterprise is regarded more seriously. Technology in itself cannot alter that scholastic "balance of payments." But through a considered reorientation of our educational mission, and the judicious design and use of technology that meshes with that mission, we – and other nations – can achieve far more success with much larger numbers of students. The application described in this chapter represents but one of a growing number of promising innovations – ones that can be readily implemented, enjoyable to use, and susceptible to rigorous assessment.

Acknowledgment

Reprinted with permission from Shirley Veenema and Howard Gardner, "Multimedia and Multiple Intelligences," *The American Prospect*, 7, (29), November 1st, 1996. The American Prospect, 11 Beacon Street, Suite 1120, Boston, MA 02108. All rights reserved.

CHAPTER 10

THE THREE FACES OF INTELLIGENCE

Daedalus, 2002, 139–42.

Once, at an American gathering called Renaissance Weekend, I found myself on a panel with a U.S. senator, a congressman, and a policy wonk. As a cognitive psychologist with an interest in education, I was non-plussed to be surrounded by this distinguished but (to me) exotic company. About halfway through the hour, the mystery was abruptly solved. One of the panelists used the word "intelligence" and another immediately responded by citing the failures of the CIA during the past quarter-century. As was later confirmed, the panels had been constituted by noting key words in our biographies, and both I and the other panelists had described themselves as experts on "intelligence."

While individuals from many backgrounds describe themselves as interested in intelligence, for those of us trained in psychology "intelligence" has a quite specific history and connotation. For nearly a century the word has largely been owned by psychometricians. These individuals devise, administer, and score short-answer tests of intelligence that require subjects to perform tasks associated with school: define words, select antonyms, remember passages, supply general information, manipulate geometric shapes, and the like. Those who consistently do well on measures of intelligence (often called IQ tests) are considered smart – and indeed, so long as they remain in school, they are likely to have that characterization confirmed.

A surrounding web of assertions often accompanies this seemingly objective information. As stated sharply in the bestselling book *The Bell Curve* (Herrnstein and Murray, 1994), individuals are thought to be born with a certain intellectual potential; it is difficult to change that potential; and psychometricians can tell us from an early age how smart we are. Authors Richard Herrnstein and Charles Murray went on to trace various social ills to those with low intelligence levels and to hint that IQ scores may be related to race. The latter claims led to the sales and the furor surrounding the book.

During the latter years of the twentieth century, the psychometric hegemony over intelligence was increasingly challenged. Computer specialists began to develop theories and applications of artificial intelligence; some of their systems were general problem-solvers, while others featured well-delineated expertise. Neuroscientists and geneticists focused on the evolutionary origins and the neural representations of various mental faculties. And within the field of psychology, alternative perspectives were introduced as well.

According to the theory that I have developed, it is misleading to think of humans as possessing but a single intellectual capacity, which almost always amounts to an amalgamation of linguistic and logical-mathematical skills. Rather, examined from an evolutionary perspective, it makes more sense to conceptualize human beings as having several relatively autonomous mental faculties, including musical intelligence, spatial intelligence, bodily-kinesthetic intelligence, and naturalist intelligence. I also propose two forms of personal intelligence, interpersonal and intrapersonal.

When I was developing this pluralistic theory, I still thought that intelligence was a singular concept. It has taken me years to realize the importance of distinguishing between three distinct meanings of intelligence, which are captured in the following sentences.

1   In view of the close resemblance between chimpanzee and human genetic material, it has become challenging to delineate the defining characteristics of human *intelligence*.
2   On most dimensions of interest, Susan simply displays more *intelligence* than John.
3   What distinguishes Alfred Brendel's piano playing is not his technique per se, but the sheer *intelligence* of his interpretations.

When invoking the first meaning of intelligence, we attempt *a general characterization of human (or non-human) capacities*. We might, for example, speak of human intelligence as the capacity to solve complex problems, or to anticipate the future, or to analyze patterns, or to synthesize disparate pieces of information. A major disciplinary tradition, begun with Charles Darwin's studies of the "descent of man" and continuing with Jean Piaget's investigation of children's minds, seeks to capture what is unique and generic about intelligence.

The second meaning of intelligence is the one that has been most widely employed by psychologists. Those in the psychometric tradition – whether unitarians or pluralists – assume that intelligence is a trait, like height or extroversion. Individuals can be usefully compared with one another on the extent to which they exhibit this trait or ensemble of traits. I term this tack *the examination of individual differences on a trait of interest*. Much of my own work on MI has entailed descriptions of the differing profiles of intelligence across individuals.

The third meaning of intelligence has been the least explored, though it may be the most intriguing. As suggested in the Brendel example, the focus here falls on *the manner in which a task is executed*. We often speak in this way; we talk about whether a decision was wise or ill-advised, whether the manner in which the decision was reached was clever or foolish, whether a leadership transition was handled intelligently or ineptly, whether a new concept was introduced intelligently into a lecture, and so forth.

What distinguishes this third connotation of intelligence? We cannot characterize an act or decision as intelligent without some sense of the goal or purpose at issue, the choices involved in a genre, and the particular value system of the participants. Alfred Brendel's playing may not be technically more accurate on some objective index. Rather, in view of his own goals, the choices available in piano performance, and the values of the listener, one can validly speak of his interpretations as intelligent or wanting in intelligence. Moreover, I could dislike Brendel's interpretations and still concur that they were intelligent, if you could convince me of what he was trying to achieve and why it made sense in his terms. Or I could convince you that Glenn Gould's performance of the same piece was intelligent, whether or not you personally liked it. There do not exist example-independent criteria for what constitutes a wise or foolish decision, planning process, leadership transition, introduction of a topic in a class, and so on. Yet, armed with information about goals, genres, and values, we can make assessments about whether these tasks have been performed intelligently – even as we can agree to disagree about the particular instantiations that emerged.

How does the third sense of intelligence relate to MI? I speculate that different tasks call on different intelligences or combinations of intelligences. To perform music intelligently involves a different set of intelligences than preparing a meal, planning a course, or resolving a quarrel.

So, one might ask, what is achieved by this exercise in the "semantics of intelligence"? Let me suggest three possible dividends. The first is lexical. It is useful and important to distinguish the three distinct definitions of intelligence; otherwise we risk speaking past one another, with a Piagetian needlessly clashing with a psychometrician, or a literary critic believing that she is engaged in the same kind of endeavor as a school psychologist.

The second dividend concerns research. There is little question that scholars and researchers will continue to examine the nature of intelligence. We can expect to read about new tests of intelligence, new forms of artificially intelligent machinery, and even about genes (if not *the* gene) for intelligence. Some researchers will be quite clear about what they mean in using the term "intelligence," but we can expect there to be considerable confusion as well, unless scholars take care to indicate which aspect of intelligence they are studying and how (or whether) it relates to the other ones.

Finally, and most important for me, are implications for education. When an educator speaks about intelligence in the first sense, she is referring to a capacity that can be assumed to exist in all human beings. Perhaps it is manifest more quickly or dramatically in one person than in another, but ultimately we are dealing with part of the human birthright and so no special measures are needed. In contrast, intelligence in the "individual difference" sense involves judgment about the potentials of individuals and how each might be taught in the most effective manner. If (following Richard Herrnstein and Charles Murray) one assumes that Sally has little intellectual potential in general or (following the theory of MI) little potential for the development of spatial intelligence, one is faced with clear-cut educational choices. These can range from giving up to working much harder to searching for alternative ways to deliver instruction, be the topic geometry, ancient history, or classical music.

And what of doing something intelligently or stupidly? The greatest educational progress could be achieved here. All too often we ignore goals, genres, or values, or we assume that they are so apparent that we do not bother to highlight them. Yet judgments about whether an exercise – a paper, a project, an essay response on an examination – has been done intelligently or stupidly are often difficult for students to fathom. And since these evaluations are not well understood, few if any lessons can be drawn from them. Laying out the criteria by which judgments of quality are made may not suffice in itself to improve quality; but in the absence of such clarification, we have little reason to expect our students to go about their work intelligently.

CHAPTER 11

MI AFTER 20 YEARS

Paper presented at the American Educational Research Association, Chicago, April 21st, 2003.

I have often been asked how I first got the idea of the theory of MI. Probably the most truthful answer is "I don't know." However, such an answer satisfies neither the questioner nor, to be frank, me. With the benefit of hindsight, I would mention the following factors, some remote, some directly feeding into my discoveries.

1   As a young person I was a serious pianist and enthusiastically involved with other arts as well. When I began to study developmental and cognitive psychology, I was struck by the virtual absence of any mention of the arts. An early professional goal was to find a place for the arts within academic psychology. I am still trying! In 1967 my continuing interest in the arts prompted me to become a founding member of Project Zero, a basic research group at the Harvard Graduate School of Education begun by a noted philosopher of art, Nelson Goodman. For 28 years I was the co-director of Project Zero and I am happy to say that the organization continues to thrive (see Chapter 3).

2   As my doctoral career was drawing to a close, I first encountered the neurological research of Norman Geschwind, a notable behavioral neurologist (see Chapter 4). I was fascinated by Geschwind's discussion of what happens to once normal or gifted individuals who have the misfortune of suffering from a stroke, tumor, or some other form of brain damage. Often the symptoms run counter to intuition: for example, a patient who is alexic but not agraphic loses the ability to read words but can still read numbers, name objects, and write normally. Without planning it that way, I ended up working for 20 years on a neuropsychological unit, trying to understand the organization of human abilities in the brain.

3   I have always enjoyed writing, and by the time I began my post-doctoral work with Geschwind in the early 1970s, I had completed three books. My fourth book, *The Shattered Mind*, published in 1975, chronicled what happens to individuals who suffer from different forms of brain damage. I documented how different parts of the brain are dominant for different cognitive functions. After I completed *The Shattered Mind*, I thought that I might write a book that describes the psychology of different human faculties – a modern reformulation of phrenology. In 1976 I actually wrote an outline for a book with the tentative title *Kinds of Minds*. One could say that this book was never

written – and indeed I had forgotten about it for many years. But one could also say that it eventually arose from the file cabinet and transmogrified into *Frames of Mind* (1983).

So much for the more remote causes of the theory.

In 1979 a group of researchers affiliated with the Harvard Graduate School of Education received a sizable grant from a Dutch foundation, the Bernard van Leer Foundation. This grant was designed for a grandiose purpose, one proposed by the foundation. Members of the Project on Human Potential (as it came to be called) were expected to carry out scholarly work on the nature of human potential and how that potential could best be catalyzed. When we carved out our respective projects, I received an interesting assignment: to write a book about what had been established about human cognition through discoveries in the biological and behavioral sciences. Thus was born the research program that led to the theory of MI.

Support from the Van Leer Foundation allowed me to carry out an extensive research program with the aid of many colleagues. I saw this as a once-in-a-lifetime opportunity to collate and synthesize what I and others had learned about the development of cognitive capacities in normal and gifted children as well as the breakdown of such capacities in individuals who suffered some form of pathology. To put it in terms of my daily calendar, I was seeking to synthesize what I was learning *in the morning* from my study of brain damage with what I was learning *in the afternoon* from my study of cognitive development. My colleagues and I combed the literature from brain study, genetics, anthropology, and psychology in an effort to ascertain the optimal taxonomy of human capacities.

I can identify a number of crucial turning points in this investigation. I don't remember when it happened, but at a certain moment I decided to call these faculties "multiple intelligences" rather than abilities or gifts. This seemingly minor lexical substitution proved very important; I am quite confident that if I had written a book called *Seven Talents* it would not have received the attention that *Frames of Mind* received. As my colleague David Feldman has pointed out (2003), the selection of this word placed me in direct confrontation with the psychological establishment that cherishes IQ tests. However, I disagree with Feldman's claim that I was motivated by a desire to "slay IQ"; neither the documentary nor the mnemonic evidence suggests to me that I had much interest in such a confrontation.

A second crucial point was the creation of a definition of an intelligence and the identification of a set of criteria that define what is, and what is not, an intelligence. I can't pretend that the criteria were all established a priori; rather, there was a constant fitting and refitting of what I was learning about human abilities with how best to delineate what ultimately became eight discrete criteria. I feel that the definition and the criteria are among the most original parts of the work, but neither has received much discussion in the literature.

When I began the book, I was writing as a psychologist and that remains my primary scholarly identification. Yet, given the mission of the Van Leer Foundation, it was clear to me that I needed to say something about the educational implications of MI theory. And so, I conducted some research on education and in the concluding chapters touched on some educational implications of the theory. This decision turned out to be another crucial point because it was educators, rather than psychologists, who found the theory of most interest. (See Chapters 6 to 8 for details of the theory.)

By the time that *Frames of Mind* was published in 1983, I had already published half a dozen books. Each had had a modestly positive reception and a reasonable sale. I did not expect anything different from *Frames of Mind*, a lengthy and (for a trade audience) somewhat technical book. But within a few months after its publication, I realized that this book was different. Not that the reviews were that exuberant or the sales that monumental. Rather, there was a genuine "buzz" about the book. I got invited to give many talks, and when I showed up at a site, people had at least heard about the theory and were eager to learn more about it. Echoing the artist Andy Warhol, I sometimes quip that "MI theory" gave me my fifteen minutes of fame. While I have done many other things in my professional life, I realize that I am likely always to be known as the "father of MI" or, less palatably, as the "MI guru."

For the first decade following the publication of *Frames of Mind*, I had two primary relations to the theory. The first relationship was that of a bemused observer. I was amazed at how many individuals said that they wanted to revise their educational practices in the light of MI theory. Within a year or so I had already met with the teachers from Indianapolis who would shortly begin the Key School, the first school in the world organized explicitly around MI theory. I began to receive a steady stream of communications asking or telling me how to use MI theory in various kinds of schools or for various populations. While I tried to be responsive to these communications, I always maintained that I was a psychologist and not an educator, and did not presume to know how best to teach a class of young persons or how to run an elementary or secondary school.

My second relation was as a director of research projects that grew out of MI theory. The most ambitious effort was Project Spectrum, a collaboration with David Feldman, Mara Krechevsky, Janet Stork, and others (Gardner, Feldman, and Krechevsky, 1998). The goal of Project Spectrum was to create a set of measures whereby one could ascertain the intellectual profiles of young children – preschoolers and those in the primary grades. We ended up devising fifteen separate tasks that were designed to assess the several intelligences in as natural a manner as possible. We had a great deal of fun devising the Spectrum battery and using it with different populations. We also learned that creating assessments is a difficult task and one that requires a great investment of money and time. I decided, without saying so in so many words, that I did not myself want to be in the assessment business, though I was very pleased if others chose to create instruments in an effort to assess the various intelligences.

Let me mention a few other research projects that grew out of the first wave of interest in MI theory. Working with Robert Sternberg of Yale, another critic of standard views of intelligence, my colleagues and I created a middle-school curriculum called Practical Intelligences for School (Williams *et al.*, 1996). Working with colleagues from the Educational Testing Service, my colleagues and I developed a set of curriculum-and-assessment instruments designed to document learning in three art forms (see Chapter 13 and Winner, 1992). There were also collaborative efforts in the use of computers in education.

To my surprise and pleasure, interest in MI survived the transition to the 1990s. By that time I was prepared to undertake several new activities. The first was purely scholarly. Building on the notion of different kinds of intelligences, I carried out case studies of individuals who stood out as remarkable in terms of their particular profile of intelligences. This line of work led to my books on creativity (*Creating Minds*, 1993a), leadership (*Leading Minds*, 1995a), and extraordinary achievement more broadly (*Extraordinary Minds*, 1997). You can see that I was getting a lot of mileage by injecting book titles with the term "mind"!

The second was an extension of the theory. In 1994–5 I took a sabbatical and used part of that time to review evidence for the existence of new intelligences. I concluded that there was ample evidence for a naturalist intelligence; and suggestive evidence as well for a possible existential intelligence, "the intelligence of big questions" (Gardner, 1999). I also explored much more deeply the relation between intelligences – which I construe as biopsychological potentials – and the various domains and disciplines that exist in various cultures. What we know and how we parse the world may well be in part a reflection of the human intelligences. I also introduced three distinct uses of the term "intelligence" (see Chapter 10):

- a property of all human beings (all of us possess these eight or nine intelligences)
- a dimension on which human beings differ (no two people – not even identical twins – possess exactly the same profile of intelligences)
- the way in which one carries out a task in virtue of one's goals (Joe may have a lot of musical intelligence but his interpretation of that piece made little sense to us).

A third activity featured a more proactive relationship to the uses and interpretations of my theory. For the first decade I had been content simply to observe what others were doing and saying in the name of MI theory. But by the middle 1990s I had noticed a number of misinterpretations of the theory – for example, the confusion of intelligences with learning styles and the confounding of a human intelligence with a societal domain (e.g. musical intelligence being equated with mastery of a certain musical genre or role). I had also taken note of practices that I found offensive – for example, describing different racial or ethnic groups in terms of their characteristic intelligences. And so, for the first time, I began to differentiate my "take" on MI from that of others who had learned about and tried to make use of the theory (see Chapter 7).

A final feature of this second phase entailed a more active involvement with educational reform. This involvement took both a practical and a scholarly form. On the practical level, my colleagues and I at Harvard Project Zero began working with schools as they attempted to implement MI practices and other educational programs that we have developed, such as teaching for understanding. We also launched an annual Summer Institute. On the scholarly side, I began to articulate my own educational philosophy. In particular, I focused on the importance in the precollegiate years of achieving understanding in the major disciplines – science, mathematics, history, and the arts. For various reasons, achieving such understanding is quite challenging. Efforts to cover too much material doom the achievement of understanding. We are most likely to enhance understanding if we probe deeply in a small number of topics. And once the decision is made to "uncover" rather than "cover," it is possible to take advantage of our MI. Put concretely, we can approach topics in a number of ways; we can make use of analogies and comparisons drawn from a range of domains; and we can express the key notions or concepts in a number of different symbolic forms.

This analysis has led to a perhaps surprising conclusion. Doing "MI" should not in and of itself be an educational goal. Educational goals need to reflect one's own values, and these can never come simply or directly from a scientific theory.

Once one reflects on one's educational values and states one's educational goals, however, then the putative existence of our MI can prove very helpful. And, in particular, if one's educational goals encompass disciplinary understanding, then it is possible to mobilize our several intelligences to help achieve that lofty goal.

This, then, is how the first 20 years of MI look to me. I am grateful to the many individuals who have taken an interest in the theory – both within my research group and across the country and the globe. I have tried to be responsive to their inquiries and to build on what they have taught me. And I have come to realize that once one releases an idea – a "meme" – into the world, one cannot completely control its behavior – any more than one can control those products of our genes called children. Put succinctly, MI has and will have a life of its own, over and above what I might wish for it, my most widely known intellectual offspring.

MI turned 20 in the same year that I turned 60. I do not know how much time I will have left to work on the theory. In any event, this moment is an excellent one for me to step back and to suggest some future lines of analysis and practice.

To begin with, there will be efforts to propose new intelligences. In recent years, in addition to the explosion of interest in emotional intelligences, there have also been serious efforts to describe a spiritual intelligence and a sexual intelligence. My colleague Antonio Battro (2002) has proposed the existence of a digital intelligence and has indicated how it may fulfill the criteria that I have set forth. Recently, the noted cognitive neuroscientist Michael Posner has challenged me to consider "attention" as a kind of intelligence (2004). I have always conceded that, in the end, the decision about what counts as an intelligence is a judgment call and not an algorithmic conclusion. So far, I am sticking to my 8½ intelligences but I can readily foresee a time when the list could grow, or when the boundaries among the intelligences might be reconfigured. For example, to the extent that the so-called Mozart effect gains credibility, I might want to rethink the relation between musical and spatial intelligences.

Much work needs to be done on the question of how the intelligences can best be mobilized to achieve specific pedagogical goals. I do not believe that educational programs created under the aegis of MI theory lend themselves to the kinds of randomized control studies that the U.S. Federal Government has now called for in education. But I do believe that well-choreographed "design experiments" can reveal the kinds of educational endeavors where an MI perspective is appropriate and where it is not. To state just one example, I think that MI approaches are particularly useful when a student is trying to master a challenging new concept – say, gravity in physics, or the Zeitgeist in history. I am less persuaded that it can be useful in mastering a foreign language – though I admire those teachers of foreign languages who claim success using MI approaches (see Haley, 2004).

Were I to be granted more time and energy to explore the ramifications of MI theory, I would devote those precious gifts to two endeavors. First of all, as indicated above, I have become increasingly fascinated by the ways in which societal activities and domains of knowledge emerge and become periodically reconfigured. Any complex society has 100–200 distinct occupations at the least; and any university of size offers at least 50 different areas of study. Surely these domains and disciplines are not accidents; nor are the ways that they evolve and combine random events. The culturally constructed spheres of knowledge must bear some kind of relation to the kinds of brains and minds that human beings have, and the ways that those brains and minds grow and develop in different cultural settings. Put concretely, how does human logical-mathematical intelligence relate to the various sciences, mathematics, and computing software and hardware that have emerged in the past few thousand years, and those that may emerge one year or 100 years from now? Which makes which or, more probably, how does each shape the other? How does the human mind deal with inter-disciplinary studies – are they natural or unnatural cognitive activities? I would love to be able to think about these issues in a systematic way.

Second, from the start, one of the appealing aspects of MI theory was its reliance on biological evidence. At the time, in the early 1980s, there was little relevant evidence from genetics or evolutionary psychology; such speculations were mere handwaving. There was powerful evidence from the study of neuropsychology for the existence of different mental faculties, and that evidence constituted the strongest leg on which to justify MI theory.

Twenty years later, knowledge is accumulating at a phenomenal rate in both brain science and genetics. At the risk of seeming hyperbolic, I am prepared to defend the proposition that we have learned as much from 1983 to 2003 as we did in the previous 500 years. As a sketchily trained neuroscientist and geneticist, I have tried as best I can to keep up with the cascade of new findings from these areas. I can say with some confidence that no findings have radically called into question the major lines of MI theory. But I can say with equal confidence that, in light of the findings of the past two decades, the biological basis of MI theory needs urgently to be brought up to date.

Whether I will be in a position to do this myself, I cannot say. But I would like to throw out a speculation.

At the time that MI theory was introduced, it was very important to make the case that human brains and human minds are highly differentiated entities. It is fundamentally misleading to think about a single mind, a single intelligence, a single problem-solving capacity. And so, along with many others, I tried to make the argument that the mind/brain consists of many modules/organs/intelligences, each of which operates according to its own rules in relative autonomy from the others.

Happily, nowadays, the argument for modularity has been well made. Even those who believe strongly in "general intelligence" and/or neural plasticity feel the need to defend their position, in a way that was unnecessary in decades past. But it is time to revisit the issue of the relationship between general and particular intelligences.

This revisiting can and is being done in various intriguing ways. Psychologist Robbie Case (1991) proposed the notion of central conceptual structures – broader than specific intelligences but not as all-encompassing as Piagetian general intelligence. Philosopher Jerry Fodor (2000) contrasts impenetrable dedicated modules with a permeable central system. The team of Marc Hauser, Noam Chomsky, and Tecumseh Fitch (2002) suggests that the unique quality of human cognition is its capacity for recursive thinking; perhaps it is recursion – informally, the potential of a system to refer to itself and to generate novel instances of itself – that characterizes advanced thinking in language, number, music, social relations, and other realms. Electrophysiological and radiological studies indicate that various brain modules may already be activated in newborns. Neural imaging studies of individuals solving IQ-style problems suggest that certain areas of the brain are most likely to be drawn on for these kinds of problems; and there may be evidence for genes that contribute to unusually high IQ, as there clearly are genes that lead to retardation. And our own case studies of unusually high performances suggests a distinction between those who (like musicians or mathematicians) are outstanding in one area, as opposed to those generalists (politicians or business leaders) who display a relatively flat profile of cognitive strengths. I think it would be worthwhile to study in detail the differences between those who deploy a focused *laser* intelligence and those who display an ever-vigilant and shifting *searchlight* intelligence.

Were I granted another lifetime or two, I would like to rethink the nature of intelligence with respect to our new biological knowledge, on the one hand, and our most sophisticated understanding of the terrain of knowledge and societal practice, on the other – another Van Leer Project on Human Potential, perhaps! I don't expect this wish to be granted. But I am glad to have had the chance to make an opening move some 20 years ago; to have been able to revisit the gameboard periodically; and to lay out this problematic so that other interested players can have their chance to engage.

PART 3

ARTS EDUCATION

CHAPTER 12

ARTISTIC INTELLIGENCES

Art Education, National Art Education Association, 1983, 36 (2), 47–9.

Scratch a school principal or, for that matter, an experimental psychologist, and you are likely to encounter a standard view of how humans participate in the arts. From dance to drama the arts are seen as matters of emotion – arising from and stimulating feelings. Some individuals are endowed with talents in the arts, and, if so blessed, they simply wait until inspiration strikes. No realm of experience seems further away from formal schooling, from rationality, from scientific progress; how appropriate it is that the arts are listed in the newspaper as amusements and that one enters a concert hall or a museum with the same unreflective awe that one brings to church.

Scratch an unreflective or defensive artist, and you are likely to garner yet further testimony in support of such an affective and inspirational view of the arts. But most artists know better. They must certainly be aware of the training and discipline which enters into and permeates their craft, of the difference between occasional inspiration and daily toil. Indeed, in their own informal conversations, artists speak frequently about the development and deployment of a wide range of abilities and skills. Yet there has been almost a conspiracy of silence among artists concerning the arduous training and the keen mental efforts involved in artistic practice. Just why this has been so is a difficult matter to assay, but, in any case, most artists have hesitated to acknowledge the cognitive dimensions and demands of their chosen field.

Given these commonly encountered opinions both in and outside "the trade," it is not surprising that the prevailing wisdom about participation in the arts was for many years studiously non- (or even anti-) cognitive. But in the past few decades there has been significant change in the way in which aestheticians, artists, art educators, and others conceptualize the activities of artistic creators, performers, and audience members. Art is being seen anew – or, once again, as a matter of the mind. Some credit should go to the Zeitgeist, to the rise of the cognitive sciences, which sometimes threaten to overwhelm all human-oriented disciplines. Considerable credit should go to a few insightful commentators – Nelson Goodman, Ernst Gombrich, Rudolf Arnheim, Leonard Meyer, I.A. Richards – who have stressed (and exemplified) the cognitive facets of artistry. And part of the credit should go to that small but spirited phalanx of empirical researchers who have provided detailed evidence in support of such a cognitive view.

Just what is entailed in a cognitive view of the arts? As we have developed this perspective at Harvard Project Zero, artistry is first and foremost an activity of the mind. Like much other mental activity, artistic perception and production involve the use of symbols – a deployment which may well constitute the hallmark of human cognition. But artistry centers on the use of certain kinds of symbols (for example, paintings rather than chemical formulae), which are used in certain kinds of properties. To attain competence in the arts, it is necessary to gain *literacy* with these symbol systems. And so the artistically competent individual is one who is able to "read" and to "write" symbols in such realms as literature, music, or sculpture. On this cognitive view, the role of the emotions is certainly acknowledged, but emotions are seen as aiding in the processes of symbol encoding and decoding, rather than as somehow opposed to "sheer" cognitive activity. That different works may have different value or merit is also acknowledged, but attention focuses on how one interacts with (or "comes to know") artistic symbols, and not on whether one symbol is intrinsically better or worse, more or less beautiful, than another.

In light of these considerations, a research agenda readily follows. The investigator of artistic knowledge studies the ways in which skilled (and unskilled) individuals handle artistic symbols: the goals they set, the problems they encounter, the steps through which they pass in fashioning or interpreting artistic symbols. Those interested in human development probe the stages through which children pass in gaining artistic mastery. Those interested in adult performance compare novices with experts, or study highly competent performance on a moment-by-moment basis. And those whose interests focus on educating artistic vision examine various methods for enhancing an individual's capacity to encode and decode artistic symbols. Such is the program which we have attempted to follow at Harvard Project Zero, a program which, happily, is being embraced by an increasing number of researchers.

Having sketched something of the contour of artistic symbolization – its adult facets, its development trajectory, its educational regimen (Gardner, 1973a, 1982a; Perkins, 1981; Winner, 1982) – we (as well as other researchers) have been thrown back to an important question, which, for a while, it was prudent to bracket. This is the question of the relation between artistic and other forms of knowledge. How do the arts relate to other pursuits – to business, to athletics, to politics, and above all to the sciences? Are the arts a domain apart, perhaps even a domain that has captured one half of the brain, or one half of the mind? Or does the cognitive division of labor prove more complex, with the relations between the arts and other pursuits still largely uncharted territory?

In an effort to sort out these questions, I have recently reviewed a large body of the literature about human cognition which has accrued over the past decades. My special goal has been to cull insights from bodies of knowledge that had not hitherto been brought to bear upon one another. Included in this survey have been reviews of the development of cognition (as described by Piaget and many developmental scholars); the breakdown of cognitive capacities following various kinds of brain injury; the nature of abilities (and disabilities) in special populations, including prodigies, *idiots savants*, autistic children, and others who exhibit unusual cognitive profiles; the cross-cultural literature chronicling *which* cognitive abilities are valued in diverse societies, as well as relevant (though necessarily scattered) information about the evolution of cognition and about the intellectual capacities of other species. By means of this review of various lines of evidence, I have sought to determine whether there are certain cognitive proclivities which especially characterize human beings. My conclusions are summarized in *Frames of Mind* (see also Chapters 6 to 8). I put forward some tentative conclusions here, in the hope that they may help to illuminate the relation between artistic and other forms of knowledge.

I believe that human beings are capable of developing capacities of an exquisitely high order in several semi-autonomous intellectual realms. That is, as a species, we have the potential to develop our intellectual potentialities in the following realms: 1) language; 2) music; 3) logic and mathematics; 4) visual-spatial conceptualization; 5) bodily-kinesthetic skills; 6) knowledge of other persons; 7) knowledge of ourselves. This list may well not be exhaustive and, as evidence accumulates, it may be advisable to revise or otherwise refashion this list (see Chapters 8, 10, 11). But the general point – that we are capable of developing some, or perhaps all, of these competences to a high degree – seems a relatively robust outcome of the survey which I've conducted.

It must be noted that, even in affixing these relatively colorless labels, I am already classifying these potentials in a culturally tinted way. My claim, expressed more precisely, is that humans possess a set of semi-autonomous information-processing devices – one may think of them as "dumb" but reliable computers – which, when exposed to certain forms of environmental information, will carry out certain kinds of operations upon that information. The computational "core" of linguistic intelligence is phonological and syntactic analysis; the "core" of musical intelligence is rhythmic and pitch analysis; the "core" of logical-mathematical intelligence is the perception of certain recurrent patterns, including numerical patterns, and so on.

Human beings live in cultures, and these cultures can only survive if certain roles are filled and if certain functions are carried out. One means of survival is to ensure that these critical functions are passed on from one generation to the next. For this transmission to occur, various intellectual potentials must be mobilized. In my view this mobilization occurs through the invention and dissemination of various kinds of symbolic products – books and speeches, pictures and diagrams, musical compositions, scientific theories, games, rituals, and the like.

For educational as well as scientific purposes, an analysis in terms of symbolic products turns out to be a judicious undertaking. On the one hand, these entities are sufficiently tangible so that the culture can assess whether roles are being fulfilled and knowledge transmitted. On the other hand, symbolic products are susceptible to brute information-processing in the sense that "computational devices" can be brought to bear on them. To put it concretely, the human brain is equipped to process stories, while at the same time these stories prove an excellent cultural means of transmitting knowledge from one generation to another. The same can be said of number systems, musical songs, or religious rites. The "socialization" or "enculturation" of the aforementioned human intellectual proclivities is, to my mind, the major task of our education system.

Even if this rough-and-ready sketch of an aspiring theory of intelligence has some validity, the question remains about how such a formulation may bear upon the delineation of artistic domains. In my view, the "intelligences" are not, either separately or jointly, preordained to be involved in the arts, the sciences, or any particular specific cultural area. Instead they are raw computational mechanisms, which can be marshaled by artistic symbols or for artistic ends, if that seems appropriate, or, equally, for other kinds of symbols and other kinds of ends, when that seems indicated.

Thus, to take the case of language, there is no particular reason why an individual's linguistic potential needs to be harnessed in the service of metaphor, poetry, stories, or dramas. Yet, clearly, if these kinds of symbolic products are available, and if the culture (via its members, institutions, or values) chooses to highlight the literary use of language, this particular artistic faculty will be developed. Spatial intelligence is similarly "blind"; it can be exploited for geometry, physics, engineering, or sailing, on the one hand, or it may be marshaled in the production of sculpture, painting, or choreography, on the other. Indeed, it turns out that each of the "multiple intelligences" I have proposed can be entrained in artistic activities; some, like music, are typically involved in this way, while others, like logical-mathematical abilities, are only rarely so deployed (see the paintings of M.C. Escher or 12-tone music). But there is no imperative that any given intelligence be sculpted into an aesthetic form; that turns out to be an accident of cultural history.

Such a portrayal of human intellectual competences has a number of implications for the way that we think of mind. For a start, this portrait proves far more pluralistic than the cultural stereotype of a single form of intelligence, with which each individual is endowed (for better or worse) at birth. Presumably individuals do differ in their potential in each of these intelligences, but there is ample room for developing several intelligences, alone or in combination, and an individual's peculiar profile of development will give rise to a wide array of complex skills. This framework also highlights the extent to which the surrounding culture determines the uses to which one's raw intellectual potentials are put. Clearly, a society can opt for a highly artistic diet – as Bali or Japan appear to have done – or a society can choose to adopt a far more scientific, technological, or economic regimen, thereby minimizing the incidence and importance of artistic symbolic products. Some would allege that our own society has veered in a non-aesthetic vein, though there are certainly noteworthy exceptions to this charge.

Educational implications follow as well. One interesting implication is that we should stop regarding perception, memory, and learning as extremely general capacities, applicable equivalently to every manner of content. According to my analysis, there may be specific forms of perception, memory, and the acquisition of new knowledge for each of the intellectual competences. At the very least there is no reason, *a priori*, to assume that a heightened memory in one particular domain implies anything about one's mnemonic capacities in a neighboring (or contrasting) domain.

Another implication pertains to early detection of an individual's intellectual profile. My own guess is that individuals differ in their potentials in various domains and that an individual's strengths can be identified quite early: the ability to recognize patterns, and then to retain them, is probably discernible in the first years of life, and these capacities may serve as a sensitive measure of one's inherent talents in one or another intellectual domain. Such an assessment of an individual's "intellectual profile" should be thought of as informative rather than limiting. Armed with this kind of knowledge, parents and educators have the option of developing a child's strengths and of supplementing weaker areas, either through special training or through the use of prosthetics, which can often supplant modest endowment in a given intellectual domain.

According to my analysis, we have tended in our own society to accord excessive weight to linguistic and logical-mathematical intelligences, while giving relatively short shrift to other intellectual domains. Our aptitude and achievement tests are also far more sensitive to accomplishments in these domains. In order to test an individual's ability in the bodily or musical domains, for example, it is clearly inadequate simply to use paper-and-pencil measures which can be administered in an hour. Rather, one should ask individuals to participate in activities that actually call in significant measure on these "intelligences" – to dance, play a sport, to sing, to learn an instrument. It should be possible to develop intrinsically compelling activities (for example, simple games) that allow a ready assessment of an individual's interest, and potential for development, in a given intellectual domain. Identifying such "crystallizing experiences" in the arts is an important task for educators. Properly deployed, such experiences can be used to assess a child's "zone for potential development" and to increase the likelihood that the assessed potential gets actualized.

This novel view of intelligence suggests that the arts may be especially suited to encompass the range of individual intellectual profiles. No matter how idiosyncratic an individual's intellectual skills, there should be art forms and products which can mobilize them. The menu of choices – literature and music, painting and dancing, acting, carving, and sculpture – prove sufficiently variegated to allow virtually every individual to gain pleasure and to achieve competence. To be sure, art educators should not force-feed these activities; that would be as misguided as a diet of all sciences, all sports, or all commercial endeavors. But to the extent that we wish children to have the opportunity to develop their full range of intellectual potentials, it is virtually an imperative that we facilitate involvement in one or more art forms. Involvement with the arts proves one of the best ways in which children can come to know the greatest achievements of which human beings are capable; it is also an excellent avenue to allow them to contribute to their own culture. If children have these opportunities, they will certainly be using their minds to the fullest. At the same time, they may gain those emotional pleasures, those moments of inspiration, and those feelings of mystical involvement which commentators once thought were the special province of the arts.

Acknowledgment

Reprinted with permission from the National Art Education Association, © 1983.

CHAPTER 13

ZERO-BASED ARTS EDUCATION
An introduction to ARTS PROPEL

Studies in Art Education, Blackwell,1989, 30 (2), 71–83. Reprinted in *The Journal of Art and Design Education*, 8, 167–82.

In this chapter I introduce a new approach to curriculum and assessment in the arts, called ARTS PROPEL. While a number of the features of ARTS PROPEL are shared with other contemporary initiatives, the approach differs both in terms of its intellectual origins and its particular mix of components. Thus the current chapter also serves as an introduction to the general approach to arts education devised over the past decades at Harvard Project Zero and to a particular form it has currently assumed in the practical arena.

It is appropriate to introduce the lines of analysis within the Development Group that I headed in the 1970s and 1980s; these led most directly to the ARTS PROPEL undertaking. In early work we adapted the pathbreaking methods of investigation devised by Jean Piaget (1983) in his study of children to the kinds of symbol-using competence which had been described by Nelson Goodman. This focus eventually gave rise to three principal lines of investigation. First of all, we carried out cross-sectional experimental studies of specific capacities (such as style sensitivity or metaphoric competence) in order to determine the "natural" developmental trajectory of these important skills (Gardner, 1982a). Second, we carried out naturalistic longitudinal studies of the development in early childhood of various kinds of symbol-using capacities (Wolf and Gardner, 1981, 1988; Wolf *et al.*, 1988). Third, in a scientifically related body of work, we investigated the breakdown under conditions of brain damage of the very symbolic skills whose ontogenesis we had been probing (Gardner, 1975; Kaplan and Gardner, 1989).

A number of important and sometimes unexpected findings emerged from these studies, undertaken principally during the 1970s.

1   In most areas of development, children simply improve with age. In several artistic spheres, however, evidence suggests a surprisingly high level of competence in young children, followed by a possible decline during the years of middle childhood. This jagged or "U-shaped" curve in development is particularly evident in certain areas of artistic production, though it can perhaps be manifest as well in selective areas of perception (Gardner and Winner, 1982).

2   Notwithstanding certain deficiencies in their performances, preschool children acquire a tremendous amount of knowledge about and competence in the arts. As is the case with natural language, this acquisition can occur without explicit tutelage on the part of parents or teachers. The evolution of children's drawings constitutes a particularly vivid example of this self-generated learn-

ing and development (Gardner, 1980). In this respect artistic learning stands in sharp contrast to most traditional school subjects.

3   In nearly every area, an individual's perceptual or comprehension capacities develop well in advance of productive capacities. Once again, however, the picture in the arts proves far more complex, and, at least in some domains, comprehension actually appears to lag behind performance or production capacities (Winner *et al.*, 1986). This finding underscores the importance of giving young children ample opportunity to learn by performing, making, or "doing."

4   According to classical developmental theory, children's competence in one cognitive sphere should predict the child's level of competence in other spheres as well. Along with other investigators, we discovered much less synchrony across areas. Indeed, it was entirely normal for children to be strong in one or two areas (e.g., art form x) while being average or below average in their attainment in other areas (including art form y – Gardner 1983; Winner *et al.*, 1986).

5   It has been thought for some decades that the brain was "equipotential," with each area capable of sub-serving the range of human capacities. Neuro-psychological research called this finding into severe doubt. A better descrip-tion indicates that specific areas of the cortex have particular cognitive foci, and that, particularly after early childhood, there is little "plasticity" in the representation of cognitive capacities in the nervous system (Gardner 1975, 1986b).

It would be misleading to suggest that we now understand artistic development, even to the same extent that researchers have illuminated scientific development or the development of linguistic competence. As our taunting "zero" reminds us, research on this topic is still in its infancy. Our work has established that artistic development is complex and multi-vocal; generalizations are hard to come by and often fall by the way. Still, it has been important for us to try to tie together our major findings about artistic development and this we have attempted in a number of places (Gardner, 1973a; Winner, 1982; Wolf and Gardner, 1980).

The Project Zero approach to art education

Given our cognitive approach to artistic education, we believe that students need to be introduced to the ways of thinking exhibited by individuals involved in the arts, by practicing artists and by those who analyze, criticize, and investigate the cultural contexts of art objects. Yet, in contrast to some advocates of "discipline-based arts education," we introduce a number of nuances in our position. These points have led us to put forth our own approach to education in the various art forms. While not pretending to speak for all of Project Zero – past or present – I would call attention to the following points.

1   Particularly at younger ages (below, say, ten), production activities ought to be central in any art form. Children learn best when they are actively involved in their subject matter; they want to have the opportunity to work directly with materials and media; and, in the arts, these strengths and inclinations almost always translate into the making of something. Moreover, young children

have considerable gifts for figuring the crucial components or patterns in an artistic object, and they should have the opportunity to do such "ferreting out" on their own (Bamberger, 1982). This accent is the legacy of the progressive era which deserves to endure, even in a more "disciplinary epoch" (cf. Dewey, 1958; Lowenfeld, 1947).

2　Perceptual, historical, critical, and other "peri-artistic" activities should be closely related to, and (whenever possible) emerge from, the child's own productions. That is, rather than being introduced in an alien context to art objects made by others, children should encounter such objects in relation to the particular artistic products and problems with which they are themselves engaged and, whenever possible, in intimate connection to the child's own art objects. (Older students and adults can also benefit from such contextualized introductions to peri-artistic activities.)

3　Arts curricula need to be presented by teachers or other individuals with a deep knowledge of how to "think" in an artistic medium. If the area is music, the teacher must be able to "think musically" – and not merely introduce music via language or logic. By the same token, education in the visual arts must occur at the hand – and through the eyes – of an individual who can "think visually or spatially" (cf. Arnheim, 1969). To the extent that teachers do not already possess these skills, they ought to enroll in training regimens which can develop these cognitive capacities.

4　Whenever possible, artistic learning should be organized around meaningful projects, which are carried out over a significant period of time and allow ample opportunity for feedback, discussion, and reflection. Such projects are likely to interest students, to motivate them, to encourage them to develop skills; and they may exert a long-term impact on the students' competence and understanding. As much as possible, "one-shot" learning experiences should be spurned.

5　In most artistic areas it will not be profitable to plan a Kindergarten to Grade 12 sequential curriculum. (I have in mind here undemanding but all too frequent curricular goals: can provide four color names; can sing three intervals; can recite two sonnets.) Such a formula may sound attractive, but it flies in the face of the holistic, contextually sensitive manner in which individuals customarily gain mastery in crafts or disciplines. Artistry involves a continuing exposure, at various developmental levels, to certain core concepts, such as style, composition, or genre; and to certain recurrent problems, like performing a passage with feeling or creating a powerful artistic image. Curricula need to be rooted in this "spiral" aspect of artistic learning. A curriculum may be sequential in the sense that it revisits concepts and problems in an increasingly sophisticated way, but not in the same sense that there exists one set of problems, concepts, or terms at grade two, another set at grades three or four.

6　Assessment of learning is crucial in the arts. The success of an arts program cannot be asserted or taken on faith. However, assessments must respect the particular intelligences involved – musical skill must be assessed through musical means and not via the "screens" of language or logic. And assessment must probe those abilities and concepts which are most central to the arts. Rather than crafting the curriculum to suit the assessment, we must devise assessments which do justice to what is most pivotal in an art form.

7   Artistic learning does not merely entail the mastery of a set of skills or concepts. The arts are also deeply personal areas, where students encounter their own feelings as well as those of other individuals. Students need educational vehicles which allow them such exploration; they must see that personal reflection is a respected and important activity; and their privacy should not be violated.

8   In general, it is risky – and, in any case, it is unnecessary – to teach artistic taste or value judgments directly. However, it is important for students to understand that the arts are permeated by issues of taste and value that matter to anyone who is seriously engaged in the arts. These issues are best conveyed through contact with individuals who do care about these issues, who are willing to introduce and defend their values, but who are open to discussion and who countenance alternative points of view.

9   Art education is too important to be left to any one group, even that group designated as "art educators." Rather, art education needs to be a cooperative enterprise involving artists, teachers, administrators, researchers, and the students themselves.

10   While ideally all students would study all art forms, this is not a practical option. There are simply too many subjects – and, in my terms, too many intelligences – competing for attention on the calendar, and the school day is already excessively fragmented. In my view, no art form has any intrinsic priority over others. Thus, at the risk of offending those involved in a particular art form, I assert that students should all have extended exposure to some art form, but that it need not be one of the visual arts. Indeed, I would rather have an individual well versed in music, dance, *or* drama than one with a smattering of knowledge across the several lively arts. The former student will at least know what it is like to "think" in an art form and will retain the option of assimilating other arts forms in later life; the latter individual seems consigned to remain a dilettante.

The above points could give rise to any number of programs in arts education. In the present instance, they have contributed to a new approach called ARTS PROPEL. In 1985, with encouragement and support from the Arts and Humanities Division of the Rockefeller Foundation, Harvard Project Zero joined forces with the Educational Testing Service and the Pittsburgh public schools. The goal of the resulting multi-year project was to devise a set of assessment instruments which can document artistic learning during the later elementary and high school years. I want to stress that the ideas of ARTS PROPEL have been worked out in collaboration with the partners I've just named.

As anyone involved in educational experiments can readily appreciate, it has proved easier to state than to implement our goal. We began by attempting to delineate the competences that we sought to measure in our students. We decided to work in three art forms: music, visual art, and imaginative writing. And we decided to look at three kinds of competences; PRODUCTION (composing or performing music; painting or drawing; engaging in imaginative or "creative" writing); PERCEPTION (effecting distinctions or discriminations within an art form, "thinking" artistically); REFLECTION (stepping back from one's own perceptions or productions, or those of other artists, and seeking to understand the goals, methods, difficulties, and effects achieved). PROPEL captures acronymically this trio of competences in our three art forms, with the final L emphasizing our concern with LEARNING.

Ideally, we would have liked simply to devise adequate assessment instruments and to administer them to students in the target age groups. However, we soon arrived at a simple but crucial truth: there is no point in assessing competences or even potentials unless the student has had some significant experience in working directly with relevant artistic media. Just as baseball scouts look at students who are already playing baseball, it is necessary for educational assessors to examine students who are already engaged in artistic activities. And just as baseball rookies need well-trained and skilled coaches, so too art students require teachers who are fully acquainted with the goals of an educational program and able to exemplify the requisite artistic skills and understandings.

To bring about these goals, therefore, we elected to devise curriculum modules and link these to assessment instruments. We implemented a careful procedure of curriculum-and-assessment development. In each art form we assembled an interdisciplinary team, which together defined the central competences in an art form. In writing, we looked at students' capacities to create instances of different genres – e.g., writing a poem, creating dialogue for a play. In music, we examined the ways in which students learn from rehearsals of a work-in-progress. And in the area of visual arts (from which I will draw most of my examples here), the competences include sensitivity to style, appreciation of various compositional patterns, and the ability to create a work which satisfies certain constraints.

Let me flesh out our mode of operation. For each of these nominated competences, we generate a set of exercises called a "domain project" – a set which must feature perceptual, productive, *and* reflective elements. Domain projects do not in themselves constitute an entire curriculum but they must be curriculum-compatible; that is, they should fit comfortably into a standard art curriculum. The domain projects are first explored and critiqued by teachers. Following revision, they are administered in pilot form to students. A preliminary assessment system is then tried out by the teachers. An iterative process is involved until the domain project is considered adequate from the perspective of each of its audiences. Once the project has been completed, it can be used "as is" by teachers or adapted in various ways to fit a particular curriculum or the teaching style or goals of a specific teacher. Part of the assessment procedure is rough and ready – simply giving students and teachers a feeling for what the student is learning. However, it is also possible to make more fine-grained analyses (for research purposes), even as it is possible to produce a summary score for use by the central school administration.

As one example, let me briefly describe the "composition" domain project, which has been used quite widely in ARTS PROPEL. This project is designed to help students notice how arrangements and interrelationships of shapes affect the composition and the impact of artistic works. Students are given an opportunity to make compositional decisions and to reflect on the effects of such decisions in their works and as well in works created by acknowledged artistic masters. In an initial session, students are given a set of ten odd black geometric shapes. They are asked simply to drop those shapes on a piece of white paper. The exercise is then repeated, except that on the second trial students are asked to put together a set of shapes which they find pleasing. They are then asked to reflect on the differences between the "random" and the "deliberate" work. In a notebook they record the differences which they see and state the reasons which motivated their own "deliberate" choices. Most students find this exercise fun, though at first many do not quite know what to make of it.

In a second session, students encounter informally certain principles of composition. The teacher introduces the students to a number of artistic works of different styles and periods which differ significantly from one another in the kinds of symmetry or balance which they epitomize or violate. Students are asked to describe the differences among these works as they appear to them and to develop a vocabulary which can capture these differences and convey them effectively to others. Achievements (or violations) of harmony, cohesion, repetition, dominant forces, radial patterns, surprise, or tension are noted. At the conclusion of the session, students are asked to jot down in a notebook similarities and differences in contrasting sets of slides. They are also given an assignment. During the next week they should search in their daily environment for instances of different compositions – both those compositions already achieved by an artist and those which they can themselves create by "framing" a scene in nature.

In a third session, students report on the "compositions" they observed in their own environment and discuss them with reference to those observed in the art classes. The students then return to the deliberate composition of Session one. Now they are asked to make a "final work." Before proceeding, however, they are asked to indicate their plans for this work. Then they go about realizing and, if they wish, revising their final composition. On a worksheet they indicate what they found most surprising about their composition and what further changes they might want to make in a future work.

In addition to the students' own compositions, perceptual discriminations, and reflections, the teacher also has his or her own assessment sheet. There the teacher can evaluate the student in terms of the kinds of compositions attempted or achieved. Other kinds of learning – for instance, the student's success in discovering interesting compositions in his environment or his ability to connect his own compositions with those of well-known artists – can also be assessed. This domain project can be repeated, in its initial or in altered form, to determine the extent to which the student's grasp of compositional issues has developed over time.

The "composition" domain project works with a traditional element of the visual arts – the arrangement of form – and seeks to tie this element to the students' own productive and perceptual experiences. A quite different approach is taken in a second domain project called the "biography of a work." In this instance our goals are much broader. Indeed, we want to help students synthesize their learning from previous domain projects in composition, style, and expression; and to do so through tracing the development of a complete work.

In this domain project the students are asked to draw their room at home in a way that expresses something about themselves. They are given a range of media (paper, pencil, charcoal, pen and ink, etc.) as well as some pictorial material such as magazines and slides. In the first session students are asked to choose any element(s) of their room and to add whatever props or objects might be revealing about themselves. They are asked to use these in preparing a preliminary sketch. Their focus should fall on composition, but they are encouraged to think about how the range of artistic elements can express *themselves* and not just what is represented literally in the picture. A few examples are given of how aspects of form can convey metaphorically a property of an individual.

In the second session, students begin by examining slides that show how artists have used objects metaphorically in their work and also how particular objects or elements can carry a multiplicity of meanings. They are also shown slides of artists' studios or rooms and asked how these rooms might bring out something about the artists' view of their particular world. Students then return to their own preliminary sketches and are asked to make provisional decisions about the media which they wish to use and the style, color, line, texture, etc., they plan to employ. As in the earlier session, students fill out worksheets in which they are asked to reflect on the choices they have made, the reasons for them, and their aesthetic consequences.

In the third session, students review all of their preliminary sketches and "trial sheets," think about whether they are satisfied with them, and then begin their final work. Students discuss their works-in-progress with other students. Then, in a final session during the following week, the students complete their works, critique one another's efforts, and review their sketches, trial sheets, and reflections. The activities in this final week serve as a model for the kinds of reflections that are used as well in the student portfolio compilations (see below).

It has been our aim in ARTS PROPEL to create an ensemble of domain projects for each art form. These prototypes should encompass most of the important concepts in an art form. We seek as well to develop a *general theory* of domain projects: what set of exercises qualifies as a domain project, what kinds of learning can one expect to take place, how best can the student be assessed within and across domain projects.

In addition to the ensemble of domain projects, we have also introduced a second educational vehicle – the portfolio (which I have sometimes called the "process-folio"). Most artists' portfolios contain only the very best works by an artist, the set by which the artist would wish to be judged in a competition. In contrast, our portfolios are much more like "works-in-progress." In these portfolios, students include not just finished works but also original sketches, interim drafts, critiques by themselves and others, art works by others which they admire or dislike and which bear in some way on the current project. Students are sometimes asked to present the whole folder of materials; at other times they are asked to select only those pieces which appear particularly informative or pivotal in their own development (cf. N. Brown, 1987; Wolf, 1986, 1988a, 1988b).

Though the assessment of domain projects is by no means simple, it at least bears a family resemblance to other kinds of assessment routinely carried out by educators and psychologists. When it comes to the assessment of portfolios – and particularly ones which focus on the processes of learning rather than on the quality of the final products – we are charting unfamiliar territory in the schools.

Nonetheless we have isolated some areas to examine systematically. We can evaluate such components as the individual features (or personal profile) of the student's output; his or her ability to conceptualize and carry out a project; the inclusion of historical and critical materials which are related to, or which help to explicate, the student's own work; the regularity, relevance, and precision of portfolio entries; the capacity to think directly in an artistic medium (e.g., by systematically varying one aspect of a work in order to monitor the effect of such manipulation); signs of development and linkage from one work, or set of works, to another; the student's own sensitivity to his or her development; the ability to express personal meanings and to give them some kind of universal form. We realize that it will not be easy to judge each of these dimensions in an objective way, but even an attempt to monitor their initial inclusion and their development across years seems worthwhile.

As noted above, an important aspect of artistic learning is the opportunity to become involved in meaningful projects, in which one's own understanding and growth can come to the fore. It is already clear to us that both students and teachers find these portfolio activities engaging, exciting, and useful in their own right. Their classrooms come alive. By encouraging the development of portfolios, and by looking at them sympathetically and systematically, we may be able to increase the use of these materials and activities in schools. While it may be too much to expect that colleges will ever base admissions decisions chiefly on such portfolio information, we hope that such educational vehicles may allow students to put forth their own cognitive strengths.

Educators and educational critics frequently lament the gap between theory and practice – and between theories and practitioners. It is no doubt true that the professional goals of the two groups *are* different – that the theorist's triumph often leaves the practitioner untouched, while the practitioner's pleasures seem uninteresting to the theorist. For some time, it was fashionable to criticize Project Zero for its remoteness from educational practice, remoteness in two senses: (a) our work focused more on "natural" development than on what could be explicitly taught in the classroom; (b) our ideas, whether or not they were appealing, had little or no direct implications for what happened in the classroom on Monday morning.

While these charges sometimes left us a bit offended and made us a shade defensive, we are on the whole comfortable with our process. We feel that it is important to look at "natural" development before one examines interventions; and we believe that it is important to establish the psychological facts and to develop one's educational philosophy before one attempts to influence practice – especially since it is always possible that one might influence practice for the worse!

Having had the luxury of relatively "ivory tower" exploration in arts education, it has certainly been opportune for us to become more directly involved in educational experimentation. ARTS PROPEL represents one concerted effort to do just that. It is too early to know how successful this effort will prove to be and, even if successful in its "hot-house" atmosphere, whether it can be successfully transported to more remote soils. But it is not premature to indicate that researchers can learn a great deal from attempting to implement their ideas in a school setting. So long as we are on the alert for any disruption that we may cause, this intermingling of theory and practice should redound to the good of those involved in arts education.

CHAPTER 14

ILLUMINATING COMPARISONS IN THE ARTS

Henle, M (ed), *Vision and Artifact*, New York: Springer, 1976.

During the summer of 1973 the Minneapolis Institute of Arts mounted an exhibit of several hundred works of art drawn from diverse persons and schools; included were representatives of several aesthetic media, ranging from paintings and drawings to book covers and pottery. The show was billed as an "educational exhibit." This struck me as a curious designation from one point of view, since a non-educational museum exhibit is difficult to envisage. And yet, as the exhibit lent itself superlatively to pedagogical purposes, perhaps the description is justified. I had the opportunity to attend the exhibit on a number of occasions; it proved a singularly entertaining and edifying aesthetic experience. In these paragraphs I will seek to uncover the reasons for my positive reaction and consider whether some wider principles might be culled from this experience. Using the exhibit as a point of departure, I will examine the technique of the "illuminating comparison" as a means of heightening aesthetic awareness.

Fully half of the works on display in Minneapolis would normally have been a source of keen embarrassment to the curator and trustees of a museum. For the director and the "curatorial staff had assembled a collection of 'Fakes, Forgeries, and other Deceptions' "; deceits of every variety were conveniently juxtaposed alongside the originals they were purporting to represent. By this happy arrangement, the viewer was granted the invaluable opportunity to compare and contrast originals and forgeries.

Unquestionably, such a collection constituted a veritable feast for the connoisseur. Not only did he have the opportunity to examine works seldom on display, but he could also bring to bear varied tools of technical analysis, ranging from knowledge of the methods and materials available in different historical periods to details of the ways in which specific artists signed, dated, and otherwise incorporated distinctive marks onto canvases. Indeed, a wide array of scholars and critics visited the Minneapolis show, delivered suitable lectures, praised its catalogues, and urged the preservation of the displays in one form or another.

Too often, however, exhibits are mounted just for the cognoscenti. The hypothetical average viewer may well feel alienated or abandoned by such professional *tours de force*. Lacking the necessary background and training in analytic procedures, the untrained observer cannot fully appreciate the rationale for the show, the significance of particular selections (and omissions), the technical language of the catalogue, and the intent and impact of this or that curatorial aside. At best, the typical gallery-goer may gain some pleasure from one or another work, or from the elegance with which the show was curated.

The special power of the Minneapolis assemblage lay in its vast potential for aiding the unsophisticated but motivated viewer to gain insights hitherto available exclusively to the connoisseur. The expert is equipped to honor Rembrandt, for she understands the master's technical innovations, heightened expressive powers, special use of color, unsurpassed capacity to capture an emotion and compose a scene. What the average viewer had only glimpsed in a traditional show could now become manifest; as if magically supplied with the critic's lens, he too became capable of contrasting Rembrandt with his lesser contemporaries and, more especially, with those poseurs of later periods who unsuccessfully attempted to pass for the Dutch master. And particularly when given the opportunity to examine in tandem several fakes, forgeries, and deceptions, the audience member could gain a feeling for the range and depth of Rembrandt's powers; he had the invaluable chance to survey a variety of artists, each failing (in instructive ways) to achieve a desired effect.

Derogating the fake may be unnecessarily argumentative. To be sure, when it comes to a genius of Rembrandt's proportions, almost any comparison is likely to be at the expense of the deceptive work. But prior to, and perhaps more important than, the ultimate evaluation in terms of good and bad, better and worse, is the vital capacity to *discern, to appreciate differences.* What renders the work effective or ineffective to the viewer is the manner in which the numerous choices and challenges confronting the artist were resolved. Viewing the finished products, we confront records of the artists' choices – the differences in the final canvases – and from these derive our final evaluation.

All judgment, all evaluation, necessarily presupposes and depends upon comparison. In most exhibitions and displays the comparisons are implicit; the viewer must compare what he sees with what the artist might have done, given similar goals and means, but different abilities, plans, or techniques. The connoisseur is prepared for these implicit comparisons, for she has seen the absent works so many times that they have been deeply engraved on her mind's eye, but the average viewer is only rarely so equipped. At the "Fakes" show all viewers had the opportunity to be connoisseurs. The raw materials were provided from which informed comparisons could be made and reasoned judgments achieved.

Indeed, the opportunity was more than merely present; the invitation to compare was compelling. For faced with two apparent Botticellis and with the knowledge that only one is the "real thing," a virtually irresistible temptation arises to examine both closely, to peer back and forth, to focus on respective attempts to realize details, capture expressions, achieve certain hues, and, after detecting the differences, to make an informed guess about which is the "real Botticelli." Cleverly exploiting the pervasive human proclivity to enter into such a game, the museum placed in every municipal bus a poster bearing two Mona Lisas with the enticing caption "Will the real Mona Lisa please stand up?" The stagers of the exhibit had exploited the human tendency to search for similarities and differences among objects or displays, to represent to oneself the meanings of such resemblances and disparities, and to evaluate works on the basis of such a survey. In a way, adoption of the phrase "illuminating comparisons" may yield a deceptively simplified view of this process; in fact, achievement of such comparisons is a lengthy, painstaking process, fraught with the possibility of uninstructive contrasts and misleading conclusions. By no means will any set of objects or art works lend themselves to comparisons, let alone to relevant and enlightening ones. Rather, like the physician who draws on the details of his memory in making a difficult diagnosis, a curator or instructor must search through a mental (or physical) catalog of many hundreds of objects in order to select that pair or trio which drives home to even the most uninitiated individual the salient points of a lesson or a comparison.

Had the Minneapolis exhibition contained an endless series of originals juxtaposed to fakes, it would have been interesting and at least moderately entertaining, but not to my mind especially memorable. Again, however, the unseen hand which mounted the exhibit was guided by a basic tenet of human psychology: that there are many ways to stimulate a comparison, and that our minds are well served by a multiplicity of exploratory routes. Thus a wide array of comparisons was featured. Nearly every set of works posed a new challenge; no solution generalized automatically to the succeeding alcove; and yet there were enough possibilities for success and sufficient emerging patterns for the viewers so that, rather than despairing, they were instead stimulated to proceed on their course through the gallery.

Let me record a few of the pedagogical techniques that effectively stimulated comparisons. To begin with, one might speak of a *distance* principle. Some works were directly juxtaposed to facilitate comparison; others were mounted at some remove so that one had to stroll back and forth to effect a comparison. This device brought home the lesson that the expert does not always have the original available to him; it stimulated the viewer to remember or reconstruct the original, so that she might achieve the present comparison and be better equipped for future ones. In addition to geographical distance, disparities in quality were included. Sometimes the difference between the original and fake was quite evident – so that even the least trained eye could detect it; at other times it was so subtle that tools were needed. The museum provided a magnifying glass in one such instance, and it was constantly employed by visitors.

Further cognitive exercise was ensured by the inclusion of a wide variety of comparisons. The sets included, for instance, an original and a fake, an original and two or three fakes, lithographs produced in different periods, an original and a copy by a member of the artist's own school, innocently produced copies which had been provided with a false signature, copies supervised by the artist himself, and a whole group of fakes collected by one individual. These assemblages revealed that the expert is continually confronted with new problems and questions, that there is no unequivocal line among fakes, forgeries, and harmless exercises. The viewer was challenged to take on the task of the expert and to learn from each of these confrontations. Every set conveyed new messages or presented old messages in slightly new ways.

Furthermore, to warn the viewer against facile conclusions, some presentations were deliberately misleading: originals without signatures; originals of poor quality; a whole set of fakes without any original. Again these unexpected twists provided special insights into the expert's dilemmas and conferred a light touch upon the exhibit as well. Finally, the show featured some unfrocked forgeries, in which the forged work is only partially removed, revealing part of the older worthless painting on top of which the forger had labored. An apparent Greco or a Holbein which has been partially defaced served as a dramatic and jarring reminder of the manner in which forgers work.

A third distinctive feature of the exhibit was the way in which it emphasized diverse historical and stylistic features. Included were several works by a single forger (e.g., van Meegeren) as well as attempts by different artists to imitate one artist (several fake Rembrandts). The viewer gained a feeling for the style of the forger (who often reveals his own time when sufficient examples of his work are gathered in one place) and also an appreciation for the subtlety of the original artist's style (by seeing the manifold ways in which it is possible to disfigure a Rembrandt).

Forgeries date back to ancient times, and fakes have been elicited by diverse circumstances at different epochs in history. The special problems raised by contemporary forgeries were clarified by the exhibit: we have no distance from our own era; sophisticated methods of mechanical reproduction are available; certain works (such as conceptual or pop art) seem particularly easy to duplicate, at least to our own eyes. Nonetheless, clear differences could be seen between the original and a copy of Claes Oldenburg's *Baked Potato*.

Finally, the exhibit conveyed a sense of the task an expert faces when she encounters a suspected deception. Insights were provided into the different cues available to the expert: methods of signature, size of work, age of canvas, x-ray methods, tiny details of shading, awareness of anachronistic details or colors, construction of the frame, knowledge that an artist favored certain themes and spurned others, failure to capture a certain facial expression. These methods differ greatly in their objectivity, their reliance on technology, their dependence on acquaintance with other works by the artist, but all are helpful. The exhibit also revealed that some attributions are disputed; and it illustrated how a convergence of reasons, none of which is individually decisive, can nonetheless lead to authoritative conclusions. The viewer was thus enabled to draw on multiple criteria in making his own judgments.

Though tremendously impressed with, and delighted by, the stunning exhibit, I was conscious of a number of problems that it raised. Although described as educational, it is unclear that the exhibit educated anyone. I believe that it did, and so do those at the museum, but there is no proof. It does not suffice merely to assume that displays intended to stimulate comparisons have had that effect; they may have had unintended consequences or no consequences at all. To evaluate the educational success of an exhibit, no elaborate machinery or high-power statistical techniques would be necessary. A common-sense approach and perhaps consultation with a psychologist should yield suitable and unobtrusive measures of audience learning.

Another difficulty centered around the level of audience sophistication assumed by the displayers. Though, in my view, most visitors enjoyed and profited from the exhibit, a significant number commented that it was too difficult. Some viewers failed to see the differences alluded to in captions; others expressed disillusionment about the whole connoisseurial enterprise: "Well, if the experts make all these mistakes, how can I ever hope to tell?" "Who knows, perhaps half the pictures we admire are fakes." "The experts don't know any more than we do." These latter comments are particularly disconcerting. They suggest that, for certain viewers, the curator-intended comparisons may have failed in their intended effects. True, the viewers' awe of art may have been healthily reduced, but at the price of cynicism.

The expert's role vis-à-vis the audience is a challenging one. It does not suffice to say, "I have chosen this work, therefore you must like it." After all, the expert does not casually decide which classical vase to display. She knows and she cares about mythology, Greek methods of sculpture, the materials available to artists of two millennia ago, the clothing, religion, philosophy, mores, likes, and prejudices of individuals of that era. It is not enough simply to declare her knowledge to the viewer; such technical detail cannot be absorbed by the unprepared mind. Rather, an exhibit should be so staged that the viewer is led, subtly and entertainingly, yet authoritatively and convincingly, into the reaches of the expert's own knowledge. Only then can the non-expert appreciate why *this* art work is worth examining today. The Minneapolis exhibit was most successful when it made the world of the expert come alive for the viewer, less successful when it simply paraded knowledge or assumed understanding.

Finally, some comments are also in order about the supplementary information sources – the labels and program guides – that adorned the exhibit. There is no question that some labeling is essential in an exhibit of this type; how else can one tell if one's guesses are correct or what features to look at if one is incorrect? Without good labels, the exhibit would not work. The labels should be not placed in a prominent spot. Indeed, it might be optimal if the viewer were not allowed to scan the label until she had spent some time examining the canvas. It is too easy to conclude that you have seen what you are supposed to see after you have been told what it is and where to look for it.

In general, I encountered two difficulties with the labels in the "Fakes" show, difficulties by no means restricted to the present exhibit. First of all, there was a fair amount of technical material – recondite references to the styles of painting, characters from mythology, methods of production and detection, which were doubtless devoid of meaning to many viewers. Such references could intimidate them. Second, there was an unwarranted display of erudition.

An effective label is one which points to a difference which can then be seen by the viewer: "In the original the shading runs directly into the clouds; in the fake there is a gap of two millimeters." "In the original the numeral five has been printed backwards." An ineffective label is one which is too vague or which requires specialized knowledge. I have listed some labels which I found unhelpful:

> "The dullness of A vs. the vibrancy of B."
> "The piece is mechanical and dull, displaying nothing of the fine concern for life and death which characterizes Aztec religion."
> "The difference between the pieces is in essence, not in substance."
> "While superficially Renaissance in style, the triptych is really purest nineteenth century."
> "The artist expresses awe whereas the copy is merely coy."
> "The forgery captures none of the subtle qualities of the original."
> "Out of character in terms of the artist's true style."
> "It fails to capture the artist's deeply felt religious feeling."

It might have been helpful to categorize the kinds of differences cited; at least then label-writer and viewer alike would acknowledge the differences between an objective technical reason (age of frame), an objective non-technical reason (the shading doesn't reach to the clouds), an interpretation which is readily verified ("The Madonna in the original is looking directly into the eyes of the child"), an interpretation that does not lend itself to such verification ("The forger fails to capture the religious spirit of the original"). I do not mean to imply that the latter reason is irrelevant, only that in the present context it could have so many possible meanings that it does nothing to sharpen the viewer's appreciation.

Discussion of labels and their applicability to works of art raises the vexing question of the relationship between visual displays and linguistic instruction. The question is especially crucial in the present context, given the goal, on the one hand, of improving the viewer's perceptual skills, and the risk, on the other hand, that the viewer fails to draw valid inferences from the comparison before him. And yet the question is extremely controversial. One school of thought is deeply suspicious of any linguistic comments about "ineffable" works of art, while another equally vociferous group considers verbal instruction the optimal means for enhancing aesthetic sensitivity.

In this dispute the views of Rudolf Arnheim are especially instructive. As one who has devoted a lifetime to the understanding of art, and who writes eloquently on the subject, he is keenly sensitive to the advantages and the drawbacks of linguistic and non-linguistic modes of communication. Arnheim has offered a needed corrective to the uncritical overuse, and frequent misapplication, of linguistic instruction in our educational system. Without questioning the essential communicative role of language and its appropriateness for transmitting certain subject matters, he challenges the widespread belief that language provides the optimal means for presenting the full range of information and capturing the entire gamut of thought processes. Arnheim demonstrates that thought processes rely heavily on the effective functioning of our sensory modalities and on the role of nonlinguistic symbol systems.

By theoretical conceptualization, as well as by example, Arnheim has helped to specify the appropriate role of ordinary language in explicating the arts. Often, as at certain points in the Minneapolis exhibit, the correct point will be grasped without recourse to verbal documentation; at such times linguistic elaboration is neither necessary nor desirable. At other times, however, a pictorial display may be subjected to numerous interpretations, and the intended pedagogical principle, the illuminating comparison, is likely to be missed. At such times verbal labels can provide useful supplements, directing the viewer toward points worthy of his consideration, helping to explicate the significance of elements that have been but dimly discerned.

The shortest distance to effective communication is not always a direct or literal line, however. Metaphors, personifications, and other figures of speech may well succeed in conveying a crucial point in an especially succinct and effective manner. Particularly in the arts, the connotative and allusive qualities of language constitute a rich resource for the sensitive teacher or writer. Certainly, we must not delete words from artistic instruction; we must only deploy them with the precision and care with which a brush is wielded or a violin bowed.

A case could be made that all learning necessitates contrasts and comparisons. Where there is no change, no discrepancy, no gap, no perceived distinction, we cannot learn. The Minneapolis exhibit overshadowed most other cultural and educational experiments because, by means of a simple yet elegant technique, the viewer was enticed into effecting comparisons; owing to the aptness of the comparisons, significant new aesthetic insights could be gained. A simple example, or an illuminating comparison of two works, can form the beginning of a deeper understanding of a principle. But the future application of this principle requires that its underlying features be detected and formulated with some precision.

The inquiry prompted by my visit to Minneapolis suggests certain conclusions about the role of comparisons in artistic knowledge. First, the teacher or exhibitor must be clear in her own mind about what educational point is to be made and have some confidence that the point is worth making. Next, she should select a variety of examples that illustrate the point in a number of different and accessible fashions. She should consider the use of various linguistic and nonlinguistic supplements for conveying the point; and if such supplements are used, she must take care that they direct attention to the relevant details, rather than serve to obfuscate the point or to signal the brilliance of the writer. And, finally, she should engage in some modest experimentation in order to determine whether the point at issue has indeed been grasped by the intended audience. In addition to a set of guidelines like this, however, some models or examples of aesthetic education are also desirable. To those in search of such models, I can point with enthusiasm to the Minneapolis exhibit and to the works of Rudolf Arnheim, in which are exemplified many principles touched on in this essay.

Acknowledgment

This chapter first appeared in a *Festschrift* dedicated to Professor Rudolf Arnheim.

CHAPTER 15

THE KEY IN THE KEY SLOT
Creativity in a Chinese key

Gardner, H. *To Open Minds: Chinese Clues to the Dilemma of Contemporary Education*, Basic Books, 1989.

At the Jinling, a comfortable hotel in Nanjing where the Gardner family spent a month in the spring of 1987, the key to our hotel room was attached to a large plastic block with the room number embossed on it. When leaving the hotel, guests were encouraged to turn in the key, either by handing it to an attendant standing behind the desk or by dropping the key into a slot. Because the key slot was rectangular and narrow, the key (with its plastic pendant) had to be carefully aligned by hand so that it would fit into the snug slot.

Our 20-month-old son Benjamin, whom we had adopted from Taiwan a year earlier, loved to carry around the key and shake it in his hand. He also liked to attempt to place the key in the key slot. Whenever my wife or I approached the hotel registration desk with Benjamin in our arms, he would bring the key to the vicinity of the slot and then try to shove it into the hole. Because of his tender age and limited understanding, he would usually fail to insert it into the slot. This lack of success did not bother Benjamin in the least. He loved to bang the key on the slot and enjoyed the sound it made, and the kinesthetic sensation it produced.

My wife Ellen Winner and I were both perfectly happy to allow Benjamin to bang the key in the vicinity of the key slot. But I soon observed an interesting phenomenon. Frequently, when there was a Chinese attendant nearby – and sometimes even when there was merely a Chinese passerby in the vicinity – that individual would come over to watch Benjamin. As soon as the observer saw what our son was doing and noted his lack of immediate success, she attempted to intervene. In general, she would hold onto his hand and, gently but firmly, guide it directly to the slot, reorient it as necessary, and then press the key-clutching hand into the slot. She would then smile somewhat expectantly at Ellen or me, as if awaiting a thank you.

Alas, we were not particularly grateful for this intervention. After all, it was not as if Benjamin were running around wildly without supervision; clearly we – his parents – had been aware of what he was doing and had not ourselves intervened. However, it also became clear to us that we were dealing with a very different set of attitudes – assumptions concerning not only what children should be doing, but also the proper role of other adults in their socialization. Perhaps indeed, this recurring incident held part of the key to the mysteries of arts education which had brought us to China.

Over the course of the months that we spent in China, as part of the U.S.A China Exchange in Arts Education, it became clear to us that babies are "fair game" in China. Adults (and even adolescents) feel little compunction about inter-vening in the child rearing process. It was equally clear that the Chinese had a con-sensus on what was right or wrong in most situations, and in their casual encounters with Benjamin they were simply exhibiting their commonly held beliefs.

After I had gleaned what was going on, I began to incorporate this little "key-slot" anecdote into my talks to Chinese teachers, parents, and administrators. I would relate what had happened and seek audience reactions. With very few exceptions my Chinese informants shared the opinions of the attendants at the hotel. They put it this way. Since adults know how to place the key in the key slot, since that is the ultimate (if not the only) purpose of approaching the slot, and since the baby is not old (or clever) enough to consummate the action on his own, what possible gain is achieved by having the baby flail about? Why not show him what to do? He will be happy (those around will also be happy), he will learn how to do it sooner, and then he can proceed to more complex activities. We agreed that sometimes it is important to show the child what to do and that we certainly did not want to frustrate him. But we also pointed out that Benjamin was rarely frus-trated by his attempts to insert the key in the slot – delight was a more common reaction. We then tried to communicate to our Chinese hosts that we had quite a different view about the significance of our son's behavior.

First of all, we did not care whether he succeeded in inserting the key into the slot; it was not important. He was having a good time and was exploring, which we liked. But the more important point was this: we *were* trying to teach Benjamin something in the process – that one can solve a problem by oneself. This lesson reflects a principal value of child rearing in middle-class America. So long as the child is shown exactly how to do things – whether it be placing a key in a key slot or drawing a rooster – he is less likely to figure out himself how to do it. He is cer-tainly less likely to arrive at an original way of doing it. And, in general, he is less likely to view life – as we do – as a series of situations in which one has to learn to think for oneself.

In reflecting on the episodes with the Jinling key, I discerned a key to some of the most fundamental differences between Chinese and American society. I have described these differences in terms of five points or assumptions. I see these five points as interconnected and perhaps inseparable, a series of interlocking concepts which fuse into a greater, one might almost say Confucian, whole. One could dis-cuss them in any order and reach the remainder of the set by several routes. Taken together, they help to explain not only differences which we continually observed in arts education but also more pervasive differences which influence the range of activities in society. Again, I must stress that these are *relative* differences and that one finds examples of the opposite assumptions in each society. In approved peda-gogical fashion I will state the five assumptions of Chinese society succinctly and baldly here and then review each of them at somewhat greater and more nuanced length (see also Gardner, 1989b).

1   Life should unfold like a performance, with carefully delineated roles.
2   All art should be beautiful and should lead to good behavior.
3   Control is essential and must emanate from the top.
4   Education should take place by continual careful shaping.
5   Basic skills are fundamental and must precede any efforts to encourage cre-ativity.

The high value placed in China on performance dates back a long time. Nearly 2,500 years ago Confucius put forth a composite portrait – in words and in his own example – of how a gentleman should behave. Procedures for study, for the transmission of knowledge, and for the leading of a proper life were laid out carefully. The tradition of indicating the exact dimensions of a desirable performance has survived in China over the centuries. Indeed, by the time of the Ming dynasty (1368–1644) prescribed performances were expected of cultivated gentlemen or literati; one had to be able to make music, paint, compose poems, and render calligraphy according to culturally agreed-upon standards, and one had as well to display proper responses to these performances.

But simply to talk about expected behaviors, or roles to be fulfilled, does not begin to convey the Chinese commitment to performance. As we mentioned to the Chinese educators with whom we met, nearly everything that the visitor sees publicly in China appears to be a performance – and a very refined and finished one at that. From the young children sitting with hands folded at their desks or walking rhythmically into a room, to the headmaster describing her school with punctilious detail in a morning briefing, to the student answering questions with vivid expressiveness in a discussion with visitors, everything has been carefully scripted in advance. As children are performing, adults sit there mouthing the exact same words and gestures, as if to ensure that there is a model present for any confused child to consult. In addition, the arrangement and layout of these scenes look as if they could be the scenery for a play or if they could be put onto "live" television. Everyone knows just about what to expect and how it should look; any deviations are readily noticed and quite troubling to those who have "staged" the performances.

It is this commitment to an elegant and well-executed performance which prompts the Chinese to correct Benjamin. His banging the key about is disorderly and offends the sense of a smooth performance. The goal of the adults in correcting him is to ease his way to a well-executed key-slotting performance as soon as possible – a performance which all can admire.

We were impressed by the performances which we constantly encountered, not only in arts classes but throughout our journey through the educational system. Yet we were also frustrated. To carry out our research mission, we wanted to see *how polished performances came to be achieved* – in other words, to peer behind the scenes, to see some rehearsals en route to the final version, to learn about curriculum selection, planning, and evaluation. We clearly saw instances of Chinese children learning new things which were, in that sense, not performances. My guess is that it was not easy for Chinese to show us this, since it permitted us to go "backstage."

Yet even these non-performances struck us as performances. This is not, I think, because they were necessarily "put-ons." Rather, teaching in China takes place at such a fine level of detail, and one lesson builds so integrally and compulsively upon the previous ones, that few stretches are required. And so, even a new class is simply a tiny variation on an old performance ... as if the director had merely changed a few lines or a few entries in an old and well-mastered script. At times, however, it was clear that we were being told that something was spontaneous when in fact it had been carefully rehearsed. At these times we became genuinely annoyed.

Of course, an emphasis on performance is not necessarily an isolated or bad thing. In times past, our society had much more of a "public performance" dimension.

During the age of nobility, the West featured public selves as stylized as those perceived today in China, but now there is much more of an emphasis on informality. Many Asian cultures continue to feature this penchant for performance, well described by Clifford Geertz in his studies of Indonesia. Educated Chinese people often like to read European novels such as those of Jane Austen or American novels like those of Edith Wharton, possibly because these works document a society which placed a premium on performances.

I feel that it is good to foster performing skills, and I advocate the development of oratorial skills in American children. But performing skills are not the same as a performing society. American students are often better at informal situations and at critical discussions; they are usually comfortable, where Chinese are not, at talking with strangers, at criticizing their own papers and those of other students. These are situations which cannot, by their nature, be rehearsed. But some American teachers, while agreeing with me, point out that Chinese students master the factual material much better and commit arguments to memory with greater accuracy.

In the United States, and in the West more generally, one may contrast performance with *understanding*. We want, above all, for our students to dig beneath the surface and become able to grasp the meaning, including the underlying meaning, of writings, texts, scientific principles, works of art. This emphasis is really as old as the focus placed on Confucius in China. It dates back to Socrates (roughly a contemporary of Confucius), who valued knowledge and argument above all things, who was himself slovenly and did not care about "superficial" performance matters (though he was an effective performer) but was obsessed about the quality of thought and reasoning.

It is not surprising, of course, that I would emphasize the cognitive and "understanding" aspects of education in general and artistry in particular. I am a committed cognitive psychologist, who views art as a matter of the mind. I am a committed Westerner as well – and I remember a colleague's wry definition of the West as that place where Socrates is a culture hero. Understanding, of course, is not inherently inconsistent with performance; indeed, elsewhere I call for "performances of understanding." But the usual connotations of Understanding and Performance do seem to pull in different directions. If one is to follow the direction of one's cognitive powers, and to focus on understanding and misunderstanding, one may well find oneself on a collision course with certain performance standards, which have survived for a long time but which may reflect little or no understanding.

In putting forth this picture of China as a performing society, I am well aware of one criticism which could be directed at me. I was a "high-level" visitor to China; perhaps the performances I witnessed had little relation to what goes on in China normally, in the absence of observers from abroad. It is of course not possible for me to conduct the experiment of being in China without being there. However, for two reasons I feel that my characterization is not merely a function of the particular conditions under which I visited China. First of all, the Chinese went to such great lengths to make sure that everything I saw was polished that they thereby revealed the great premium they placed on performance. (Despite enormous efforts, most Americans could simply not have matched these performances.) Second, I am here describing what I take to be an ideal state, one that is striven for rather than one that is regularly achieved. Just as we in the West today value informality, casualness, and directness, the Chinese seem in comparison to value roles and rituals which are perfectly realized.

The arts as beautiful and good

A focus on art as performance fits hand in glove with a view of art as entailing beauty and proper behavior. Now in espousing this view of things, Chinese scarcely hold a monopoly. Most individuals anywhere in the world, when asked about the reason for the arts, would say that they are dedicated to, and indeed exemplify, beauty; and few would object initially to attempts to link the true, the beautiful, and the good.

But once again, just as the Chinese today take performance further than most other peoples, they also have a conception of beauty which is more precisely delineated, and more aggressively invoked, in artistic matters. We can see from an early age that Chinese parents and teachers convey to their charges very clear ideas about what a painting should look like, how a story should be told, how an instrument should be played, a dance step executed, a calligraphic passage completed. There is one right way (or perhaps a small set of right ways) and many wrong ways; the right way is beautiful and should be enacted, while the wrong ways are ugly and should be spurned. So completely are students indoctrinated in these prescribed ways that they continue to exemplify them even when they are given free rein to do what they wish.

We see these views in operation in the Benjamin-key incident. There is a correct way to place the key in the slot and that way is also beautiful. These canons of beauty need to be instilled early and completely so a child is not tempted to carry out activities in an ugly or disruptive way (for example, by banging the key against the slot).

We also receive insight into why only certain forms of art are sanctioned in contemporary China. So long as art is representational, so long as music refers to content, it is possible for censors to ensure that the works subscribe to evident canons. But if abstract art were allowed, how could one judge it and determine whether it was beautiful and good? Rather than open up that Pandora's box of normlessness, it is far better to restrict art to things which everyone can perceive and on which consensual beauty judgments can readily be rendered. Of course not all artists in China endorse these views uncritically; but they entertain a risk if they challenge them publicly.

In contrast to a Chinese view of art as beauty, what do Westerners espouse? Consistent with my argument that we in the West have assumed an increasingly cognitive stance toward matters, I contend that art is now expected to be interesting, powerful, compelling – and that art exists in the first instance to allow individuals to see, to hear, to conceive of elements in new and perhaps initially unsettling ways.

What we seek (and find) in our great artists is not – or not *merely* – the exemplification of some form of beauty, and not beauty, certainly, in some fixed or preordained sense. Canons cannot be handed down. What, after all, is beautiful about a military scene from Goya or a bombed ruin by Picasso? Do T.S. Eliot and James Joyce write about beautiful subjects and use florid language in doing so? Is Stravinsky's *Rite of Spring* or are Bartok's string quartets conventionally beautiful?

No – at least in the past century or two, such artists compel because they make us rethink our conceptions and even re-experience the art of the past in new ways. After we hear Stravinsky's or Bartok's music, it may change our experience of other music and other sounds. Far from providing a respite, as one expects in a comfortable ritualized setting, the works of art we have come to admire function more like a powerful new political or scientific theory which we must try to assimilate and then somehow incorporate into the rest of our understanding.

And so, particularly with reference to the arts of today, we would not speak – as the Chinese still do – about a painter who makes beautiful birds or a composer who composes lovely songs about spring. We talk instead about a creator with an interesting or arresting perspective on the world – a *Weltanschauung* that would presumably come through whether one is working in one genre or in quite another one. To the extent that such changes in conception have taken place in China, they have occurred over much longer spans of time and are distinctly evolutionary rather than revolutionary.

When I put forth some of these ideas in China, I was called a formalist – someone only interested in abstract formal matters and unconcerned with connections to life. As one cadre put it: "In America you are interested in art for art's sake; in China we are interested in art for life's sake." I had a retort for this gentleman. "Actually," I pointed out, "we are not interested in art for the sake of art; we are interested in art for the sake of mind." I then explained that many observers regard art as a cognitive endeavor and as another way to expand our knowledge of what the world can be and what it might be – as in some ways closer to Science than to Nature. And I sought to explain as well our interest in joining, in education, the skills of producing, perceiving, and reflecting, as a better means of coordinating the various forms of knowledge which flow from artistic experience.

The Chinese proclivity for linking art and morality – the beautiful and the good – is more difficult for me to expound, perhaps because it lacks a parallel in the contemporary West. As Chinese have sought to explain it to me, involvement in the arts is part of being a good person. If you make beautiful paintings or beautiful sounds on an instrument, these performances contribute to your becoming a worthy person. Apparently there is a spill-over from being involved in the arts to becoming a desirable kind of person. Thus in the past the same Confucian gentlemen who painted and performed well were also good human beings.

Now, as a cynical Westerner, I could not resist picking apart these claims. I pointed out that many individuals who are great artists were despicable and immoral individuals; and I pointed out that individuals without any aesthetic proclivities can be highly moral. While my Chinese colleagues listened patiently to my comment, I soon got the impression that my remarks were beside the point. We are not dealing here with an empirical claim but rather with a belief system, a conviction that there is a certain notion of a good life, which includes art and morality, and that these things ought to – and do – go together. Indeed, much more so than Western intellectuals, and perhaps more like religious fundamentalists, Chinese believe that all good traits come together, and that if one is lacking on one dimension, one is unlikely to excel elsewhere. Education is supposed to develop as one piece an individual's body, knowledge, sense of beauty, *and* morality; it fails if it does not accomplish all of these, and the clear implication is that it is not even possible to develop one virtue without the others.

The importance of hierarchy

Turning from performance and beauty, the next two conceptions convey the desired structure of society and the way of passing down information and performance standards from one generation to another. Any observer of Chinese society over the millennia has to be impressed by the extent to which it is hierarchically organized. Except during times of upheaval it has always been all too clear who is at the head of the society – generally an emperor or a warlord – and where everyone else fits in relation to the center, and the apogee, of power. Hand in hand with this sense of organizational structure comes the educational conviction that individuals need to be carefully molded from the first to conform to societal values and practices.

In China traditionally "the people" must look in two directions: upward, toward those who hold authority, and backward, to the traditions of the past. This dual orientation is brought together neatly in the practice of ancestor worship, where one looks up to those who are "higher" than one in the family and "back" to those who are most remote in time. The one direction in which Chinese have *not* habitually looked is outward, since China has traditionally been considered to be the Center of the World – the Middle Kingdom.

The structure of the school, both professionally and politically, reflects these notions. In the class, the teachers are considered the center of all activity, and students' behaviors and words are directed toward them. As I came to put it, the teacher is the sun and the students are the planets which revolve around her. All knowledge is assumed to exist in the Chinese past and the teacher's job is to transmit that knowledge to her charges as faithfully and efficiently as possible. The ubiquitous proverbs, enumerated lists, and frozen phrases are simply efficient distillations of that knowledge. Sometimes, as a thought experiment, I asked teachers what they would do if they were not allowed to model behavior or to present the right answer; their difficulties in responding indicated how alien were these "progressive" notions of education in a non-Western context.

While Confucian classics no longer dominate the curriculum, parroting back the past remains a staple of most Chinese classrooms. The burden of the past is simply overwhelming. When I had a protracted discussion with a teacher during which I challenged the rationales offered for some of the things which she did, she effectively closed the conversation by asserting: "Well, we have been doing this for so long that we just *know* that it is right."

In the episode with Benjamin and the key, one can see this set of values at work. The older and more powerful person knows how to carry out the desired behavior, and it is his or her role to show the younger person how to do it – both transmitting the superior knowledge of the past and establishing the authority of his or her generation in the process. Why cast about for new approaches, why try to orient the key in the slot differently, when the best ways have long since been discovered and fashioned to perfection?

This hierarchicization has profound implications for scholastic activities. In a society where the standards for excellence (or beauty) are quite clear, an individual can situate himself easily vis-à-vis the rest of his countrymen. Take violin performing, for example. If a child is the best in his class, he will be placed in a group with other skilled individuals of his age at the school; if identified as the best in that group, he is absorbed into a group with the best in the school as a whole; and as he continues to stand out, he will ultimately be grouped with others in his district, municipality, province, and, if among the *very* best, with students from the rest of the country. In fact the best musical students will end up at the Beijing or Shanghai conservatories, universally considered to be the best in the country and therefore having their pick of the best of the young.

Thus, in music, and in any other sphere worth tallying (from mathematics to political power), the existence of common standards and of regular competitions ensures that any individual knows at least his approximate rank and can plot his progress or lack thereof. This ranking procedure is simply a contemporary manifestation of the ordering which was possible at the time of the imperial examination system.

The existence in contemporary China of a single curriculum to which all must subscribe – and the extreme difficulty of introducing changes to it – reflects the fact that Chinese feel like members of one gigantic family or clan (the Han people, who constitute over 90 percent of the population). It is important for all members of this group to be able to share experiences and a common heritage. To some extent this commonality is impressive and allows all Chinese (at least in principle) to feel at one with their countrymen. (Today many Americans lament the absence, or loss, of a similar common culture in our country.) The situation is not, however, so pleasant for members of the fifty or so minorities. Nor is it palatable to individuals who might want to suggest some improvements or changes to the current social or educational order. Even to suggest changes is difficult because, as in some American paramilitary organizations, one is only allowed to address suggestions to the next level up, and one has no means of reaching people near the top. The options that we might have in the U.S., of writing a public article or switching to another organization, are not readily available in China.

Authoritarian, hierarchical, and patriarchal ways may be common in China, from Confucian to communist epochs, but they are quite remote from dominant credos in the West. In our democratic systems, and particularly in the pluralistic and often fragmented United States, we have never had such a well-defined power structure nor such a common set of values and attitudes. I speak relatively again, but it is assumed that the past can be as much a burden as a source of knowledge; that placing great power in the hands of a single leader is dangerous; that one needs checks and balances; that the young can be a source of inspiration and information and ought perhaps to be placed on a pedestal rather than put in their place. When there is nostalgia for control, for a return to the past, the case always needs to be made with special persuasiveness, because it runs in the face of prevailing wisdom. And in general the trend quickly reverts toward a more meritocratic and pluralistic environment. (Reviewing these words in 2005, I am less sure that they still apply to the United States.)

Shaping and molding from birth on

One of the most impressive accomplishments of the Chinese educational and training system has been its capacity to take even the most complex activity, break it down into its component parts, start the child out on the simplest part, have him perfect it, and then move on gradually but inexorably to more complex and more impressive performances. Every educational system uses this procedure, of course, but few have carried it through as relentlessly as the Chinese.

Thus when our well-meaning Chinese observers at the Jinling Hotel came to Benjamin's rescue, they did not simply push his hand down clumsily, hesitantly, or abruptly, as I might have done. Instead, they guided him with extreme facility and gentleness in the desired direction. These Chinese were not just molding and shaping Benjamin's performance in any old manner; in the best Chinese tradition they were "ba je shou jiao" ("bazhishoujiao") – teaching by holding his hand – so much so that he would happily come back for more shaping. To borrow another Chinese phrase, they were inducing change through the chocolate offered in one hand – but if necessary, they would have used the whip that is traditionally clutched in the other.

Lurking behind and inspiring such shaping practices is the long-established procedure for mastering calligraphy – a dauntingly complex process which nonetheless has been mastered millions if not billions of times over the centuries. Since this training course has worked so well for an invention about which the Chinese feel justifiably proud, it ought to be marshaled for as many other uses and in as many other circumstances as possible.

In general, child rearing in China proceeds as if following a chapter in Ivan Pavlov, B.F. Skinner, or J.B. Watson (the founder of behaviorism). Reward, or positive reinforcement, is the preferred mode of training, though punishment (or negative reinforcement) is certainly not unknown. "The whip" is in fact inflicted quite brutally when older children do not study, fail to obey, or do not practice their musical instruments. (All of this punitiveness is very "backstage" and is certainly not part of the public Chinese performance.) Ultimately, after years of supervised study, Chinese individuals are expected to internalize these methods and to continue to study (more broadly, to cultivate themselves) without prodding for the remainder of their lives.

Consistent with the prevalent associationist psychology, all teachable performances in China are broken down into the smallest possible units, for presentation and mastery one step at a time. And, again consistent with an empiricist (as opposed to a rationalist) view, there is relatively little interest in cognition, ideas, thinking, abstract knowledge; instead, what is at issue is attainment of the correct observable performance – be it the polished performance of a dance or the proper placement of a key. A school lesson is not considered successful unless all students achieve a perfect performance. Chinese educators cannot understand the pleasure experienced by American educators when we succeed in conveying a lesson to "most" of our students.

This state of affairs has led me to the radical conclusion that, save in a few academic pockets, there is really no developmental psychology in China and perhaps no concept of childhood as we know it. To be sure, Chinese have in the past treated very young children differently from older children; for example, they have indulged children until the age of four or so and have then instilled a much stricter adult-oriented regimen (Levy, 1968). But this differentiation is still remote from the kinds of views associated with John Dewey or Jean Piaget, individuals who saw childhood in a positive way, rather than simply as a necessary period en route to adulthood.

According to this influential Western view, childhood is a very special time and each child exhibits for a time a form of genius. Children are already born knowing certain things and, more importantly, they have been adequately equipped by Nature to know how to figure things out, how to construct knowledge on the basis of their explorations. Children pass through a series of stages, also preordained, and at each stage they perceive the world in a different but intellectually respectable way. Those charged with rearing children should respect these stages and allow children to develop in their own way at their own pace.

Consistent with this psychology comes an educational regimen. Schools should supply and nourish, but they should not try to dictate or to mold. Such intrusions by civilization can be brutal and stultifying. The child has his own creative genius which should be allowed to flower. There is sufficient structure in the child's mind, enough chemistry in the contact between a child and an interesting material, that there is no need to intervene. Hence Benjamin can be left to play with the key – he will figure out the important things in due course.

These views – which I happen to cherish – are largely foreign to China. (I hasten to add that they are scarcely pervasive in the United States either, but many good schools endorse and attempt to implement them.) Those artful scribbles and early metaphors for which I have remained alert in my own research are dismissed in China as mistakes which should be ignored. School is important precisely because it exorcises these mischievous, unpredictable, unproductive, and possibly pernicious elements as soon as possible. School is also important because it is society's most reliable way of assuring quality control and bringing about the Confucian ideal of a socially and politically harmonious society. That learning which takes place in the U.S. from the examples of peers and at the behest of media such as books, comic books, movies, and television is considered much less trustworthy. And of course, whenever possible, these "media materials" are reworked by the State in China, so that they will be consistent with, rather than antagonistic to, the lessons promulgated in school.

There are some signs that a way of teaching and molding which has worked, more or less well, for several thousand years may not be most appropriate for dealing with an uncertain future. Such a realization may have led to the interest in the 1920s and 1930s in the works of John Dewey, to various experimental schools and programs over the years, and to the burgeoning interest in MI which I observed in a return visit to China in May 2004.

Basic skills before creativity

Attempts to change the basic structure of the Chinese classroom, or of Chinese society, touch directly on the issue which brought us to China, and which remained centrally on our agenda throughout our stay: the relative importance of, and the relationship between, basic skills and creativity.

There are few issues about which attitudes have differed so sharply. In the United States many aspects of the society are so designed as to encourage innovation and creativity. From its foundation, the United States has looked to its frontier and to its youth to forge new and unanticipated forms of living and of knowledge. Though the U.S.'s schools are not its most innovative institutions, they have long tolerated experiments of various sorts. And in the view of many Americans, schools are but one of the socializing influences, along with parents, siblings, peers, various media of communication, and life in the broader society – each of which may be transmitting its own idiosyncratic messages.

As the oldest continuing civilization in the world, China has witnessed innovations over centuries, rather than decades, as they unfold at a distinctly evolutionary pace. Oriented to tradition, Chinese have generally striven to adhere to what has gone before. Even under a radical (in some ways) new political system, the continuities with the past are striking, and nowhere more so than in those inherently conservative institutions called schools.

To the extent that change occurs in every society, the preferred mode also differs. In the U.S., as in other parts of the West, we place a premium on radical departures from the recent past and, at least over time, honor the Beethovens, Picassos, Joyces, and Einsteins who have within one lifetime remade or at least radically altered our world view. Interestingly, some of these same individuals are also revered in China, but the kind of iconoclasm which they epitomize is not similarly prized and is actively discouraged during the frequent "swings" to the left.

While no one would nominate Benjamin's session with the key as a prototype of creative behavior, this little incident captures something telling about attitudes toward creativity in our two cultures. The Chinese approach to this task is straightforward: for Benjamin to succeed, he needs to acquire basic skills of manipulation, orientation, and placement. Since the means for acquiring these are well known and unproblematic, they ought simply to be passed on to him as efficiently and constructively as possible. Should he at some later date wish to make modest modifications in his form of attack, that is OK too. Indeed, this toleration of minor modifications comes close to my notion of how "creativity" is understood in China – as neither a massive dislocation nor a radical reconceptualization but rather as a modest, continuous, and cumulative alteration of existing schemes or practices.

The American approach is epitomized in Ellen's and my reaction to the Episode of the Key. On this view, the best way to approach a new area is to have ample opportunities to explore it, with encouragement but relatively little direct supervision or instruction on the part of an elder. Such unstructured exploration is considered the optimal way to come to know the parameters of a problem and to discover one's own competence with reference to it. It is all to the good if an individual can solve the problem without any help; and indeed it is praiseworthy if he can do so in a new way, or even discover along the way an unanticipated problem worthy of solution.

If the individual becomes frustrated or makes no progress, then some modest intervention or aid may be appropriate. And if, later on, the person himself craves instruction, then his masters may draw on relevant stores of knowledge from the past. Increasingly, however, educators look askance at the provision of direct models for slavish copying; it is far preferable to offer hints or suggestions, or to provide a menu of possible approaches, than to intimate that there is a royal road to the acquisition of a particular skill. Too often it has been found in the West that the individual who on his own ventures in a new direction, or who himself decides what merits copying, effects the most impressive or innovative achievements.

One way of summarizing the "American position" is to state that we value creativity more and will readily postpone the acquisition of basic skills for a later time. Yet it can also be argued that, for us, *other* skills are basic – skills such as devising a new problem, looking at one's work critically, or drawing upon one's own feelings. One society's skills may be another society's residuals.

But assuming that the antithesis I have developed has validity, and that the fostering of both skills *and* creativity is worthwhile, the important question becomes this: can we glean, from the Chinese and the American case studies, a superior way to approach education, perhaps striking an optimal balance between the poles of creativity and basic skills?

I'll begin my answer by suggesting that each country has proved that its way can succeed. There is ample evidence in the United States that one can begin by fostering creativity in a "progressive" environment and yet turn out individuals who master basic skills fully and go on to achieve in an innovative manner in some cultural domain. Based on my experiences in China I can vouch for the fact that it is possible as well to follow a regimen of strict skill development and still end up with products which are highly distinctive and creative. I have observed this in the case of individual students and teachers; and many of us in the West rub shoulders with Chinese students who were reared in a skill-oriented milieu and yet go on to become creative artists, scientists, or businessmen.

A first answer, then, is that it is not essential to begin one way, as opposed to the other. So long as the society wants to develop both basic skills *and* creativity, it can have both. It *is* important that the alternative approach be kept in mind, lest an exclusive orientation toward creativity, or a total commitment toward skill development, preclude the possibility of developing the other facility. But so long as such extremes are avoided, there seems to be no necessary edge to one approach.

Yet I am not satisfied with the simple answer "Either approach will do." My own opinion, based on general studies in developmental psychology and on my observations in these and other countries as well, is that there is a preferable or optimum *sequence*. I find it preferable to devote the early years of life – roughly speaking, up to the age of seven – to a relatively unstructured or "creative orientation" where students have ample opportunity to proceed as they wish and to explore media on their own. (In traditional China some individuals apparently held similar views [Levy, 1968], but I never heard these referred to during my trips to China.) Thereafter, given the child's increasing inclination toward the learning of rules, it is both appropriate and advisable to inculcate basic skills. This is a time when children readily acquire skills and have some appreciation of the reasons for doing so.

With the advent of adolescence, particularly in our society, youngsters want to be able to put their skills to a public and, possibly as well, a personal use. It is therefore important that by this time they have acquired sufficient skills so that they will not be disappointed or embarrassed by their own efforts. Building on the early experience with unhampered exploration, and in the light of the subsequent honing of skills, they should be in a favorable position to form novel products which make sense to them and which can also speak to others in their culture.

There is one more point to this scheme. Even though the focus should ideally shift from creativity to basic skills and then back again, it is crucial that the other alternative be kept in mind during each developmental phase. The early years of life ought to feature at least some areas of skill acquisition, some development of useful working habits. By the same token, the years of middle childhood should incorporate some open-ended exercises, some free productions, as well as constant reminders that there is never a single best way to do something. So long as these alternative options – the accent on skills and the flair for creativity – are kept in mind at all times, the growing child is likely to be able to capture the best of both orientations.

The idea of a shift in emphasis at some point in development is central to my case. It is possible, in fact, that the Chinese might want to begin with more of a stress on skill development (as they in fact do) and then shift to periods of more free-ranging explorations (which they rarely do). What is least desirable is an exclusive emphasis on one end of the continuum. If there is too great a leaning in the direction of untrammeled creativity – the American risk – the child may end up without skills and thus able to communicate only with himself (and perhaps an overly indulgent parent). On the other hand, if there is an unrelieved focus on skill development – the Chinese danger – the child may end up unable to depart from the models that he has absorbed.

In seeking to acquire a more balanced pedagogical portfolio on this issue, each country can learn from the other. And it is important that each country watch carefully and experiment prudently. Too many efforts in creativity training in China are destined to fail because they are based on a superficial understanding of how to sustain a playful atmosphere, how to challenge received wisdom, how to welcome new ideas in an educational setting. And too many attempts to institute the training of basic skills in the United States do not work because they underestimate the degree of drill and dedication needed on the part of both teacher and pupil if a complex skill is to be thoroughly mastered. If attempts are not to be caricatures, they need to be based on rigorous study and patient practice. Exchange visits among artists and scholars, such as the one in which we were privileged to participate in the 1980s, provide an excellent means for understanding the techniques of an alien culture and the reasons why they work as effectively as they do.

Acknowledgment

Originally published in *To Open Minds: Chinese Clues to the Dilemma of Contemporary Education*, by Howard Gardner. Copyright © 1991 by Howard Gardner. Reprinted by permission of Basic Books, a member of Perseus Books, L.L.C.

PART 4

DISCIPLINARY UNDERSTANDING

CHAPTER 16

THE UNSCHOOLED MIND
Why even the best students in the best schools may not understand

This chapter was first presented as the Peterson Lecture to the International Baccalaureate Organization, December 1992. The transcript of the talk was published in *IBWorld* in April 1993.

I'm trained in developmental psychology, a field in which the contributions of Jean Piaget are unequalled. I have had a very lively career during which I challenged Piaget on several issues. My three principal arguments with him are as follows.

First of all, Piaget believed that if you studied children, you had to know what they were going to become – what the end state of development is. Piaget thought it was to be a scientist; that's what Piaget was. However, in my own training I had spent a lot of time working in the arts. I felt that there was something wrong with a theory which only talked about the mind of the scientist as being the end-all of a child's development. So I began to explore what development would be like, if one thought of participation in the arts as an artist, or a critic, or a performer, or a connoisseur as being a viable end state. This is not to say that human beings should develop to become artists any more than they should develop to become scientists, but rather that we can develop many different kinds of human beings.

The second argument I had with Piaget, and the one that I gained recognition for, was with respect to the notion that there is a single thing called intelligence which can be measured by an intelligence test. Now it's not widely known that Piaget studied in Alfred Binet's laboratory, specifically with Théodore Simon who had worked with Binet. Piaget became interested in children's minds because of the mistakes the children made on the intelligence tests. Piaget explained the general intelligence that all human beings share (see Chapter 1).

I define intelligence as the ability to solve a problem, or to fashion a product which is valued in at least one culture or community. Psychologists of intelligence concede that solving problems is important, but they shy away from any concern about making something – like writing essays, staging plays, designing buildings, and other human feats. Moreover psychologists get upset when you talk about an ability being valued in a culture; that is because it suggests that, unless a culture provides certain opportunities, a person might not seem to be smart. Most psychologists believe that intelligence is completely in the brain ... and if you know exactly where to stick the measurement device, you can figure out how smart that person is.

In my view intelligence is always an interaction between potentials and what's available in a culture. For example, Bobby Fischer is one of the greatest chess players in the history of the world. But if Bobby Fischer had been born in a culture where there was no chess, he would just be an awkward geek; he has a brain that was perfectly matched to something in his culture, namely chess, but mismatched to just about everything else. It is worth pointing out that Piaget thought he was studying *all* of intelligence. But I believe he was studying logical mathematical intelligence (later in his life I think he came to the same conclusion about the focus of his own work). In contrast, I talk about intelligence which artists have as well as those intelligences which are crucial in the human sphere – something of great concern to educators as we begin to deal with global issues, moral issues, issues of value and the like.

My third argument with Piaget concerns the most interesting claim that he made. If you remember your studies of Piaget, you will remember that he maintained that children pass through stages of cognitive development. So infants "know" the world in one way, five-year-olds in another way, ten-year-olds in another way, and 15-year-olds in still another way. When you go from nine to 11 or from 13 to 16 years old, not only do you see the world in a very different way, but you can't even remember how you used to construe the world.

An example. At age seven you don't believe that you ever embraced certain ideas: if a ball of clay were squished, there would be less clay there; or that if water were poured into a different kind of vessel, there will be more or less water depending on the shape of the receiving vessel. Yet every four-year-old in the world believes those things. Where Piaget was wrong, I believe, was in his argument that when people get older, they see the world in a different way and they no longer have access to earlier ways of knowing. I argue that most of us, except in areas where we are expert, continue to think the way we did when we were five years of age. We continue to think the way we did before we went to school. That's a pretty radical thesis.

So my remarks focus on the subject of education for understanding. If I said to you: what *is* understanding and *how* can we determine whether understanding has been achieved? – that is a much more difficult question.

I define understanding as the capacity to take knowledge, skills, concepts, facts learned in one context, usually the school context, and use that knowledge in a new context, in a place where you haven't been forewarned to make use of that knowledge. If you were only asked to use knowledge in the same situation in which it was introduced, you might understand, but you might not; we can't tell. But if something new happens out in the street or in the sky or in the newspaper, and you can draw on your earlier knowings, then I would infer that you understand. I'll introduce my "problématique" with three quite common-sense examples.

In the first five years of life children all over the world, with very little formal tutelage, learn to speak, to understand, to tell stories, to tell jokes, to draw, to sing, to invent new tunes, to engage in pretend play – all the things which Piaget and other psychologists demonstrated. Even though nobody knows how to teach these things, young people still learn them all. Then they go to school and suddenly, in the very place where we are supposed to know how to teach them, it's very hard and many of them don't do well. That's a paradox.

One more example. Students at the very best universities in the United States (places like MIT and Johns Hopkins), with very high grades in physics, ultimately leave their class and are given a problem to solve on the street, or a game to play, each of which involves various physical principles. Not only do the students use what they learned in school, but they actually answer in the same way that five-year-olds do.

Ask almost anybody what happens, what forces obtain, when you flip a coin. Most people will come up with the following answer (even people who have taken physics courses): you've got a certain amount of force in your hand and you transfer that force to the coin; for a while that force makes the coin go up and then, when the force kind of gets spent, the coin is tired and kind of flips to the ground. However, physics teaches us that the second you release the coin, the only force that obtains on the coin is gravity. That authoritative account goes against a very powerful intuition that you develop when you're young. And it's not the intuition that's abandoned. It's Newton's and Galileo's laws of motion that prove very difficult to master.

A third vignette is a personal one. My daughter, a very good student, telephoned me when she was a sophomore in college, crying. I said, "Why are you crying?" She said, "It's my physics; I don't understand it." I said, "Well, you know" (and I was telling the truth) "I really respect you for taking physics because it's difficult and I wouldn't have taken it in college." I then added, "I don't even care what grade you get, but it's really important that you understand your physics." So I said, "Go to your instructor and have him or her explain to you what it is you don't understand." And she said, "Dad, you don't get it! I've never understood."

This exchange had a profound impact on me. My daughter was not saying that she was a faker or a "poseur." What she was saying is what I think most of us experience: we know the moves to make in school, to get good grades and even to be successful, but we know that if people put the questions to us in another way, if they push to see how much we have really understood, the whole house of cards might fall.

At least in the United States, there are formidable obstacles to understanding.

1 *Short-answer assessments*, or what I call a "text/test context." You read a textbook. The test is based on the textbook, and the textbook tells you the answers you have to give.
2 *The correct answer compromise* is an "entente" between the teacher and the student. No matter how you respond, nobody should ask any further question. No one is made uncomfortable, but deeper understanding is avoided.
3 *The pressure for coverage*, which means: there are 37 chapters in the book and you must get through all 37 chapters by the end of the term.

So, three vignettes. The young child learns so easily; the school child has difficulty. The students who get "As" at the best universities in the world are still Aristotelians in their models of the physical world. And then, of course, the most powerful evidence from my own daughter. What's going on here? I call it cognitive Freudianism.

Freud convinced people that, as adults, we continue to have the same personality traits as we did when we were children. We fight the same battles we fought in the nursery with our parents and our siblings. Most people who live in a modern Western society believe this. (If you don't believe it and you pay me $100 an hour, I will convince you that it's true.) That's what psychoanalysis is all about. I'm making the claim that Freud was correct in an area that he wasn't expert in, and where Piaget was allegedly the authority. Namely, except in areas where we are experts, most of us continue to think the way we did when we were five years old.

An expert is a person who comes to understand the world differently. But that is very difficult to do and I'm going to argue today that it's not done very often.

This is the thesis of my remarks. I'm going to provide evidence that no matter where you look in the curriculum, you will find students who don't understand: physics, mathematics, biology, literature, art. It's ubiquitous. Later I will chronicle things we can do about this situation. It *is* possible to educate for understanding.

My analysis of the potency of the five-year-old mind has three foci, which I have introduced to you already. There is the young natural learner: the three, four or five-year-old who absorbs and constructs so much about the world without formal tutelage. There is the student in most schools who basically masters what school requires so that he or she can get to the next level. But I will argue he doesn't really understand. Then there's the individual we want: the person who can use knowledge in new situations. That's my definition of an expert.

A form of knowing (a theory of knowledge) goes with each of these three foci. The expert is a person who can use the skills that are valued in his or her culture. So when an historical example comes up, he can draw on history; when a physical example comes up, he can draw from physics, and so on. That's what we want; that's why we go to school. If people are not going to be able to use the knowledge acquired, then we may as well close schools down. Scholastic knowledge is what we are very good at doing in school; but unless that scholastic knowledge can be activated in new circumstances, it remains inert and essentially useless.

We teach people notations, squiggles on a paper, formal concepts – what is gravity, what is density, what is force. People who have no sense of what it's like in the world can nonetheless give you a formula and a definition if that's what is called for in class. Then, if you're lucky and you attend an International Baccalaureate (IB) school, you get epistemic forms. Epistemic forms constitute the ways in which people think in the different disciplines. To think like a historian is not the same as to think like a literary critic or a biologist.

In the first years of life a natural learner benefits from what Piaget so brilliantly described: sensory motor knowledge, learning about the world, using your hands and your eyes, exploring the world of objects, the world of liquids poured from one container to another, and what I call first-order symbolic competence. People use words, pictures, gestures to communicate meanings. That's what every five-year-old can do.

That's the good news. However, five-year-olds do one thing which is troublesome: they form intuitive conceptions or theories – theory of matter, theories of mind, theories of life. Every normal five-year-old develops these theories. And those theories can prove serviceable for getting along in the world. However, all too often the theories are wrong. School is supposed to replace the erroneous theories with better theories.

So what's a theory of matter? A theory of matter is: if I have a heavy object in this hand, a light object in this hand and I release them at the same time, the heavier one will fall more quickly. That's what you learn intuitively. Heavy things fall more quickly. However, Galileo went to the top of the tower of Pisa, dropped two objects, and since then informed individuals understand that that's not in fact what happens. We understand that the laws of acceleration are independent of weight (density). But as children we develop a very powerful theory of matter, and that's very hard to shake.

Here's a theory of life: every five-year-old believes if it's moving, it's alive; if it's not moving, it's dead. This is a very useful theory. However, it doesn't help for sleeping dogs, and computers pose a real problem. Are computers which display moving images alive or dead? It's very hard to say.

Here's a theory of mind. I've got a mind; you've got a mind. If we look the same, our minds are the same. If we look different, our minds are different. If you look like me, you've got a good mind; if you look different, you've got a bad mind. This is a very powerful theory which is very entrenched. It shows up in all kinds of places. Just turn on the television for evidence. It's a conception like this that education is supposed to deal with, and it's this, I maintain, that education has, by and large, failed to deal with.

Why do these misconceptions arise and endure? I claim it happens because there are different kinds of constraints operating on us.

The first constraint has to do with the kind of species we are. We learn certain things very easily. We develop certain theories very readily, and other ones prove very hard for us to acquire. It's a whole interesting evolutionary question why that should be the case.

There are institutional constraints. If you put 30 to 50 people in a room like this and one person in front of them, it's very hard to explain things so that all who are present can understand. For every person who is nodding, three are nodding off.

There are also disciplinary constraints. The moves that have been developed over the centuries for analysis in one discipline are very different from the moves in other disciplines. Physical causality is not like historical causality or literary causality.

Anticipating what we might do, there is some hope. The hope lies in two institutions. One of them is very old: the apprenticeship. There are many powerful clues about how to educate for understanding contained in the apprenticeship. The other is a new institution, more familiar in the United States than in most other countries, but it is spreading rapidly: the children's museum, the science museum, the discovery museum, or the San Francisco *Exploratorium*. Very powerful education implications lurk in those two institutions.

Let me try to summarize this argument.

The natural learner displays what I call *intuitive understanding*. He or she is very promiscuous with the theories already developed in the young mind. Whenever anything happens, the young child draws on the theories of mind, matter, and life to explain them, whether or not those theories are appropriate at all.

In contrast, the scholastic learner never tries to apply the theory anywhere, except where he or she is told to. So, the scholastic learner gives a ritualized performance. The teacher asks the question, the student gives the prescribed answer or is told that she is wrong, and you go on to the next student.

The disciplined learner, the expert, produces a discipline of understanding, which means that not only can he or she draw on knowledge when it's appropriate but, equally importantly, doesn't draw on that knowledge when it's not appropriate. The five-year-old is too promiscuous and uses it always. The ten-year-old is repressed (the opposite of being promiscuous) and never uses it. But the person with disciplined understanding has good taste and uses the knowledge just when it's appropriate.

I've argued that there are some deep, if you will some epistemological, reasons why it's very difficult to teach for understanding. These limitations cover every discipline. I've already mentioned physics. Most people remain 5-year-olds or Aristotelians even though they studied physics. Here is a wonderful example, actually from astronomy. Twenty-five Harvard students have just graduated, all wearing their gowns and their mortar boards. An interviewer says to the students: "Tell me, why is the earth warmer in the summer than it is in the winter?" Twenty-three out of the 25 students immediately came up with the same answer, the answer which you would come up with if you didn't know what I was speaking about, namely that the earth is closer to the sun in the summer than it is in the winter. Now if we think about it, that doesn't make any sense because it wouldn't account for the seasons in different parts of the earth. The right explanation has to do with the angle of the earth on its axis as it spins around. But 23 out of 25 students forget to apply what they have learned in their astronomy classes and give the same five-year-old kind of answer.

You might say physics is hard. How about biology? Research shows that students who have taken not one but two or three courses in biology focusing on the topic of evolution still do not understand the basics of evolution. They still believe that something in one generation can be passed on to the next, even if it was acquired in the former generation. They are also still perfectionists. They think that each organism is trying to get more perfect, and that there is an unseen hand that's guiding that perfection rather than simply variation and selection within a particular ecological niche. So problems encountered in physics extend to biology and to the other sciences as well.

What about mathematics? Mathematics is all abstract. It has nothing to do with the real world. So maybe people don't have misconceptions in the area of mathematics. What they have instead is what I call rigid algorithms. They learn to fill in numbers into a formula.

Consider this problem. There are six times as many students as professors. If there are ten professors, how many students are there? Anyway, that is quite a simple problem. The answer is 60. If I ask you to capture the above information in a written equation where S stands for students and P stands for professors, most people will write the following equation: $6S=P$. This is because if you parse the sentence it says there are six times as many students as there are professors. However, what they are actually writing is "six times sixty equals ten," which is clearly an absurd result.

What happens in mathematics is that students learn how to plug numbers into formulas, how to solve equations. As long as the information is presented to them in a certain canonical order, they will get the answer right. If, however, the problem is presented in a new way, in a way which actually requires understanding of the formalism, most people will not get it right because they will not understand the formalism.

I think back to my own education. I studied the quadratic equation, and I must have solved 500 problems with the quadratic equation. I'm sure by the time I finished school, I could do the quadratic equation in my sleep. Never did anybody give me any education of what a quadratic equation stood for. Nowadays if I ran into a problem, I wouldn't have a clue that it involved the quadratic equation, even though I might, on a dark and stormy night, remember what a quadratic equation was. But I got very good grades in mathematics because I wasn't expected to know where to use this kind of formalism.

So, the problem in science is misconceptions. The problem in mathematics is rigidly applied algorithms. How about in the arts, in the humanities?

In the arts and the humanities the problem is different. It's what I call *scripts* or *stereotypes*. Early in life children develop very powerful theories about the world. A favorite script is the restaurant script. Every four-year-old knows that if you go to a restaurant, somebody comes and seats you. You are given the menu; you order. Food comes. You eat it and then you call for the check, and you leave.

If you go to McDonald's, you pay first but that's an exception to the script. Every four-year-old also knows about birthday parties: who comes, what you serve, that kind of thing. The rules are different in different cultures, but everybody knows about birthday parties in their vicinity.

Another script which you develop when you are very young is the Star Wars script – named both after the movie of that name and after President Reagan's strategic defence initiative. Star Wars says: "it's good to be big; you should be big yourself; if you're not big, align yourself with somebody who is big." If you look like that person, you will be good and people who look different will be bad. That's the Star Wars script and it's very very powerful!

You can have people who've studied world history, and you ask them about the causes of the First World War. They say: "Oh, it's very complicated. There was colonialism, imperialism, ethnic strife and long-term rivalries," and they give you a very nuanced response. Then you say to them: "Well, what's happening in the Gulf war of the early 1990s?" They will say: "Well, there is this bad guy named Saddam Hussein and if we get rid of him, everything will be OK." Now, that's a Star Wars type of explanation.

Perhaps the best example of the unschooled mind in the arts comes out of the University of Cambridge in the UK. In the 1920s a literary critic and poet named I.A. Richards did a study of Cambridge undergraduates. He reported it in a book called *Practical Criticism* (1929). He took Cambridge undergraduates who were the best and brightest literary students. He gave them poems and he asked two questions about the poems:

- What do they mean?
- Are they any good?

He performed one manipulation on the poems. He removed the names of the poets. (It's like touring the Louvre without the labels.)

What did Richards find? He found that the students didn't have a clue about which poems were good (according to the critics) and which were bad. They rejected John Donne. They rejected Gerald Manley Hopkins. They embraced a Sunday poet who couldn't get into the *Cambridge Chronicle* and, when they were asked what accounted for the quality, they replied: if a poem rhymed, scanned, dealt with a pleasant subject, but was not too sentimental, it was good. But if it dealt with philosophy or anything tragic or anything abstract, it was bad. So, here you have good students who have studied literature. When the authorial clue is removed (namely this is by a good poet, this is by a bad poet or by a non-poet), these elite students display the same taste that someone with no education in literature would exhibit.

I've argued that in every area of the curriculum you have real problems, revealing how difficult it is to educate for understanding. You have misconceptions in the sciences, rigidly applied algorithms in mathematics, and scripts and stereotypes in social studies, humanities, and the arts. I'm going to argue that there is some hope after all. One source of hope entails taking some lessons from the old institution of apprenticeships and the new institution of children's museums.

Now I want to be very clear about this point. People misunderstand me to say that we should institute seven-year agreements between the apprentice and the master, where the apprentice is indentured and has to sweep the floor and that kind of thing. Or that we should close schools down and put everybody in children's museums. That's not what I mean.

I contend that there are very powerful educational messages in these two institutions. In the case of the apprenticeship, a young person works for someone who is the master of his or her discipline or craft, and who uses that discipline or craft every day in the course of genuine problem-solving. The master poses the problems and requires products from the apprentice at his or her level of competence; when the apprentice becomes more competent, the standards are raised accordingly. The master never has to take kids and test them at the end of the week, or the end of the year, because essentially he and the student are assessing every day. Moreover the master embodies the learning that he or she wants the child to acquire.

In the United States every teacher can read and write but very few of our elementary school teachers actually *do* read and write regularly. In fact, the average American schoolteacher reads one book a year. People who live in a literate world who read and write and talk about what they are reading and writing will have youngsters who do the same. People who simply say you should read but turn on the TV for seven hours give a very different message.

Until 25 years ago there were almost no children's museums. These locales contain very lively demonstrations of many of the principles that students learn about in school. Museums allow children to explore those principles, those ideas, at their own pace and in ways that are comfortable for that child. Frank Oppenheimer, who founded the *Exploratorium* in San Francisco, said: "Nobody flunks museum."

I became a devotee of children's museums because when I took kids to children's museums, I sometimes found that kids who were called bright in school could not engage with the "hands-on" opportunities. They were very unschooled. But kids who were not considered bright in school could often learn very well in those contexts.

For each of the areas of the curriculum in which I have diagnosed a problem, there is a move that we can make as educators that can be helpful.

In the case of misconceptions I recommend Christopherian encounters, named after Christopher Columbus. If you believe the world is flat, but every month or every year you travel around the world and you come back to where you started, that tends to belie the notion that the world is flat. In a Christopherian encounter, you expose your theories to disconfirmation. If your theories are consistently disconfirmed, you will slowly abandon them and hopefully construct better theories.

Most schoolkids believe that the reason that you are warm when you put on a sweater is because that sweater has warmth in it. If every year in school during the winter you put a sweater outside and you come in the morning and find it is freezing cold, that tends to disconfirm the notion that warmth inheres in the sweater.

Christopherian encounters have to happen over and over again. Think about the brain/mind as a surface which, earlier in life, becomes engraved with these primitive theories. What school usually does is simply to put some powder over that engraving so you can't see it any longer. And as long as you're in school, the powder is what the observer notices. When you leave school, and you slam the door, the powder disperses and the engraving is still there, the early theory. What happens in the Christopherian encounter is that you slowly upgrade that early engraving and you put a new and better one in its place.

But note that it doesn't happen in one time. Let me tell you what's wrong with the "one time" thing. If you ask my son Benjamin, at age seven, what's the shape of the world, he will tell you it's round. This makes you think he's very smart. But if you asked Benjamin where he is standing, he will say: "That's easy. I'm on the flat part underneath." His theory has been totally unaffected but he has absorbed the powder that is required: namely, if you want to shut up your father, you say that the world is round because that's what grownups say, but who could believe it?

Thus Christopherian encounters challenge those notions every day.

In mathematics the cure for a rigidly applied algorithm is what I call rich exploration of the relevant semantic domain. You must know what the equation stands for. You have to understand the formalism. So if you are going to do distance, rate and time problems – a common algebra exercise – you do a lot of experimenting. You try to predict how long it will take for something to get from one point to the other. You develop an intuition for the formalism so that when you learn the formalism, it actually refers to something that you already have an intuition for, that you already have an understanding for.

This has been done quite brilliantly with calculus. Before any of the formalism is introduced, students learn to make predictions about their bodies moving at various speeds, and the kind of graphs that would be produced over the course of time, and procedures like that.

A mathematician is not somebody who remembers all the formalisms. A mathematician is somebody who doesn't care if he/she remembers because, if necessary, he/she can derive it again because he/she understands what it stands for. That's why most of us are not mathematicians.

In the case of the humanities, the cure for stereotypes is the regular adoption of multiple stances. If it becomes a regular habit of mind to look at things from many different points of view, you will gradually abandon stereotypical thinking.

During the Gulf war, one of my sons went to school where there were youngsters from many different countries. The teacher had a very good idea. Rather than everybody just affirming what the cable news network reported, he had a student from Iran and a student from Kuwait and a student from Israel, etc., each convey his understanding of what was happening every day. Then, a few weeks after that, the teacher asked the kids in the school: "What do you think Moshe will think about this and what do you think Omar will think about this?" That's giving students the opportunity to put themselves into other people's minds.

If you study any revolution from the point of view of the vanquished as well as the victors, you get a very different story. If you study the American revolution from the point of view of the British, where it was seen as a colonial uprising, and from the point of view of the French, where it was seen as a good opportunity to get at the British, it's a very different story than if you just read the average American textbook. That's how you break down stereotypical thinking, but it has to become a regular habit of mind, otherwise it won't work at all.

Let me, in conclusion, describe a project that I'm involved in to educate for understanding. It is based upon three core ideas which I have worked out in conjunction with colleagues at Harvard:

1   the identification of rich, generative ideas – nutritious topics on which it's worth spending a lot of time;
2   the development of different kinds of teaching languages – multiple ways to approach those topics, so we can be sure that students have maximum access to those ideas; and
3   what I now call "ongoing assessment."

"Ongoing assessment" (see Chapter 19) means assessment is taking place all the time by students and by peers as well as by the teacher.

We believe that if you can identify rich ideas, explore them in multiple ways, and give students much opportunity to assess their own learning, there is a chance for education for understanding.

I now want to flesh out those ideas.

First of all, the greatest enemy of understanding is *coverage*. If you are determined to cover everything in the book, you virtually guarantee that very few students will understand. So, if you want to educate for understanding, you've got to make tough choices about what to focus on. And obviously you should focus on those things which have the biggest payoff. If you're teaching a course in history or social studies and you decide, say, to focus on democracy, or if you're teaching a course in biology and you choose to focus on evolution, you can cover a lot of the important material in those subjects by focusing on those topics. It will mean, however, if you're doing history, you're not going to get through every decade. If you're doing biology, you're not going to get through every cycle or through every part of the cell, or every part of the tree. It's a hard choice, but it's a choice worth making. If you have rich concepts and you spend time on them, you can approach them in different ways.

Growing out of my theory of MI, I claim that almost any topic which is worth spending time on can be approached from at least six different "windows" into the same room:

1   Narrational: the story mode.
2   A quantitative, logical rational way of dealing with numbers, principles, causality.
3   A foundational way, asking basic kinds of questions such as: Why is this important? How does it relate to what came before? How is it related to our lives today?
4   Aesthetic: What does it look like? What does it sound like? What appearance does it make? What patterns and configurations? How does it impress you?
5   Hands on: What is it actually like to be this thing, to do this thing? If you're studying evolution, what is it like to breed *Drosophila*? If you're studying democracy, what's it like to be in a group that decides by consensus as opposed to one that decides by autocracy, oligarchy or some other political principle?
6   Personal: Can you integrate this topic through debate, role play, projects, jigsaw participation and other joint interactions?

There are two advantages of using these multiple entry points. First of all, you're more likely to reach every child, because not every child learns most readily in the same way. That's one of the burdens of the theory of MI. Second of all, and equally important, if you approach a topic from many different vantage points, you're modelling for a student what it is like to be an expert. Because an expert is somebody who can always represent knowledge in more than one way. No expert can think about his or her topic in only one way. Experts have very flexible ways of thinking about their topics. You're modeling as a master to your apprentices if you approach a topic in a number of different ways.

That leaves assessment.

In authentic assessments we get far away from short answer examinations. We move toward what I call performance-based exams, where you actually demonstrate what it is that you're supposed to be able to do. Projects, exhibitions, portfolios, and "process folios" provide good ways of assessing whether the students are really understanding.

In work with teachers in local schools we ask them first to define "understanding goals" – these are the broad things that we want to achieve in a course. They will be very familiar things to you, like having a sense of the scientific method or understanding something about the nature of revolution.

What we then do, which may not be so familiar to you, is define a whole family of "performances of understanding" – these are performances which, if a student can carry them out, will count as evidence for understanding.

This entails a play with language, but I think it's an important play, because people tend to think of understanding as something that happens in the head. Perhaps it does, but we don't know you understand unless you can perform your understanding publicly. So, your performance involves analyses, critiques, debates, projects that you create, exhibitions that you put on, things like that.

Finally, given the "understanding goals" and the "performances of understanding," how are those performances going to be assessed? You make the assessment criteria absolutely clear. People know exactly what they are going to have to be able to do in order to perform an understanding. There are no surprises, no mysteries, no key to the answers, but rather examples all around of what a good performance is and what are not such good performances, from apprentice level all the way to that of a master.

I'm going to finish with a number of thoughts that I have had recently.

- After working for 25 years in psychology and education, I realized that I've been interested primarily in two things. One is how to observe students carefully, and MI theory is a way to look at students more carefully. The other is how to observe student work more carefully – and that is done by having assessment that looks at student performances very carefully.

- In most of the schools that I visit, not much time is spent watching the students and developing a model of how particular students learn; not nearly enough time is spent looking at student work. This is what I call the teacher's fallacy. I taught a great class, therefore the students understood. I teach, therefore you understand. The only way you can find out if students are understanding is to have them actually do some work.

- One technique that has become very popular in the U.S. is the minute paper. At the end of a topic, and sometimes at the end of every session, you ask the student to write down one thing that he or she learned in the period and one question that he or she still has. It's a revelation! I never cease to learn when I do the minute paper. And the misconceptions are revealing. But unless misconceptions get out in the open, they sit there underneath accumulating that powder.

- Portfolios are great – but I don't have time to look at my students' work! I'm too busy, too much pressure for coverage, too many faculty meetings. I've a second job. If you don't have time to look at students' work, you shouldn't teach. Because if you don't look at your students' work, you have no idea whether they are learning anything.

- I used to think that if we simply change the assessment, everything else will be fine. But if the curriculum isn't good, the assessment is worthless. You can have wonderful assessment *and* curriculum, but if the staff isn't well instructed, teachers aren't educated even before or during the experience, the assessment and curricula are worthless.

- Finally, "school doesn't have to be the way you remember it." Unfortunately, the unschooled mind even applies to parents and teachers; we have a stereotype formed by the age of five about what school is like. Namely, somebody at the front of the room is talking just as I am, and you're sitting in your seat, trying to be quiet, and all the knowledge is in the teacher's head and the purpose is to put it into your head. That's a very powerful idea. Whether people love school or hate school, most have that stereotype.

Unless we can help people think differently about what school can be like, what can be studied, how it can be taught, how it can be learned, then the opportunity for education for understanding is not going to be seized.

Now Piaget said one valuable thing which I didn't adhere to. He said that developmental psychologists should not try to be educators. And he steered clear of proposing educational theory. I have stepped into the lion's den today and offered you an educational theory that comes out of developmental psychology. Only time will tell whether I should have adhered to Piaget's admonition.

CHAPTER 17

TEACHING FOR UNDERSTANDING IN THE DISCIPLINES – AND BEYOND

Howard Gardner and Veronica Boix-Mansilla

Teachers College Record, Blackwell,1994, 96 (2), 198–218

The notion of discipline is doubly dual-edged. The popular version of discipline denotes the requirement that individuals behave according to a strict regimen. While many in our culture recognize the need for disciplined training ("that child needs discipline"), few (except perhaps for masochists) wax enthusiastic about a disciplined life. The academic version of discipline refers to domains of knowledge or competence within a society; individuals enroll in scholastic or informal apprenticeships and eventually achieve a certain degree of expertise in a discipline. While most educators recognize the need for the acquisition of academic disciplines, a rather widespread conviction obtains that such disciplines are good for you ("that child needs to master the disciplines before going to college") rather than enjoyable to pursue, ultimately useful, or essential for full development.

In this chapter we adopt a positive view of both disciplinary terrains. We believe that individuals will be most fully engaged and most productive when they lead a life in which disciplined training has become a regular, predictable feature. Relatedly, we maintain that the scholarly disciplines represent the formidable achievements of talented human beings, toiling over the centuries, to approach and explain issues of enduring importance. Shorn of disciplinary knowledge, human beings are quickly reduced to the level of ignorant children, indeed to the ranks of barbarians.

One hundred years ago a defense of the disciplines would have been unnecessary. In the current climate, however, there has been much criticism of the organization of precollegiate curricula, and the disciplines have often been a flashpoint for that criticism. Criticism of the disciplines in schools typically takes several forms. Sometimes it becomes a call for inter-disciplinary or thematic curricula, even when students could not yet have mastered individual disciplines; at times it suggests that disciplines are an outmoded way of organizing knowledge and are better replaced by a focus on "ways of knowing," "learning styles," or even "intelligences." Finally, criticism of the disciplines cites shifting definitions of disciplines or "blurring of genres" as additional reasons for discarding a disciplinary focus in the curriculum.

More responsible critics do recognize the contributions of the disciplines, but often their critiques lead educators to conclude that the disciplines constitute a significant part of the problem in schools today (Jacobs, 1989; Hirst, 1972; Phenix, 1964; and Sizer, 1992). We, in contrast, find the disciplines to be indispensable in any quality education, and we urge individuals not to throw away the "disciplinary" baby with the "subject matter" bathwater.

While adopting this decidedly more benign view, we do concur in one respect with those who harbor reservations about discipline. We assert that disciplinary competence is hard to come by, indeed much more difficult than observers have hitherto believed. Indeed, so powerful are our early "pre-disciplinary" ways of knowing that the achievement of genuine disciplinary mastery proves highly demanding.

In what follows we undertake three principal tasks. To begin with, we review the accumulated evidence that disciplinary knowledge represents an impressive yet elusive attainment. Next, we sketch out an educational approach designed to engender effective understanding within and across the disciplines. We illustrate this "ideal type" sketch by reporting preliminary results from a study in which teachers are attempting to enhance student understanding across the disciplines. This discussion includes a brief consideration of understanding that transcends individual disciplines – hence, the "and beyond" of our title. Finally, we return to the practical difficulties that arise in attempting to educate for understanding and indicate how some of these obstacles might be dealt with.

While most observers would endorse the goal of "teaching for understanding," there have been only scattered attempts to define what is meant by this phrase and set up programs that explicitly address this goal (Cohen *et al.*, 1993). In our own work we define "understanding" as the capacity to use current knowledge, concepts, and skills to illuminate new problems or unanticipated issues (Gardner, 1991c; Perkins, 1992). So long as one is drawing on such knowledge only to illuminate issues that have already been encountered, it is not possible to tell how much genuine understanding has been achieved. But one can with some confidence conclude that genuine understanding has been achieved, if an individual proves able to apply knowledge in new situations, without applying such knowledge erroneously or inappropriately; and if he or she can do so spontaneously, without specific instruction to do so.

Copious research documents how difficult it is to demonstrate such understanding in even our best students (see Gardner, 1991c, and Chapter 6). Wherever one looks in the curriculum, one finds very little evidence of deep understanding. At most, students show extremely threadbare forms of understanding. In the sciences, misconceptions abound. Students of physics believe in forces that can be mysteriously transmitted from one substance or agent to another; students of biology think of evolution as a planful, teleological process, culminating in the perfect human being; students of algebra plug numbers into an equation with hardly a clue as to what the equation means or when (and when not) to invoke it; students of history insist on applying the simplest stereotypical models to the elucidation of events that are complex and multifaceted; students of literature and the arts prefer works that are simple, realistic, and sentimental over those that deal with seemingly abstruse philosophical issues or that treat subject matter that is not overtly beautiful.

Why the robustness of these unproductive habits of mind? Why does it prove so difficult to educate for understanding? We argue that, during the early years of life, children form extremely powerful theories or sets of beliefs about how the world works – theories of mind, theories of matter, theories of life. Some aspects of children's early understanding of the world, such as their genuine questions and inquisitive spirit, provide a promising grounding for future disciplinary understanding. However, many other aspects constitute obstacles to be overcome. Children construct powerful stereotypes about persons and events (people who look different from oneself are seen as more likely to be evil; events are conceived as having single causes or are interpreted from self-centered perspectives). They establish habits of learning facts and procedures in a reflexively syntactic manner, overlooking the meaning or implications of particular statements or processes; the result is ritualistic memorization of meaningless facts and disembodied procedures.

These theories, ideas, and procedures become so deeply entrenched in the human mind that they prove very difficult to eradicate in favor of the more comprehensive and more veridical views that have been painstakingly constructed in and across the disciplines. Rather, like the proverbial Trojan Horse, these powerful yet erroneous notions remain quietly in hiding during the school years until their opportunistic moment arises. At that point they rise up and assert themselves with considerable force, in the process documenting an enduring lack of genuine understanding on the part of most students.

To educate the unschooled mind, two kinds of disciplines are necessary. First of all, the classical academic disciplines, ranging from physics to poetry, offer well-established means for understanding the world. If individuals pursue these disciplines assiduously, they ought to be able to replace their misconceptions with more appropriate ideas and practices. Indeed, experts may be thought of as individuals who really do succeed in replacing their earlier, imperfect notions with more serviceable ones. Such experts exemplify cases in which intuitive and common-sense ideas that were once engraved on the mind/brain have been gradually smoothed away; ultimately these initial configurations have come to be replaced by a new and more appropriate set of engravings. To achieve such expertise, students require ample doses of discipline in the alternative sense of the term: regular practice, with feedback, in applying those habits of mind that yield understanding.

It is important to specify what we mean by disciplines. Disciplines consist of approaches devised by scholars over the centuries in order to address essential questions, issues, and phenomena drawn from the natural and human worlds; they include methods of inquiry, networks of concepts, theoretical frameworks, techniques for acquiring and verifying findings, appropriate images, symbol systems, vocabularies, and mental models. Over the centuries human beings have developed these particular ways to look at the past, to understand biological beings, or to understand ourselves, that now proceed under the label of history, biology, or psychology. Disciplines are dynamic. Their objects, methods, theories, or accounts stimulate controversy and evolve in time. In order to socialize our youngsters into these bodies of knowledge and practices, we need to focus on the disciplines' essential features at this point in history, while acknowledging their dynamic and continually evolving nature.

Defining disciplinary boundaries is a complex epistemological and sociological enterprise that lies beyond the scope of our discussion. Whereas some concepts and methods are prototypical features of specific disciplines, others are shared by two or more disciplines. Assumptions about the nature of knowledge as well as particular theoretical positions within disciplines shape the discussion about disciplinary boundaries (Schwab, 1978). Despite these wrinkles, we believe one can still identify the essential questions that each of these disciplinary approaches is trying to address as well as the "rules of the game" that help students develop appropriate habits of mind and understanding.

Disciplines are not the same as subject matters or Carnegie units. At best there is a rough correspondence between any list of school subjects and the disciplines that underlie them. Whereas subject matters are seen as collections of contents that students need to learn, disciplines entail particular modes of thinking or interpreting the world that students need to develop. In disciplinary work, concepts or theories are not disembodied from the knowledge-building process through which they emerge.

With reference to these disciplinary considerations, what actually happens in most schools, for most students, is a curious form of *détente*. Certainly, students do learn facts, memorize concepts, come to master practices and performances in the classroom or in the laboratory. However, by and large such "subject-matter knowledge" is superficial. Students master knowledge encoded in textbooks and spew that knowledge back in tests that are yoked to the textbook. Teachers and students agree to honor the "correct answer compromise." That is, both partners in the educational conversation agree to accept certain formulations as evidence of mastery, while not pushing one another any further on what the particular issue in question genuinely entails: "If you don't push me on what energy (or photosynthesis or negative numbers or the Russian Revolution) really means, I won't hold you accountable for such sophisticated understanding in the final exam."

And, finally, many teachers succumb to what one might term the "teacher's fallacy;" in its most familiar form, this fallacy entails the chain of reasoning: "I taught a great class; therefore the students must have understood." In truth, of course, unless the teacher has the opportunity to look carefully at student work, to probe for both understandings and non-understandings, it is just not possible to ascertain how successful one's teaching has actually been. In our view, even teachers who know a great deal about their disciplines and about general learning principles need to diagnose students' conceptions regularly, if they are to gauge the effectiveness of their teaching.

Despite this searing indictment of most schools in most countries, we believe that there are schools in which teaching for understanding does occur. In general, such institutions aim for "uncoverage" rather than for "coverage"; they embrace the contemporary aphorism that "less is more." Certainly, the greatest enemy of understanding is coverage – the compulsion to touch on everything in the textbook or the syllabus just because it is there, rather than taking the time to present materials from multiple perspectives, allowing students to approach the materials in ways that are initially congenial to them but that ultimately challenge them, and assessing understandings in as direct and flexible a manner as possible. To the extent that various schools, ranging from English boarding schools to French *lycées* to John Dewey's progressive schools, have adopted a less frenetic and more thoughtful approach to the curriculum, the opportunities to educate for understanding can be seized.

At least in the United States, much of what happens inside classrooms happens for reasons unconnected to educational effectiveness. Teaching content is determined by an externally mandated syllabus. Practices endure because they had been carried out in the past, or because they satisfy the putative requirements of the College Board, a regimen of Carnegie units, or the curricular ideas endorsed by the local school board.

It is possible to envision an education that assumes a totally different form. In such an approach, one rooted in the progressive tradition of John Dewey, Theodore Sizer, and others, the curriculum is built from the first around gritty central questions or generative issues (Dewey, 1964a, 1964b; Sizer, 1992). These are issues that thoughtful human beings all over the world have posed, issues for which answers of various degrees of adequacy have been promulgated over the centuries in diverse cultures.

These basic questions are articulated by young children, on the one hand, and by seasoned philosophers, on the other; they are addressed by the disciplines created by the scholars, the roles adopted in the society, the artwork, poetry, and religion forged by the culture. Among the essential questions, grouped roughly by conceptual domains, are these:

Identity and history: Who am I? Where do I come from? Who is my family? What is the group to which I belong? What is the story of that group? Of other groups? Who are the other people around me, and in other parts of the world? How are they similar to and different from me? How do they look? What do they do? What is their story?

Relations to others: How should you treat other people? How should they treat you? What is fair? What is moral? How do you cooperate? How do you handle conflicts? Who is the boss and why?

My place in the world: Where do I live? How did I get here? How do I fit into the universe? What will happen to me when I die?

The psychological world: What is my mind? Do others have minds? Are they like mine? What are thoughts, dreams, feelings? Where do my emotions come from? How can I handle them? How do I remember things? How do I communicate?

The biological world: What about other creatures? What does it mean to be alive? Dead? Do animals think? What about plants? How are animals related to one another, to the world of plants, to humans? Is there a substance of life? How is it created? Is it immortal?

The physical world: What is the world made up of? Why do things move? What do we know about the sun, the stars, the waters, the rocks – their origins, their fate?

Forms, patterns, sizes: Why do things look and feel the way that they do? What regularities are there in the world? How do they come about? What is big, biggest? How can you tell?

In an education geared toward understanding, such issues are introduced in forms that reflect relevant aspects of disciplinary inquiry from the earliest ages. Youngsters approach these questions in ways appropriate to their age, developmental stage, and learning style. Much, if not most, of the curriculum is tied directly to these questions; students and parents, as well as teachers, should be able readily to discern the connections among today's homework assignment, tomorrow's projects, and the questions that have animated them. Indeed, in a school geared toward understanding, one should be able to stop anyone in the halls, find out what he or she is doing, and behold that individual relating a current activity to the questions that inspired it and to the long-term goal of achieving a sophisticated understanding of that question. This state of affairs can come about only if agreement obtains across the grade levels on the principal understandings to be cultivated.

How does one introduce the perennial tasks of education into a framework organized around questions? To begin with, students encounter instances of individuals (preferably "live," but if necessary on film or transmitted electronically) who are themselves addressing these issues in a serious and engaged way. These include disciplinary experts, of course, but also ordinary men and women at work as well as individuals featured in works of art. If a society values the question "What are human beings made of?" the student in that society should observe basic scientists attempting to answer that question; and to the extent that meaningful approaches to this question are being pursued by artists, technologists, spiritual leaders, or philosophers, these perspectives should be on ready display as well.

Having seen experts at work contemplating or solving these problems and questions, what should children do? Certainly it is important for students to master the basic literacies – to be able to read, write, and compute, with increasing ease, confidence, and automaticity. However, such literacies need to be seen as means – means for approaching the questions, means for learning the disciplines that represent the society's sustained attempts to tackle basic questions. This is the genius of "whole language" classrooms or of "project-based education" – students have the opportunity of acquiring literacies and disciplines not as unmotivated ends in themselves, but rather as part of an effort to gain leverage on questions with which thoughtful persons have long wrestled.

However, there are attendant risks to such holistic methods. To the extent that such projects do not build on the literacies and the disciplinary curriculum, to the extent that they wander off in other directions, the school is functioning in a fragmented fashion. In an integrated educational environment, literacies and disciplinary knowledge readily make their way into students' projects and exhibitions. Even for those who have mastered the basic literacies, the road to disciplinary mastery is by no means uncluttered. Indeed, in thinking about the skills that individuals require to approach essential questions in an increasingly sophisticated way, we find it important to isolate several distinct approaches to knowing.

Early common sense: From the very first, youngsters are able to utilize their incipient theories and explanatory frameworks in order to approach essential questions. We see these simple notions at work when the child explains the movement of the cloud in terms of a motor contained within it or the breath of a flying monster propelling it across the sky. Early common sense is a wonderful capacity, and it can both charm and disarm. Its exercise reflects the species' proclivity for using available symbolic forms to make sense of our surrounding world. Yet, as the philosopher Nelson Goodman once quipped, much of common sense is actually common nonsense, and it needs to be recognized as such.

Enlightened common sense: Still at the level of common sense, yet more sophisticated than the garden-variety common sense of the toddler, is what we term "enlightened common sense." This variety is a result of experience in the culture and incipient habits of reflection and questioning. It develops spontaneously with little need for specific instruction. The difference between the eight-year-old and the four-year-old is not so much the greater disciplinary knowledge of the eight-year-old but rather his or her potential for reflecting critically on an answer, for drawing on relevant daily experience, for engaging in discussion and dialogue, and benefiting from such interchange.

Proto-disciplinary knowledge: By the middle years of elementary school, most children are ready to adopt some of the habits of the disciplinary thinker. As budding scientists, they can think about empirical claims and the evidence that supports or undercuts them; as incipient historians, they can understand the difference between a historical and a fictional account and appreciate the role of records and texts in the creation of a historical account; as aspiring artistic practitioners, they can assume the role of the critic as well as that of the creator. We term this approach "proto-disciplinary" because it does not require a full-fledged immersion in the texts and the methods of the disciplines. Indeed, the roots of proto-disciplinary knowledge lie in the habits of common sense as leavened by discourse with other persons and by casual attention to the practices of reflective adults. Proto-disciplinary knowledge extends beyond common sense in that it includes some of the salient features of a discipline-based approach. At this point, there is no need for a formal delineation of disciplines – and indeed the disciplinary terrain at this point consists of but a handful of distinct approaches to knowledge. Gross distinctions between understanding the social realm (social studies) and understanding the natural world (natural science) may be enough. In further developing disciplinary understanding, finer distinctions among disciplines (history, sociology, political science) will emerge. Given certain literate or scholarly environments, one can count on some youngsters to achieve proto-disciplinary knowledge without direct tutelage; such an expectation is not realistic when it comes to the mastery of "normal" disciplinary knowledge.

Normal disciplinary knowledge: Scholars over the centuries have accumulated the knowledge, the theories, the concepts, and, above all, the methods that constitute the disciplines of today. It would be clearly impossible for any individual starting from scratch to assemble and organize that knowledge on his or her own. Therefore, schools are in a privileged position to introduce students to normal disciplinary knowledge – its texts, its problem sets, its ritualized procedures – since it would be unrealistic to expect youngsters to achieve such understandings on their own. Normal disciplinary knowledge constitutes the main course of middle school and beyond (Kuhn, 1970). And it is regularly enacted "discipline," in the aforementioned popular sense of the term, that allows individuals to move toward disciplinary mastery.

Most schools achieve a measure of success in conveying to most students the procedures of the major disciplines. However, disciplines tend to be conveyed (or at least to be apprehended) in a superficial way. Often, the focus falls on the mastery of facts, and facts, it turns out, are remarkably bereft of genuine disciplinary content. That is, to know the atomic weight of fluorine does not differ epistemologically from knowing the date of the fall of Constantinople or the materials out of which the murals on the ceiling of the Sistine Chapel were painted. Thus, so long as the telltale cues or frames are presented, it looks as though students genuinely understand the disciplines – or at least have mastered the required subject matter. But once a question or issue is phrased in an unfamiliar way, or posed at an unexpected time, one is likely to find that genuine understanding is absent. In fact, as has been amply documented, when facing new situations, even students who score well on standard tests fall back on the kinds of answers given by the five-year-old "unschooled" mind. Disciplinary tactics and terminology are likely to stick, but disciplinary understanding has not been achieved.

The distinct approaches to knowledge described above suggest a developmental trend from early common sense to disciplinary understanding. It is worth noticing that this development is not linear. A single individual may elicit different simultaneous approaches within or across specific disciplines depending on factors such as mastery of a particular topic, the context in which he or she works, or the extent of scaffolding received.

In moving beyond the disciplines, three additional forms of knowing need to be kept in mind: multi-, inter-, and meta-disciplinary knowledge. Because performing understanding in these realms requires mastery in specific disciplines, these forms of knowing are not often achieved successfully in the precollegiate educational systems.

Multi-disciplinary work: It is possible to approach a topic or issue by employing, seriatim, a number of disciplines. An individual interested in the Renaissance who approaches this era first as a historian, then as a scientist, then as an artist, is employing a multiplicity of disciplines. And yet, so long as no attempt is made at synthesis, the whole will not be greater than the sum of its parts.

Inter-disciplinary work: An individual who not only applies more than one discipline but actually strives to combine or synthesize these stances is engaging in that rare but precious practice called inter-disciplinary work. Many questions or problems can be approached only in a pluri-disciplinary way, and many of our most honored thinkers are those who can synthesize disciplines.

However, it is crucial to note that inter-disciplinary work can be carried out legitimately only after the individual has become at least somewhat conversant in the relevant disciplines. Much of what is termed inter-disciplinary or multi-disciplinary work in the early grades is actually pre-disciplinary "theme-based" work – drawing chiefly on common sense.

Meta-disciplinary work: In meta-disciplinary work, rather than using disciplines to illuminate a topic or question, one focuses on the nature of disciplinary thought itself – of what the disciplines consist, how they interact, to what uses they can be put, and allied meta-cognitive concerns. It is possible to be an excellent disciplinarian without engaging in meta-disciplinary work; yet some reflectiveness about the nature of disciplinary activity should aid most students (and all teachers!). For instance, students can receive a variety of insights when they compare a historical novel or film with a piece of historical writing or a cinematic documentary; and such a meta-disciplinary stance is certainly at a premium in the reading and writing of a paper like this.

While this sequence is suggestive rather than lock-step, it is not easy – and not advisable – to speed up or to alter it. In a single high school class, one might well have students who are pre-disciplinary as well as ones who have already become deeply involved in the discipline. Moreover, the same student may be a pre-disciplinary thinker in one domain, yet exhibit considerable disciplinary understanding in another. Each student needs to be addressed at his or her level of disciplinary sophistication. At the same time, however, it is advisable to expose students of all degrees of sophistication to genuine disciplinary work, so that they receive an image of what it is like to use one's disciplinary knowledge – one's developed mind – in a productive manner. While the disciplinary sequence may be developmental, the educational setting should be holistic.

To flesh out this discussion, consider two fictional, though plausible, situations.

- It was announced today in the *Hometime Newspaper* that the current Queen of England has abdicated and that the House of Windsor has decided to disestablish itself. What are the likely consequences of such a decision?

- The *New England Journal of Medicine* described a study on the origins of colds. Two groups of students were randomly assigned to matched groups. Group I played sports together in the indoor gym after school. Group II worked individually at terminals in the computer room. A follow-up of all students revealed that students in Group I were twice as likely to contract colds as students in Group II. The results are being reported in the popular media as evidence that indoor sports can cause illness.

In the terms introduced earlier, each of these examples centers on an essential question or topic. The first one focuses on the "body politic" – the nature of power, rule, control. The second one focuses on the "physical body" – the meaning of health, strength, sickness. These questions qualify as essential because they prove of enduring interest to individuals of different ages, backgrounds, and cultures. To be sure, the particular examples that we have contrived may not intrigue every person. But at the very least, these questions can be posed in terms understandable by every schoolchild: how does one get sick? Can one get sick by standing near someone who is sick? Who is the boss? How does one get to be the boss? What happens when the boss dies or relinquishes power?

Let us suppose, then, that one were interested in the extent to which students understood these questions, or questions like them, from the various disciplinary perspectives reviewed above. How would one broach the questions? What performances of understanding could one reasonably expect from youngsters of different degrees of sophistication, reflecting different levels of development?

Early common-sense understanding   At this level one asks whether students can draw on their intuitive theories with respect to the issues at hand. In the case of the physical body, one observes whether a student is able to apply an intuitive theory of health (a person is healthy if he or she feels and looks good; a person is sick if he or she looks or feels bad; people get sick because they are bad or because they have done something that makes them sick). In the case of the body politic, one observes whether a child invokes a theory of power (the person in power is the strongest and can boss others around; persons cease to hold power if they tire of it or they lose strength, and one would have to find a new boss to replace them). Note that no particular tutelage is needed to approach these questions – just sufficient understanding of the question so that one's intuitive theories of health or power can be invoked in as adequate a fashion as possible.

Enlightened common-sense understanding   By the end of the primary grades, a child can typically go beyond an uncritical invocation of his or her intuitive theory. Instead, the child can be somewhat critical of the theory (does one always have to be the strongest to be the boss? Does one always need to have a boss?). In the case of health, the student might ponder whether one could be sick even if one looked healthy, or whether one would be more or less likely to avoid infection if one had recently been ill. In such instances children begin to go beyond their strictly phenomenological and *ad hoc* accounts to begin to raise relevant questions, issues, and tests.

Proto-disciplinary knowledge   At this point, generally reached in the later years of elementary school, the youngster can be introduced to the questions in essentially the form they have been presented here. As a start, one wants to make sure that the child understands the example well enough to paraphrase it or to explain it to someone else. Then, encroaching on the disciplinary area of social studies, one might ask the youngsters to read a book about English royalty and to note who secured the crown following previous abdications and how the investiture was made and enforced. Students could also compare earlier cases of divine right-based absolute monarchies with current "symbolic" monarchies. Such a tactic would help students to go beyond their tendency to think of political power as based on personal features and to appreciate its institutional basis. At the same time, one would be fostering students' proto-disciplinary historical knowledge by directing them to use sources and reason from a historical perspective.

In the case of the physical body, a proto-disciplinary approach establishes that the child has mastered the basic facts of the cases. One asks the student to describe how the study was done and to suggest some of the reasons why the students playing in the gym were more likely to get sick. In so doing, the students are introduced to the rudiments of understanding of experimental science (how one finds out what causes something) as well as the beginnings of a theory of infection that builds on biological knowledge.

"Normal" disciplinary understanding   Much of what is presented in middle school, high school, and college calls for disciplinary understanding. With reference to our illness example, one expects a young disciplinarian to be able to describe some of the strengths and weaknesses of rival experimental designs, differences between causation and correlation, and basic knowledge about the nature of disease, infection, bodily defenses, contagion, and allied concepts. Note that understanding of these concepts is never fixed; moreover, a disease process will be explained in an entirely different way in a culture that lacks the science (or the art) of medicine.

In the case of the body politic, one expects at a minimum that the students understand the nature of the governmental system in England, the relationship between the parliamentary system and the monarchy, the actual rights and responsibilities of the monarch, the rules or precedents for abdication, its most probable consequences. Since our hypothetical class is located in the United States, one can reasonably expect students to compare the British situation with an analogous one in our own country.

Beyond individual disciplines   It is legitimate to look for higher degrees of sophistication in the disciplines and for thinking that transcends the individual discipline. Sophisticated disciplinary thinking might involve recognition of the pros and cons of different governmental systems; or, in the case of the English example, a consideration of the symbolic power of the monarchy and of which institutions might be expected to fill the void caused by abdication and disestablishment.

Examples of inter-disciplinary thinking include the consideration of both biological and psychological explanations for the different incidences of illness in the two groups of students; psychosomatic phenomena are particularly interesting from this perspective. In the case of political power, inter-disciplinary understanding can be pursued by considering poetry and art, as well as history, in examining the role of the monarchy in British life. Whether multi- or inter-disciplinary performances are issued depends on the extent to which students attempt to synthesize ideas and methods from more than one discipline.

Meta-disciplinary thinking can be brought to bear, for instance, as one contemplates the difference between (1) the investigation of disease, which might ultimately produce both an explanation of and a cure for colds, and (2) the study of a one-time historical event, where it is not possible to use control groups, where one can never hope to explain events fully, and where the course of future events cannot be predicted.

In the end, each of us should arrive at our own personal resolution of essential questions. A student might put his or her own values into practice, perhaps indicating whether physical exercise is so important that it is worth the risk of getting sick, or defending the proposition that a monarchy is inherently preferable to other forms of government. Were the student to wax philosophical, he or she could meditate about the similarities and differences between physical and psychological bodies – a whimsical motivation for including this pair of yoked examples.

It is possible to organize a sizable part of a curriculum around essential questions and to examine disciplinary understanding of such questions at a number of levels of development. Such an ideal-type scheme conveys a view of education quite different from that which normally prevails. Yet, in educational writings, visions are common, evidence of their realization much less so.

Working with a large number of colleagues at Harvard Project Zero and elsewhere, we have been engaged in a number of efforts to educate for understanding. In our view, teaching for understanding is grounded in four essential elements that interact dynamically with each other (Blythe, 1998; Wiske, 1998; see also Chapter 16).

1   *Essential questions or generative issues*   These are rich and engaging topics that hold the interests of students (and of non-students!). They become the core ideas in a curriculum, can be featured in projects, and can be approached from a number of different perspectives. They invite probing and reveal depth when so investigated. While any idea can be generative, the goal is to arrive at issues that are seminal in the disciplines and that readily engage most students. The essential questions listed above, as well as the two curricular instances reviewed, are instances of generative topics.

2   *Goals of understanding*   Any course, indeed any lecture or exercise, ought to have one or more goals of understanding. Goals of understanding specify just what we want students to understand as a result of taking a unit or course of study. A course in British history might have as its aim that students understand the changing nature of the monarchy over the centuries; a course in biology might be so designed that students will understand prevailing models of sickness and health and the scientific method that is used to investigate these models. Of course, a curriculum can feature many goals, ranging from the learning of facts and skills to the enhancement of self-esteem, but none of these would be goals of understanding. Goals of understanding will vary from preschool to college – hence the challenges of assessing the variety of levels of understanding of a generative issue that our students spontaneously exhibit and of defining goals that help them to move toward a more disciplined reinterpretation of these topics.

3   *Performances of understanding*   Goals of understanding set a general context for education, but it is necessary to specify just what students need to do in order to demonstrate that they have in fact achieved requisite understandings.

In the above discussion we have indicated some of the performances that one should expect students at different levels of development to exhibit if they are to demonstrate an understanding of the monarchy, or of sickness and health. Specifically, a performance of understanding in biology might require a student to delineate the several factors that could have led to the reported experimental results and to design an experiment that might adjudicate among these competing factors. A performance of understanding in a history class might ask students to delineate the similarities and differences that obtain between the seventeenth-century beheading of Charles I and the resulting protectorate; the twentieth-century abdication of Edward VIII and his replacement by George VI; and the circumstances that surround the hypothetical disestablishment of the House of Windsor.

From the beginning of the course, teachers and more proficient students may perform in ways that demonstrate these desired disciplinary understandings. Novice students may elicit partial or pre-disciplinary understandings in their attempts to accomplish these tasks. Such performances of partial understanding offer room for more knowledgeable individuals to scaffold and model more sophisticated instances of understanding.

4   *Ongoing assessments*   In the typical school of today, students master a great deal of material – usually factual – and are then required on specific dates to reproduce that material in the class or on an externally devised examination. Not infrequently, the material is forgotten almost immediately after the course is over. Performances of understanding provide opportunities for teachers to assess students' understanding. For instance, when students delineate the similarities and differences between cases of monarchic abdication in history, teachers may detect one student's present-centered interpretation of the past or another student's ability to grasp the complexity of power struggles inherent in an abdication. In an education geared for understanding, the desired goals and performances are shared with students from the beginning, and teachers will assess the work. Students have ample opportunity to acquire and rehearse them. For the process to work effectively, both students and teachers need to have available:

a   *Instances of the mature, desired performances and of high-quality exhibitions and projects*   The more examples that are available, the more likely that students will stretch cognitively and discern ways in which they themselves can grow. Their understandings should accordingly be enhanced.

b   *Benchmarks along the way*   Simply to see the final, full-blown performance is not enough – indeed, it can be intimidating and may even turn off the students. Students and teachers need to encounter numerous signposts or markers along the way, instances of novice as well as journeyman and master-level performances. It is also advantageous to have available less skillful performances and critiques thereof.

c   *Processes and models for how to progress from one benchmark to the next*   Even paradigmatic examples of end states and intermediate points may not suffice. A detailed road map is helpful. The more that one can specify what it takes to get from one milestone to the next, and how best to navigate the intervening terrain, the more likely it is that students and teachers will achieve success.

Armed with formulations like the above, we have worked with a variety of teachers, across a variety of settings, in an effort to help them to teach for understanding. Here are some early findings from the field.

1   Education for understanding is a challenging undertaking. Even individuals who desire ardently to teach for understanding find that it is a difficult and demanding undertaking for all concerned. The difficulty comes not only from potent and enduring misunderstandings in the various disciplines but also from the habits of teaching and learning that have been ingrained in most of us in the educational system. When educators – be they primary-school teachers or university professors – say that these ideas are familiar and that they are already teaching for understanding, it is usually the case that they have something quite different in mind, or that they are confusing desire with achievement.

2   In the absence of well-crafted and appropriate measures, it is impossible to determine whether understanding has occurred. Many of us fall prey to the aforementioned teacher's fallacy: "I taught a great class; therefore the students understood." Indeed, unless one has available authentic assessments with relevant and reliable criteria that examine performances of understanding directly, it is quite possible that one will be deceived into inferring understanding where little or none exists. It is also possible that standardized short-answer examinations may obscure instances of mis- or partial understanding.

3   Many students at first recoil at the requirement of understanding, but they can eventually be energized by its challenges. Even if one does not receive a satisfactory score, it is much easier to take a standard examination. Teaching for disciplinary understanding entails breaking the tacit agreement of the "correct-answer compromise" between instructor and students. So, initially, many students feel that unfair requests are being made of them when they must actually perform their understandings. Yet, if students have the opportunity to see what they are learning, and that they can make use of what they are learning in a wider – and even an unfamiliar – context, then the disaffection may be transmuted into enthusiasm.

4   The greatest enemy of understanding is coverage. So long as a teacher (or student or parent or administrator) is determined to cover everything in the curriculum, at the expense of moving at a measured rate and giving students many opportunities from many angles to exhibit their understandings as well as their misunderstandings, it is virtually guaranteed that little genuine understanding will ensue.

5   If teachers themselves have not had the opportunity to understand disciplinary materials, they must themselves go through a process much like that outlined here. Needless to say, the degree of understanding, and of familiarity with teaching for understanding, varies enormously among teachers, even among teachers with the same training who have worked alongside one another for years in the same department. If teachers have not partaken of a liberal arts education, where the questions posed may be more important than the answers given, they will need practice in this educational approach. Fortunately, even those teachers who may have had an education that was bereft of understanding will have achieved pockets of understanding in their own lives; moreover, they certainly will have encountered examples of experts

who do understand. It is possible to build on, to cobble together, these bits and snatches of understanding. Moreover, once teachers themselves discover that their own passion for learning has been reactivated, their enthusiasm for this more ambitious form of education becomes enhanced.

6   There is a surprising tension between the degree of structure of a discipline and the resistance to teaching for understanding. On an intuitive basis, it had seemed to us that, in those subjects where later lessons depend on earlier ones, there would be more dogged efforts to ensure that understanding has taken place. So far, however, our studies suggest the reverse. In cumulative subjects like mathematics or science, there is great pressure to proceed through the curriculum in lock-step fashion, independent of any evidence that documents students' understanding. Conversely, in history and especially in English, subjects that feature more open-ended inquiry and where there is less of a delineated knowledge base through which to proceed, teachers find it easier to allow the time and exploration needed for understanding.

In various waves of reform, there has been an almost purposeful avoidance of the most crucial set of questions. What is education for? How can we tell whether we have achieved success in attaining this goal? In this chapter we have argued that the purpose of education should be to enhance understanding. We provided evidence that such understanding is hard to achieve, both because educators have little accumulated knowledge of how to teach for it and because students harbor many potent habits of mind that stand in the way of performances of understanding.

Still, it is possible to envision an education that places understanding centrally in the curriculum. Once this decisive step has been taken, it becomes possible – despite many obstacles – to move in the direction of greater understanding. One must activate two powerful allies: the disciplines of knowledge that have developed painstakingly over the centuries, and the habits in which students work regularly and determinedly to master knowledge and skills and to activate them in the service of understanding. The distinguished British educator Paul Hirst once argued that disciplines do not train the mind; rather, they let us see what it is to have a mind. And that is certainly a goal worth aiming for and, perhaps, even an end to which one might meaningfully devote one's life.

CHAPTER 18

MULTIPLE APPROACHES TO UNDERSTANDING

Instructional-Design Theories and Models, Lawrence Erlbaum Associates, 1999, 2, 69–89.

Let me introduce the core ideas of the educational approach that I embrace. I believe that every person ought to master a central body of curricular materials and approaches, though I am not thereby wedded to a specific canon. For this chapter I have selected the examples of evolution and the Holocaust – though they are not without controversy – because I think that they lie comfortably within the ensemble of ideas that every educated person should have encountered, grappled with, and mastered. (In my book *The Disciplined Mind* [2000] I have added to the true [evolution] and the evil [the Holocaust] an example of the beautiful [the music of Mozart]). I depart from traditional educators – and from their allies in psychology – in the assumption that such topics need to be taught or assessed in a single way.

Because of their biological and cultural backgrounds, personal histories, and idiosyncratic experiences, students do not arrive in school as blank slates, nor as individuals who can be aligned unidimensionally along a single axis of intellectual accomplishment. They possess different kinds of minds, with different strengths, interests, modes of processing information. While this variation (a product of evolution!) initially complicates the job of the teacher, it can actually become an ally in effective teaching. For if the teacher is able to use different pedagogical approaches, there exists the possibility of reaching more students in more effective ways.

Differences among students can be described in innumerable ways and it is a simplification to prioritize any. For my purposes, I will speak of students as highlighting different intelligences. However, to follow this argument, one need not endorse my particular theory of intelligences. Any approach that recognizes and can somehow label or identify differences in intellectual proclivity or potential will suffice.

Assume that our educational goals include an enhanced understanding of the theory of evolution and the events called the Holocaust – topics drawn respectively from biology and from history. Specifically, we want students to appreciate that evolution, a process of random mutation in the genotype, is the driving force behind the variety of species that have existed historically and contemporaneously. The diverse phenotypes yielded by genetic variation result in organisms that are differentially able to survive in specific ecological contexts. Those that survive to reproduce in abundance have a competitive advantage over those that, for whatever reason, are less prone to adjust adequately to a given ecological niche. If these trends continue over the long run, the survivors prevail while those who cannot compete successfully are doomed to extinction. The fossil record documents the course and fate of different species historically; one sees the gradual increase in variety of species, as well as the increasing complexity of certain lines of descent. It is possible to study the same processes contemporaneously, with relevant research ranging from the breeding of *Drosophila* of various strains to experimental investigations of the origin of genes.

Turning to the Holocaust, we want students to appreciate what happened to the Jewish people, and to certain other condemned minorities and political dissidents, during the Nazi Third Reich, from 1933 to 1945. Efforts to castigate and isolate the Jewish people began with simple verbal attacks and laws of exclusion, gradually evolved into more violent forms of abuse, and ultimately culminated in the devising of camps whose explicit goal was the extinction of European Jewry. The contours of anti-Semitism were laid out in Hitler's early speeches and writings; but the historical course from plans to actualities took several years and involved hundreds of thousands of individuals in various capacities. Genocide – the effort to eliminate a people in its entirety – is hardly a new phenomenon; it dates back to biblical times. Yet the systematic way in which an allegedly civilized, modern nation proceeded to eradicate 6 million Jews is without precedent.

In brief form, these understandings would constitute a reasonable goal for a course or unit. Sheer memorization or faithful paraphrase of these paragraphs, of course, does not count for understanding. Rather, as noted above, students exhibit understanding to the extent that they can invoke these sets of ideas flexibly and appropriately to carry out specific analyses, interpretations, comparisons, critiques. An "acid test" of such understanding is the student's ability to perform his understandings with respect to material that is new – perhaps as new as today's newspaper.

How to approach these formidable topics? From the vantage point of MI, I propose three, increasingly focused lines of attack.

Entry points

One begins by finding a way to engage the student and to place her centrally within the topic. I have identified at least six discrete entry points, which can be roughly aligned with specific intelligences. In each case, I define the entry point and illustrate it with respect to our two topics.

1 *Narrative*   The narrational entry point addresses students who enjoy learning about topics through stories. Such vehicles – linguistic or filmic – feature protagonists, conflict, problems to be solved, goals to be achieved, tensions aroused and, often, allayed. Evolution invites treatment in terms of the story of Darwin's voyages (as it contrasts with the story of origins told in the Bible) or of the "course" of a particular species. The Holocaust can be introduced through a narrative account of a particular person, or through a year-by-year chronicle of events in the Third Reich.

2 *Quantitative/numerical*   The quantitative entry point speaks to students who are intrigued by numbers, the patterns that they make, the various operations that can be performed, the insights into size, ratio, and change. From an evolutionary perspective, one can look at the incidence of different individuals or species in different ecological niches, and how those aggre-

gates change over time. With respect to the Holocaust, one can look at the movement of individuals to various camps, the survival rates at each, the comparisons of the fates of Jews and other victim groups in different cities and nations.

3 *Foundational/existential* This entry point appeals to students who are attracted to fundamental "bottom line" kinds of questions. Nearly all youngsters raise such questions, usually through myths or art; the more philosophically oriented come to pose and argue about issues verbally. Evolution addresses the question of who we are and where we come from – and whence all living matter emanates. The Holocaust addresses the question of what kinds of beings humans are, and what are the virtues and vices of which they/we are capable.

4 *Aesthetic* Some individuals are inspired by works of art, or by materials arranged in ways that feature balance, harmony, a carefully designed composition. The tree of evolution, with its many branches and interstices, may attract such individuals; Darwin himself was intrigued by the metaphor of the "tangled bank" of nature. Many efforts have been undertaken to portray the Holocaust in works of art, literature, film, and music, both by those who were subsequently killed and by those survivors and observers who have tried to capture its horror.

5 *Hands-on* Many individuals, particularly young persons, find it easiest to approach a topic through an activity in which they become actively engaged – one where they can build something, manipulate materials, carry out experiments. The chance to breed generations of fruit flies (*Drosophila*) gives one the opportunity to observe the incidence and fate of genetic mutations. Holocaust displays can provide a harrowing introduction to this event. When students receive an alternative "identity" upon their entrance to a Holocaust exhibit and later ascertain what happened to this person in the course of the Holocaust, the personal identification can be very powerful. Being a subject in a psychological experiment that documents the human proclivity to follow orders can be a jarring experience as well.

6 *Social* The entry points described thus far address the individual as a single person. Many individuals learn more effectively, however, in a group setting, where they have the opportunity to assume different roles, to observe others' perspectives, to interact regularly, to complement one another. A group of students can be given a problem to solve – for example, what happens to various species in a given environment following a dramatic change in climate; or how would the Germans have reacted, had the Allies blown up the train tracks that led to a concentration camp. Or they can be asked to role-play different species in a shifting ecology, or different participants in a rebellion in a ghetto that is under siege.

Telling analogies

An "entry point" perspective places students directly in the center of a disciplinary topic, arousing their interests and securing cognitive commitment for further exploration. The entry point, however, does not necessarily inculcate specific forms or modes of understanding.

Here the teacher (or the student) is challenged to come up with instructive analogies, drawn from material that is already understood, that can convey important aspects of the less familiar topic. In the case of evolution, for example, analogies can be drawn from history or from the arts. Societies change over time, sometimes gradually, sometimes apocalyptically. The processes of human social change can be compared with those of biological change within and between species. Evolution can also be observed in works of art. Characters change within the course of a book and, sometimes, over a series of books. Themes in a fugue evolve and develop in certain ways, and not (ordinarily) in others.

One may search for analogies to the Holocaust. The effort to annihilate a people can be analogized to the eradication of traces of an event or even of an entire civilization. Sometimes these efforts at eradication are deliberate, as when the criminal seeks to hide all evidence of a crime. Sometimes these efforts occur as a result of the passage of time, as happens when the traces of an ancient city are virtually destroyed (absent relevant historical records, we do not know, of course, about those cities whose vestiges have altogether disappeared as the result of natural disaster or a vengeful enemy).

Analogies can be powerful, but they can also mislead. Analogies are an excellent way to convey important facets of a topic to individuals who have little familiarity with it. However, each analogy can also suggest parallels that do not hold – for example, the informing intelligence that constructs the theme of a fugue differs from the random nature of biological evolution; a murderer working in isolation differs from a large sector of society working secretly but in concert. The teacher is obliged to qualify each analogy as appropriate and to make sure that the misleading parts of the analogy are not allowed to distort or cripple the students' ultimate understanding.

Approaching the core

Entry points open up the conversation; telling analogies convey revealing parts of the concept in question. Yet the challenge to convey the central understandings still remains.

We come to the most vexing part of our analysis. Traditionally, educators have relied on two seemingly opposite approaches. Either they have provided quite explicit instructions – usually didactic – and assessed understanding in terms of linguistic mastery of materials (Evolution is ... The five central points about the Holocaust are ...). Or they have supplied copious information to the student and hoped that, somehow, the student would forge his own synthesis (On the basis of your reading, our trip to the museum, and various classroom exercises, what would you do if ... ?). Some teachers have pursued both approaches, either simultaneously or successively.

Here we encounter the crucial educational question: Can one use knowledge about individual differences in strengths and modes of representations to create educational approaches that can convey the most important, the "core notions" of a topic in a reliable and thorough manner?

First off, one must acknowledge that there cannot be a formulaic approach. Every topic is different – just as every classroom context is different – and so each topic must be considered in terms of its own specific concepts, network of concepts, issues, problems, susceptibilities to misconception.

A second step recognizes that topics do not exist in isolation – they come from and are, to some extent, defined by the ensemble of existing and emerging disciplines. Thus, a study of evolution occurs within the domain of biology and, more generally, within the realm of scientific explanation. As such, it involves the search for general principles and for models that will apply to all organisms under all kinds of circumstances (though some ideographically-oriented scientists seek to explicate specific events like the disappearance of dinosaurs). In contrast, a study of the Holocaust occurs within history – and, sometimes, within literary or artistic efforts to render this historical event. Parts of the Holocaust may resemble other historical events, but a foundational notion about history is that it offers an account of specific events, occurring in specific contexts. One can neither expect general principles to emerge nor build models that can be tested (though some scientifically oriented historians have attempted to construct and test such models).

The third step acknowledges commonly used ways of describing and explaining a concept. Thus evolution is typically described using certain examples (e.g., the disappearance of Neanderthal man, the branching tree of evolution), while the Holocaust is typically presented in terms of certain key events and documents (e.g., Hitler's *Mein Kampf*, the formulation of the Final Solution at the January 1942 Wannsee Conference, the records kept at Auschwitz, the reports by the first Allied soldiers to liberate the camps, the chilling photographs of the survivors). These familiar examples are not randomly chosen: rather, they have helped scholars to define these topics in the past, and they have proved effective pedagogically with at least a reasonable percentage of students.

But while these examples have their reasons, one must not infer that such examples are uniquely or permanently privileged. One can certainly feature these examples without ensuring understanding; and, by the same token, it is surely possible to enhance understanding of evolution or the Holocaust by using other examples, other materials, differently formulated causal accounts. We know that this ensemble changes, because there are new historical or scientific discoveries, as well as novel pedagogical approaches that prove effective. (Thus, for example, the opportunity to simulate evolutionary processes in a computer program, or to create virtual realities, spawns educational opportunities that could not have been anticipated a generation or two ago.)

The key step to approaching the core is the recognition that a concept can only be well understood – and can only give rise to convincing performances of understanding – if an individual is capable of representing that core in more than one way, indeed in several ways. Moreover, it is desirable if the multiple modes of representing draw on a number of symbol systems, intelligences, schemas, and frames. Going beyond analogies – indeed proceeding in the opposite direction – representations seek to be as accurate and comprehensive as possible.

Several implications follow from this assertion. First of all, it is necessary to spend significant time on a topic. Second, it is necessary to portray the topic in a number of ways – both to illustrate its intricacies and to reach an ensemble of necessarily diverse students. Third, it is highly desirable if the multiple approaches explicitly call upon a range of intelligences, skills, and interests.

It may seem that I am simply calling for the "smorgasbord" approach to education – throw enough of the proverbial matter at students and some of it will hit the mind/brain and stick. Nor do I think that such an approach is without merit. However, the theory of MI provides an opportunity, so to speak, to transcend mere variation and selection. It is possible to examine a topic in detail, to determine *which* intelligences, *which* analogies, *which* examples, are most likely *both* to capture important aspects of the topic *and* to reach a significant number of students. We must acknowledge here the cottage industry aspect of pedagogy – a craft that cannot now and may never be susceptible to an algorithmic approach. It may also constitute the enjoyable part of teaching – the opportunity continually to revisit one's topic and to consider fresh ways in which to convey its crucial components.

Educators and scholars may continue to believe that there is still an optimal mode for representing the core of a topic. I respond as follows. The history of disciplinary progress makes it inevitable that experts will think about a topic in terms of privileged considerations – perhaps genetic mutations and ecological niches in biology, perhaps human intentions and worldwide demographic and ecological forces in the case of history. Such consensual portrayal is reasonable. However, one should never lose sight of the fact that evolution did not occur in biology, and the Holocaust did not occur in history; they are events and processes that happened and became available for observers and scholars to describe, interpret, and explicate as best they could. New discoveries, as well as new disciplinary trends, gradually undermine today's orthodoxy; tomorrow's scholar might remake our understandings. Just as Darwin rewrote Lamarck's view of evolution, the believers in punctuated equilibrium aim to overthrow Darwinian gradualism (Gould, 1993). By the same token, Daniel Goldhagen's *Hitler's Willing Executioners* (1996) gives a far more "ordinary Germanic" cast to the Holocaust than had historians of earlier decades.

Generalizing the approach

Even if I have achieved some success in suggesting how best to approach two gritty topics of education, I evidently have left untouched the vast majority of the curriculum. My focus has been on a high school – perhaps a college – pair of topics; I have drawn from biology and European history, rather than from mathematics, music, or meteorology; and I have focused on topics or issues rather than, say, specific chemical reactions, or metrical analyses, or geometric proofs.

I would be remiss were I to imply that the approach sketched here could be applied equivalently to every topic of the syllabus. Indeed, I deliberately selected two topics that are relatively rich and multi-faceted, and that readily allow consideration from several perspectives. I suspect that no pedagogical approach is going to prove equally effective for the full range of topics and skills that need to be conveyed; teaching French verbs or the techniques of Impressionism is simply not commensurate with covering the Russian Revolution or explicating Newton's laws of mechanics.

Still, the approach sketched here can have wide utility. First of all, it raises the question of *why* one is teaching certain topics and what one hopes that students will retain at some time in the future. Much of what we teach recurs through habit; it makes sense to teach fewer topics and to treat them in greater depth. Such an approach allows one to relate materials to a few central themes – such as evolution in biology or the Holocaust in history (or energy in physics or character in literature) – and to eliminate topics if they cannot be reasonably connected to some powerful themes or throughlines. After all, we cannot conceivably cover everything; we may as well strive to be coherent and comprehensive in what we do cover.

Having determined which topics require sustained attention, one can then exploit an ensemble of pedagogical approaches. To recapitulate, one begins by

considering which entry points might succeed in attracting the interest and attention of diverse students. One then considers which kinds of examples, analogies,
and metaphors might convey important parts of the topic in ways that are powerful and not misleading. Finally, one seeks to find a small family of literally appropriate representations that, taken together, provide a rich and differentiated set of
representations of the topic under consideration. Such an ensemble conveys to students what it is like to be an expert. And to the extent that the family of representations involves a range of symbols and an array of schemes, it will prove far more
robust and useful to students.

Presenting materials and fostering multiple representations is one component of
effective teaching; the complementary component entails the provision of many
opportunities for performance, which can reveal to the student and to interested
observers the extent to which the material has been mastered. In stimulating performances of understanding, teachers need to be imaginative and pluralistic. While
it is easy to fall back on the tried and true – the short-answer test, the essay question – there is no imperative to do so. Performances can be as varied as the different facets of the topic, and the diverse sets of skills of students. A variety of
sanctioned performances not only provides more students with an opportunity to
show what they have understood; it also ensures that no single "take" on a topic
exerts an inappropriate hegemony on students' (or test-makers'!) understandings
of that topic.

With respect to our present examples, then, I encourage teachers to have students engage with one another in debates – on the causes of the Holocaust or
the merits of Lamarckianism; carry out experiments that probe different aspects
of the evolutionary process; interview individuals who have survived the
Holocaust or various others of the global conflicts of our time; create works of
art that commemorate heroes of the Resistance; design a creature that can survive in an environment that has become highly toxic. Perhaps most challeng-
ingly, they might need to be asked to discuss the factors that permitted the
Holocaust in terms of what we know about the evolution of behavior in that
line called *Homo sapiens sapiens*. Hence, at last our two topics would be joined.
Consultation of curricular guides and conversations with other teachers should
stimulate the imagination with respect to other kinds of performances for other
specimen curricula.

Just another call for projects – the sins of the Progressive movement, as casti-
gated by E.D. Hirsch (1996)? Quite the contrary. Student projects need to be
considered critically in two respects: 1) adequacy as an example of a genre (Is it
a coherent essay? Is it an effective monument? Does it qualify as a causal explanation?); 2) adequacy as an occasion for performing one's understandings (Does
the debater stick to the consensual facts or does she distort what is known?
Does the newly designed species have a life span that allows reproduction and
rearing of offspring?). Far from being a superficial measure of understanding,
such projects and performances hold the students to high standards – the key
features of the concept should be performed in vehicles that meet the test of cultural viability.

I have restricted myself until now almost entirely to the simplest forms of
technology – books, pencils, paper, perhaps a few art supplies, a simple bio-
chemical laboratory. This is appropriate – fundamental discussions of educational goals and means should not be dependent upon the latest technological
advances.

Yet the approach outlined here promises to be enhanced significantly by current and future technologies. It is no easy matter for teachers to provide individualized curricula and pedagogy for a class of thirty elementary school students, let alone several high school classes totaling more than 100 students. Similarly, it is challenging to have students provide a variety of performances and then provide meaningful feedback on this potpourri.

Happily, we have in our grasp today technology that will allow a quantum leap in the delivery of individualized services for both students and teachers. It is already possible to create software that addresses the different intelligences; that provides a range of entry points; that allows students to exhibit their own understandings in symbol systems (linguistic, numerical, musical, graphic, just for starters); and that begins to allow teachers to examine student work flexibly and rapidly. Student work can even be examined from a distance, thanks to electronic mail, video conferencing, and the like. The development of "intelligent computer systems" that will be able to evaluate student work and provide relevant feedback is no longer simply a chapter from science fiction.

In the past it might have been possible to argue that individualized instruction – while desirable – was simply not possible. That argument is no longer tenable. Future reluctance will have to be justified on other grounds. My strong hunch is that such resistance is not likely to persuade students and parents who are not experiencing success "in the usual way" and who might benefit from alternative forms of delivery; neither will such resistance satisfy scholars who have arrived at new ways of conceptualizing materials, nor teachers who are themselves dedicated to a variety of pedagogies and assessments.

Educators have always tinkered with promising technologies, and much of the history of education chronicles the varying fates of paper, books, lecture halls, film strips, television, computers, and other human artifacts. Current technologies seem tailor-made to help bring into reality the kind of "MI approach" that I have endorsed here. Still, there are no guarantees. Many technologies have faded, many others have been used superficially and unproductively. And we cannot forget that some of the horrible events of human history – such as the Holocaust – featured a perversion of existing technology.

That is why any consideration of education cannot remain merely instrumental. Not merely computers, we must ask – but computers for what? More broadly, education for what? I have taken here a strong position – that education must ultimately justify itself in terms of enhancing human understanding. But that understanding itself is up for grabs. After all, one can use knowledge of physics to build bridges or bombs; one can use knowledge of human beings to liberate or to enslave them.

I want my children to understand the world, but not just because the world is fascinating and the human mind is curious. I want them to understand it so that they will be positioned to make it a better place. Knowledge is not the same as morality, but we need to understand if we are to avoid past mistakes and move in productive directions.

An important part of that understanding is knowing who we are and what we can do. Part of that answer lies in biology – the roots and constraints of our species – and part of it lies in our history – what people have done in the past and what they are capable of doing. Many topics are important, but I would argue that evolution and the Holocaust are especially important. They bear on the possibilities of our species – for good and for evil. A student needs to know about these topics not primarily because they may appear on an examination, but rather because they help us to chart human possibilities. Ultimately, we must synthesize our understandings for ourselves. The performances of understanding that truly matter are the ones that we carry out as human beings in a world that is imperfect but one that we can affect – for good or for ill.

PART 5

FUTURE THEMES

CHAPTER 19

ASSESSMENT IN CONTEXT
The alternative to standardized testing

Gifford, B.R and M.C. O'Connor (eds), *Changing assessments: Alternative views of aptitude, achievement and instruction*. Boston: Kluwer, 1991.

Contrasting models of assessment

A familiar scene almost anywhere in the United States today: several hundred students file into a large examination hall. They sit nervously, waiting for sealed packets to be handed out. At the appointed hour, booklets are distributed, brief instructions are issued, and formal testing begins. The hall is still as students at each desk bear down on number two pencils and fill in the bubbles which punctuate the answer sheets. A few hours later, the testing ends and the booklets are collected; some time later a sheet bearing a set of scores arrives at each student's home and at the colleges to which the students have directed their scores. The results of a morning's testing become a powerful factor in decisions about the future of each student.

An equally familiar scene in most pre-industrial societies over the centuries: a youth of ten or 11 moves into the home of a man who has mastered a trade. Initially, the lad is asked to carry out menial tasks as he helps the master to prepare for his work or to clean up the shop at the end of the day. During this initial phase, the lad has the opportunity to watch the master at work, while the master monitors the youth to discover his special talents or serious flaws. Over the months the apprentice slowly enters into the practice of the trade. After initially aiding in the more peripheral aspects of the trade, he eventually gains familiarity with the full gamut of skilled work. Directed by tradition, but also guided by the youth's particular skills and motivation, the master guides his charge through the various steps from novice to journeyman. Finally, after several years of supervised training, the youth is ready to practice the craft on his own.

While both of these scenes are idealized, they should be readily recognizable to anyone concerned with the assessment and training of young people. Indeed, they may be said to represent two extremes. The first "formal testing" model is conceived of as an objective, decontextualized form of assessment which can be adopted and implemented widely, with some assurance that similar results will be obtained. The second "apprenticeship" model is implemented almost entirely within a naturally occurring context in which the particularities of a craft are embedded. The assessment is based upon a prior analysis of the skills involved in a particular craft, but it may also be influenced by subjective factors, including the master's personal views of his apprentice, his relationship with other masters, or his need for other kinds of services.

It should be evident that these two forms of assessment were designed to meet different needs. Apprenticeships made sense when the practice of various crafts was the major form of employment for non-rural youths. Formal testing is a contemporary means of comparing the performance of thousands of students who are being educated in schools. Yet these forms of assessment are not limited to the two prototypical contexts described above. Despite the overwhelmingly agrarian nature of Chinese society, formal tests have been used there for over 2,000 years in selecting government officials. And, by the same token, in many art forms, athletic practices, and areas of scientific research (Polanyi, 1958), apprenticeships and the concomitant ongoing, context-determined forms of assessment continue to be used in our highly industrialized society.

Thus, the choice of "formal testing" as opposed to "apprenticeship" is not dictated solely by the historical era or the primary means of production in the society. It would be possible in our society to utilize the apprenticeship method to a much greater extent than we do. Most observers today (myself included) do not lament the passage of the obligatory apprenticeship system, with its frequent excesses and blatant sexism; from several points of view, contemporary formal testing represents a fairer and more easily justifiable form of assessment. And yet aspects of the apprentice model are consistent with current knowledge about how individuals learn and how their performances might best be assessed.

Our society has embraced the formal testing mode to an excessive degree; I contend that aspects of the apprentice model of learning and assessment – which I term "contextualized learning" – could be profitably reintroduced into our educational system (see Collins, Brown, and Newman, 1989). Following an account of the origins of standardized testing and the one-dimensional view of mentation often implied by such testing methods, I review several lines of evidence from the cognitive, neural, and developmental sciences which point to a far more capacious view of the human mind and of human learning than that which informed earlier conceptions.

Our task here is to envision forms of education and modes of assessment which have a firm rooting in current scientific understanding and which contribute to enlightened educational goals. I describe in general terms the characteristics of these novel forms of assessment. I then introduce educational experiments in which my colleagues and I have become engaged, at levels from preschool to college admissions. These educational experiments demonstrate alternative ways in which information relevant to guidance and selection could be obtained. I conclude with a description and endorsement of a possible "individual-centered" school of the future, in which the lines between assessment and curriculum, students and disciplines, school and community are newly drawn. Such a school can be fashioned within a society that spurns standardized testing in isolation and favors assessment in context.

Accompanying a fealty to formal testing is a view of education which I have termed the "uniform view of schooling." This view does not necessarily entail the wearing of uniforms, but it does call for homogenized education in other respects. According to the uniform view, as much as possible students should study the same subject matter. (This may include a strong dosage of the values of the dominant culture or subculture – see Bloom, 1987; Hirsch, 1987; Ravitch and Finn, 1987.) Moreover, as much as possible, that subject matter ought to be conveyed in the same way to all students.

In the uniform view, progress in school ought to be assessed by frequent formal tests. These tests should be administered under uniform conditions, and students, teachers, and parents should receive quantitative scores which detail the student's progress or lack thereof. These tests should be nationally normed instruments, so that the maximum comparability is possible. The most important subject matters are those which lend themselves readily to such assessment, such as mathematics and science. In other subjects, value is assigned to the aspects which can be efficiently assessed (grammar rather than "voice" in writing; facts rather than interpretation in history). Those disciplines which prove most refractory to formal testing, such as the arts, are least valued in the uniform school.

In putting forth this picture of the uniform view of schooling, I am aware that I am overemphasizing certain tendencies and lumping together views and attitudes in a way which is not entirely fair to those who are closely associated with formal testing. Some individuals intimately involved with testing have voiced the same concerns (Cronbach, 1984; Messick, 1988). Indeed, had I put this picture forth a few decades ago it might have seemed an outrageous caricature. However, the trends within American education since the early 1980s bear a strong resemblance to the views I have just sketched. At the very least, these views serve as a necessary "contrast case" to the picture of contextualized and individualized assessment and schooling which I present later in the chapter; they should be taken in that contrastive spirit.

While the testing society has responded more to pragmatic needs than to scientific dictates, it does reflect a certain view of human nature. The scientific ideas on which the testing society has been based derive from an earlier era in which behaviorist, learning theoretical, and associationist views of cognition and development were regnant (see Gardner, 1985a for a summary). According to these views, it made sense to believe in "inborn" human abilities, in a smooth, probably linear curve of learning from infancy to old age, in a hierarchy of disciplines, and in the desirability of assessing potential and achievement under carefully controlled and maximally decontextualized conditions.

Over the past few decades, however, the various assumptions on which this testing edifice was based have been gradually undermined by work in developmental, cognitive, and educational studies, and a quite different view has emerged.

The desirability of assessing learning in context

When standardized tests and paradigmatic experimental designs were first introduced into non-Western cultural contexts, they led to a single result: preliterate individuals and others from non-Western societies appeared to be much less skilled and much less intelligent than Western control groups. An interesting phenomenon was then discovered. Simple alterations of materials, test setting, or instructions frequently elicited dramatic improvements in performance. The "performance gap" between the subjects from another culture and the subjects from our own culture narrowed or even disappeared when familiar materials were used, when knowledgeable and linguistically fluent examiners were employed, when revised instructions were given, or when the "same" cognitive capacities were tapped in a form that made more sense within the non-Western context (Laboratory of Comparative Human Cognition, 1982).

Now a huge body of experimental evidence exists to indicate that assessment materials designed for one target audience cannot be transported directly to another cultural setting; there are no purely culture-fair or culture-blind materials. Every instrument reflects its origins. Formal tests that make some sense in a Western context do so because students are accustomed to learning about materials at a site removed from the habitual application of such materials; however, in unschooled or lightly schooled environments, most instruction takes place in situ, and so it only makes sense to administer assessments which are similarly in context.

Building upon this cross-cultural research, there is also an accumulation of findings about the cognitive abilities of various kinds of experts. It has been shown that experts often fail on "formal" measures of their calculating or reasoning capacities but can be shown to exhibit precisely those same skills in the course of their ordinary work – such as tailoring clothes, shopping in a supermarket, loading dairy cases onto a track, or defending one's rights in a dispute (Lave, 1980; Rogoff, 1982; Scribner, 1986). In such cases, it is not the person who has failed but rather the measurement instrument which purported to document the person's level of competence.

Locating competence and skill outside the head of the individual

The research just reviewed has yielded another novel conceptualization. In many cases it is erroneous to conclude that the knowledge required to execute a task resides completely in the mind of a single individual. This knowledge can be "distributed"; that is, successful performance of a task may depend upon a team of individuals, no single one of whom possesses all of the necessary expertise but all of whom, working together, are able to accomplish the task in a reliable way (Scribner, 1986). Relatedly, it is too simple to say that an individual either "has" or "does not have" the requisite knowledge; that knowledge may show up reliably in the presence of the appropriate human and physical "triggers" but might be otherwise invisible to probing (Squire, 1986).

It makes sense to think of human cognitive competence as an emerging capacity, one likely to be manifest at the intersection of three different constituents: the "individual," with his or her skills, knowledge, and aims; the structure of a "domain of knowledge," within which these skills can be aroused; and a set of institutions and roles – a surrounding "field" – which judges when a particular performance is acceptable and when it fails to meet specifications (Csikszentmihalyi, 1988; Csikszentmihalyi and Robinson, 1986; Gardner and Wolf, 1988). The acquisition and transmission of knowledge depends upon a dynamic which sustains itself among these three components. Particularly beyond the years of early childhood, human accomplishment presupposes an awareness of the different domains of knowledge of one's culture and the various "field forces" that affect opportunity, progress, and recognition. By focusing on the knowledge that resides within a single mind at a single moment, formal testing may distort, magnify, or grossly underestimate the contributions which an individual can make within a larger social setting.

The foregoing research findings point to a differentiated and nuanced view of assessment, one which, in at least certain ways, might more closely resemble traditional apprenticeship measures than formal testing. An assessment initiative being planned today, in light of these findings, should be sensitive to developmental stages and trajectories. Such an initiative should investigate human symbolic capacities in an appropriate fashion in the years following infancy and investigate the relationship between practical knowledge and first- and second-level symbolic skills. It should recognize the existence of different intelligences and of diverse cognitive and stylistic profiles, and it should incorporate an awareness of these variations into assessments; it should possess an understanding of those features which characterize creative individuals in different domains. Finally, a new assessment initiative should acknowledge the effects of context on performance and provide the most appropriate contexts in which to assess competences, including ones which extend outside the skin of the individual being assessed.

It is a tall order to meet all of these needs and desiderata. Indeed, an attraction of formal testing is that one can bracket or minimize most of the features which I have just outlined. However, if we seek an assessment which is both true to the individual and reflective of our best understanding of the nature of human cognition, then we cannot afford to ignore the lines of thinking which I have just outlined.

General features of a new approach to assessment

If one were to return to the drawing board today and lay out a fresh approach to assessment, one might attempt to incorporate the following principal features.

Emphasis on assessment rather than testing

The penchant for testing in America has gone too far. While some tests are useful for some purposes, the testing industry has taken off in a way which makes little sense from the point of view of a reflective society. Many who seek to understand the underlying theoretical or conceptual basis of findings of validity are disappointed. It seems that many tests have been designed to create, rather than to fulfill, a need.

While I have ambivalent feelings about testing, I have little ambivalence about assessment. To my mind, it is the proper mission of educated individuals, as well as those who are under their charge, to engage in regular and appropriate reflection on their goals, the various means to achieve them, their success (or lack thereof) in achieving these goals, and the implications of the assessment for rethinking goals or procedures.

I define assessment as the obtaining of information about the skills and potentials of individuals, with the dual goals of providing useful feedback to the individuals and useful data to the surrounding community. What distinguishes assessment from testing is the former's favoring of techniques that elicit information in the course of ordinary performance and its general uneasiness with the use of formal instruments administered in a neutral, decontextualized setting.

In my view, those in the psychological and educational communities charged with the task of evaluation ought to facilitate such assessment (see Cross and Angelo, 1988). We ought to be devising methods and measures which aid in regular, systematic, and useful assessment. In some cases we would end up producing "formal tests." But not in most cases, I expect.

Assessment as simple, natural, and occurring on a reliable schedule

Rather than being imposed "externally" at odd times during the year, assessment ought to become part of the natural learning environment. As much as possible it should occur "on the fly," as part of an individual's natural engagement in a learning situation. Initially, the assessment would probably have to be introduced explicitly; but after a while much assessment would occur naturally on the part of student and teacher, with little need for explicit recognition or labeling on any-one's part.

The model of the assessment of the cognitive abilities of the expert is relevant here. On the one hand, it is rarely necessary for the expert to be assessed by others unless engaged in competition. It is assumed that experts will go about their business with little external monitoring. However, it is true that the expert is constantly in the process of assessing; such assessment occurs naturally, almost without conscious reflection, in the course of working. When I first began to write, I was highly dependent upon the detailed criticism of teachers and editors; now most of the needed assessment occurs at a preconscious level as I sit at my desk scribbling, or typing a first draft, or editing an earlier version of the material.

As assessment gradually becomes part of the landscape, it no longer needs to be set off from the rest of classroom activity. As in a good apprenticeship, the teachers and the students are always assessing. There is also no need to "*teach* for the assessment" because the assessment is ubiquitous; indeed, the need for formal tests might atrophy altogether.

Ecological validity

A problem for most formal tests is their validity, that is, their correlation with some criterion (Messick, 1988). As noted, creativity tests are no longer used much because their validity has never been adequately established. The predictive validity of intelligence tests and scholastic aptitude tests is often questioned in view of their limited usefulness in predicting performance beyond the next year of schooling.

Returning to our example of the apprenticeship, it would make little sense to question the validity of the judgments by the master. He is so intimately associated with his novice that he can probably predict the novices' behaviors with a high degree of accuracy. When such prediction does not occur reliably, trouble lies ahead. I believe that current assessments have moved too far away from the territory that they are supposed to cover. When individuals are assessed in situations which more closely resemble "actual working conditions," it is possible to make much better predictions about their ultimate performance. It is odd that most American schoolchildren spend hundreds of hours engaged in a single exercise, the formal test – when few if any of them will ever encounter a similar instrument once they have left school.

Instruments that are "intelligence-fair"

As already noted, most testing instruments are biased heavily in favor of two varieties of intelligence – linguistic and logical-mathematical. Individuals blessed with this particular combination are likely to do well on most kinds of formal tests, even if they are not particularly adept in the domain actually under investigation. By the same token, individuals with problems in either linguistic or logical-mathematical intelligence or both may fail at measures of other domains, just because they cannot master the particular format of most standard instruments.

The solution – easier to describe than to realize – is to devise instruments which are "intelligence-fair," which peer directly at the intelligence in operation rather than proceed via the detour of language and logical faculties. Spatial intelligence can be assessed by having an individual navigate around an unfamiliar territory;

bodily intelligence by seeing how a person learns and remembers a new dance or physical exercise; interpersonal intelligence by watching an individual handle a dispute with a sales clerk or navigate a way through a difficult committee meeting. These homely instances indicate that "intelligence-fairer" measures could be devised, though they cannot necessarily be implemented in the psychological laboratory or the testing hall.

Uses of multiple measures

Few practices are more nefarious in education than the drawing of widespread educational implications from the composite score of a single test – like the Wechsler Intelligence Scale for Children. Even intelligence tests contain subtests, and, at the very least, recommendations ought to take into account the "scatter" on these tests and the strategies for approaching particular items (Kaplan, 1983).

Attention to a range of measures designed specifically to tap different facets of the capacity in question is even more desirable. Consider, for example, the admission standards of a program for gifted children. Conservatively speaking, 75 percent of the programs in the country simply admit on the basis of IQ – a score of 129 and you are out, 131 and you are in. How unfortunate! I have no objection to IQ as one consideration, but why not attend as well to the products which a child has already fashioned, the child's goals and desire for a program, performance during a trial period with "gifted" children, and other unobtrusive measures? I often feel that enormous educational progress would be made simply if the Secretary of Education appeared in front of the television cameras not accompanied by a single one-dimensional chart, but against the backdrop of a half-dozen disparate graphic displays, each monitoring a distinctly different aspect of learning, motivation and productivity.

Sensitivity to individual differences, developmental levels, and forms of expertise

Assessment programs which fail to take into account the vast differences among individuals, developmental levels, and varieties of expertise are increasingly anachronistic. Formal testing could, in principle, be adjusted to take these documented variations into account. But it would require a suspension of some of the key assumptions of standardized testing, such as uniformity of individuals in key respects and the penchant for cost-efficient instruments.

Individual differences should also be highlighted when educating teachers and assessors. Those charged with the responsibility of assessing youngsters need to be introduced formally to such distinctions; one cannot expect teachers to arrive on their own at empirically valid taxonomies of individual differences. Such an introduction should occur in education courses or during teaching apprenticeships. Once introduced to these distinctions and given the opportunity to observe and to work with children who exhibit different profiles, these distinctions come to life for teachers.

It then becomes possible to take these differences into account in a tacit way. Good teachers, whether they teach arithmetic to second graders, piano to toddlers, or research design to graduate students, have always realized that different approaches will be effective with different kinds of students. Such sensitivities to individual differences can become part of the teacher's competence and can be drawn upon in the course of regular instruction as well as during assessment. It is also possible – and perhaps optimal – for teachers to season their own intuitive sense of individual differences with judicious occasions of assessment, crafted with the particular domain of practice in mind.

Use of intrinsically interesting and motivating materials

One of the most objectionable, though seldom remarked upon, features of formal testing is the intrinsic dullness of the materials. How often does *anyone* get excited about a test or a particular item on a test? It was probably only when, as a result of "sunshine" legislation, it became possible for test takers to challenge the answer keys used by testing organizations that discussion of individual test items ever occupied space in a publication that anyone would voluntarily read.

It does not have to be that way. A good assessment instrument can be a learning experience. But, more to the point, it is extremely desirable to have assessment occur in the context of students working on problems, projects, or products which genuinely engage them, which hold their interest and motivate them to do well. Such exercises may not be as easy to design as the standard multiple-choice entry, but they are far more likely to elicit a student's full repertoire of skills and to yield information that is useful for subsequent advice and placement.

Application of assessment for the student's benefit

An equally lamentable aspect of formal testing is the use made of scores. Individuals receive the scores, see their percentile ranks, and draw a conclusion about their scholastic, if not their overall, merit. In my own view, psychologists spend far too much time ranking individuals and not nearly enough time helping them. All assessment should be undertaken primarily to aid students. It is incumbent upon the assessor to provide feedback to the student that will be helpful at the present time – identifying areas of strength as well as weakness, giving suggestions of what to study or work on, pointing out which habits are productive and which are not, indicating what can be expected in the way of future assessments, and the like. It is especially important that some of the feedback take the form of concrete suggestions and indicate relative strengths to build upon, independent of rank within a comparable group of students.

Armed with findings about human cognition and development, and in light of these desiderata for a new approach to assessment, it should be possible to begin to design programs which are more adequate than those which exist today. Without having any grand design to create a "new alternative to formal testing," my colleagues and I at Harvard Project Zero have become engaged in a number of projects over the past several years which feature new approaches to assessment. In the following sections of this chapter I touch on our two principal efforts. I then attempt to place these efforts within a broader picture of assessment in schools and in society as a whole.

Project Spectrum assessment at the preschool level

Project Spectrum is a collaborative project undertaken by several researchers at Harvard Project Zero in conjunction with our colleague David Feldman at Tufts University and the staff and students of the Eliot-Pearson Children's School in

Medford, Massachusetts. The project was originally designed to assess the different intellectual strengths or "intelligences" in a representative group of three- and four-year-old children. As I will indicate, however, it evolved over its four-year history into a preschool curriculum, with assessment aspects folded in at various points (see Gardner, Feldman, and Krechevsky, 1998).

When we first undertook Project Spectrum, we were interested in whether the cognitive profiles of children aged three or four could be distinguished from one another. Stated differently, we were searching for early indices of the seven intelligences identified in *Frames of Mind*. It soon became apparent, however, that far more than seven intellectual capacities wanted examination; moreover, it was also clear, at least for that age group, that it is important to examine cognitive or working styles (such as attention, planfulness, ability to reflect upon a task) as well as "sheer" cognitive strengths. Thus, we monitor in our population a score of different cognitive strengths as well as over a dozen stylistic features (see Table 19.1 on the next page).

Even as we had to broaden the ensemble of skills at which we were looking, we also came to reconceptualize the nature of our assessment project. Like many others in the assessment field, we had initially assumed that one could assess "potential" or "gifts" directly, without the need for involvement in curriculum or teaching. We have come to believe, however, that this assumption is flawed. There is no "pure potential" apart from some experience in working with a domain or symbol system. As soon as one assesses, one is assessing some form of prior learning, whether or not it has been deemed relevant to the particular target domain. And so if one wants any assurance that one is assessing the domain of interest, it is advisable to present individuals with an ample set of experiences in that domain.

Let me use an example. Suppose that one is interested in assessing talent at chess. One could see how quickly the person can respond to a light flash, or one might examine the size of the person's vocabulary. It is conceivable that these two measures might correlate with chess talent, though I would not be surprised if neither did. One could also try to break down chess into its components and assess an individual's spatial imagery or logical reasoning skills or interpersonal skill in outwitting an opponent. Conceivably one or more of these measures might foretell chess wit or wisdom.

What is clear is that, in both of these examples, one is assessing something, whether or not it turns out to be related to facility in chess. One could simply give a chessboard to children and see how well they play, but in the absence of knowing the rules of chess the children are as likely to play chess as the proverbial monkeys are likely to pen the plays of Shakespeare.

This presentation of the chessboard does, however, point to the path that I would endorse. If you want to assess chess potential, you should teach your subjects the rules of the game and let them play chess with one another over a period of months. I have little doubt that the students would soon sort themselves quite reliably in terms of "chess aptitude" and that the distribution of chess talent in this population would emerge after thirty or forty games.

My colleagues and I have followed this line of thinking in surveying a variety of intellectual domains, including those which utilize linguistic, musical, and bodily intelligences. In each case our approach has been to expose students to experiences in the particular domain of interest and to observe the way in which they become engaged in that domain. The ensuing record provides a powerful indication of how much talent or potential the students exhibit in the domain of interest.

Table 19.1 Dimensions examined in Project Spectrum

Activities which sample different cognitive strengths:

Music	Production measures	Happy Birthday
—	—	New songs – up in the air
—	—	Animal song
—	Perception measures	Montessori Bells
—	—	Incidental music task
Language	Narrative measure	Storytelling board
—	Descriptive measure	Reporter task
Numbers	Counting measure	Dinosaur game
—	Calculating measure	Bus game
Science	Hypothesis-testing measure	Water table activity
—	Logical inference measure	Treasure hunt game
—	Mechanical measure	Assembly task
—	Naturalist measure	Discovery area
Visual Arts	Drawing measures	Art portfolios
—	—	Farm animal, person, imaginary figure
	3-D measure	Clay activity
Movement	Creative movement measure	Biweekly movement curriculum
—	Athletics measure	Obstacle course
Social	Social analysis measure	Classroom model
—	Social roles measure	Observations of children's interactive styles

(Table 19.1 continued)

Measures of working style:

Child is	• easily engaged /reluctant to engage in activity
	• confident /tentative
	• playful /serious
	• focused /distractible
	• persistent /frustrated by task
	• reflects on own work/impulsive
	• apt to work slowly/apt to work quickly
	• conversational/quiet
Child	• responds to visual/auditory/kinesthetic cues
	• demonstrates planful approach
	• brings personal agenda/strength to task
	• uses materials in unexpected ways
	• shows pride in accomplishment
	• shows attention to detail/is observant
	• is curious about materials
	• shows concern over "correct" answer
	• focuses on interaction with adult
	• transforms task/material

Having said a bit about the general philosophy and approach of Project Spectrum, let me indicate how it operates in practice. A Spectrum classroom is equipped with a rich set of materials. There are musical instruments, a fantasy play area, puzzles and games which stimulate numerical and logical thinking, a naturalist area in which students can examine different kinds of biological preparations, and the like, all of which are designed to engage the interest of students and to encourage them to play with these materials. There are also regular activities – like "Weekend News" – which give observers the opportunity to observe the child's oral language skills. A careful observer, watching children interact with these materials and participate in the activities over a semester or a year, gains considerable information about the profile of interests of each child and should also be able to perceive the degree of sophistication with which the materials have been plumbed.

Complementing these enriched classroom materials and activities is a set of tasks and measures which we have designed to look specifically at different intellectual spheres. These tasks are engaging to children and can be introduced in the course of a natural classroom interchange. In the area of number, for example, we feature two games. The dinosaur game pits the child against the experimenter in a race to escape from the dinosaur's mouth to his tail. The number and direction of moves is determined by two dice, one bearing numbers, the second featuring plus and minus signs. The players shake their dice and, at times, the child is allowed to "fix" his or her own or the experimenter's dice. The child's success at this game can be fully quantified, and the score provides a "user-friendly" index of the child's numerical sophistication.

For children who "ceiling" on the dinosaur game, there is the bus task. In this game the child plays the role of bus driver while the experimenter is "the boss." The bus proceeds on its route and, at each stop, some children and adults mount the bus and some depart. Every once in a while "the boss" telephones and asks the driver for a count of how many adults and children are currently on the bus. Tokens are available to aid in the counting. Children of this age do not ordinarily have written numbers or other tally systems at their disposal, but sheer involvement in this game stimulates the more able among them to develop "online" a system whereby they are better able to keep track of the comings and goings on the bus.

In other areas, analogous games and exercises have been devised (see Table 19.1). Some of these exercises feature a fully quantifiable scoring system; others call for more holistic and subjective scoring, as appropriate. In certain areas, it is not necessary to devise special exercises. For example, we evaluate talent in the visual arts by rating a collection of "spontaneous" drawings made by the child; and we evaluate social strengths through a checklist which probes how children respond to certain "charged" situations which arise in the ordinary course of events (for example, a new child coming to school, a fight breaking out, a bossy child throwing his weight around). While we wish for our scoring systems to be as precise and reliable as possible, we recognize that rough-and-ready measures can be useful as well.

The school year is divided into biweekly intervals during which a particular set of measures is taken on the children. When the classroom is an experimental one, the exercises are administered and assessed by the experimenter; in an ordinary classroom each teacher decides how to approach the targeted assessments. It is our expectation that most teachers will not wish to administer most tasks formally, nor will they generally assess them using our score sheets. Instead, they will monitor children's activities in an informal way, using our tests and sheets chiefly in instances where there is uncertainty about the child's competence. (I believe that the same philosophy should be followed in the case of standardized instruments, such as intelligence tests, which can be helpful when children appear to be "at risk.")

By the end of the year, the teachers or experimenters will have amassed a great deal of information about the intellectual strengths and working styles of all the children in the classroom. This material becomes the basis of Spectrum Reports, brief essays which describe the particular pattern exhibited by the child: strengths, weaknesses, stylistic features, and the like. This information is presented relativistically; that is, each child's strengths are described with reference to the child's other strengths and weaknesses. In the less frequent case in which the child stands out in comparison to the entire population of preschoolers, an "absolute" strength or weakness is indicated.

As important as the trajectory of strengths illustrated in the Spectrum Report is the list of recommendations which are offered. Consistent with our belief that psychologists should help rather than rank students, we include in the report concrete suggestions about what might be done at home, in school, and/or in the community, in light of a particular profile of competences and proclivities.

With its detailed assessments and its year-end reports, Project Spectrum raises a number of questions, including the advisability of such an undertaking. Is such detailed assessment really necessary and might it in some way be injurious? Recall that our initial goal was to find out whether individual differences do exist and can be documented at this early age. However, we posed this question not only out of curiosity but because of our belief that such information can be educationally beneficial. The mind of the preschooler is both flexible and trainable; thus, if difficulties can be identified at an early age, they are much more likely to be remediable. By the same token, if our scales identify unusual strengths that have somehow been missed before, the parents or teachers gain the option of seeking special help or training.

However, there is a clear risk to the early labeling by Spectrum, particularly in view of our current practice of describing a child's abilities in terms of readily recognizable adult "end states" (for example, dancer, naturalist, mediator). The danger is of premature billeting, by which an early attempt at description ends up by becoming a self-fulfilling prophecy. This risk is best mitigated by two procedures. The first is to stress to consumers of Spectrum Reports that these are descriptions at a particular historical moment; especially when children are young and active, the profile of abilities and disabilities can change dramatically from one year to the next. The second is to maintain Spectrum-like procedures each year. So long as students continue to be exposed to a variety of inviting materials and exercises, and so long as assessment is not a one-shot affair, there is every reason to believe that the cognitive profile will evolve – not remain static – and that subsequent reports will capture the new profile accurately.

Another question concerns the ultimate purpose of Project Spectrum. Is it simply an assessment program, or can it fulfill a broader and more integrative function? The explicit purpose of Project Spectrum has always been assessment, and the bulk of our efforts have been directed at the production of tasks and instruments which are reliable and which can be used by classroom teachers. For those reasons we have issued a set of handbooks (see Gardner, Feldman, and Krechevsky, 1998). Note, however, that Spectrum can constitute a valuable intervention even apart from any formal assessment. That is, the range of exercises provided and the number of intellectual spheres touched upon compare favorably with offerings in most preschool programs. Even if teachers were to decide that they were not primarily interested in the Spectrum assessment materials but simply in the games, or if they used the assessment tools only in cases of children with special problems, these materials could still fulfill an important educational goal.

Indeed, this potential for curricular as well as assessment use is consistent with our belief that the line between curriculum and assessment ought ordinarily to be blurred, particularly at the younger age levels. Moreover, it is our expectation that teachers who regularly use the Spectrum materials would develop that "sixth sense" of individual differences which would allow them to make online assessments without necessarily having to use our formal procedures. Thus the Spectrum materials can be seen as potentially shaping teacher understandings and consequently affecting teacher practices in ways that we hope will foster the development of individual potential.

In the current political climate in America, there is tremendous pressure for good programs for preschool children. Most programs either serve as extensions upward from homecare (attachment and social ties) or as extensions downward from school (pre-literate skills). Only a few programs, like the Montessori approach, seem to be fashioned with the particular strengths and needs of the "typical" preschooler in mind. Thus another potential purpose of the Spectrum materials may be to aid in the development of an innovative, developmentally sensitive, and student-centered preschool curriculum. We feel that our program speaks to the wide range of potentials in the preschool child and fosters creative growth and imaginativeness without constraining development in artificial ways. No matter how well conceived, however, our program is unlikely to be adopted if its efficacy cannot be demonstrated. The existence of an extensive battery which assesses student growth in several areas of competence can document whether a Spectrum program achieves its stated goals.

ARTS PROPEL: assessment at the middle and high school levels

For a description of this effort at assessing student learning on several art forms, please see Chapter 13.

Our assessment experiments have been designed largely as a means of improving the quality of education in America (and possibly elsewhere). The use of these instruments for purposes of selection has been a secondary consideration. In principle, of course, the materials developed for Spectrum and for ARTS PROPEL could be employed by elementary or high school teachers for placement purposes and, in the case of PROPEL process-folios, for college admissions. I am comfortable with such usages because I think that these forms of information could usefully supplement – and perhaps even replace – the more common standardized testing instruments. In addition, and not incidentally, the assessment techniques on which we are working can provide useful feedback to students, independent of their selection or non-selection. They have a valuable educational purpose in themselves.

Assessment at other ages

Our major research efforts have been devoted to Project Spectrum and ARTS PROPEL. It is certainly feasible to envision parallel assessment projects for other ages and in other subject domains. Here I would like to mention briefly a number of related assessment efforts, focusing on those in which our research group has had some involvement. I organize the discussion around the areas of assessment not explored above. Of course, the entire program of research and implementation sketched in this chapter is not comprehensive; we have, however, set down some of the major issues that must be explored further in a wide range of teaching and assessment contexts.

Early childhood

In my view there is no pragmatic reason to assess the intellectual proclivities or styles of infants or young toddlers. Children of that age have little experience with most materials used in assessment, and the results of such assessments could well be misused or overinterpreted.

For research reasons, however, it could be extremely instructive to sample a broader survey of human abilities than are tapped by standard psychological or psychometric measures. One could examine the capacities of one- and two-year-olds to habituate to (or to distinguish among) different kinds of sensory information, linguistic sounds, musical sounds, musical rhythms, abstract pictorial patterns, numerical configurations, and so on. Skill at learning various kinds of motor or sensori-motor sequences could also be assayed. While one should guard against attaching undue significance to such early cognitive markers, it would be informative to trace continuities, or the lack thereof, between such early signs and the later profile of abilities detected in Project Spectrum.

The early elementary years

The methods used with three- and four-year-olds in Project Spectrum might well be extended upward to kindergarten and to the early years of school. Providing environments for rich exploration, offering tasks with which children can become engaged, devising unobtrusive means of assessing growth, and preparing detailed Spectrum-style reports for parents are all activities which could easily be implemented at the older levels and which might well provide information of use to parents and teachers. Indeed, a chief value of the Spectrum approach is the possibility that it can be carried over from one year, or perhaps even from one quinquennium, to another.

Just as the Project Spectrum ideas could "trickle up" to the primary grades, the ARTS PROPEL approach might profitably "trickle down" to elementary school. Domain-projects, process-folios, and other kinds of reflective activities might be useful tools for teachers working with students aged eight to 12. A record of student growth extending across annual boundaries is as valuable for older children as it is for younger ones (Carini, 1987).

In Indianapolis the Key Learning Community is dedicated to the fostering of the whole spectrum of human intelligences. To this end, teachers offer regular instruction in such areas as music, dance, visual arts, computing, and Spanish, as well as the "basic" subjects of reading, math, and social studies. But what distinguishes the school as well are a number of special offerings and organizing schemes.

To begin with, each child participates in the "flow area," a rich Spectrum-like corner of the school, where youngsters can play with games and engage in activities appealing to their specific profile of intelligences and interests. Students also participate on a daily basis in small cross-age groups called "pods," in which they have the opportunity to carry out an apprenticeship in an area of special interest, ranging from architecture to astronomy to Hispanic culture. To help tie together the disparate strands of the school, there is also a school-wide theme which changes every nine weeks – initial themes have included "connections" and "changes in time and place."

Thus far, the kinds of assessment which take place in the Key School occur chiefly during the course of regular class activities. As in other elementary schools, the teachers intervene when a problem or difficulty arises. One special feature of the school, however, is the involvement of all children in an individual project during each nine-week period. These objects give the children a chance to mobilize their abilities in the service of the "school theme." Children then present, and record on videotape, the results of their project. The videotape becomes part of the archival material maintained by the school; at graduation each child receives a tape in which all of her project presentations have been recorded. These visual records should prove of use to future teachers and of considerable interest to the now grown students.

Other schools, like the Putney School in Vermont, have featured major student projects over the years; and a few selected schools, such as the Prospect School (also in Vermont), have maintained student portfolios indefinitely (Carini, 1987). There is little question that this activity has intrinsic value for the school and the students, emphasizing as it does that learning is intensive as well as extensive, and it accrues gradually over long periods of time. The portfolios at the Prospect

School also help teachers to think about student work and about the special characteristics of individual students.

Surprisingly, to my knowledge little assessment of these records themselves, or of their use by students and teachers, has taken place, probably due to the considerable expense of such assessing activities and the other competing interests of the school staffs. However, these already assembled materials provide a repository of invaluable information which could be drawn on for many purposes and which might be assessed by techniques now being developed in ARTS PROPEL. The utility of such methods of learning and documentation was demonstrated in the 1930s by the Eight Year Study, a blue-ribbon investigation undertaken to determine the efficacy of non-traditional methods of education (Aiken, 1942). I suspect that if this study were replicated today, these educational procedures would once again be vindicated.

Computer support for domain-projects

At Project Zero we have developed an additional set of domain-projects for use with computer software. According to our analysis, there is much powerful software available for use by individuals with pre-existing expertise in a domain. Just to mention a few instances, there is software which allows musicians to compose, artists and architects to draft, programmers to solve problems, and the like.

We have found that novices are typically unable to make use of this software, even if they are motivated to engage in the activities for which the software has been designed. The novices lack the prerequisite skills and concepts, while the software itself does not provide sufficient clues as to its possible uses. We have therefore devised "computer domain-projects" – sample problems and solutions which are provided as databases accompanying the software, as well as manuals which instruct the novices in how to use these problem sets to "educate themselves."

The computer domain-projects have been used only on a pilot basis, but the results are encouraging. Individuals with a moderate amount of musical knowledge and with the desire to compose music have been able to compose and "orchestrate" limericks after just a few hours at the computer terminal. The computer domain-projects provide enough support so that the novice can perform at a journeyman, if not a master, level. Similar domain-projects are being created in the areas of computer programming (aiding students in learning to use PASCAL) and social studies (allowing students to recreate and solve the problems faced by Boston immigrants in the mid-nineteenth century).

Once again, we find that an ingenious curriculum approach can engage students and bring them directly into contact with the "stuff" of a culturally valued domain. And once again, the border between curriculum and assessment becomes blurred, if not irrelevant. In the case of the computer domain-projects, there is no need for extensive separate assessment. Assessment of progress and evaluation of products can be built directly into the use of the domain-project itself. The research can therefore focus directly on the questions of which factors allow some domain-projects to operate successfully and how the domain-projects, as a class of educational vehicles, can be improved.

An individual-centered school

Earlier in this chapter I outlined the assumptions of the "uniform school," where students encounter an identical curriculum, all subjects are taught according to the same procedures, and students are evaluated according to the same formal "standard" instruments. Even though current research throws each of these assumptions into question, they still constitute an ideal in our society.

At one time, when the amount of formal knowledge to be conveyed was considerably smaller and when less was known about individual differences in human beings, the uniform school might have made sense. Nowadays, however, it is evident that no individual can learn even an infinitesimal percentage of extant knowledge; choice is inevitable and it might as well be informed, Moreover, now that we know something of the many differences among individuals, it is increasingly indefensible to treat them (to treat ourselves) as if no such differences exist.

On the basis of our foregoing analysis, it is possible to imagine a different school – one which I have termed the "individual-centered school." Such a school recognizes the need for certain basic skills and certain bodies of common knowledge for all students. At the same time, however, this school takes seriously the need for choices in education and the documentable differences among students, and strives to make these factors central to the educational process (see Chapters 6 to 9).

In implementing such a school, one would be advised to delineate three distinct roles which can be realized in a number of ways: (1) the assessment specialist, (2) the student-curriculum broker, and (3) the school-community broker.

The assessment specialist

It is the job of this individual to carry out regular and appropriate forms of assessment of the children in the school, to document these assessments, and to make the results available in appropriate form to teachers, to parents, and (eventually) to students themselves. The assessments would cover a range of materials, procedures, and instruments. Because assessments would be regular and ongoing in such a school, the descriptive reports should be constantly updated to provide current information. Of course, in cases where there are special problems, needs, or skills, a more aggressive intervention may be necessary.

Our projects have suggested a number of forms that assessment might take in an individual-centered school. But even when "formal standard assessment techniques" are utilized, the emphasis should always fall on making the results of the assessment useful to the consumers – in other words, on the formulation of concrete suggestions about what the student ought to do next.

The student-curriculum broker

The student-curriculum broker takes the results of the observations and analyses carried out by the assessment specialist and translates them into concrete suggestions for students. These suggestions include courses and electives which the student might take, given his or her particular strengths and weaknesses, as well as which versions (or sections) of a course the student ought to take, in light of his or her particular style of learning.

I am sympathetic to the idea of course electives. These choices might as well be informed ones, and the student-curriculum broker is in an excellent position to guide students to courses that they would find interesting and from which they might profit. However, I would certainly not endorse the *assignment* of students to particular electives – in fact, this would be a contradictory notion. Students should be given options and allowed to make their own choices. If students bypass courses which ought to be of interest to them or elect courses for which they apparently have little aptitude, this practice is perfectly legitimate. Indeed, many individuals – myself included – are energized by the challenge of studying areas for which they apparently have little natural talent. Obstinacy is fine so long as it has been properly put "on notice."

Of course in any school, including this "idealized" one, there will be required courses. The issue is whether these required courses need to be taught in the same manner to all students. To the extent that there are teachers who favor different teaching styles or who themselves can offer instruction in more than one way, information about these options ought to be used to guide students to the appropriate "section." Most subjects in a core curriculum can be presented in a variety of ways, and there is no reason why this should not happen.

Even where "custom-teaching" cannot take place, it is still possible to help individual students learn in the most effective way. Many educational and technological inventions can aid students who exhibit a characteristic learning style to deal with information or to carry out analyses which might otherwise cause difficulties. To take just one example, students with deficient or limited spatial imagery have often encountered difficulties with geometry and physics. Now the existence of software which can supplement imagery by providing it "on-line" should make these subjects easier and far more palatable to these students. The task of the student-curriculum broker is to increase the chances that such salubrious student–software matches can be effected.

The school-community broker

Even though it would be optimal if all educational needs could be met within the walls of each school, such comprehensive service is not feasible. Schools can do a good job in covering the traditional curriculum and in developing some of the intelligences, but it is unrealistic to expect them to meet all needs, nourish all intelligences, and to cover all subjects.

Here the school-community broker comes in. It is this person's job to survey the educational opportunities that are available in the community – apprenticeships, mentorships, clubs, professions, arts organizations, big sisters, big brothers, and so on – and to organize them in a database. Information about print and media resources ought to be incorporated as well. This information can then be made available to students, who will have the option of broadening their learning in after-school programs or, perhaps, during the school day itself. If the broker is successful, the students are more likely to develop a range of intelligences and to find an appropriate vocational and avocational niche within their community.

In truth, I do not worry about those students who are excellent in linguistic and logical pursuits. They will likely find their rewards within the school, in standard gifted programs, or in special advanced sections or honors groups. The educational challenge is to provide comparable opportunities for students who have cognitive and personal strengths that are not well addressed by the standard school curriculum.

In the past, these students "found themselves" – if they did at all! – by accident or happenstance. The crystallizing experiences which can be so crucial in helping an individual to discover a life-long vocation or avocation were rarely brought about through planning (Walters and Gardner, 1986). To my mind, the most important educational event in a student's life is the discovery of some situation or material which excites and motivates the student to make a commitment to master the materials necessary for a deeper grasp of this area. It is the job of the school-community broker to engender more frequent crystallizations in more different fields, and most especially those crystallizations that are valued in the community at large but are often invisible in the school.

The question may be raised about the advisability of promoting matches in domains which do not appear to be viable vocational options for students. Certainly, efforts should be made to locate options which are both compatible with the student's proclivities and relevant for careers. Yet, I do not feel that the danger of "useless" matches need concern us. First of all, it is better for a student to have some kind of engagement than none at all; the very feelings of competence and experience of mastering a domain may turn out to have considerable transfer value. Second, the scholastic matches that are currently valued in school do not necessarily forecast vocational success in later life; the personal intelligences may well be more important for such success. Third, it is short-sighted to try to calculate in advance just which combinations of intelligences will be valued in the future or which amalgamation can be drawn upon profitably by a specific individual. Finally, even if a match cannot point the way directly to a career choice, it can at least delineate an area in which the individual can expect to gain satisfaction of a personal or avocational sort in the future.

I have described these curricular, assessment, and educational opportunities in terms of individual roles only as a convenience. School systems can evolve comfortable means of realizing these roles, perhaps by drawing on guidance counselors or other existing personnel or by creating centralized sources of information.

Implementing these roles, however, is of little avail if the school and the surrounding community are not dedicated to education across a broad spectrum of areas and abilities. Taken in combination with a supportive educational community, these roles ought to aid in the realization of a school in which individual differences are taken seriously, cherished, fostered, and mobilized to worthwhile personal and community ends.

My description of one school of the future should lay to rest any lurking fears that I am out to abolish the role of testing and assessment in schools. If anything, the program I have laid out would call for the development of a cadre of specialists that does not now exist and that would be called on to carry out work even more pivotal than that now being carried out by psychologists, guidance counselors, and testing experts. I am not lobbying for the decimation of testing but for a broadening and a deepening of the assessment roles.

At the same time, I have no aim to minimize the role of teachers. Indeed, it is my hope that this scheme will free teachers to teach as expertly as possible in the ways that they find comfortable. This kind of education can only take place if teachers are highly professionalized and have responsibility for planning their curricula and for orchestrating their classes. The improvement of teaching conditions and the upgrading of the quality of teacher-training programs central to this enterprise are topics of signal importance in our society.

Toward the assessing society

This chapter has been an extended essay in favor of regular assessment occurring in a natural fashion throughout the educational system and across the trajectory of lifelong learning. I have reviewed a sizable body of theoretical innovations and experimental evidence, which, by and large, points up problems with standard formal testing as an exclusive mode of assessment. Many of these findings suggest that it would be more fruitful to create environments in which assessments occur naturally and to devise curricular entities, like domain-projects and process-folios, which lend themselves to assessment within the context of their production. It would be an exaggeration to say that I have called for a reintroduction of the apprentice method. Yet I do claim that we have moved too far from that mode of assessment; contemporary assessment might well be informed by some of the concepts and assumptions associated with traditional apprenticeships.

Indeed, if one considers "formal testing" and "apprentice-style assessment" as two poles of assessment, it could be said that the United States today has veered too far in the direction of formal testing without adequate consideration of the costs and limitations of an exclusive emphasis on that approach. Even outside the realm of physics, an excessive action calls for a reaction – one reason why this chapter stresses the advantages of more naturalistic, context-sensitive, and ecologically valid modes of assessment. Standard formal tests have their place – for example, in initial screening of "at-risk" populations – but users should know their limitations as well.

Some objections to the perspective introduced here can be anticipated. One is the claim that formal testing is, as advertised, objective and that I am calling for a regression to subjective forms of evaluation. I reject this characterization for two reasons. First of all, there is no reason in principle to regard the assessment of domain-projects, process-folios, or Spectrum-style measures as intrinsically less objective than other forms. Reliability can be achieved in these domains as well. The establishment of reliability has not been a focus of our pilot projects; however, the conceptual and psychometric tools exist to investigate reliability in these cases. Moreover, these assessment measures are more likely to possess "ecological" validity.

A second retort to this characterization has to do with the alleged objectivity or non-bias of standard formal tests. In a technical sense, it is true that the best of these instruments avoid the dangers of subjectivity and statistical bias. However, any kind of instrument is necessarily skewed toward one kind (or a few kinds) of individual and one (or a few) intellectual and cognitive styles. Formal tests are especially friendly to those individuals who possess a certain blend of linguistic and logical intelligences and who are comfortable in being assessed in a decontextualized setting under timed and impersonal conditions. Correlatively, such tests are biased against individuals who do not exhibit that blend of intelligences, those whose strengths show up better in sustained projects or when they are examined *in situ*.

I believe that, especially when resources are scarce, every individual ought to have the opportunity to show her or his strengths. There is no objection to a "high scorer" being able to show off a string of perfect scores to a college admissions staff; by the same token, individuals with other cognitive or stylistic strengths ought to have their day (and their lives) as well.

There are those who might be in sympathy with the line of analysis pursued here and yet would reject its implications because of considerations of cost or efficiency. According to this argument, it is simply too inefficient or expensive to mobilize a nation around more sustained forms of assessment; and so, even if formal testing is imperfect, we will have to settle for it and simply try to improve it as much as possible.

This line of argument has a surface plausibility, but I reject it as well. To be sure, formal testing is now cost effective, but it has taken millions, perhaps billions, of dollars expended over many decades to bring it to its current far-from-perfect state. Nor do I think that more money spent on current testing will improve it more than marginally.

The major obstacle I see to assessment in context is not availability of resources but rather lack of will. There is in the nation today an enormous desire to make education uniform, to treat all students in the same way, and to apply the same kinds of one-dimensional metrics to all. This trend is inappropriate on scientific grounds and distasteful on ethical grounds. The current sentiment is based in part on an understandable disaffection with some of the excesses of earlier educational experiments, but, to a disturbing degree, it is also based on a general hostility to students, teachers, and the learning process. In other countries, where the educational process is held in high regard, it has proved possible to have higher quality education without subscribing to some of the worst features of one-dimensional educational thinking and assessment.

It is not difficult to sketch out the reasons for the tentative national consensus on the need for more testing and more uniform schools. Understandable uneasiness with poor student performance in the early 1980s resulted in a general indictment of contemporary education, which was blamed for a multitude of societal sins. Government officials, especially state administrators and legislators, entered the fray. The price paid for increased financial support was simple: do more testing and more accountability based on testing. The fact that few students of education were entirely comfortable with the diagnosis or the purported cure was not relevant. After all, political officials rarely pore over the relevant literature; they almost reflexively "search for scapegoats" and call for the "quick fix."

It is unfortunate that few public officials or societal leaders have put forth an alternative point of view on these issues. If significant forces or interest groups in this country were to dedicate themselves to a different model of education, which subscribes to the assessment-and-schooling philosophy outlined here, I have every confidence that they could implement it without breaking the bank. It would be necessary for a wider gamut of individuals to "pitch in"; for college faculties to examine the process-folios that are submitted; for community members to offer mentorships, apprenticeships, or "special pods"; for parents to find out what their children are doing in school and to work with them (or at least encourage them) on their projects. These suggestions may sound revolutionary, but they are daily occurrences in excellent educational settings in the United States and abroad. Indeed, it is hard to imagine quality education in the absence of such a cooperative ambience.

To my way of thinking, the ultimate policy debate is – or at least should be – centered on competing concepts of the purposes and aims of education. As I have intimated above, the "formal standard testing" view harbors a concept of education as a collection of individual elements of information which are to be mastered and then spewed back in a decontextualized setting. On this "bucket view" it is expected that individuals who acquire a sufficient amount of such knowledge will be effective members of the society.

The "assessment view" values the development of productive and reflective skills, cultivated in long-term projects. The animating impulse seeks to bridge the gap between school activities and activities after school, with the thought that the same habits of mind and discipline can be useful in both kinds of undertakings.

Especial attention is paid to individual strengths. On this view, assessment should occur as unobtrusively as possible during the course of daily activities, and the information obtained should be furnished to gatekeepers in useful and economical form.

The "assessment view" fits comfortably with the vision of individual-centered schooling that I have outlined above. Some individuals sympathetic to a focus on assessment might still object to the individual-centered view, seeing it as an impractical or romantic view of education; they would prefer more naturalistic modes of assessment in the service of a rigorous curriculum. To these individuals I would respond, perhaps surprisingly, by unequivocally endorsing the importance of rigor. There is nothing in an "individual-centered" approach which questions rigor; indeed, in any decent apprenticeship rigor is assumed. If anything, it is the sophomoric "multiple-choice-cum-isolated-fact" mentality that sacrifices genuine rigor for superficial conformity. I fully embrace rigorous curricula in an individual-based school; I simply call for a broader menu of curricular options.

The assessment approach and the individual-centered school constitute a more noble educational vision. Both are more in keeping with American democratic and pluralistic values (Dewey, 1938). I also think that this vision is more consistent with what has been established in recent decades by scientific study of human growth and learning. Schools in the future ought to be so crafted that they are consistent with this vision. In the end, whatever the forms and the incidence of "official assessments," the actual daily learning in schools, as well as the learning stimulated long after "formal" school has been completed, should be its own reward.

Acknowledgment

Reprinted with kind permission of Springer Science and Business Media. Copyright © 1991.

CHAPTER 20

THE AGE OF INNOCENCE RECONSIDERED

Preserving the best of the progressive traditions in psychology and education

Howard Gardner, Bruce Torff, and Thomas Hatch

Olson, D.R and N. Torrance (eds), *The handbook of education and human development*. Blackwell, 28–55, 1996.

A canonical view in psychology and education at mid-century

Both the passage of time and the exigencies of argument can conspire to yield a past that appears appealingly simple. Succumbing to those pressures, one can readily compose views of the child and of education that are optimistic in tone and in harmony with one another. While scarcely going unchallenged, such views associated with an earlier time have done much to frame current discussions of the nature of childhood and the preferred course of education.

From the discipline of developmental psychology, which arose in significant measure out of a Rousseauian tradition, there emerged a view of the child as a relatively free-standing spirit, one destined to pass in the fullness of time through a series of preordained stages. Assuming only a non-abusive environment, the Piagetian child (Piaget, 1983) would first learn about the world directly through spontaneous and natural actions upon the physical world; then, acquiring a set of more complex cognitive structures in a preordained fashion, that child could perform "mental operations" of increasing abstraction and power on the representations of the world that she had constructed. Moving along parallel lines, the Eriksonian child (1963) would confront in turn a set of psychosexual and psychosocial tensions; and again, assuming a relatively supportive environment, the child would emerge as trustworthy, autonomous, competent, and a viable member of the community. While putting forth less totalistic schemes, other developmentalists subscribed to this basic linear and progressive view (Bruner, 1965; Kohlberg, 1969; Werner, 1948), and some added a distinctly social dimension to the developing child (Mead, 1934; Vygotsky, 1978).

A related intellectual tradition underlay that view of education which has been particularly celebrated among those with a deep interest in childhood. Dewey (1916, 1938) and, perhaps even more, his "progressivist" successors saw the child as the centerpiece of the educational firmament. Children learned best through their explorations of the world around them; the opportunity to pursue their own interests at their own pace was a crucial ingredient. In a manner that recalled the developmental tradition, Dewey asserted that youngsters must construct their own meanings out of daily school and community experiences.

Armed with a more determinedly social vision than that of the prototypical developmentalist, Dewey emphasized the importance of the support of other human beings, especially well-trained teachers, and the desirability of learning about the roles and practices featured in one's community. Yet he did not fundamentally question the need to educate youngsters in the major disciplines; he assumed that there would be a natural and typically unproblematic progression from more project-centered activities in the community to the more scholastic regimen of academic disciplines.

Though these developmental and educational traditions evolved in relative independence of one another, it is important to underscore their essential compatibility. Both focused on children's interests and personally initiated activities; both expected relatively smooth progress toward scholastic mastery and toward full citizenship in the community. While each perspective acknowledged that children differed from one another, both in terms of their interests and in terms of their native intellectual potential, neither dwelled on these differences; "the child" was a more natural way of speaking than "the children." And perhaps not surprisingly, both of these traditions reflected the environments in which they were wrought, ones which from today's perspective can be seen as comfortably middle class and ensconced in a democratic society, be it a Swiss canton or a New England village.

Since we shall here assume a somewhat critical stance toward this canonical view, it is important to indicate the kinds of conceptions against which these progressive views were reacting. Within child study, scholars like Piaget and Erikson were critiquing strong forms of environmentalism, on the one hand, and biological determinism on the other. Against the "blank slate" empiricists of a Lockean or Skinnerian persuasion, they were acknowledging organismic constraints on the ways in which human beings develop. Against committed hereditarians, they were underscoring the need for interactions with a specific environment, as well as the possibility that development might not proceed at a proper pace or in a proper direction. More positively, they saw the child as passing through a set of ordered but qualitatively different stages, each with its own organization and integrity. Children were not merely shorter or less intelligent adults; they embodied particular views of reality and engaged cognitive and emotional problems in ways that were appropriate for their life situation. Indeed, it was important to see the various facets of the child – cognitive, emotional, social – as working together to yield an integrated person.

"Child-centered" educators were analogously engaged in characteristic responses to previously prevalent perspectives. They opposed the view of faculty psychologists who saw the child as a collection of separate mental abilities, each to be independently fostered. They rejected with equal fervor the atomistic views of pedants who sought to present curricula as a set of isolated facts or of disparate skills. Particularly problematic from their point of view was a factory model of education, where children were marched through their paces so that they could ultimately be sorted into their proper roles in an increasingly industrialized society. Progressivists rejected the classroom in which an adult, her head filled with information, sought to transmit as much information as possible, as efficiently as possible, into the small but growing head of the child; in its place progressivists sought to configure educational spaces in which children actively explored materials, working with other youngsters in a socially supported environment, "rehearsing" for life in a democratic society.

New insights

It has been important to delineate the forces against which the psychological and pedagogical progressives were aligned; we [the authors] share the antipathy of the progressives to adultocentric views of children, on the one hand, and to a transmission view of education on the other. Indeed, we continue to cherish much of the vision that was forged earlier in the century by such scholars as Dewey and Piaget. Yet in the several decades since the canonical "innocent" view was first consolidated, an ensemble of new perspectives has arisen (or, to put it less grandly, some earlier perspectives have received fresh attention). In what follows we first list the set of ideas that have emerged during recent decades. We then introduce a new approach – the "symbol systems approach" – which purports to preserve the strengths of the canonical view while drawing upon the insights of more recent times. We examine the ways in which views of human development and approaches to education might be reformulated in the light of the symbols systems approach, yielding a new and perhaps more powerful intellectual and practical synthesis.

Among the perspectives that have emerged in the past several decades, we single out for special mention six insights that have pointed the way toward a new perspective.

1   *The existence of domains beyond universals*   The broad spectrum of work in developmental psychology has, perhaps appropriately, begun by examining those conceptions and domains that are part and parcel of the experience of every human being. Thus Piaget focused on the development of conceptions in what might be termed the Kantian realms, such as time, space, and causality. Other scholars, such as Kohlberg (1969) and Arnheim (1974), have investigated other putatively universal domains, such as morality and the arts. However, much of what is most valued within a culture is not necessarily esteemed or even shared by other cultures. That literacy which is virtually required within Western culture has until recently not been known in many indigenous cultures (Olson, 1994). And other activities, ranging from the playing of chess to the mastery of calculus to the execution of various dances and rituals, prove peculiar to specific cultures or subcultures. Thanks to the work of Feldman (1980), we are far more cognizant of those domains that, while of import in one or several cultures, are not valued universally; and we consider as well the possibly quite particularistic trajectories of development that obtain across these disparate domains.

2   *The importance of specific knowledge and expertise*   Just as there has been increasing recognition of the existence of domains that range beyond the universal, there is growing skepticism about the existence of general knowledge and general skills (Carey and Gelman, 1991; Gunnar and Maratsos, 1992; Resnick, 1989). Rather than there being "general thinking" and "general problem-solving" skills, it is now widely believed that most skills are far more task-specific, with ready transfer across contexts being questionable at best. Individuals acquire expertise by working regularly over long periods of time on tasks and skills in particular domains; and the attainment of high levels of skill in one domain is by no means a guarantor of any significant level of skill in other domains, unless they happen to be quite closely related to one another. While this line of work has some superficial resemblance to the older

faculty psychology, the particular faculties possess psychological coherence, and the processes of skill acquisition are described in ways that honor the different "domain-specific" conceptions of expertise (Ericsson and Charness, 1994).

3   *The need to explain individual differences*   The concern with difference across domains and tasks has been paralleled by an interest in the differences among individuals. While differences among individuals have always been noted in both lay and scientific circles, of course, these differences have either been viewed along one dimension (more or less intelligent) or in a very general way (individuals have different personalities, temperaments, styles, and the like). Of late, however, far more specific proposals have been put forth about differences that may be important: among those interested in stylistic issues, differences in field-dependence or independence (Witkin *et al.*, 1962); among those interested in temperament, differences in shyness or impulsivity (Kagan, 1993). Of special importance for our work is the possibility that individuals may differ in their profiles of intellectual strengths. The "theory of multiple intelligences" posits that individuals may foreground quite different sets of mental skills, having disparate strengths and weaknesses, and that these in turn are important for the ways in which individuals learn and the kinds of creative or expert achievements that they may ultimately realize (Gardner, 1983, 1993c, and Chapters 6–9).

4   *The existence of potent, enduring misconceptions*   Part of Piaget's (1929) enduring legacy was his demonstration that young children often exhibit quite distinctive conceptions of the world, including ones that are poignantly animistic, artificial, or otherwise egocentric. Because Piaget was concerned primarily with universal domains, he was able to document the spontaneous disappearance of these misconceptions. Recent work on the acquisition of disciplinary expertise has established an unsettling phenomenon. Put succinctly, except for experts, most individuals continue to adhere to early misconceptions, even in the face of considerable tutelage and counter-evidence (Gardner, 1991c). Thus, even college physics students often retain Aristotelian notions of force and agency, just as advanced students in the humanities and social sciences continue to adhere to the most simplistic forms of stereotypical thinking. The pedagogical moves needed to dissolve these misconceptions and to place in their stead more well-grounded, complex, and comprehensive views, turn out to be quite demanding (see Chapters 16–18).

5   *The critical role of contextual and mediated experiences*   Every behavioral and cognitive scientist at least pays lip service to the importance of the surrounding context. However, in the progressive developmental tradition, such contexts were discussed only in the broadest terms, because universal properties were of primary interest; because differences across contexts were thought to be (and perhaps were at the time) of lesser consequence; and because there did not exist a conceptual apparatus for analyzing contextual influences in any detail or with any precision. Stimulated by the work of Vygotsky and other contextualists, researchers have now provided convincing documentation that the society into which one is born, the styles and values of the family in which one lives, the procedures of the cultural and educational institutions of one's community, and perhaps especially nowadays the messages transmitted by the dominant media exert an enormous influence on the kind of person that each child becomes (Bruner, 1990; Collier, 1994; Geertz, 1983; Heath,

1983; Rogoff, 1990). To be sure, certain universal cognitive and emotional milestones may differ little across contexts. But once one begins to attend to the values held by individuals, the ways in which such individuals organize, reflect upon, and symbolize their experiences, and the manner in which individuals interact with others, the pervasive role played by contextual and mediated factors cannot be ignored.

6   *The application of standards in the judgment of work*   Midst the welter of contextual factors and agents that surround every developing human being, one strand deserves to be singled out for separate mention. We refer here to those individuals and institutions – sometimes called "the field" (Csikszentmihalyi, 1988) – that render judgments about the acceptability and quality of human work. Every culture transmits explicit and implicit signals about the products and behaviors that it values, and these values permeate schools and other educational and cultural institutions. But within these institutions there are specific individuals – ranging from master teachers to admissions officers to prize-givers to encyclopedia writers – who exert massive influence on who and what gets recognized. Indeed, the set of standards and values beheld by the next generation is determined largely by the actions of members of the field in the present generation. A scholarly handbook represents an effort to control the signals or "memes" that will be available for digestion by the next generation of researchers and educators.

These six insights, along with others that could have been mentioned, amount to the legacy which a new generation of workers must encounter, master, and evaluate. To use a Piagetian analogy, it is possible to assimilate these lines of work to an existing educational or psychological framework. However, it is also possible to use these fresh insights as the basis for creating a new synthesis, one which may be better suited for the research and practical issues of today and tomorrow.

The symbol systems approach

We introduce here an approach to the study of human development that grows out of the canonical tradition sketched above, but which, in our view, is better able to make use of the new lines of investigation and better suited to constructing an educational approach that is valid for our times. We term our approach the "symbol systems" approach, and, without making undue claims for its originality, we set forth here its basic assumptions and implications.

For at least a century it has been recognized that a distinctive property – perhaps *the* distinctive property – of human beings has been the species' capacity to employ various kinds of symbol systems: physical or notional elements that refer to, denote, express, or otherwise convey various kinds of information, various strands of meaning. Initially, the interest of scholars centered around the symbols of language and of logic – those coherent sets of systems that make possible everyday communication as well as the mastery of the crucial domains of mathematics and the sciences. But since the seminal writings of Cassirer (1957), Langer (1942), and Goodman (1968), the existence of other kinds of symbol systems has also been recognized. While artistic symbol systems may lack the precision and unambiguity of more conventional symbol systems, their capacities to create and transmit powerful and otherwise inexpressible meanings is now appreciated within the scholarly community. Moreover, scholars have become attuned not only to the syntactic and semantic properties of symbol systems but also to their uses – their pragmatics; and they have come to note both the potential of symbol systems to be combined with one another and the capacities of human beings to create new personal or even public symbol systems (Feldman, 1980; Gardner and Nemirovsky, 1991; and Chapters 3, 6, 7).

To mention symbol systems to developmental psychologists is to invoke a widely acknowledged phenomenon. Practitioners of different strands all recognize the crucial milestone in the life of the child when that individual becomes able to capture and convey meanings not only through direct physical contact or through personal regard but through such mediated vehicles as words, pictures, numbers, and the like.

So much work has been done of late on the nature of symbolization in general, and on the ontogenesis and development of symbolization in particular domains, that one could virtually rewrite developmental psychology – or at least cognitive developmental psychology – in terms of the mastery of symbolic systems. And yet, strangely, the crucial nature of symbol systems, and their implications for how we think about children, development, and education, have not been sufficiently pondered.

A focus on symbolization makes profound sense from both a substantive and an analytic point of view. There is a sense in which one can speak of the infant as pre-symbolic: both her interactions with the physical world and her relations with the world of other human beings occur primarily in terms of direct, unmediated contact, using mechanisms that have presumably been programmed into the species. (This statement is neutral with respect to the issue of the forms of mental representations or "mentalese" used by the infant [cf. Mandler, 1983].) By the end of the first year of life, however, overtly symbolic processes begin to come to the fore, and they remain prevalent for the remainder of life. Some of these forms of meaning-making are distinctly personal. Every child, every family develops its own forms of signaling and symbolizing (Bruner, 1990). But the vast majority of symbolic forms are public, reflecting modes of meaning-making that have evolved over many centuries within and across cultures and that all children must gradually internalize (Vygotsky, 1978).

Until the age of five or so, assuming a sufficiently rich environment, the development of competence within symbolic systems occurs without the necessity for much direct instruction or crafted mediation. Children are so constructed as species members that they readily pick up the various languages that are expressed around them, and also begin to use them productively and fluently (Heath, 1983). Researchers differ on the extent to which they endorse a single, comprehensive story of symbolization – a so-called "semiotic track" – as opposed to an account that invokes instructive and telling differences in the trajectories of different symbolic competences (Karmiloff-Smith, 1992). (Our own view is that the developmental paths are quite different in matters of syntax but have stronger parallels in their semantic and pragmatic dimensions – cf. Gardner and Wolf, 1983). But whether one is a unitarian or a pluralist, the increasing domination by symbolic codes during the course of early childhood is difficult to dispute (Bates, 1976; Bruner *et al.*, 1966; Olson, 1994; Mandler, 1983; Werner and Kaplan, 1963).

Symbolic development continues throughout childhood but takes on different colors after the first quinquennium of life, and particularly so in a literate culture. Education in the use of the most important symbol systems comes to take place in more formal settings – in apprenticeships, in craft-learning, in religious training, and, of course, in those institutions called schools (Scribner and Cole, 1973). Some education consists in a refinement of the first-order symbol systems. But literate cultures are defined by their employment of second-order symbol systems – notations/marks that themselves refer to first-order symbolic codes. And in the reaches of higher education, ever more subtle and higher-order symbol systems come to be used, a phenomenon exemplified by complex mathematical and computational systems.

Until this point, we have ignored an important ambiguity in the use of our term "symbol systems." In fact the term has two distinct meanings and disciplinary histories. Within the area of philosophy, and in such allied disciplines as semiotics and linguistics, a symbol system consists of a publicly examinable set of marks, whose syntax and semantics can be identified and dissected by trained analysts. Codes ranging from written language to dance notation to scientific diagrams all function as *external* symbol systems (Eco, 1976; Goodman, 1968). Within psychology and various cognitively oriented disciplines, *symbol systems* are thought of primarily in *internal terms* – as cognitive representations in some kind of mentalese or language of thought (Fodor, 1975; Gardner, 1985a; Newell, 1980). Fierce debate obtains about the exact nature and specificity of this internal symbolic representation, but that there exists some kind of mental code is the defining assumption of cognitive science (except, one must note, in its recent, parallel-distributed guise – Rumelhart and McClelland, 1986; Smolensky, 1989).

In noting the internal/external contrast in any discussion of symbol systems, we segue to a discussion of the analytic role that can be assumed by a symbol systems perspective. Academic disciplines play an important, indeed indispensable, role in our inquiries and in our institutional life. Yet few would question the assertion that many important issues do not respect disciplinary boundaries and that a key goal of research is to forge appropriate connections among disciplinary perspectives.

It is here, we claim, that a symbol systems approach exhibits special virtues. Any thorough understanding of the mind of the child and the process of education must span the gamut from human biological and evolutionary heritage, on the one hand, to the operation of human cultural institutions and practices, on the other. Yet the distance between genes and gods is simply too great to be casually bridged.

Consider, however, the role that can be played in such disciplinary conversation by the analytic construct of "symbol systems." As a species, human beings are programmed in their genes and equipped in their nervous systems to become symbol-using creatures. Rather than positing a single general cognitive capacity, however, we find it more useful to think of the nervous system as congenial to the development of a number of different cognitive systems that process different kinds of information; we term these systems "multiple intelligences" (see Chapters 6 and 8).

The multiple intelligences commence as a set of uncommitted neurobiological potentials. They become crystallized and mobilized by the communication that takes place among human beings and, especially, by the systems of meaning-making that already exist in a given culture (Bruner, 1990). It is the existence of spoken language, sung music, and communal number systems, respectively, that convert linguistic, musical, and numerical potentials into discretely operating and interacting intelligences. Here the encounter of brain with sounds, sights, or marks in the world brings about a dialectic between external symbol systems – present for all to behold – and internal symbol systems – the particular variants of mentalese that allow individuals to participate in, make use of, and even come to revise the evolved symbol systems of their cultures.

One may ponder, from an anthropomorphic perspective, the following assertion: the functioning culture must ensure that it continues to exist – the survival of memes proves to be as important for the culture as the survival of genes is for the species. The culture cannot observe genes, brains, or even intelligences, but it can observe the presence and the use of external symbols. And indeed, the culture determines the extent of its survival by creating institutions which monitor whether, to what extent, and how appropriately symbol systems are being learned, absorbed, utilized, and transformed by the younger members of the society. Put more concretely, responsible adults note the appearance (or non-appearance) in growing children of the myths, adages, rituals, art works, scientific practices, and philosophical systems of the community.

Here, then, we may begin to see the powerful analytical role that can be played by symbol systems in any comprehensive human science. Put directly, symbol systems serve as an indispensable *tertium quid* for the analyst – a safe, respected, and hallowed "middle ground" between the genes and the gods. To look at it schematically, consider the location of symbolic systems within the continuum of the human sciences:

GENES	BRAIN	INTERNAL SYMBOL SYSTEMS	EXTERNAL SYMBOL SYSTEMS	CULTURAL ROLES, INSTITUTIONS, FIELD
		(mental representations in one or more codes)	(external marks, patterns, sets of behaviors)	

But how does this symbol systems approach unfold in a concrete fashion, spanning the gamut from early biological predispositions to the preservation and transmission of culture, typically through a formal or informal educational system?

In what follows we examine in some detail the application of the symbol systems approach in two domains – that of musical cognition and that of spatial cognition. In each case we begin by noting the kinds of adult end states which competent practitioners within a culture might expect to attain. We then trace specimen developmental courses within those domains, taking into account the biological predispositions, the cultural messages, and the ways in which initial apprehensions of the domain may prove insufficient to permit the smooth attainment of expertise. The purpose of these surveys is to indicate the complex trajectory that must be followed for the realization of valued forms of competence, and, in the process, to suggest that a symbol systems approach may obviate some of the limitations of earlier unabashedly "progressivist" tacks in the disciplines of developmental psychology and education. We turn in the final section to a more direct concern with pedagogical issues.

Musical cognition

In Western society, the course of musical development results in a number of end states. To begin with, individuals become competent to participate in the surrounding music culture; most if not all people develop the ability, for example, to tackle perceptual tasks like distinguishing musical styles (e.g., jazz vs. rock) and to render a reasonable vocal version of "Happy Birthday." The more widely heralded end states of musical cognition are, however, in the professional realm – mastery of one of the musical disciplines, which include performance, composition, musicology, and music theory. Professional musicians demonstrate a set of rudimentary skills and literacies (e.g., ear training, notation reading) as well as elements specific to particular disciplines (e.g., instrumental technique).

Designed to encourage individuals toward these end states, music educational practices are based, often implicitly, on a particular "folk psychology" and "talk pedagogy" of the musical mind. In Western society, the predominant "folk pedagogy" advances a relatively simple model of musical achievement: inborn talent revealed through years of practice. The "talent model" predicts that the individual, given the appropriate genetic gifts and sufficient instruction/practice, will enjoy unproblematic accrual of musical skill.

Below we suggest that the view of a smooth path to musical mastery may be unduly optimistic. By looking at music from the vantage point of symbol systems, we see that different representations of music may conflict with one another, but that particular steps can be taken to address the resulting problems. In order to make this argument, we will briefly summarize the symbol systems approach to music and then discuss its educational implications.

The claim of universal and innate capacities for musical symbolization is supported by three lines of research (Gardner, 1983). First, nearly all children reveal remarkable vocal skill early in life. After a period of melodic and intonational as well as phonological experimentation, children begin at the age of about a year and a half to engage in "spontaneous song" – individual explorations relatively untouched by environmental input. Second, infants are able to make impressive intonational discriminations: by the age of one, and perhaps earlier, children can match pitch at better than chance rates and are also capable of imitating intonational patterns (Kessen, Levine, and Peindich, 1978). Third, studies of prodigies (e.g., Feldman, 1986) and "savants" with severe learning deficits (e.g., Viscott, 1970) document advanced performances not easily attributable to practice or training alone.

Consistent with views of a "modular" mind, other evidence suggests that musical intelligence is largely autonomous – distinct from other intellectual competences, most notably language. Studies of music perception provide evidence that the mechanisms by which pitch is apprehended are different from the mechanisms that process language (Aiello, 1994; Deutsch, 1975, 1982). Moreover, neuropsychological research employing brain-imaging techniques (e.g., Sergent, 1993) and studies of individuals with brain damage (e.g., Basso and Capitani, 1985; McFarland and Fortin, 1982) suggest "functional autonomy of mental processes inherent in verbal and musical communication and a structural independence of their neurological substrates" (Sergent, 1993, p. 168).

Vast individual differences in musical behavior from the earliest years of life suggest that musical intelligence has high heritability (Gardner, 1982a; Torff and Winner, 1994; Piechowski, 1993). Biologically based "talent" *is* a factor in musical achievement, but, as we shall see, cultural and training considerations play an indispensable role as well.

Exposed regularly to recorded music and the singing of adults, the young child in the West is immersed in song. This exposure provides the catalyst for several years of musical development that occurs without much formal instruction – development that finds the child increasingly in tune with the particular musical symbol systems embraced by the surrounding culture.

At about the age of 2½, the child begins to exhibit more explicit and extended awareness of tunes sung by others (Gardner, 1982a). The child attempts to reproduce familiar nursery rhymes, initially by matching the rhythmic structure, later by following the contour of the melody, and finally by singing discrete pitches (Davidson, 1994). As "learned song" comes to dominate, "spontaneous song" becomes less frequent and eventually all but disappears.

Picking up expressive as well as contextual meanings from the world around her, the child acquires the symbolic forms of the ambient music culture. One example is the linkage of harmonies and moods; in the course of everyday life in Western culture, the child comes to appreciate that major tonalities symbolize happiness while minor tonalities convey sadness. Another example connects music to situations: one tune denotes the onset of *Sesame Street*, another a birthday party or a religious ceremony.

This story of spontaneous musical development draws to a close when the child reaches school age, when everyday immersion in the music culture appears to lose its power to catalyze further. At least in Western culture, there is little evidence to suggest that, in the absence of instruction, musical development continues beyond the age of seven or so (Gardner, 1973a; Winner, 1982). Thus, musical intelligence demonstrates the same kind of developmental plateau reached by the "five-year-old mind" in other domains (Gardner, 1991c).

The result is a musical mind which is at once powerful and limited. Competent to participate as consumers in a music culture, musically untrained individuals demonstrate impressive abilities on tests of perception (Dowling, 1994; Dowling and Harwood, 1986; Krumhansl, 1990), production (Sloboda, 1994; Swanwick and Tillman, 1986), and representation (Bamberger, 1991; Davidson and Scripp, 1988). At the same time, marked limitations are also evident. First, stereotypes may be forged. For example, research indicates that college students value poems with regular meter, rhyme, and an upbeat tone – restrictions disciplinary experts do not embrace (Richards, 1929). As children are typically oriented toward the lyric content of songs and to songs that honor a canonical form (Gardner, 1982a; Gardner, 1973b), similar stereotypical predilections seem to prevail in music. Second, misconceptions may emerge, such as the notion that songs must begin and end on the same note (Davidson, Scripp, and Welsh, 1988). Finally, should instruction commence, conflicts may emerge between intuitive and disciplinary conceptions of music.

Disciplinary expertise and instruction in music

In music classes and apprenticeships, the child confronts the concepts and moves of the discipline and becomes more deeply enmeshed in symbols and symbol systems of the music of her culture. To begin with, first-order symbol systems are elaborated. For example, in typical apprenticeship settings in music performance, coaching of performances yields understanding of more subtle shades of expression or of programmatic aspects of compositions (Davidson, 1989). In addition, second-order symbols come into play. For example, linguistic symbols are seen in performance directives (e.g., "*legato*") and metaphor (e.g., "like a butterfly"). Finally, notation systems are used in "second-order" musical cultures (as opposed to "traditional" cultures and Western subcultures such as blues and rock).

Instruction brings the symbol systems of the discipline into contact with the intuitive musical mind. In some instances, the result is a smooth path to disciplinary expertise marked by improved performance/composition, perceptual acuity, and reflective skills. In other cases, however, the transition proves more problematic.

In a revealing line of work, Bamberger (1991, 1994) reports a conflict between intuitive "figural" understandings embedded in particular contexts and "formal" systems such as music notation. Trained and untrained subjects were asked to create an invented notation of the rhythmic pattern of "one, two, pick up shoes, three, four, shut the door." This pattern features two claps (grouping A) followed by three claps (grouping B), followed by a silence (a "rest") that is as long as the time between the two claps in grouping A or between the first and third claps in grouping B.

The untrained subjects typically created notations that group the claps appropriately but ignore the length of the rests:

.. ..

A person attempting to "read" this notation would reproduce groupings of two and three but would fail to reproduce the rests in a consistent fashion. In contrast, trained subjects follow metrical patterns, recognizing how much time is taken by both the pulses and rests:

. / . / . . / . / . / . / . . / .

This rendering is literally correct. However, when asked to perform the pattern itself, the trained subjects may fail to re-create the feeling of rhythmic grouping ("phrasing") that is highlighted in the naive notations and performances. Crafting a notation that is metrically accurate but fails to capture the phrasing, the trained subjects produced a "correct-answer compromise" rather than a fully appropriate and comprehensive notation. In Bamberger's terms, "formal" knowledge (the notation system) overwhelmed the intuitive "figural" knowledge of the pattern. While the expert musician is not limited to either the figural or formal interpretation, Bamberger argues, students encounter difficulty matching intuitive knowledge of "how the song goes" to its notation. The culture's formal symbol system clashes with intuitive musical competence.

In a vein similar to Bamberger's work, Davidson, Scripp, and Welsh (1988) report that students demonstrate a conflict between perceptual knowledge and conceptual knowledge in a notation task. Attempting to notate the song "Happy Birthday" using the standard notation system of Western music, the students produced an inaccurate notation. They opted to alter the key of the final phrase of the song, based on the misconception that songs must begin and end on the same note. Asked to sing from their notations, the students reproduced the canonical version of the song, while detecting no errors in their notations. In their notations, the students disregarded accurate perceptual knowledge of the song in favor of misconceived conceptual knowledge. In their singing, they drew on the perceptual knowledge and overlooked the inaccuracy in their notations. According to the authors, the students experience a disjunction between perceptual knowledge of music and the formalism of music notation.

The foregoing examples point up tensions that may exist between different forms of representation or understanding in music. Many of these persist despite instruction. The progressive movement encouraged music educators to downplay direct transmission of knowledge (e.g., readings, lectures) about music in favor of experience-based learning. Accordingly, there is a tendency in music education to place overwhelming emphasis on performance – the immediately audible aspect of musicianship. Often resulting in impressive but essentially unanalyzed performances, typical pedagogy restricts student access to the full range of skills required of disciplinary experts and allows misconceptions to remain unconfronted.

The symbol systems approach reveals how an appropriate pedagogy can result in *understanding* that goes beyond intuition by fostering the skills exemplified by expert musicians. To begin to sketch such a music pedagogy (while making no undue claims that our suggestions are original or comprehensive), we seek to combine the best of the traditional apprenticeship model with emerging ideas about teaching for understanding in music.

Around the world, musicians cut their teeth by apprenticing to a master performer for an extended period. Affording the learner sustained interaction with the disciplinary conventions (e.g., moves, techniques, concepts, values, categories, aesthetics) used by expert musicians, the apprenticeship *contextualizes* learning in several important respects.

To begin with, the teacher is often an active musician who may perform or compose in the lessons. In addition, the learner is often charged to analyze recordings and performances. *Modeling* makes visible to the student the procedures and rules that are immediate and overt as well as values and goals that are distant and covert. However, it is not enough that the student is simply exposed to models; she must also have ample opportunity to imitate. Thus, the apprenticeship affords the learner the opportunity to engage in *successive approximation* – a two-step sequence in which the learner consults the model and attempts to render a performance similar to the model. As the cycle is repeated, the learner edges closer to the modeled behaviors. In addition, the student benefits from *coaching* – personalized feedback (verbal and musical) adapted to the individual learner by the teacher. Often taking the form of comments and demonstrations concerning the student's performance, coaching points up strengths in the learner's performance as well as addressing what to improve and how to improve it.

Beneficial as the traditional apprenticeship may be, the existence of enduring misconceptions points up the need for additional steps designed to teach for genuine understanding in music. Given the all-too-common overemphasis on performance in contemporary pedagogies, it is essential to specify "Understanding Goals" and "Performances of Understanding" that encourage students to encounter and rethink intuitive conceptions about music (see Chapters 17–18). This is the procedure that we followed in ARTS PROPEL (see Chapter 13) and other educational experiments, combining *production* (performance or composition), *perception* (skills of aural discrimination), and *reflection* (focusing critical judgment on perception or production).

Combining the strengths of the traditional apprenticeship model with proactive steps to foster understanding in music, our approach encourages students to encounter disciplinary conventions and confront misleading intuitive conceptions about music, with the goal of moving students toward the genuine understanding epitomized by master musicians.

Spatial cognition

In talking about the art works of young children, Picasso exclaimed, "When I was their age I could draw like Raphael, but it has taken me a whole lifetime to learn to draw like them" (Gardner, 1993a p. 145). Picasso's remark reinforces the popular mythology surrounding artists by leaving the impression that artistic ability does not have to be developed – it has to be unleashed. In such a conception there seems to be little room for education. A similar point of view seems to apply to many other aspects of spatial development. We are more familiar with the seemingly spontaneous demonstrations of chess prodigies than with the years of preliminary drill and match that lead to championships. More mundane spatial abilities, like those evident in the use of maps, are assumed to develop relatively easily and without explicit instruction.

The abilities and understandings that are central to the spatial domain certainly originate in tendencies that have become a part of our genetic endowment. However, in order to become a painter or a geographer, or to achieve any one of a number of the "end states" of spatial development, such predispositions are not sufficient. To become a geographer, one has to overcome a natural tendency to assume an iconic relationship between maps and the aspects of the world they represent. The geographer has to get beyond the surface features – how things look – and come to understand why they look that way. Such an understanding involves mastering the symbols and symbolic relationships that have developed in the discipline. It means that one can do more than recite place names or recall the routes between them, instead demonstrating mastery in such "Performances of Understanding" as reading novel maps and creating new geographical representations.

Similarly, becoming an expert visual artist involves mastering such cultural conventions as perspective drawing. Achievement also depends on the development of the understandings of how color, form, and composition can be used to create aesthetic effects. Further, artists have to go beyond the literal, realistic representations that most people can learn to create; they have to demonstrate their understandings in the way they address and challenge the cultural conventions that obtain in their time. In each case, the developmental course includes some useful predispositions, substantial obstacles, and the possibility of ultimate mastery of the representations, practices, and roles of the spatial domain.

A wide variety of research suggests a strong biological component to such spatial abilities as learning new routes, forming and manipulating mental images, and creating spatial representations. For example, studies have shown that a wide variety of animals and insects – including honey bees, ants and rats – have innate tendencies that help them to carry out such specialized spatial functions as route-finding (Cheng, 1986; Dyer and Gould, 1983; Gallistel *et al.*, 1991; Margules and Gallistel, 1988).

Evidence is not limited to non-human species, however. In fact the concordance of findings in research with animals and humans is among the most powerful evidence for the biological basis for spatial abilities. Such investigations have shown that specific parts of the brain (especially regions of the right hemisphere) of both humans and monkeys are "prepared" to carry out particular spatial functions (Stiles-Davis, 1988). In addition, there is extensive evidence of a link between sex differences in human performances on spatial tasks and biological factors like hormone levels and rates of physical maturation (Harris, 1981; Witelson and Swallow, 1988). In a task in which subjects have to find their way through a maze, Bever (1992) has even shown analogous sex differences in the performances of humans and rats. Females of both species rely more heavily on landmarks, while males focus more on the configuration of space.

This ecological endowment enables infants to begin their lives ready to explore and exploit the spatial world. As they grow older, however, and encounter the representations and knowledge that have evolved in the spatial domain, young children experience a variety of situations that evolution has failed to anticipate. Maps and perspective drawing are two examples of the challenges that symbolic representations provide for development.

Maps are not simply repositories of place names or references for distant journeys. They are notations that represent the knowledge that has accrued over hundreds of years about relationships that obtain over wide spaces. Although young children – both sighted and blind – can use some simple maps (Landau, 1988; Landau *et al.*, 1984), mastery of these means of representation involves a variety of achievements. Among the most important is the realization that there is not a direct or iconic relationship between maps and their referents (Bluestein and Acredolo, 1979; Gregg and Leinhardt, 1994; Liben and Downs, 1991). In the absence of such an understanding, children exhibit a host of misconceptions. Common misconceptions include the belief that islands float on top of the ocean, and that lines separating states and countries are marked on the earth (Gregg and Leinhardt, 1994; Hewes, 1982). Even as they learn the conventional properties of graphic representations, children overgeneralize, assuming that grass in an aerial photograph must be at the bottom of the photograph while the sky must be at the top.

Unfortunately, human biological heritage provides no more reliable preparation for the challenges that visual artists must surmount. The accurate depiction of perspective is a particularly problematic step in the development of spatial abilities. Not until the Renaissance did human beings figure out how to represent objects and scenes from a unitary viewpoint. Even now that this spatial problem has been solved, it takes most children considerable time before they can accomplish this feat.

In young children's drawings, items that should be on top of one another are likely to be drawn as if they are floating on the page. Only about the age of nine do most children attempt to draw in three dimensions, and not until the teenage years are most able to render perspective somewhat properly in their art works (Willats, 1977). The overall development of children's cognitive abilities in a scholastic environment certainly plays a part in this achievement, but it is likely that some exposure to the art works and conventional solutions evolved in our culture is a necessary part of this development as well (Gombrich, 1960; Goodman, 1968).

Education and achievement in the spatial domain

Even though most people do manage to gain some proficiency in reading maps and drawing in perspective, few of us achieve the kinds of understandings that are required to become expert geographers or artists. Without some informal or formal educational experiences, misconceptions and rote performances are likely to persist.

While most adults have learned that maps are not iconic representations, they continue to manifest a variety of incorrect assumptions about our world and its representation. At least in part, such misconceptions in adults arise from our "common sense" of the way the world should look and a tendency to use simple heuristics to aid in perception and recall (Gregg and Leinhardt, 1994). Thus, adults who know that the Atlantic Ocean is east of the Americas and the Pacific to the west, incorrectly assume that the Atlantic entrance into the Panama canal is further east than the Pacific entrance (Stevens and Coupe, 1978). Similarly, many adults, expecting some geographical symmetry, believe that North America is situated directly over South America (Tversky, 1981). Even with a map in front of them, the common association of the shape of Italy with a boot leads people to create representations that are somewhat distorted and gloss over important details (Rock, 1974). Some errors also result from a tendency to use maps without a clear understanding of how they are constructed. For example, those who do not understand that reducing three dimensions to two involves some distortions fail to recognize that Greenland – which appears quite large on most maps – is actually the size of Saudi Arabia (Liben and Downs, 1991).

Such misconceptions are undoubtedly promoted by conventional approaches to geography in which maps are simply reference tools used to teach place names and locations. Such instruction fails to get at the underlying spatial relationships or the sophisticated reasoning that goes into their representation. In contrast, in an exemplary third-grade geography lesson, a teacher structures her lesson by addressing three generative questions – "Where?"; "Why there?"; "So what?" (White with Rumsey, 1993). In the process, her students get beyond rote knowledge and gain an understanding of what connects the places on a map. Such an activity provides a key to the robust knowledge that will enable students to demonstrate their understanding by carrying out such tasks as constructing their own maps and interpreting representations of unfamiliar areas.

Geography in an Urban Age (GUA) (Association of American Geographers, 1965, 1979), a curriculum developed in the late 1960s, provides an example of how a deeper understanding of maps and geography can be achieved (Gregg and Leinhardt, 1994). The GUA curriculum engages students in case studies of real problems. In the process, students are asked to consider a variety of questions, including: Where is it? Where is it in relation to others of its kind? How did it get there? What factors influence growth in that place? What difference does it make to me, to society, that it is there? What else is there, too? How are these things related to each other in place? How is it connected to things in other places? In pursuing such questions, students encounter a reason for using maps. They are required to carry out performances of their understanding of spatial relationships by finding places, relating them, and representing them.

In the visual arts, many people learn to draw fairly realistic representations that respect rules of perspective, color, and composition. This achievement begins to come about in middle childhood, when children grapple with the cultural conventions of the discipline. It is at about this time that children become preoccupied with accuracy and with making their representations "realistic" (Gardner, 1982a; Winner, 1982). This "literal stage" is apparent across domains as children become concerned with conforming to the standards and rules of the dominant culture.

Many adolescents and adults never get beyond the literal stage, nor are they likely to get beyond a reliance on simple forms or conventional strategies in using perspective. Those who do become artists have to master well-known techniques as well as invent new ones of their own. They have to hone their understanding of color and form in studies and sketches, constantly assessing the results until desired effects are achieved.

As a young child, Picasso showed considerable spatial skills, as he drew constantly, noticed visual details and arrangements, and recalled almost every live and painted scene that he had ever witnessed (Gardner, 1993a). But just like music prodigies who must transcend manual virtuosity, Picasso had to develop more than technical skills. Formal education in art school was a part of Picasso's education, but for the most part he learned in more informal ways. In visits to museums, he explored the works of earlier masters such as Goya and Velázquez; in his journals, he tried out new ideas and reflected on them; in countless sketches and studies for paintings like *Les Demoiselles d'Avignon*, Picasso played with different shapes, colors, and placements in order to achieve particular aesthetic effects. In collaboration with Georges Braque, he tested traditional modes of representation. Through these experiences Picasso confronted the conventions of the discipline and came to deeper understandings of how to represent the properties of objects in two dimensions and how to bring out the psyche of his subjects and the emotions underlying scenes of all varieties.

Beyond such "informal" learning experiences, many artists have benefited from apprenticeships similar to those that musicians may undertake. Often apprentices in the visual arts join the studio of an accomplished master and begin their training simply through observation. As they stretch canvases, mix paints, or carry out other simple tasks, they have the opportunity to see how master artists approach the activity of painting or drawing, how they grapple with the conventions of the discipline, and the moves they make in revising their work. At the same time, the apprentice may also have the opportunity to imitate the master by making copies, filling in sketches, or creating works according to instructions. While it is difficult to know how much coaching actually goes on in the artist's studio, there is ample opportunity for the apprentice to secure some guidance from the master. In addition, the assignment of work of gradually increasing complexity by the master is an act of coaching that scaffolds the apprentice's growing spatial abilities.

Both alone and in collaboration with peers and mentors, artists and geographers develop their abilities as they grapple with the problems and conventions of their discipline. One could argue that our biological heritage prepares humans to draw and even to read simple maps. But in our culture artists have to go beyond their initial perceptions of what looks "good" and overcome an unreflective affinity for literal representation in order to master the moves and strategies that contribute to aesthetic achievements. Similarly, geographers have to see beneath the surface similarities that lead to misconceptions and learn how to interpret and use the notations and second-order symbols that represent abstract spatial relationships. Without formal and informal educational experiences that guide young artists and geographers through their disciplines and the symbol systems they encompass, any "natural" talents are likely to remain unrealized.

The view from education

From one vantage point it has been argued that scientific findings – including ones from psychology – are not strictly relevant to educational practice (Egan, 1992). Nearly every social scientific finding or perspective harbors within it a number of possible educational implications, not all of which are necessarily consistent with one another. Moreover, it is hardly the case that educational practitioners need to peruse scientific journals, avoiding the classroom until they have digested the latest finding from the theorist's study or the experimentalist's laboratory. Plato's Academy introduced quite powerful educational notions without any "research base"; neither Locke nor Rousseau (the ancestors of current educational practice) ever conducted a formal experiment; and most educators rely as much on careful observation of their own (and others') practices as on lectures or monographs.

Yet, even if there is not (and perhaps should not be) a unidirectional path from psychological insights to educational practice, representatives of both lines of work do rightfully participate in constant conversations about principles and practices. Nearly all of the psychologists mentioned above have been interested in educational issues; and few of the educators of influence in this century have proceeded in ignorance of current psychological work. It is perhaps better to think of both psychologists and educators as reflecting the predominant intellectual trends of their time. And in this spirit, many contemporary psychological ideas, including those about symbolization, have come to exert influence on the beliefs and practices of educators.

In our own case, we have tried to forge an approach to educational practice that draws upon the strength of the progressive movement, cherishes features of more traditional approaches, and remains mindful of newly emerging insights about human cognitive functioning. These ideas have been worked out, in part, on the theoretical level. But they have been tested as well within schools – as embodied in experimental programs that we and our colleagues have set up; as parts of model school programs, instituted by practitioners "in the field"; and by recent collaborative work with other educational reformers, most especially in the ATLAS project, a collaboration of our research-and-development group with Theodore Sizer's Coalition of Essential Schools at Brown University, James Comer's School Development Program at Yale University, and the Education Development Center directed by Janet Whitla (ATLAS, 1994; Comer, 1980; Gardner, 1991c, 1993c; Sizer, 1984, 1992).

Sketched in the ideal, what are the principal features of the "new progressivism" in education? To begin with, the goals and processes to be adopted by a school or school system need to be negotiated by the principal stakeholders – educators, families, and community members. Schools are unlikely to be effective unless they reflect the input and "stake" of those responsible for the life of the community. These parties – in this case the "field" – need to agree on what kinds of knowledge, skills, and understandings should be exhibited by students when they have completed their education. In our terms, there should be extended conversation and ultimately consensus about the symbolic competences to be achieved and exhibited. And "exhibition" is an operative word here. Students can be said to be educated when they are able to display publicly to an acceptable level of accomplishment what they have been able to understand and to master, whether it be performing a new composition on the piano or creating a map of an unfamiliar region of one's community. Of course the adoption of exhibitions as occasions for assessment presupposes at least two conditions: the existence of a community that has developed a sense of what constitutes an acceptable performance, and the constitution of a group of judges who can apply standards in a reliable way.

What should be the focus of such an education? As we see it, all human beings are motivated to understand better certain basic issues and questions: Who are we? To what group do we belong? Where do we come from? Where are we headed? How does our group relate to others? What is the physical world made of? How about the biological and social worlds? What is true, what is beautiful, what is good? Youngsters bring versions of these questions with them to school – and both graduates and older individuals hope that they will be able to come up with satisfactory and satisfying answers to these "essential" questions.

Even the five-year-old mind has constructed an approach to these questions, but, as we noted earlier, this approach is limited and flawed. Human beings have, over the centuries, devised more sophisticated approaches to the "essential questions" and have in a number of ways fashioned more comprehensive and satisfactory responses. The principal path to these privileged approaches is through the mastery of disciplines and domains – organized approaches to knowledge that make use of the existing symbol systems and that, when necessary, revise those systems, or proceed to devise new ones.

A principal purpose of school – indeed, we would argue, the principal purpose of school – is to acquire facility and fluency in the use of the disciplinary symbol systems, moves, and understandings. Not for its own sake – though the cultivation of such skill can be rewarding; but rather because such accumulated corpora of wisdom represent human beings' hard-won efforts to gain leverage on deep and subtle questions and issues. Individuals demonstrate their education by exhibiting understandings of the approaches, and the resolutions, that have been arrived at over the centuries; and, to the extent possible, by putting forth their own more personal (though still disciplinary-grounded) responses to these issues. In pursuing this path, they are mastering the symbolic processes and products wrought by those who have worked within and across the disciplines.

So far this educational regime seems quite traditional, and we make no apologies for that fact. To deny tradition is to turn one's back on the very best work done by countless individuals over many hundreds of years. And yet, while the program of disciplinary mastery is one to which we subscribe, we have little sympathy with most of the established pedagogical moves – for instance, strings of lectures, memorization of text, issuing of short-answer tests as a measure of one's learning.

Indeed, it is here that we gladly revisit some of the principal practices of the progressive movement, though with a newly cut key. To begin with, youngsters possess different interests and these must be taken seriously, if one wants to involve them integrally in the foundational experiences of exploring the physical and symbolic worlds. Relatedly, they also subscribe to different belief and causal theories, held with varying degrees of explicitness, and these must be taken into account as well. Finally, youngsters also learn in different kinds of ways, exhibiting different profiles and blends of intelligences, which result in different representations of bodies of knowledge. In all of these senses, education must be personalized.

Following a period of initial romance, as Whitehead (1929) termed it, a time when interests are first crystallized, there can be no substitute for years of disciplinary training. The classical apprenticeship, where an individual worked for several years at the foot of a master artist or craftsperson, remains an unequalled route toward mastery of a discipline. Still, there is no reason whatsoever why this experience of skill acquisition needs to be dull or dulling. Individuals can gain disciplinary (and inter-disciplinary) skills through working with others, through engagement in rich projects, through public exhibitions of their understanding complete with informative and supportive feedback. Apprenticeships come in many flavors. There is at least as much to be learned from time spent within the institution of the children's museum as from hours at the traditional school, church, or factory. The power of personalization, the miracle of motivation, can be marshaled to the ends of disciplinary mastery.

Nor need mastery occur at the expense of creativity and individuality. Even as there are common elements which need to be mastered by every individual, there are alternative routes to mastery, as well as costs and benefits for every road taken and every road spurned. So long as both students and masters remain cognizant of these pluralities and these tradeoffs, the goal of creativity can continue alongside the goal of skill development and disciplinary mastery.

Even well-set-up educational environments, with exciting materials and stimulating teachers, may not suffice to produce genuine understandings. The research on misconceptions, alluded to earlier, has documented the robustness of early conceptions and the sometimes overwhelming obstacles in the face of genuine disciplinary understanding (Gardner, 1991c).

Neither we nor others have discovered a royal road to genuine understanding. But our research has suggested a number of pointers. To begin with, individuals must be brought face to face with their misconceptions and stereotypes – they have to be exposed repeatedly to the nonsensical implications of these uncritically held beliefs. At the same time, they need multiple opportunities to develop more complex notions and to see the ways in which these conceptions more adequately address the questions and issues at hand. A combination of exposure to models of understanding, on the one hand, and regular opportunities to work out the consequences of one's own beliefs and conceptions, on the other, seem necessary prerequisites for a deeper understanding.

So far in this discussion it may appear that we have sidestepped the most nagging question of curriculum: What topics should be covered, what books should be read, which subjects are mandatory, which optional, which expendable? Particularly when we are calling for a sharp reduction of coverage, it may seem derelict to avoid the listing of the most important topics, subjects, and themes.

Here we adopt a distinctly non-traditional approach. Once the basic literacies have been acquired, once individuals are comfortable in the crucial symbol systems of reading, writing, and reckoning, we discern no necessity to place a special premium on one subject as opposed to another (biology vs. chemistry; American history vs. world history), let alone particular topics (light vs. gravity) or library works (Homer vs. *Hamlet*). Far more important, in our view, is the experience of approaching in depth *some* key topics or themes in the broadest disciplinary areas – math and science, history and philosophy, literature and the arts. Students need to learn how to learn and how to probe deeply into one or another topic. Once they have achieved these precious insights, they are in a position to continue their own education indefinitely. And if they have not mastered these lessons, all the facts, factoids, and mandated tests will not save their souls. Assessment should look for evidence of deep understanding; the teacher and student should be afforded wide latitude in the topic that is to be assessed (see Chapters 17 and 19).

Progressive education, in its innocence, had too optimistic a view of education – giving rise to the belief that all students could learn, without much scaffolding, ignoring the conceptual obstacles en route, all too often minimizing the need for disciplinary mastery, skill building, and milestones and markers along the way (Gardner, 1993b; Graham, 1967). For committing these sins of omission, we may cast a critical eye on some of our predecessors. Yet on the bigger picture – the need to establish interest, the openness to various ways of learning, the conviction that one can benefit from work on rich projects set in context, the perceived relationship in a democratic society between the conditions of learning and the conditions of citizenship – Dewey and his associates arrived at profound and enduring truths.

Closing the loop: innocence recaptured

Even given our ambitious charge, we have sought to cover here a wide terrain. At the end of the day, what do we hope to have achieved? Scholarship and practice is greatly indebted to the giants of our world; upon the life works of Jean Piaget and

John Dewey, who inhabited the same chronological periods and adjoining intellectual spheres, there is much to build. While we have devoted at least as much energy to critique, we trust that such criticism has not masked our profound respect for their achievements.

Perhaps as penitence, perhaps as proof, we suggest – admittedly with some timidity – that the developmentalists and the pedagogues of mid-century would not reject the picture that we have put forth here. Modify perhaps, quibble here and there, raise a few objections and point in a few new directions – but not challenge it in a fundamental way. And that is because, by and large, the fresh insights about human nature and the keener sensitivities to educational complexity in no fundamental way contradict the picture forged at mid-century – instead they deepen and complexify it in relatively congenial ways. Moreover, the emerging dialectic between researchers and school personnel is in its deepest respects congenial to the vision of society and knowledge that was embraced by Piaget, Dewey, Bruner, and their associates.

In putting forth the symbol systems approach, as a privileged perspective for the broad understanding of human development, and as a central element in conceptualizing the purposes of education, we again make no claim for a revolutionary change of direction. Both the psychological and the educational traditions have been sensitive to the importance of symbolic vehicles and systems. Yet we do believe that the picture of symbolization put forth here has the potential to bring about a greater degree of order and a more reliable synthesis of knowledge and practice than has been available heretofore.

It is our deepest belief that the human mind comes prepared – we might even say "well prepared" – to be open to new ideas. It is the obligation of any society in which we would choose to live to maintain that openness and to facilitate the routes to new insights and new understandings. We oppose those psychological and educational approaches that threaten that openness or presume to deny its importance and even its existence. The approaches that we choose to build on are those that share with us this fundamental theme, this "world hypothesis" (Holton, 1988; Pepper, 1942). It is because we believe that creativity is not possible in the absence of disciplines and discipline, and that new knowledge must be based upon a deep mastery of tradition, that we have sought to leaven the more innocent aspects of progressivism – the better to preserve its core vision.

CHAPTER 21

HOW EDUCATION CHANGES
Considerations of history, science, and values

Suarez Orozco, M. and D. Qin-Hilliard (eds), *Globalization: Culture and education in the new millennium*. Berkeley: University of California Press, 2004.

The transmission of knowledge and skills to the next generation, the process of education in formal and informal settings, is inextricably bound with the emergence of *Homo sapiens* over the past several hundred thousand years (Bruner, 1960; Donald, 1991; Tomasello, 2000). Formal schools, however, are just a few thousand years old, and the notion of universal education, in which all young persons in a society receive several years of competent schooling, is still a distant dream in many corners of the globe (Bloom, 2003; Bloom and Cohen, 2001).

For the most part, institutions change slowly. Such gradual change may be a positive element. The practices associated with an institution tend to be worked out by trial and error over long periods of time. While such experimentation does not guarantee a stronger and more effective institution, at least the most problematic structures and procedures are eliminated. When it comes to educational institutions – which have come to bear a primary responsibility for the intellectual and moral health of the next generation – such conservatism is especially to be recommended. We do not – or at least we should not – want to sacrifice our children to the latest fad. On occasion, shock treatments are administered to an educational system – for example, consider the dramatic changes that took place in Japan after the Second World War or in China following the Communist Revolution in 1949. Such changes may achieve their initial goal. But less welcome consequences can also occur, for example hiding large parts of history in the case of Japan or alienating children from their parents in the case of the Cultural Revolution in China.

Education stands out in one crucial way from most other societal institutions. Put directly, education is fundamentally and primarily a "values undertaking," and educational values are perennially in dispute. Members of a society can reach agreement with relative ease about the purpose of medicine – to deliver high-quality healthcare to all citizens; nor need the purposes of the military or the monetary system be perennially disputed. However, except for certain fundamentals, the purposes of education, and the notion of what it means to be an educated person, are subjects about which individuals – both professional and lay – hold distinctive and often conflicting views. Clearly, the values that undergirded the educational system in imperial Japan or China differed radically from those that came to motivate the system in a fledgling democratic society like that of Japan in 1950 or an experimental socialist society in China at the same time. As I have put it whimsically, "in the United States in the early twenty-first century, how could we possibly create an educational system that would please the three Jesses – conservative

North Carolina senator Jesse Helms, charismatic African American leader Jesse Jackson, and flamboyant Minnesota wrestler-turned-governor Jesse Ventura?"

While the gradual change of educational institutions can readily be justified, we must also ask what can, and should, happen to educational institutions when dramatic alterations take place in the ambient society. Such changes can take place as a result of a shift in values; that is what prompted changes in East Asia a half century ago. However, changes can also take place as a result of scientific findings that alter our understanding of the human mind or because of broader historical forces, such as globalization, that affect regions all over the world. At such times, the tension between the pace of institutional change, on one hand, and the pace of scientific discoveries and historical forces, on the other, can become acute.

For much of its relatively short history, formal schooling has been characterized by a religious orientation. Teachers were typically members of a religious order; the texts to be read and mastered were the holy books; and the lessons of school were ethical and moral in character. (The madrasas of the Islamic world, the cheders that have accompanied the Jewish diaspora in recent decades, and the rise of fundamentalist schools in the United States would have seemed much less anomalous a few centuries ago.) Religious instruction, or a state religion, is still common in many European countries, while the "state religion" of communism is only gradually waning as an educational staple on the Chinese mainland. (It remains alive and well in Cuba.)

Yet, despite the persistence of such religious or quasi-religious strains, most of the developed world, and much of the developing world, has converged on a form of precollegiate education that is largely secular in thrust. The major burden of the first years of school – the primary grades – is threefold: (1) to introduce children to the basic literacy systems of the ambient culture – the "three Rs," to use the English parlance; (2) to acclimate youngsters to the milieu of decontextualized learning, where – in contradistinction to the learning that is most readily accomplished by human beings – one learns about events and concepts outside of their naturally occurring contexts (Bruner *et al.*, 1966; Resnick, 1987); (3) to give children the opportunity to play and work together civilly with those individuals with whom they can expect to grow and eventually spend their adult years. While such processes used to begin around the age of six or seven, it is notable that many countries now attempt to inculcate these skills in the preschool years, sometimes as early as the fourth or fifth year of life.

A century ago only a small percentage of the population received even this much education before those with "basic education" returned to the farm or proceeded to the factory. Bloom and Cohen note that in "recent decades progress towards universal education has been unprecedented. Illiteracy in the developing world has fallen from 75% of people a century ago to less than 25% today" (2001, p. I). Still, the amount of education in the developing world is modest: the "average number of years spent in school more than doubled between 1965 and 1990, from 2.1 to 4.4, among those age 25 and over in developing countries" (Bloom and Cohen, 2001, p. I). In contrast, in the developed world nearly all youngsters receive education at least through some secondary school, and in some lands a third to a half or even more receive some form of post-secondary education.

Following the years of primary school, the burden of education shifts. Complementing the missions stated above, most formal educational institutions also strive to help students obtain fluency in the basic literacies, so that they can deal readily with all manner of texts, assist them in mastering the fundamentals of several key disciplines, particularly mathematics and the sciences, and provide tools so that students can understand and participate in the formal and informal social, economic, and political systems of their country. This latter goal is achieved both through direct instruction in history, literature, and civics and through a demonstration of these processes in the manner in which the school operates. Specifically, in authoritarian cultures almost all of the processes of education are dictated by a central authority, such as the Ministry of Education or the dominant religious order. In more democratic cultures, students and teachers have considerable say in the governance and activities of the school, and sometimes curricular choices are left to the local educational establishment.

It would be an exaggeration to claim that education across the developed world is centrally orchestrated. Vast and gritty differences exist across and even within nations. Yet there is surprising convergence in what is considered a reasonable pre-collegiate education in Tokyo or Tel Aviv, in Budapest or Boston. Following ten to 13 years of school, students are expected to have studied several sciences, mastered mathematics through beginning calculus, know a good deal about the history and governance of their own country, and be able to read and write fluently in their native language. Most nations have moved or are moving toward standardized curricula and assessments in these areas – another indication of globalization's momentum. Countries differ notably in the extent to which they require mastery of languages other than the native tongue(s), knowledge of the history and culture of other parts of the world, and acquaintance with "softer" subjects like the arts or literature. International comparisons, such as the International Mathematics and Science Survey (TIMSS) or the PISA tests, exert increasingly strong pressures in the planning chambers of educational ministries. And programs such as the International Baccalaureate are spreading rapidly to many countries – developing as well as developed – throughout the world (Walker, 2002a, 2002b).

From this description it may seem that large parts of the world have managed to strip education not only of its religious moorings but also of a clash among competing values. To some extent, this characterization has validity. There is little dispute across the globe that future citizens need to be literate, numerate, capable of scientific thought, and knowledgeable about the history, traditions, and governmental system of the nation in which they are being educated. Yet the specter of values still looms large in two respects.

First, competence in science, mathematics, engineering, and technical subjects has come increasingly to be valued, perhaps overvalued, in comparison, say, to the arts, literature, moral education, or philosophy. In this sense, a technical education is equally important to fundamentalist Muslims, Hindus, Christians, and Jews; piano or calligraphy lessons take place after school or on weekends for those who can afford it. Second, especially within democratic societies, there are large and unresolved disputes about what competence means. Thus, within the sciences competence can mean mastery of large bodies of factual information, familiarity with laboratory procedures, in-depth understanding of selected key concepts, and/or the ability to make new discoveries or raise new questions. And educational policy makers disagree about whether future citizens should know political or social history, embrace triumphalist or critical accounts of their own history, learn to support or to critique the status quo. The sphere of values remains alive and well in education.

Until 30 years ago, even students who received the highest-quality education typically left school during adolescence. Nowadays, however, some form of tertiary education is becoming common, even expected, especially in developed countries. The American option of some years of "liberal arts" is exceptional and may be an endangered species even in the United States; it is (perhaps reasonably in some countries) assumed that sufficient liberal arts were conveyed in the precollegiate years, and that the tertiary years should focus on professional or at least pre-professional training, again with an emphasis on technical professions. Whether or not tertiary education occurs at the end of adolescence, it is widely recognized that some forms of adult or "lifelong" learning will be necessary across the occupational spectrum. Which institutions should handle such an education and what value systems will be embodied are questions that will need to be addressed in the coming years.

For centuries significant changes in the educational system have been due largely to historical trends. The emergence of urban centers in Europe gave rise to the universities of the late Middle Ages. The invention of the printing press made possible wide-scale literacy and allowed individuals increasingly to take charge of their own education ("Just give me a library card, please"). The changing status of women both allowed more young girls into the educational system and ultimately conferred career options beyond teaching on large numbers of capable adult women.

Since the rise of psychology and other social sciences in the latter part of the nineteenth century, educational policy makers have sought to base their recommendations on emerging knowledge about human beings. Note that this is itself a values statement: the claim that scientific discoveries about human nature ought to be a basis for educational changes might seem bizarre in an educational milieu where sacred considerations are dominant.

With little question, in recent years the largest impact on educational policy making has come as a result of psychometrics. Testing has a long history, but its rationale took a sharp turn in the early twentieth century. The impetus for this turn came from the growing belief that individuals differed from one another in intellectual potential and that psychologists could measure these differences reliably through an IQ test.

Interestingly, the test makers initially embraced a range of political and social positions. Alfred Binet, the French psychologist who created the first intelligence tests, sought to identify individuals with potential learning difficulties so that these persons could achieve special help and support. American progressives who embraced intelligence tests saw them as ways of improving education generally by placing it on a more scientific basis. As Lord Kelvin famously pointed out, measurement is the key component of any scientific practice. However, testing has also been embraced by those with an affirmative political and social agenda. For many scientists and policy makers in the early twentieth century, testing was a scientifically validated way of selecting those with talent and consigning those who scored poorly to the backwaters of school and society (Gould, 1981).

Contributing strongly to educational policy and practice have been the models of human learning that have emerged in psychology. Each of the principal models has antecedents that date back to earlier philosophical positions, but each has been reinforced by researchers who draw on data and scientific ways of thinking. For example, B.F. Skinner (1938), the behaviorist, drew on studies with animals and human beings to argue that learning is best effected by a careful schedule of rewards and punishments (more technically, schedules of reinforcement). This epistemological position – which dates back to the empiricist philosophers of the seventeenth and eighteenth centuries – called for carefully calibrated curricula that guided learners smoothly from one concept or practice to the next, slightly more complex one, in a way that was as error free as possible.

Consider two contrasting pictures of human nature that derived from the psychology of cognitive development. Drawing on the famed Swiss psychologist Jean Piaget (1983), many educators have called for a system in which young individuals discover for themselves the laws that govern the physical, biological, and social worlds. According to this position, which reverberates with Rousseauian sentiments, attempts to inculcate facts and concepts directly are ill advised; only superficial learning can result. Students are better off if – like Rousseau's Émile – they can explore for themselves the operations of, say, a lever or an abacus, or the rules that govern a billiard ball, and figure out the operating principles. While not rejecting the Piagetian perspective in toto, the influential Russian psychologist Lev Vygotsky (1978) added two important components. First, he noted that there is a great deal of knowledge about such concepts already circulating within the society and that the challenge of education is to help students internalize what has already been established by previous generations. Second, he showed that proper support, or scaffolding, for the learning child is always advisable and sometimes necessary if the child is to achieve more sophisticated understandings and skills. It is illusory to believe that children can on their own figure out the major ideas that have slowly emerged in the scholarly disciplines, even though they may be able to master certain universal understandings without explicit tutelage.

Although most educators have not read Binet or Skinner, Piaget or Vygotsky in the original (and most parents have not heard of these authorities), the legacies of these intellectual giants have exerted an impact on education around the world. For at least a century, the belief in formal tests as means of selecting and comparing has proved an incredibly powerful twentieth-century virus. Behaviorist methods are widely used, particularly with populations that exhibit cognitive or emotional problems. But discovery methods are also prominent in many scientific and mathematics classes, while concern with the proper forms of support or scaffolding permeate discussions about education, ranging from Head Start programs to apprenticeships in scientific laboratories or medical schools.

Just as generals often fight the last war, many educators base their well-intentioned practices on outmoded ideas about human cognition. In the past quarter century I have had the opportunity to observe two major changes in how scientists think about human learning and to anticipate the emergence of a third. In each case, these paradigm shifts could have major educational implications, ones that remake how teachers work with students. In tracing the course and fate of these understandings, we can gain important insights into what happens when scientific discoveries meet educational practices.

From intelligence to intelligences

Let me begin with the example of intelligence. For nearly a century a consensus has obtained among those who are charged with thinking about intelligence. Put succinctly, the consensus stipulates that there is a single thing called human intelligence; individuals differ from birth in how smart they are; one's intellectual potential is largely determined by one's biological parents; and psychologists assess a person's intellect by administering a test of intelligence. These views date back to the claims of Charles Spearman (1904) and Lewis Terman (1916) at the turn of the century, and they have been espoused in recent years by such experts as the British psychologist Hans Eysenck (1986) and the American social scientists Richard Herrnstein and Charles Murray (1994).

While this consensus was challenged from early on by both scholars (Thurstone, 1938) and commentators (Lippmann, 1976), only recently has there been a more concerted critique by scientists of various stripes. Among scholars of artificial intelligence there is a growing recognition that notions such as "general problem-solving" are not well founded and that successful computer programs contain specific knowledge about specific forms of expertise. Among neuroscientists there is agreement that the brain is not a general, equipotential organ; rather, specific capacities (e.g., language, spatial orientation, understanding of other people) are associated with specific regions of the brain and have evolved over the millennia to entail specific kinds of information processing (for relevant references see Gardner 1983, 1985a, 1993a). Among anthropologists and psychologists an increasingly vocal minority has proposed the existence of several relatively independent forms of intelligence (Battro, 2003; Goleman, 1995; Mithen, 1996; Rosnow *et al.*, 1994; Salovey and Mayer, 1990; Sternberg, 1985; Tooby and Cosmides, 1991).

In a formulation developed over two decades ago, I argued that human beings are better thought of as possessing half a dozen or more separate sets of capacities that I termed "multiple intelligences" (Gardner 1983, 1993a; see Chapters 6–12). "MI theory," as it has come to be called, has two fascinating and complementary facets, and both of these can play out in the educational sphere. The first implication is that all of us possess these several intelligences; they make us human, cognitively speaking. Thus any teacher faced with youngsters who are not totally impaired can assume that the students possess all of these intelligences. If one chooses, it is possible to teach to the specific intelligences, to develop them, to draw on them in conveying consequential educational materials.

The second facet is that each individual possesses a distinctive profile of intelligences. Even identical twins – literally clones of one another with the same genetic profile – may each exhibit a characteristic "scatter" of intellectual strengths and weaknesses. These differences are due, presumably, to several factors; for example, even when two individuals have identical genetic information, they don't undergo identical experiences in the world (or even in the womb); and two individuals who appear indistinguishable on a physical basis may be strongly motivated to distinguish themselves from one another in other spheres.

The assertion that we possess a range of intelligences, with each person's profile as idiosyncratic, immediately poses an educational dilemma. One horn of that dilemma proclaims that we should ignore these differences or even try to erase them. The opposing horn holds that we should recognize these differences and try, insofar as possible, to turn them to our educational advantage.

It is important to note that, throughout most of human history, differences among individuals have been considered a nuisance factor in educational circles. We have favored uniform schools in which each person is treated the same as every other one. Moreover, this "equal treatment" appears on the surface to be fair, since no favoritism has apparently been shown. However, one can also argue – as I have – that such "uniform" schools are actually unfair (Gardner 1993b, 1999). They privilege one profile of intelligences – almost always the blend of language and logic that is probed in intelligence tests – and ignore or minimize the other ones. It would be possible to take entirely the opposite tack – one that I have labeled "individually centered education." In this alternative philosophy, one finds out as much as possible about each student and then crafts an education that helps each student learn as much as possible, in ways that are congenial to that student. I believe that such individualized education will come to fruition very soon. This outcome will occur not because of my theorizing or my preaching but because technology will make it possible to individualize education as much as we want to. And once it becomes clear that algebra or French or economics or music theory can be presented in many ways, then it will constitute malpractice to persevere in using the methods of uniform education (see Turkle 1997).

The case of MI theory makes it clear that scientific findings can readily yield educational implications. Indeed, once MI theory had been enunciated, educators in many parts of the world began to claim that they were refashioning their classes or schools in the light of the theory. I was pleased that these ideas – psychological ones – had stimulated their thinking. But it soon became clear that MI theory was like an inkblot test – an ambiguous stimulus that could be interpreted in highly idiosyncratic ways. Some educators saw MI theory as a rationale for arts education or special education; others saw it as a pretext for creating tracks, in terms of the various intelligences; still others considered MI theory as a suggestion to teach seven to eight topics and to do so in seven to eight different ways. Even the psychometricians got into the act; I was approached by several publishing companies and asked if I wanted to develop a battery of tests, one for each intelligence!

The decisions one makes in such instances clearly reflect one's own value system. One can never proceed directly and unambiguously from a scientific finding to an educational practice. Indeed, this stricture pertains even to the traditional view of intelligence. I had a chance to discuss the findings of *The Bell Curve* (1994) with its senior author, Richard Herrnstein, before his untimely death. Herrnstein and I agreed that if one premise of the book was correct – that it is difficult to change IQ – one may draw two diametrically opposite inferences. The Herrnstein–Murray inference is that it is not worth trying to raise IQ and that one should simply accept these differences and make the best of them. But an opposite, more optimistic, inference is that one should devote all one's energies in an attempt to raise IQ, and one might well hit upon a method that is successful.

The embracing of MI theory, at least at a nominal level, is an example of how a scientific finding can be readily validated by the educational community. However, such a friendly reception is not always the case.

The challenges of disciplinary understanding

Once one has acquired the basic literacies, the next educational milestone entails mastery of various subjects or disciplines. While the list of valued disciplines differs across societies, in general it features a number of sciences (biology, physics, chemistry), several branches of mathematics (algebra, geometry, precalculus), as well as a smattering of more humanistic pursuits (history, geography, one or more art forms). If the literacies represent the consensual curricula for the elementary grades, disciplinary mastery and understanding is the curriculum of choice for secondary schools and perhaps college as well.

Let me say a word about each of these terms. When I speak of disciplines, I intend a distinction between subject matter (learning the names, facts, and concepts of a particular subject) and discipline (mastering the distinctive ways of thinking that characterize a scientist, historian, humanist, or artist). Both scientists and historians offer explanations of events, but the nature of the data that they examine and the kinds of explanations that they offer are distinctively and instructively different. When I speak of understanding, I venture well beyond the simple capacity to recall what one has read or heard about. An individual who understands a disciplinary topic can apply that understanding to new situations, ones that she has never encountered before. In the absence of such performances of understanding, acquired knowledge remains inert – incapable of being mobilized for useful purposes.

In the past both traditionalists and progressives woefully underestimated the difficulties entailed in disciplinary understanding. Traditionalists saw disciplinary study chiefly as the mastery of factual and definitional information drawn from various subject matters; and such mastery entailed chiefly repetition, drill, and pre-configured problem sets (Bereiter and Engelmann, 1966; Hirsch 1987, 1996). Progressives believed that disciplinary understanding flowed naturally from the opportunity to explore topics in depth, in natural settings, at one's own pace (Bruner, 1960; Dewey, 1964a, 1964b; Jervis and Tobier, 1988). Just as literacy should arise as a matter of course following opportunities to practice in a literate environment, so disciplinary mastery should arise naturally from deep immersion in the relevant subject matter.

Alas, both of these educational perspectives have proved wrong. A large body of research from the cognitive sciences over the past few decades has documented an alarming state of affairs. It turns out that the understanding of the principal ideas in the various disciplines has proved much more challenging than most educators believed. The smoking gun can be found in the study of the sciences. Even students who get high grades in the sciences at leading secondary schools and universities turn out to have a very tenuous understanding of the principal ideas in various subject areas. This result has been ascertained by examining such students outside of their classroom environment. Not only are most students inadequate in applying properly what they have learned in class, but in many cases they give the same answers to problems and questions as are given by students who have not even taken the course in the first place! (For a summary of the relevant literature, see Gardner 1991c, 2000, and Chapters 16–18.) Thus, for example, even our high-scoring high school and college students fail to evince understanding of evolution, or the laws of motion, or the principles of economics when they are questioned outside a text–test context.

Again, the recognition of new data about the human mind should prove provocative to educators, but in this case the demonstration of misunderstanding does not immediately dictate commensurate educational practices. One could, for example, simply dodge the challenge of disciplinary mastery and remain at the level of Gradgrindian (or Hirschian) factual mastery. One could decide to challenge directly the misconceptions of the young and see whether the proper conceptions can readily arise in their place. One could let the misconceptions play out, see where they are inadequate, and let youngsters themselves contrive better understandings. One could develop targeted curricula that provide support for specific forms of disciplinary understanding. It hardly needs to be remarked that the kind of local and national assessment instruments in play will exert a powerful impact on the educational strategy that is followed. If the instrument calls for a great deal of coverage, then any chance of eradicating misconceptions will be undercut. And in my view, the latter scenario is what has happened so far. Few educators are willing to face the serious implication of the finding that genuine disciplinary under-standing is rarely found, even among our most successful students.

In the fall of 2002 both the Rhodes Scholarship and the Marshall Scholarships were announced. Seven students at Harvard University won these coveted awards, which provide support for study at a British university. What caught my eye was the fact that all seven of these students had undertaken inter-disciplinary study while undergraduates. One student was enrolled in history and literature, a second was in physics and biochemistry, a third was in philosophy and international rela-tions. All three of these individuals were also seriously involved in the arts.

While it has rarely been written about in the popular media, a sea change has occurred in the academy over the past 50 years. A large number of inter-discipli-nary centers, programs, projects, and departments have sprung up all over the edu-cational landscape, from middle school, through college and university curricula, all the way to advanced think tanks in the sciences, the humanities, and policy studies. This trend has reflected a variety of forces, ranging from the sober (so many contemporary problems demand input from a number of disciplines) to the mundane (it is attractive for a faculty member to have her own Center, in which she can explore issues of interest to her in the ways she finds congenial with col-leagues of her own choosing). And the actual work carried out under the rubric of inter-disciplinarity has ranged from pathbreaking to self-absorbed to trivial.

For the past few years my colleagues and I, complementing our studies of disci-plinary understanding, have been exploring the nature of inter-disciplinary work (Boix-Mansilla and Gardner, 1997; Gardner and Boix-Mansilla, 1994a, 1994b). There is no question that inter-disciplinarity is in the air and that much work is being carried out under its banner. What has struck us is the astonishing lack of standards for what counts as adequate or appropriate inter-disciplinary work. While standards are in place for judging the quality of work in the traditional dis-ciplines, there has not been time – and perhaps there has not been motivation – to set up analogous kinds of indices for quality work in various inter-disciplinary amalgamations. Thus one is thrown into an uncomfortable situation: accept all the work uncritically ("if it is inter-disciplinary, it must be meritorious"); or apply indices from the disciplinary world that may not be appropriate; or try to assess the impact of the work – which may not necessarily reflect its quality.

The rise of inter-disciplinary studies is not a scientific phenomenon; rather, it is a historical fact of our time. Trends in our increasingly globalized society have brought inter-disciplinary concerns to the fore. Issues such as poverty reduction, anti-terrorism, privacy, prevention of disease, energy conservation, ecological bal-ance – the list could be expanded at will – all require input from and syntheses of various forms of disciplinary knowledge and methods. Educational institutions seek, in their ways, to respond to the demand for this kind of skill; and the more adventurous students are attracted to studies that call for a blend of disciplinary expertises, Yet in a world that still believes in one kind of intelligence and that has not appreciated the difficulty of understanding even a single discipline, we are hardly in a position to mount inter-disciplinary programs and feel confident about evaluating their success. Perhaps we should first institute studies of the synthesiz-ing or inter-disciplinary mind.

Nearly everyone recognizes that the youth of today are being prepared for a world that is different in fundamental ways from the world of 1900, 1950, per-haps even 1975. In addition to the obvious differences in political alignments and technological sophistication, young people today partake of a powerful hegemonic cultural message emanating from the United States, as well as strong and divergent cultural countercurrents streaming in from major societies. Any student growing up in such a world needs to be able to navigate among these diverse and powerful messages (see Friedman, 2000; Giddens, 2000). Yet there is not even the beginning of a synthesis of how this altered world should impact education, particularly education at the primary and secondary levels (see Suarez-Orozco and Qin-Hilliard, 2003). Here I put forth some suggestions for a curriculum suitable to the era of globalization. I do so with the explicit awareness that all educational recommendations presuppose a certain set of values. Mine are based on an education that is suitable for a democratic society, in which individuals have a fair degree of say in where they live and how they live; in which the use of one's mind to the fullest is a prominent value; and in which all able-bodied individuals are expected to contribute not only to the security and well-being of their families but also to the health of the broader communities in which they live.

Beginning on a conservative note, I believe that we should not turn our backs on those methods and procedures that have been worked out over long periods of time. Though there is always room for improvement, we know a great deal about how to develop the literacies in young persons, both those who can learn in normal ways and those who have specific learning problems – for example, in the decoding of written alphabetic text.

Once we come to the mastery of disciplines, however, we can no longer afford business as usual. Now that we know the difficulties of disciplinary mastery, we need to recognize that this concern must occupy a large proportion of our pedagogical energies. My recommendation in this area is to cut down radically on the number of subjects to master in precollegiate education. I would favor all students learning at least one science, one area of history, one art form, expression and appreciation in their own language, and, especially in countries where the principal language is not widely spoken beyond its borders, expression and appreciation of English or another widely spoken tongue.

Once a sharper focus has been adopted, it is indeed possible to teach for disciplinary understanding. Such teaching is best done by focusing on the principal deep ideas in the discipline and approaching them from many different angles (Blythe, 1998; Cohen *et al.*, 1993; Wiske, 1998). A depth-over-breadth engagement with a limited number of topics and disciplines is most likely to undermine the misconceptions and to establish deep and robust forms of understanding. Interestingly, the idea of MI can be used here. For if one focuses sharply on a limited number of concepts, it is possible to approach these concepts in several ways, exploiting our various human intelligences. Such a multi-perspectival approach yields two dividends: it reaches more students and it exemplifies what it means to have expertise (Gardner, 2000). After all, the expert is the individual who can think of a topic in lots of different ways.

My focus on a few key disciplines reveals that I believe in the idea of a core curriculum. In that sense I am a traditionalist. But I am completely open to the presentation of the curriculum along any number of pathways and to the assessment of mastery in several different ways. In matters of pedagogy and assessment I am a pluralist. These ideas clash with those of people who want to revert to the ideal of uniform schools; they are congenial to those who see themselves as helping each student to realize his or her full potential in ways that are congenial.

Because of my fealty to the disciplines, I have been a strong believer that interdisciplinary work should await the mastery of a number of individual disciplines.

We would not take seriously a claim of bilingualism unless a person had mastered more than one language; and so I reason that one should not evoke the term inter-disciplinary until one has exhibited mastery of more than one discipline. Pursuing this line, disciplinary education becomes the challenge of secondary education, inter-disciplinary education the superstructure associated with tertiary and post-graduate education.

Recently, however, I have softened this line. Because inter-disciplinary work has become so important in our world, it may not be practical to withhold its practice until complete mastery of specific disciplines has coalesced. Perhaps it will be possible for an individual to achieve sufficient mastery of one discipline so that he can become part of a multi-discipline team. The challenge for this new team member is to bring a particular disciplinary perspective to bear on a problem and to boot-strap enough expertise so that he can appreciate the contributions of the other disciplines, pose insightful questions, and integrate the answers into his understanding. I see no reason why novices should not be allowed to observe these inter-disciplinary exchanges and benefit from them. However, it is vital that such novices understand that ultimately one will not be able to participate in a legitimate way on an inter-disciplinary team unless one has paid one's disciplinary dues.

Membership in such teams points up another vital desideratum for participation in a global society. Simply being the smartest person in one's discipline will no longer suffice. Individuals need to be able to work effectively and in a civil manner with individuals who have different expertises and who come from different cultural backgrounds (Murnane and Levy, 1996; Resnick, 1987; Suarez-Orozco and Qin-Hilliard, 2003). We might say that such individuals need to develop interpersonal intelligence and multicultural understanding. While there is a place for direct instruction in these realms, there is little question that youngsters are most powerfully affected by the examples that they see around them each day. To the extent that parents, teachers, and their respective communities exhibit strong forms of personal relations and cultural sensitivity, we can expect that youngsters will be equipped to participate effectively in working and playing teams. If, however, such forms of sensitivity have not been exhibited regularly by those who are closest to the young, then educational or work institutions face a daunting challenge.

Many have proposed that in our highly competitive global society, creativity, originality, and thinking "outside the box" are at a premium. Silicon Valley represents eloquent testimony to the importance – as well as the risks – of a highly creative ambience. Yet it is questionable whether the enhancing of creativity should be a task of the schools. Much depends on whether the lessons of creativity are manifest "on the street" and in commercial enterprise – as they are in Silicon Valley or Hong Kong – or whether the conformism and tradition encountered daily on the streets and in the home need to be countered boldly in the educational system.

I propose that precollegiate education in the future encompass the following relatively new skills and understandings (see Suarez-Orozco and Qin-Hilliard, 2003). These need not be transmitted by schools or by schools alone, but, unless they are passed down via other sectors of the society, their transmission will become the challenge par excellence for the precollegiate educational system.

1   *Understanding of the global system*   The trends of globalization – the unprecedented and unpredictable movement of human beings, capital, information, and cultural life forms – need to be understood by the young persons who are and will always inhabit a global community. Some of the system will

become manifest through the media, but many other facets – for example, the operation of worldwide markets – will need to be taught in a more formal manner.

2   *Capacity to think analytically and creatively within disciplines*   Simple mastery of information, concepts, and definitions will no longer suffice. Students will have to master disciplinary moves sufficiently so that they can apply them flexibly and generatively to deal with issues that could not be anticipated by the authors of textbooks.

3   *Ability to tackle problems and issues that do not respect disciplinary boundaries*   Many – perhaps most – of the most vexing issues facing the world today (including the issue of globalization!) do not respect disciplinary boundaries. AIDS, large-scale immigration, and global warming are examples of problems in need of inter-disciplinary thinking. One could take the position that it is first necessary to master individual disciplines; moving among or beyond disciplines then becomes the task of tertiary or professional education (Gardner, 2000). However, there is much to be said for beginning the process of inter-disciplinary work at an earlier point in education – as is done, for example, in the "theory of knowledge" course required of students in the International Baccalaureate or the courses in "problem-based learning" taught at the Illinois Mathematics and Science Academy. How best to begin to introduce rigorous multi-perspectival thinking into our classrooms is a challenge that we have only begun to confront, and, as noted, our psychological understanding of the mind of the synthesizer has yet to coalesce.

4   *Knowledge of and ability to interact civilly and productively with individuals from quite different cultural backgrounds – both within one's own society and across the planet*   Globalization is selecting for interpersonal competencies, including the ability to think and work with others coming from very different racial, linguistic, religious, and cultural backgrounds (see Maira, 2003; Suarez-Orozco, 2003). Mastery and cultivation of these competencies will be the cornerstone of educational systems in the most successful democracies of the twenty-first century (see Suarez-Orozco and Qin-Hilliard, 2003).

5   *Knowledge of and respect for one's own cultural tradition(s)*   The terrorists who crashed into the Twin Towers of the World Trade Center in September 2001 privileged the scientific and technical knowledge and cognitive skills that globalization makes accessible. At the same time, they despised the Western (and especially the American) values, ethos, and world view that in many regions of the world – including much of western Europe – pass as globalization's underside. Societies that nurture the emergence of the instrumental skills needed to thrive while not subverting or undermining the expressive domains of culture – values, world views, and, especially, the domain of the sacred – will endure and may even have the edge in globalization's new regime. Managing the dual process of convergence (in the instrumental domains of culture) and divergence (in the expressive domains of culture) may well be among the most critical tasks of education for globalization. Societies that can manage this psychic jujitsu will thrive.

6   *Fostering of hybrid or blended identities*   Education for globalization will select for the crafting and performing of hybrid identities needed to work, think, and play across cultural boundaries (see Suarez-Orozco, 2003). These will be increasingly indexed by multilingual competencies and transcultural sensibilities that will enable children to traverse discontinuous cultural mean-

ing systems, to metabolize, decode, and make meaning in distinct, sometimes incommensurable cultural spaces and social fields. Societies that privilege transculturation and hybridity will be in a better position to thrive, while societies that enforce a regime of compulsive monoculturism and compulsive monolingualism are likely to lose out under globalization's emerging regime.

7   *Fostering of tolerance*   Education for globalization will give those societies that tend to (1) tolerate or, better yet, privilege dissent, (2) foster healthy skepticism, and (3) provide equality of opportunity a powerful edge over societies that tend to privilege reflex-like consent and inequality of access to opportunity due to various ascribed qualities. More ominously, our world is unlikely to survive unless we become far more successful at fostering tolerant attitudes within and across nations.

Though many may wish that they would go away, the main lines of globalization are here to stay. It is difficult to envision a world in which the economic trends, communication technologies, movements of population, and cultural messages of the past few decades will somehow be reversed. Even events as epochal as those of September 11, 2001 are likely to modulate the forces of globalization rather than derail them in a fundamental way.

Yet local or national institutions, mores, and values will not necessarily disappear. Indeed, the very power of the forces of globalization will in many cases prompt strong reactions, sometimes violent, sometimes effective. Those newly emerging institutions that can respond to the forces of globalization while at the same time respecting the diversities of cultures and belief systems are most likely to have a long half-life.

Chief among those institutions will be educational systems, with those charged with precollegiate education assuming enormous importance for the foreseeable future. Educational systems are inherently conservative institutions, and that conservatism is in many ways justified. Still, just as educational systems eventually adapted to the agricultural and industrial revolutions, just as they eventually responded to the decline of established religion and the invention of print and audiovisual technologies, they will have to adapt as well to the facts of the globalized, knowledge-centered economy and society. In doing so, they will have to somehow integrate the new scientific findings, their multiple (and sometimes seemingly contradictory) educational implications, with past and present historical trends, and to do so in light of their most cherished values. This task may take 100 years or more, but as a French military leader once famously remarked when facing an especially daunting task: "In that case, we had better begin today."

CHAPTER 22

AN EDUCATION FOR THE FUTURE
The foundation of science and values

Paper presented to symposium of The Royal Palace Foundation, Amsterdam, March 14th, 2001.

Introduction

It is already a cliché to remark that our time is one of tremendous breakthroughs. I refer to new work in technology, nanotechnology, the genetics revolution, robotics, artificial intelligence, perhaps even the creation of new species, by accident or by design.

It is also a cliché to note that education is becoming increasingly important. Anything predictable and rule governed will be automated. Only those persons who are well, broadly, and flexibly educated will be able to function productively in this new world. Around the world, education leads the list of public concerns. In this chapter I present my thoughts on education of children and adolescents.

Two dilemmas

By background I am a psychological researcher who has studied mind and brain with particular reference to learning and to education. I just mentioned the consensus today about the importance of education. Alas, there is not comparable agreement about what education should be and how it should be achieved. I want to mention two dilemmas – both connected to the cognitive, or knowledge, agenda of school.

The first dilemma: What should be taught?

What should be highlighted: facts, information, data? If so, which of the countless facts that exist? Subject matters and disciplines – if so, which ones? *Which* science, *which* history? Should we nurture creativity, critical thinking? If there is to be an additional focus, should it be arts, technology, a social focus, a moral focus? If you try to have all of these foci, you would break the backs of students and teachers, even given a demanding elementary and secondary school curriculum. If knowledge doubles every year or two, we certainly cannot multiply the number of hours or teach twice as quickly. Some choice, some decisions about what can be omitted, are essential.

The second dilemma: How should we teach?

Even if we could agree on which emphases should be adopted, one must still determine whether to teach all subjects or all students the same way, or whether to individualize the curriculum for each student or group of students. How much emphasis should there be on computers, distance education, various media? What should be the role of home, school, the church, the media, or extra-curricular activities? How much responsibility should be placed on teachers, students, peers, parents, the wider community? Issues of pedagogy/instruction turn out to be as vexed as issues of curriculum/content.

Two firm foundations

Since there are far too many possibilities, we must make hard decisions. In making those decisions, I will argue that we should depend primarily on two foundations or bases: the science of learning and our own values as human beings living in communities. Let me comment on both.

Turning to the Science of Learning, consider two major findings from the field of cognitive studies, findings with which I have been personally involved.

First finding: As human beings, we have many different ways of representing meaning, many kinds of intelligence. Since the beginning of the last century, psychologists have spoken about a single intelligence that can be measured by an IQ test; my research has defined eight or nine human intelligences. We all possess these several intelligences, but no two of us – not even identical twins – possess the same profile of intelligences at the same moment. In most countries throughout history, school has focused almost exclusively on language and logic. Formal education has virtually ignored other forms of mental representation – artistic forms (musical), athletic (bodily), personal (knowledge of others and self); knowledge of natural world; knowledge of big questions. All of these "Frames of Mind" are there to be mobilized; if they are not, one could well call education "half-brained" (see Chapters 6–9).

Second finding: Facts are easy to memorize, and some of us are good at remembering them – this facility can help us win money, in fact nowadays one can win millions of dollars on a television quiz show in the U.S. But disciplinary understanding is much more elusive, much more difficult to bring about. Over the millennia human beings have developed several powerful disciplines or ways of knowing the world – chief among them scientific, humanistic, historical, artistic, mathematical forms of thought. How desirable it would be if we could simply explain these to young people ("here are the three steps to think scientifically" or "this is what it takes to think historically"); even better if we could give youngsters a shot or a pill ("here, take this mathematics pill before you go to bed on Wednesday evening"), and the students would then have mastered the discipline. In fact, however, disciplinary learning proves difficult and takes many years of guided practice and apprenticeship.

Our research has suggested one reason why. When children are young, without help from others, they develop powerful theories about the world (see Chapter 16). Many of the theories espoused by young children are wonderful; some are charming; some of them are dead wrong from the point of view of physics, biology, psychology, history. Unfortunately, these erroneous theories are also very powerful. Even the best students in the best schools adhere to these theories. In fact, when they are asked, outside the context of school, to explain a phenomenon, they typically do so in the same way as students who have never studied the subject. In education, if we want to develop better and more disciplined ways of thinking, we must first rub out or eliminate the misleading theories that children have constructed on their own. And then gradually we must help children adopt – a more accurate word is "construct" – better theories, such as the scientific theories used by contemporary biologists or physicists, many of which go directly against common sense. It does not seem sensible that human beings evolved from earlier primates; it does not seem sensible that matter exists even if it cannot be seen by the naked eye or that you could become very ill by exposure to a germ that you cannot see; it does not seem sensible that those who look very different from us could become our friends – but each of these statements happens to be true. We must help students to eradicate the wrong theories and gradually replace them with more adequate disciplinary ways of thinking.

To summarize what I've introduced thus far: disciplinary understanding is important – perhaps, in fact, it is the best justification for ten to 15 years of school! (We could keep youngsters off the street for eight hours a day with much less money.) Disciplinary understanding is also hard to achieve. Next, as human beings, we all have available different ways of representing the world, different intelligences, so to speak. The question is: can educators build on this recently established knowledge about how human beings learn? In a word, I believe that the answer to this question is "yes" and, shortly, I will try to justify my answer.

Let me turn now to the second major foundation, which complements the science of learning – that is the sphere of *values*.

As a teacher or educational policy maker, you could know all of the scientific facts about learning, and it would still not tell you what to do in class on this coming Monday morning. That is because such decisions about a course of action always involve value judgments. For example, let us say that you accept the claim that there are multiple intelligences. You could decide that you still want to make individuals as similar as possible, and so you would minimize or ignore the pluralism of intellect. Multiple intelligences are then seen as an obstacle. Many would take that "uniform" position. To honor the finding about multiple intelligences, you could decide to teach every topic in seven or eight ways. You could decide to put together all the children who are *strong* in a given intelligence, or, for that matter, if you are a pessimist, instead put together all of the children who are *weak* in a given intelligence. You could try to strengthen those intelligences that are weak, or ignore weaknesses and build instead on areas of strength. You could decide to learn about each child and personalize education as much as possible. That last option is what I personally favor – and in the age of the computer it is feasible to personalize education for every child, and not just for those from wealthy families who can afford the latest hardware and software. Take note: all these decisions entail value judgments; none of them can be decided simply because one has established that there are multiple intelligences.

Throwing caution to the winds, let me indicate my own wishes, my own value system, for education in the future. I believe that the best education must build on what has worked in the past. At the same time the best education must take into account the most contemporary findings and the needs of future generations. I put forth these views not because I'm certain they are right, but to encourage discussion and debate.

Looking in both directions

Drawing on the past

Let me first draw on the legacies of the past. I believe that the primary cognitive purpose of education for the young should be to help students understand the world around them – the physical world, the biological world, the social world, the world of personal experiences. This is best done by first training them in the three basic literacies (reading, writing, calculation) – nowadays we might add computing – and then introducing them to the major families of disciplines: science, which seeks the truths about the physical, social, and biological worlds, and which uses the powerful tools of mathematics; the study of art and nature, which tells us about the beauties of the natural and the man-made worlds and which give us the tools to produce objects that we ourselves cherish; and history and literature, which tell us about the human past, document the good and evil choices that humans have made and the consequences of these choices, and help us to determine what we ourselves should do when faced with dilemmas. In sum, the disciplines represent humanity's most determined efforts to learn and to understand what is true, beautiful, and good, and by extension to spurn falsehood, to turn away from what is repulsive, and to avoid evil deeds.

Thus far my prescription for precollegiate education is traditional and conservative, and I make no apologies for that. But my claim to be an "educational conservative" does not last long. I believe that students are most likely to develop disciplinary understanding if they investigate a limited number of topics in great depth; that is, if they give up the false dream of "coverage" (leaping from Plato to NATO in 36 weeks) in favor of intimate knowledge of a limited number of really important issues – for example, the theory of evolution in biology, or the meanings of political revolution in history, or the mastery of one art or craft. Also, I do not value the memorization of vast amounts of information. We can get all the information that we need on a single CD or a Palm Pilot that one can carry around in one's hand – thus freeing us to focus on important knowledge, important understanding, important wisdom, which cannot be so readily "packaged" in that way. You can have the list of all European sovereigns or prime ministers at your fingertips; but you can't click a mouse and suddenly think scientifically or historically, let alone make judicious decisions in these spheres. I am not arguing *against* cultural literacy – I'm arguing *in favor* of mastering the intellectual tools of the major disciplines.

The capacity to think intelligently is very different from knowing lots of information. Such intelligent thinking, such understanding is likely to come about only if one has rounded, three-dimensional familiarity with a subject, so that one can probe it in many different ways. And here at last is where our multiple intelligences can make their contribution. If we are willing to spend time on a topic and probe it penetratingly, we do not have to approach it in just a single way (which is almost always through written texts or lectures). Instead we can learn about it in many different ways, using our multiple intelligences. As a consequence, that concept or topic is much more likely to remain with us, embedded in our neural networks, and to be usable in flexible and innovative ways. In fact, I would guess that if you were asked to remember material from British history, you wouldn't remember long time-lines, but rather a few events – the Battle of Hastings, the Protectorate of the seventeenth century, or the Battle of Britain in the Second World War – that you studied in detail or encountered over and over in various contexts.

An example. You can't understand the theory of evolution by simply memorizing a definition. You can build mastery of the theory by being exposed to definitions (evolution is ...); and stories (the story of Darwin's voyage on *The Beagle* or the story of a particular contemporary species, be it mouse or man); and static pictorial accounts (a tree diagram of different lineages in the hominid line); and dynamic graphic recreations on a computer (in which one sees species evolving, morphing into others, sometimes thriving, like *Homo sapiens*, and sometimes waning, like Neanderthal man). As "entry points" to evolution, one could further mention works of art, numerical puzzles and demonstrations, and the raising of the most profound existential questions: Where do we come from, why are we here, what will happen to us and to our species in the future? Each of these "entry points," stimulating different intelligences, can yield a fuller understanding of the processes of evolution. Taken together, they stand as a model of what it might mean truly to understand a topic.

So, my recommendations can be stated simply. First obtain the literacies; then study in depth key topics in the major disciplines; approach those topics in many ways; and give youngsters many chances to master and many vehicles to exhibit their understandings. Let them use their knowledge of evolution to evaluate the discovery of a new set of dinosaur bones or the spreading of a computer virus, as seems to happen each new week, at least on my machine. Various tasks can be left for the university: a specialization in one or another discipline; work that is explicitly multi- or inter-disciplinary and the mastery of facts that may be useful to know if you want to become an expert in, say, botany or medieval history, and if you happen to lose or misplace your Palm Pilot in which the lists of information had been stored – and had forgotten to "synch it" the previous night.

Peering toward the future

I turn, finally, to the question of how education may differ in the future. The widespread availability of powerful technologies will be a great boon. Students will be able to get much information on their own, often in vivid form. They will be able to encounter multiple representations of material, for example through hypertext linkages, surfing the World Wide Web, or experimenting in virtual reality. There will be waning demand for live presentations of "straight, canned lectures," because such lectures can be recorded and accessed, if one wishes, on the Internet at any time of the day or night. In fact, I now post lectures on my website, and even an entire course, "Cognitive Development, Education and the Brain," that I co-teach is available for students on the Intranet of my university.

In the future, students and parents will expect to be able to interact with teachers, in person or via the Internet, including instructors and experts whom they have never met. (We teachers will get even less sleep than we do now!) There may well be more home schooling and more mixed forms of schooling, with students doing more at home, more with parents, more with *ad hoc* or planned groups, with only certain kinds of activity occurring each day within a single building. Flexibility is likely to prevail at school, as it is beginning to prevail in the workplace.

I find these prospects exciting. The challenge of teaching young persons is going to increase in the years ahead. Not only will students be encountering spectacular demonstrations through technology; the world itself, in its technological facets, will continue to change at dizzying rates, as I noted at the beginning. We live during the first time in history when we human beings could destroy the world through nuclear weapons. We also live at the first time in history where – through genetic engineering or nanotechnology – we could create new toxins, or new forms of bioterror, which could destroy the planet.

We also live at the first time in history where we will have machines that are at least as smart as we are in many ways – machines that can plan economies, wage diplomacy, alter politics, and, for all I know, manage our leisure life, our love life, the place and manner of our deaths and rebirths, whether and how we will be remembered. There will be experiments in cloning organs or whole human beings, and there will be attempts to merge humans and robots, for example through the implanting of silicon chips in our brains; some will even hope to achieve immortality in that way, by downloading their wet brains into a vast dry database. I will leave it to you to determine whether this prospect of lives of indefinite duration more closely approximates a dream or a nightmare!

I am not saying that these issues – that *used* to be the stuff of science fiction – should dominate the curriculum of the school. I am saying something more radical. I am saying that they are *already* beginning to constitute the curriculum of life each day. Students won't have to learn in school about cloned organs and organisms or silicon implants in the hippocampus because they will see them on television or surf past them on the Internet, or hear them argued about around the dinner table at night or at the cybercafé around the corner.

And so the tasks of educators will become dual and dually challenging: on the one hand, to inculcate the traditional disciplines and ways of thinking as I have described them; and, on the other hand, to help students cope with, and perhaps take an active role in deciding how to deal with, these dazzling developments, which, as I say, are no longer restricted to the pages of science fiction.

As I think about the future of precollegiate education, let me share a few more thoughts with you.

1   *Public vs. private education.*   Throughout the world, societies are rethinking the relationship between the world of education and the marketplace. In the United States there are many private initiatives in education. Some individuals would like to have all education choice determined by portable vouchers that pay for one's schooling, and these proponents may even look forward to the disappearance of public education as we know it.

   I believe that market control of education would be a grave mistake. Public education has much to learn from business, and I appreciate the various kinds of financial and advisory support that businesses can provide. However, the goal of business – to make a profit – is fundamentally at odds with the goal of education – to have an informed citizenry capable of independent analysis and decisions. Education is also an area of expertise and is becoming increasingly so; just as we should not entrust business people to make medical decisions, so we should not allow business people to make educational decisions.

2   *Multicultural issues.*   When a country consists primarily of a single culture, then the issues of cultural education are relatively simple. Citizens should come to understand the history, governance, art forms, and values of their particular culture. However, nowadays two new issues arise. First, many countries, such as the United States and several European societies, no longer have a dominant culture but are exquisitely multicultural. Additionally, we are all members of a global society and we all need to be prepared to deal with individuals from a diversity of backgrounds.

   It is important to learn about one's own background culture, but in my view that task can only rarely be undertaken by a school system in a multicultural society. How, in a Los Angeles high school with individuals speaking 50 or even 70 different languages, can one genuinely provide an introduction to even a small percentage of these cultures? Cultural education is better left to after-school or weekend options.

While cultural education is an option, introduction to the global society is becoming a necessity. Unless students have some grasp of trends and realities around the globe, and some sense of how to deal with individuals from diverse backgrounds and often conflicting value systems, they will be ill equipped to survive in the future. In an area like this, we in the U.S. have much to learn from the societies of western Europe and south Asia, who have, in a sense, been "globally aware" for centuries.

3   *Academic vs. practical training.*   In years past, most societies featured a fairly early "tracking mechanism," where the most successful students took an academic "Gymnasium" or "*lycée*-style" curriculum and had the opportunity for higher education, while the rest either dropped out of school, worked on farms or in factories, or entered a vocational track.

Nowadays, it is considered suspect to advocate such a tracking system. After all, most vocations run the risk of being automated, and we are living in a "learning" or "knowledge society" where individuals must be familiar with symbolic or notational systems. Otherwise they will have little chance to benefit fully from the opportunities available in a technologically sophisticated setting.

However, it is also apparent that not all students want to continue in school beyond the age of 15 or 16, nor that this is necessarily the optimal place for them to spend half of their waking hours at that stage of their life. In many cases, they and the society would be much better off if they mastered a trade, did community service, became involved in an artistic troupe, or went to work in a developing country.

My own belief is that we should not force all young people to pursue higher education before they reach the age of 20, but that we should extend the option to them throughout their lives. Just as students in all developed countries now have the opportunity for a free primary and secondary education, we should gradually extend this privilege to the tertiary level. Universally available university education should be the goal. However, it should be up to the student when and even whether to pursue that option. With the explosion of learning opportunities (e.g., distance learning, on-the-job learning, simulated learning) and with the proliferation of institutions that provide education (e.g., for-profit, corporate, the military), there is no reason for everyone to proceed along a single lock-step route from kindergarten through graduate school.

I should add, finally, that we have probably honored too sharp a division between academic and practical learning. Much academic learning can be enlivened and enhanced if it has a "real life" component, or even vivid multimedia facets. Recent experiments with project-based and theme-related curricula illustrate the power of education that activates the multiple intelligences of the learner. And by the same token, there is every reason to infuse on-the-job training with exposure to general concepts and principles that extend beyond the particular task that is being mastered. One advantage of an "MI approach" to education is that it does not simply consist of a set of hurdles designed just to pick out those individuals with a blend of linguistic-logical intelligence – though I suspect that particular blend is well represented in readers of these words!

4   *Disciplinary and inter-disciplinary studies.*   Earlier I took the position that precollegiate education should focus on the major academic disciplines. I stand by that assertion. At the same time, all of us have become aware that so much cutting-edge work in the world is focused on problems, not on disciplines; and that much of the best work combines a number of disciplines, whether it be the intersection of genetics and information science, cognitive science and neuroscience, economics and behavioral science, or arts and computers. Since postgraduate education needs to take an increasingly inter-disciplinary stance, what implications might follow for precollegiate education?

In the United States many middle and high schools claim that they are carrying out inter-disciplinary work. Yet, examined more closely, these programs typically involve treatment of a topic from a number of angles, rather than a true blending of more than one discipline in an effort to elucidate a complex topic or problem. Indeed, unless a person has mastered more than one discipline, we cannot properly speak of inter-disciplinary work. It would be like calling a person bilingual before she had mastered more than a single language.

So what about efforts at inter-disciplinary work before tertiary education? I think it is possible to lay the groundwork for inter-disciplinary education in at least three ways:

a   *Among the young*   Encourage wide reading (or even wide surfing of the Web). This is the best route to cultural literacy. When young individuals pick up ideas informally on many topics approached from many angles, they accumulate a fount of knowledge which later serves them well.

b   *During the middle school years*   Feature complex problems which require consideration from a number of different disciplinary perspectives. For example, ask students to consider what would happen if the earth ran out of oil or if computers were "hacked" by organisms from outer space. Even when students are not fully versed in a discipline, it is instructive to realize that they will have to bring more than one perspective – and more than one intelligence – to bear on a solution.

c   *In secondary school*   Devote a fair amount of time to concerted efforts at synthesis across disciplines. Most students see secondary school as a series of unrelated topics, as they wander from one class or test to the next one on the schedule. This estrangement is not essential. Particularly if there is coordination among faculty, it is possible to approach some of the same topics (e.g., light, the Renaissance, patterns) from more than one disciplinary perspective. Then, if there are special weeks or classes devoted to efforts at bridging these perspectives, students can begin to gain a feeling for what genuine inter-disciplinary work is like. The "theory of knowledge" course of the International Baccalaureate Diploma Program is a good example of an opportunity to synthesize knowledge at the secondary school level.

Let me stress that, in offering these comments on various topics, I am not speaking as a disinterested expert. Indeed, one cannot even begin to think about such issues unless one puts forth one's own value system. The answers can be guided by findings from research, but they can never be dictated solely by the results of scientific or social scientific research.

Two crucial values

In touching upon values, I want to emphasize the enduring importance of two values: the assumption of responsibility and a respect for humanity. We encourage students to carry out work, but that work needs to be *good* in two ways: exemplary in quality but also responsible. More specifically, the work that we do as adults should take into account our responsibilities to five different spheres: to our own personal set of values; to other individuals around us (family, friends, colleagues/peers); to our profession/calling; to the institutions to which we belong; and to the wider world – people whom we do not know, those who will live in the future, the health and survival of the planet. (Some would add, to our God.) Attention to these responsibilities is important for *any* worker, be he or she a physician, physicist, physical therapist, or fisherman.

Such responsible education cannot be completed in the early years of life, but it must begin there. Adult years are far too late. And so parents and teachers must embody a sense of responsibility in their own lives and seek to nurture a comparable sense of responsibility in all young people. This is especially difficult to do in uncertain and turbulent times like these, when things are changing very quickly, market forces are very powerful, there are not equivalently potent counterforces, and our whole sense of time and space is being altered by technologies like the World Wide Web.

Many people in my country and elsewhere are worried about the alienation that a lot of young people experience – alienation from the world of school and, in some sad cases, alienation from the world at large. I lack the expertise to discuss this national and perhaps worldwide phenomenon. But I do know that we must help students to find meaning in daily life; to feel connected to other individuals and to their community – past, present, and future – and to feel responsible for the consequences of their actions. We must help them to achieve the state of flow – the balance between skills and challenges – which motivates individuals to return to a pursuit time and again. Plato understood this 2,500 years ago when he stated: "Through education we need to help students find pleasure in what they have to learn."

The second value is an appreciation of what is special about human beings. Human beings have done many terrible things, but countless members of our species have done wonderful things as well: works of art, works of music, discoveries of science and technology, heroic acts of courage and sacrifice. One only need walk around the Rijksmuseum in Holland or the pyramids in Egypt or the Taj Mahal in India or the Great Wall in China to be reminded of what has been achieved over the centuries. Our youngsters must learn about these achievements, come to respect them, have time to reflect on them (and what it took to achieve them) and aspire some day to achieve anew in the same tradition – or perhaps even to found a new tradition. Learning about human heroism may be another clue to how to nurture youngsters who embody positive values. We should not be afraid to state our values; but of course it is far more important to embody them, to live them day in and day out. The scholarly disciplines are among the most remarkable of human achievements – and we must remember that they are much easier to destroy than to build up. Totalitarian societies first burn the books; then they humiliate the scholars; then they kill those who do not buckle under. As the events of the past century remind us, a Dark Age can always descend upon us.

We should remember that one of the most magnificent of human inventions is the invention of education – no other species educates its young as do we. At this time of great change, we must remember the ancient value of education and preserve it – not just facts, data, information, but Knowledge, Understanding, Judgment, Wisdom. We must use the ancient arts and crafts of education to prepare youngsters for a world that natural evolution could not anticipate and which even we ourselves as conscious beings cannot fully envision either. In the past we could be satisfied with an education that was based on the literacies; that surveyed the major disciplines; and that taught students about their own national culture. We must maintain these three foci, but we must add two more: preparation for inter-disciplinary work and preparation for life in a global civilization. And, as science and technology gain increasing hegemony over our lives and our minds, we must keep alive the important values of responsibility and humanity.

The great French playwright Jean-Baptiste Molière once declared: "We are responsible not only for what we do but also for what we do not do." We must not shirk from the responsibility to prepare children and youth for a future which we can only glimpse – as through a glass darkly. That is the challenge faced as never before by education today. Let us combine the best of physical, natural, and social science, with the most precious of human values. Let us do so on a Global Scale. Then and only then can we have an educational system that reflects the best facets of the human condition.

CHAPTER 23

THE ETHICAL RESPONSIBILITIES OF PROFESSIONALS

Hetland, L. and S. Veenema (eds), *The Project Zero classroom: Views on understanding*, 169–76. Cambridge, MA: Harvard Project Zero, 1999.

In the middle of the nineteenth century a serious proposal was made to close the U.S. Patent Office because all inventions of significance had been made. In light of the subsequent appearance of the telegraph, telephone, radio, television, airplanes, and computers, we now laugh at the naiveté of this proposal. Some years ago an American journalist named John Horgan wrote a book entitled *The End of Science* (1996). In this book he speculated that the important questions about the nature of matter and life had been answered, and that most other questions about nature and mind were not susceptible to scientific answer. A century from now, the suggestion that science was effectively at an end in the 1990s is likely to seem equally ill informed.

To be sure, we cannot predict particular advances in science and technology. At the end of the nineteenth century who could have anticipated the theory of relativity, or plate tectonics, or quantum mechanics? Turning from the physical to the biological world, who could have foreseen the revolution in molecular biology, the nature of genes and chromosomes, the structure of DNA, let alone the fact that scientists can now clone entire organisms and will soon have within their grasp the power to transform the human genetic sequence and control heredity? And in light of the progress being made in the neural and cognitive sciences, investigators will continue to unravel the mysteries of thinking, problem-solving, attention, memory, and – the most elusive prize of all – the nature of consciousness. The result of this work is likely to be of singular importance for all of us who are engaged in teaching and learning across the life span.

It is hard to deny the excitement of these enterprises. So many issues and questions that were once the lot of poets and armchair philosophers have already been answered by scientists or at least hover within their grasp. Mysteries have now become problems, and problems are susceptible to solution. And yet it is dangerous to adopt a Pollyannaish view. Science marches on, smartly but blindly. There is no guarantee that such a sequence from mystery to soluble problem will naturally contribute to the good of the public or that it will prove to be a benevolent force in the future.

Science – indeed, scholarship more generally – is morally neutral. It represents the best efforts of human beings to provide reliable answers to existential questions that fascinate us: Who are we? What is the world made of? What will happen to it? When? (Should I put the date on my calendar?) What kind of creature would ask such questions?

But what happens when these questions are answered? Sometimes the answers simply satisfy human curiosity – an important and valid goal. But at other times they lead to concrete actions – some inspiring, some dreadful. Einstein's seemingly innocuous equation $E=MC^2$ stimulated many outcomes. These ranged from powering cities with nuclear energy, to the detonation of nuclear devices at the cost of thousands of lives in Hiroshima and Nagasaki, to the spreading of fallout following the Chernobyl disaster. Following the discoveries of antibiotic agents, we behold the production of wonderful drugs that can combat dread diseases as well as the emergence of new toxic organisms that prove resistant to the effects of antibiotic medication.

Again, scholarship itself cannot decide which applications to pursue, which not. These decisions are made by human beings, acting in whichever formal and informal capacities are available to them. Einstein is a good case in point. It is doubtful that he thought about the applications of atomic theory when he was developing his ideas about the fundamental properties of the physical world. By the time the politically attuned physicist Leo Szilard approached the aging propounder of relativity theory in the late 1930s, it was already apparent that nuclear energy could be harnessed to produce very powerful weapons. Einstein agreed to sign a letter to President Franklin Roosevelt, and that action, in turn, led to the launching of the Manhattan Project and the building of the first atomic weapons. After the end of the Second World War and following the detonation of two nuclear devices over Japan, Einstein became a leader in the movement toward peace and eventual disarmament.

Such choices and dilemmas are not solely the province of those in the so-called hard sciences. For most of the twentieth century, psychologists have been involved in efforts to measure individual differences in human intelligence. Most psychologists feel comfortable using the intelligence test – an instrument developed over a century ago to help predict success or failure in school. Among the issues faced by researchers is whether to investigate group differences in intelligence – for example, between men and women or among races.

Some scholars have stayed away from these issues for one or another reason. Others have focused on them. Richard Herrnstein and Charles Murray devoted a portion of their provocative book, *The Bell Curve* (1994), to a discussion of the long-standing and widely reported difference of 15 points (one standard deviation) between the scores of Americans of Caucasian and the scores of those of African-American descent on intelligence tests. Herrnstein and Murray believe that it will be difficult to eliminate that difference and that it probably does not make sense to try. Others believe that intelligence in general can be raised and that these group differences can be narrowed or perhaps eliminated (Neisser, 1998). Even a person who believes that it is difficult to raise intelligence still faces a choice: either elect not to devote resources to such an effort, or elect to direct sizable resources to it. None of these decisions can be dictated by science; they all involve judgments of value.

In the past, scientists argued that their job was to add to permanent human knowledge and understanding, and not to make decisions about policy and action. But what factors, then, have prevented the random use, misuse, or frank abuse of technology – the so-called fruits of scientific progress?

We can identify three factors that have traditionally served as a restraint on the misapplications of science. First of all, there have been the values of the community, in particular religious values. For example, in principle a scientist could conduct experiments in which prisoners are exposed to certain toxic agents. But religion counsels the sanctity of all human life. A second balancing force has been the law. In many nations, prisoners are protected against unusual forms of treatment or punishment. Third, there is the sense of calling, or ethical standards, of professionals. For example, a scientist might take the position that a contribution to knowledge should not be secured at the expense of human or animal welfare; indeed, some scientists have refused to make use of findings obtained by the Nazis as a result of immoral experiments. Or the warden of a prison might refuse to allow his prisoners to participate in studies using inhumane treatments, even in the face of social or financial pressures to do so.

Each of these restraining factors remains operative but, alas, each seems reduced in force nowadays. At a time of rapid change, values are fragile and religious creeds may seem anachronistic. Laws remain, unless they are overturned, but often events move so quickly that the law cannot keep up. And during an era when the market model has triumphed in nearly every corner of society, it is often quite difficult for individual professionals to uphold the standards of their calling. In the 1980s physicians in France colluded in the sale of blood that they knew to be tainted by the HIV virus. It is probable that their sense of calling was not potent enough to combat financial and societal demands for the blood.

Market pressures are becoming all too familiar to educators, too. More and more, education is justified in terms of its economic leverage. Powerful politicians and policy makers call for vouchers, charters, and other market mechanisms as a means of permitting families to select schools. The arts are justified for their potential contributions to learning in skills useful in business or the professions rather than for their inherent worth. Colleges compete with one another through advertising, scholarships, and high salaries for star faculty. It is difficult to discern voices that invoke forces other than the bottom line. Nowadays few educators underscore the intrinsic value of education or point up the need for non-commercial communal values.

Ethical responsibilities of professionals

We encounter an impasse. On the one hand, science and innovation proceed apace, ever conquering new frontiers. On the other hand, traditional restraints against wanton experimentation or abuse appear to be tenuous. Must we leave events to chance, or are there ways to pursue science and education – and, more broadly, professional life – in a responsible way?

Enter the ethical responsibilities of a professional. I contend that a new covenant must be formed between professionals and the society in which they live. Society makes it possible for scientific professionals to proceed with their work – by the funding of science as well as by cooperation in its execution. In return, I submit, scientists must take on an additional task; they must relinquish the once-justifiable claim that they have no responsibility for applications, and undertake a good faith effort to make sure that the fruits of science are applied wisely, not foolishly. So it must be for all professionals, including those in education.

Let me introduce an example from my own work as a cognitive psychologist. In the early 1980s I developed a new theory of intelligence called the theory of multiple intelligences (see Chapters 6 to 9). While I thought that this theory would be of interest primarily to other psychologists, I soon discovered that it was of considerable interest to educators as well. Educators began to make all kinds of applications of the theory. I was intrigued and flattered by this interest. Yet, like most scientists, I felt little personal involvement in these applications. Indeed, if asked, I would have responded: "I developed the ideas and I hope that they are correct. But I have no responsibility for how they are applied – these are 'memes' that have been released into the world and they must follow their own fate" (cf. Dawkins, 1976).

About ten years after my book *Frames of Mind* was published, I received a message from a colleague in Australia. He said, in effect, "Your 'Multiple Intelligence' ideas are being used in Australia and you won't like the way that they are being used." I asked him to send me the materials and he did so. My colleague was absolutely correct. The more that I read those materials, the less I liked them. The so-called smoking gun was a sheet of paper on which each of the ethnic and racial groups in Australia was listed, together with an explicit list of the intelligences in which members of a particular group were putatively strong as well as the intelligences in which members of that group were putatively weak.

This stereotyping represented a complete perversion of my personal beliefs. If I did not speak up, who would? Who should? And so I went on television in Australia and criticized that particular educational endeavor as "pseudo-science." That critique, along with cautionary notes signaled by others, sufficed to result in the cancellation of the project.

I do not hold myself up as a moral exemplar. It was not a job-threatening choice to appear on a television show in a far-away country, and I was not doing work in biotechnology or rocket science – work that can literally save or destroy lives. Yet the move that I made in my own thinking was crucial. Rather than seeing applications as the business of someone else, I had come to realize that I had a special responsibility to make sure that my ideas were used as constructively as possible. And indeed, ever since that time I have devoted some of my energies to supporting work on MI of which I approve, and critiquing or distancing myself from work whose uses are illegitimate or difficult to justify (Gardner 1995b).

What can be done to forge a new covenant between professionals and the larger society? To my mind, the current impasse calls for greater efforts by each party to make clear its needs and its expectations. Professionals must continually be willing to educate the public about the nature of their enterprises and about what is needed for good work to be done within their domains. Professionals have a right to resist foolish misunderstandings of their own enterprises and to fight for the uncensored pursuit of knowledge. At the same time, they must be willing to listen carefully to reservations about their work from non-professionals, to anticipate possible misapplications of the work, and to speak out forcefully about where they stand with respect to such reservations, uses, and misapplications.

Ordinarily, neither professionals nor the general public should block the road of inquiry. Assuming that they do not harm others, individuals must have the right to follow their questions and curiosity wherever those lead. Occasionally, however, professionals may want to consider *not* exploring certain questions, even though they may be personally curious about the outcomes. In the case of my own field, I myself do not condone investigations of racial differences in intelligence, because I think that the results of these studies are likely to be incendiary. Many biological scientists are extremely reluctant to engage in experiments of genetic engineering or cloning of human beings, not because of lack of curiosity about the results but rather because some of the implications of this work could be very troubling. It is not difficult to envision serious psychological or medical problems in the light of these experiments; it is even possible to imagine how genetic experiments gone awry might threaten the viability of the species.

Steps toward responsible action

If they believe that my claim has merit – if they believe that professionals generally should become more deeply involved in ethical considerations – how might individuals act upon that belief? This is the question I have been pondering with my close colleagues Mihaly Csikszentmihalyi of the University of Chicago, William Damon of Stanford University, and several other researchers in our laboratories (Gardner, Csikszentmihalyi, and Damon, 2001; see also <http://www.goodwork project.org>. We are trying to understand how leading practitioners – individuals doing cutting-edge work – deal with the various invitations and pressures in their domains. We have been observing and interviewing scientists and professionals in other rapidly changing domains, such as journalism, business, and the arts. We want to know how their present work situations appear to such individuals "in the trenches," and we want to identify individuals and institutions that have succeeded in melding innovative work with a sense of responsibility for the implications and applications of that work.

While our study is far from complete, let me make a few comments about our findings thus far, with a particular eye on education. To begin with, professionals are not naive about their situation. They are aware of the great pressures on them and the hegemony of the market model at the beginning of the twenty-first century. They want to be ethical persons in their professional and private lives. They recognize the pressures that make it difficult for them always to do the right thing and to avoid crossing tempting lines.

Yet clear differences can be observed in how successful these innovative individuals are in maintaining an ethical sense. Not surprisingly, early training and values are important, and that includes a religious affiliation in many cases. The opportunity to work in the laboratory of an ethical scientist, to spend time in a truly distinguished institution, or to be surrounded by colleagues with individuals who "live" their values are equally important formative factors.

Once they have begun their careers in earnest, creative individuals are aided by two factors. The first is a strong sense of internal principles – lines that they will not cross, no matter what. If a scientist says – and believes – that she will never put her name on a paper unless she has reviewed all of the data herself, that virtually eliminates the likelihood that she will be an accessory to the reporting of fraudulent data. The second factor is a realization that the profession does not have to be accepted the way that it is today; as a human agent, a person can work toward changing that domain. Suppose, for example, that it has become routine practice, in the writing of grants, for the head of a laboratory to propose work that has in fact already been carried out but has not yet been published. A scientist could decide henceforth not to do this and work with colleagues to change the reigning but flawed procedures in the domain. Indeed, the installation of a process through which senior scholars apply for support by describing work that has recently been completed, rather than work that might be carried out in the future, would represent a significant alteration in the customary practices of a domain.

Similar examples can be gleaned with reference to the applications of creative work. A researcher could decide, for example, that all of her work is in the public domain and thus refuse to patent any findings. Here an internal principle wins out over the desire for personal profit. Or she could insist that science take the public interest into account. One way to do that would be for every laboratory voluntarily to set up an advisory committee, consisting of knowledgeable individuals from neighboring domains and laboratories. This advisory group would inform itself about the work of the lab, critique it when appropriate, and make suggestions about benevolent and possibly malevolent uses of findings.

The responsible educator

Plunging directly into the matter of education, let me attempt to apply the present analysis to a teaching professional who wants to devote her energies to the inculcation of disciplinary understanding in her students.

Let us suppose that you are a teacher of American history in the tenth grade. You take your calling seriously. You have decided that you want to bring about deep understanding of historical thinking in your students. And you believe the best way to do this is to study a few topics in considerable depth – say the American Revolution, the Civil War, and immigration at the beginning of the twentieth century. Your students will work with original documents, ponder essential questions, and be expected to argue about current events (e.g., recent immigration to California, the civil war in the former Yugoslavia) on the basis of their newly acquired historical understandings. You want them to understand the difficulty and the power of the venerable and venerated discipline of history.

Enter the frameworks developed in the community or state in which you reside. Working together, politicians and educational policy makers have developed a curriculum and a required set of tests for all tenth graders. The curriculum features a text that is rich in facts and figures but unsettlingly thin in ideas. The tests match the curriculum. There is no room for thoughtful analysis, for raising new questions, for applying historical insights to the current situation, for acknowledging the fragility of the historical record. Instead, the high performer becomes the student who – shades of television quiz shows – knows the names and dates of hundreds of politicians, military leaders, treaties, laws, and disputes.

What should you do as a professional embued with a strong sense of calling? Should you succumb to these new frameworks, actively fight them, conduct some kind of a guerrilla activity, or begin to scan the want-ad section (or website) of your local newspaper?

Circumstances and personalities differ, and no solution to this conundrum will work for every professional. Our study has yielded two ways of thinking about these issues that may be worth considering.

One approach could be to think about which stance you wish to assume toward the domain in which you work – in this case the teaching of American history. Recalling the reasons for your original choice of career, you could elect to pursue the domain as you initially learned it. Alternatively, recognizing the pressures of the moment, you could accept the definition of the domain imposed by others – in this case, those who write the laws and regulations and pay the salaries. A third stance could be to attempt to modify the domain – for example, organizing teachers and parents to develop an alternative view of the tenth grade curriculum, complete with its own set of standards or assessments. Yet another stance could be to try to recreate the domain in a new setting – for example, by deciding to work for, or create, a textbook company, a website, a cable television program, a new kind of testing, or an after-school program in which you teach history and current events in a quite different way.

A second way to approach this issue is to think about your responsibilities. As I mentioned in Chapter 22, every individual has a set of at least five responsibilities among which he or she must continually negotiate. One responsibility is to yourself: your own goals, values, and needs, both selfish and selfless. A second responsibility is to those about you: your family, friends, daily colleagues. A third responsibility is to your calling: the principles that regulate your profession – in this case, what it means to teach a discipline to students. A fourth responsibility is to the institution to which you belong: the particular school, or perhaps the school system or network of schools of which you are a member. A final responsibility is to the wider world: to individuals you do not know, to the safety and sanctity of the planet, and to those who will inherit the world in the future. As the American historian Henry Adams powerfully phrased it: "A teacher affects eternity: he can never tell where his influence stops." We suggest that the thoughtful professional is always wrestling with these competing responsibilities and, insofar as possible, trying to meet each one reasonably well.

Whether sage or scientist, lawyer or layperson, parent or teacher, all of us must negotiate our way among these strong and sometimes competing responsibilities. We are helped by religion, ethics, friends, and colleagues, but in the end we must do the balancing ourselves. Personal responsibility cannot be delegated to someone else. Those who have the special privilege of educating the young have an obligation to be reflective about their stance toward teaching and their negotiation of these competing responsibilities. At a time when there is so much to learn, so many new media to master, and such pressing needs in the world, these responsibilities can seem awesome. Greater mindfulness about our responsibilities has become a necessity, if we are to pass on to our progeny a world that is worth inhabiting.

BIBLIOGRAPHY

Aiello, R. (1994). Music and language: Parallels and contrasts. In R. Aiello and J. Sloboda (eds.), *Musical perceptions*. New York: Oxford University Press.

Aiken, W. (1942). *The story of the Eight Year Study*. New York: Harper & Brothers.

Arnheim, R. (1969). *Visual thinking*. Berkeley, CA: University of California Press.

Arnheim, R. (1974). *Art and visual perception: The new version*. Berkeley, CA: University of California Press.

Association of American Geographers (1965, 1979). *Geography in an urban age*. New York: Macmillan.

ATLAS (1994). *Authentic teaching, learning, and assessment for schools*. Cambridge, MA: Harvard Project Zero.

Bamberger, J. (1982). Revisiting children's drawings of simple rhythms: A function reflection-in-action. In S. Strauss (ed.), *U-shaped behavioral growth*. New York: Academic Press.

Bamberger, J. (1991). *The mind behind the musical ear*. Cambridge, MA: Harvard University Press.

Bamberger, J. (1994). Coming to hear in a new way. In R. Aiello and J. Sloboda (eds.), *Musical perceptions*. New York: Oxford University Press.

Basso, A. and Capitani, E. (1985). Spared musical abilities in a conductor with global aphasia and ideomotor apraxia. *Journal of Neurology, Neurosurgery, and Psychiatry*.

Bates, E. (1976). *Language and context: The acquisition of pragmatics*. New York: Academic Press.

Battro, A. (2003). Digital skills, globalization and education. In M. Suarez-Orozco and D. Qin-Hilliard (eds.), *Globalization: Culture and education in the new millennium*, Berkeley, CA: University of California Press.

Battro, A. and Denham, P. (2002). *Hacia una inteligencia digital*. Buenos Aires.

Bereiter, C. and Engelmann, S. (1966). *Teaching the disadvantaged in the preschool*. Englewood Cliffs, NJ: Prentice Hall.

Bever, T. (1992). The logical and extrinsic sources of modularity. In M. Gunnar and M. Maratsos (eds.), *Modularity and constraints in language and cognition*. Hillsdale, NJ: Lawrence Erlbaum.

Bloom, A. (1987). *The closing of the American mind*. New York: Simon & Schuster.

Bloom, B. and Sosniak, L. (1985). *Developing talent in young people.* New York: Ballantine Books.

Bloom, D.E. (2003). Globalization and education: An economic perspective. In M. Suarez-Orozco and D. Qin-Hilliard (eds.), *Globalization: Culture and education in the new millennium,* Berkeley, CA: University of California Press.

Bloom, D.E. and Cohen, J.E. (2001). The unfinished revolution: Universal basic and secondary education. Paper presented at the American Academy of Arts and Sciences, Cambridge, MA, July.

Bluestein, N. and Acredolo, L. (1979). Developmental changes in map-reading skills. *Child Development,* 50.

Blythe, T. (1998). *The teaching for understanding guide.* San Francisco, CA: Jossey-Bass.

Boix-Mansilla, V. and Gardner, H. (1997). Of kinds of disciplines and kinds of understanding. *Phi Delta Kappan,* 78(5).

Bower, T.G.R. (1974). *Development in infancy.* San Francisco: W.H. Freeman.

Brainerd, C. (1978). The stage question in cognitive-developmental theory. *The Behavioral and Brain Sciences,* 2.

Brooks, L.R. (1968). Spatial and verbal components of the act of recall. *Canadian Journal of Psychology,* 22.

Brown, N. (1987). Pivotal points in artistic growth. Presentation at the 1987 ARTS PROPEL summer workshop, Pittsburg, PA, August.

Brown, R. (1973). *A first language: The early stages.* Cambridge, MA: Harvard University Press.

Bruner, J.S. (1960). *The process of education.* Cambridge, MA: Harvard University Press.

Bruner, J.S. (1965). The course of cognitive growth. *American Psychologist,* 15(1).

Bruner, J.S. (1966). *Toward a theory of instruction.* Cambridge, MA: Harvard University Press.

Bruner, J.S. (1971). *The relevance of education.* New York: Norton.

Bruner, J.S. (1983). *In search of mind: Essays in autobiography.* New York: Harper & Row.

Bruner, J.S. (1990). *Acts of meaning.* Cambridge, MA: Harvard University Press.

Bruner, J.S. (1996). *The culture of education.* Cambridge, MA: Harvard University Press.

Bruner, J.S. and Cunningham, B. (1939). The effect of thymus extract on the sexual behavior of the female rat. *Journal of Comparative Psychology,* 7.

Bruner, J.S., Olver, R.R., and Greenfield, P.M. (1966). *Studies in cognitive growth.* New York: Wiley.

Carey, S. and Gelman, R. (eds) (1991). *The epigenesis of mind.* Hillside, NJ: Erlbaum.

Carini, P. (1987). Another way of looking. Paper presented at the Cambridge School Conference, Weston, MA, October.

Case, R. (1991). *The mind's staircase.* Hillsdale, NJ: Erlbaum.

Cassirer, E. (1957). *The philosophy of symbolic forms.* New Haven, CT: Yale University Press.

Cheng, K. (1986). A purely geometric module in the rat's spatial representation. *Cognition,* 23.

Chomsky, N. (1975). *Reflections on language*. New York: Pantheon.

Cohen, D., McLaughlin, M., and Talbert, J. (1993). *Teaching for understanding*. San Francisco, CA: Jossey-Bass.

Coles, R. (1997). *The moral intelligence of children*. New York: Random House.

Collier, G. (1994). *The social origins of mental ability*. New York: Wiley.

Collins, A., Brown, J.S., and Newman, S.E. (1989). Cognitive apprenticeship: Teaching the craft of reading, writing and mathematics. In L. Resnick (ed.), *Cognition and instruction: Issues and agendas*. Hillsdale, NJ: Lawrence Erlbaum.

Collins, J. (1998). Seven kinds of smart. *Time Magazine*, October 19.

Comer, J. (1980). *School power*. New York: Free Press.

Cronbach, L. (1984). *Essentials of psychological testing*. New York: Harper & Row.

Cross, K.P. and Angelo, T. (1988). *Classroom assessment techniques: A handbook for faculty*. Ann Arbor, MI: National Research Center for Research to Improve Postsecondary Teaching and Learning (NCRIPTL).

Csikszentmihalyi, M. (1988). Society, culture, and person: A systems view of creativity. In R. Sternberg (ed.), *The nature of creativity*. New York: Cambridge University.

Csikszentmihalyi, M. and Robinson, R. (1986). Culture, time, and the development of talent. In R. Sternberg and J. Davidson (eds.), *Conceptions of giftedness*. New York: Cambridge University Press.

Davidson, L. (1989). Observing a Yang Chin lesson. *Journal for Aesthetic Education*, 23(1).

Davidson, L. (1994). Songsinging by young and old. In R. Aiello and J. Sloboda (eds.), *Musical perceptions*. New York: Oxford.

Davidson, L. and Scripp, L. (1988). Young children's musical representations. In J. Sloboda (ed.), *Generative processes in music*. Oxford: Oxford University Press.

Davidson, L., Scripp, L., and Welsh, P. (1988). "Happy Birthday': Evidence for conflicts of perceptual knowledge and conceptual understanding. *Journal of Aesthetic Education*, 22(1).

Dawkins, R. (1976). *The selfish gene*. New York: Oxford University Press.

Deutsch, D. (1975). The organization of memory for a short-term attribute. In D. Deutsch and J. Deutsch (eds.), *Short-term memory*. New York: Academic Press.

Deutsch, D. (ed.) (1982). *The psychology of music*. New York: Academic Press.

Dewey, J. (1899/1967). *The school and society*. Chicago, IL: University of Chicago Press.

Dewey, J. (1916). *Democracy and education*. New York: Macmillan.

Dewey, J. (1938). *Experience and education*. New York: Collier.

Dewey, J. (1958). *Art as experience*. New York: Capricorn.

Dewey, J. (1964a). John Dewey on education. In R. Archambault (ed.), *John Dewey on education: Selected writings*. New York: Random House.

Dewey, J. (1964b). The nature of subject matter. In R. Archambault (ed.), *John Dewey on education: Selected writings*. New York: Random House.

Donald, M. (1991). *Origins of the modern mind*. Cambridge, MA: Harvard University Press.

Dowling, W. (1994). Melodic contour in hearing and remembering melodies. In R. Aiello and J. Sloboda (eds.), *Musical perceptions*. New York: Oxford University Press.

Dowling, W. and Harwood, D. (1986). *Music cognition*. New York: Academic Press.

Dyer, F. and Gould, J. (1983). Honey bee navigation. *American Scientist*, 71.

Eco, U. (1976). *A theory of semiotics*. Bloomington, IN: Indiana University Press.

Educational Leadership (February, 1994). 51(5).

Egan, K. (1992). Review of *The unschooled mind*. *Teachers College Record*, 94(2).

Ericsson, K.A. and Charness, N. (1994). Expert performance: Its structure and acquisition. *American Psychologist*, 49(8).

Erikson, E.H. (1963). *Childhood and society* (second edition). New York: Norton.

Eysenck, H. (1986). The theory of intelligence and the psychophysiology of cognition. In R. Sternberg (ed.), *Advances in the psychology of human intelligence*, Vol. III. Hillsdale, NJ: Lawrence Erlbaum.

Feldman, D. (1980). *Beyond universals in cognitive development*. New York: Ablex Publishers.

Feldman, D and L. Goldsmith. (1986). *Nature's gambit*. New York: Basic Books.

Feldman, D. (2003). The creation of multiple intelligences theory: A study in high-level thinking. In K. Sawyer (ed.), *Creativity and development*. New York: Oxford University Press.

Feldman, D., Csikszentmihalyi, M., and Gardner, H. (1994). *Changing the world: A framework for the study of creativity*. Westport, CT: Greenwood Publishing Company.

Fischer, K. (1980). A theory of cognitive development: The control of hierarchies of skills. *Psychological Review*, 87.

Fodor, J.A. (1975). *The language of thought*. New York: Crowell.

Fodor, J.A. (2000). *The mind doesn't work that way*. Cambridge, MA: MIT Press.

Friedman, T. (2000). *The Lexus and the olive tree: Understanding globalization*. New York: Anchor Books.

Freud, S. (1950). *The future of an illusion*. London: The Hogarth Press.

Gallistel, C., Brown, A., Carey, S., Gelman, R., and Keil, F. (1991). Lessons from animal learning for the study of cognitive development. In S. Carey and R. Gelman (eds.), *The epigenesis of mind: Essays on biology and cognition*. Hillsdale, NJ: Lawrence Erlbaum.

Gardner, H. (1970). Children's sensitivity to painting styles. *Child Development*, 41.

Gardner, H. (1971). The development of sensitivity to artistic styles. *Journal of Aesthetics and Art Criticism*, 29.

Gardner, H. (1972). Style sensitivity in children. *Human Development*, 15.

Gardner, H. (1973a). *The arts and human development*. New York: Wiley. Reprinted by Basic Books, 1994.

Gardner, H. (1973b). Children's sensitivity to musical styles. *Merrill-Palmer Quarterly*, 19.

Gardner, H. (1973c). *The quest for mind: Jean Piaget, Claude Lévi-Strauss, and the structuralist movement*. New York: Knopf. Vintage paperback, 1974; reprinted by University of Chicago Press.

Gardner, H. (1974a). Metaphors and modalities: How children project polar adjectives onto diverse domains. *Child Development*, 45.

Gardner, H. (1974b). The naming and recognition of written symbols in aphasic and alexic patients. *Journal of Communication Disorders*, 7.

Gardner, H. (1975). *The shattered mind*. New York: Knopf.

Gardner, H. (1976). Unfolding or teaching: On the optimal training of artistic skills. In E. Eisner (ed.), *The arts, human development, and education*. Berkeley, CA: McCutchan Publishing Company.

Gardner, H. (1977). Senses, symbols, and operations. In D. Perkins and B. Leondar (eds.). *The arts and cognition*. Baltimore, MD: Johns Hopkins University Press.

Gardner, H. (1979). Entering the world of the arts: The child as artist. *Journal of Communication*, 29(4).

Gardner, H. (1980). *Artful scribbles: The significance of children's drawings*. New York: Basic Books.

Gardner, H. (1982a). *Art, mind, and brain: A cognitive approach to creativity*. New York: Basic Books.

Gardner, H. (1982b). Artistry following damage to the human brain. In A. Ellis (ed.) *Normality and pathology in cognitive functions*. London: Academic Press.

Gardner, H. (1983). *Frames of mind: The theory of multiple intelligences*. New York: Basic Books. A tenth anniversary edition, with a new introduction, was published in 1993, and a twentieth anniversary edition, with a new introduction, in 2004.

Gardner, H. (1985a). *The mind's new science: A history of the cognitive revolution*. New York: Basic Books.

Gardner, H. (1985b). Note on the project on human potential. *Frames of mind: The theory of multiple intelligences*. New York: BasicBooks.

Gardner, H. (1985c). On discerning new ideas in psychology. *New Ideas in Psychology*, 3.

Gardner, H. (1986a). The development of symbolic literacy. In M. Wrolstad and D. Fisher (eds.), *Toward a greater understanding of literacy*. New York: Praeger.

Gardner, H. (1986b). Notes on cognitive development: Recent trends, future prospects. In S. Friedman, K. Klivington, and R. Peterson (eds.), *The brain, cognition and education*. New York: Academic Press.

Gardner, H. (1987a). An individual-centered curriculum. In *The schools we've got, the schools we need*. Washington, DC: Council of Chief State School Officers and the American Association of Colleges of Teacher Education.

Gardner, H. (1987b). Symposium on the theory of multiple intelligences. In D. Perkins, J. Lochhead, and J. Bishop (eds.), *Thinking: The second international conference*. Hillside, NJ: Lawrence Erlbaum.

Gardner, H. (1988). Mobilizing resources for individual centered education. In R. Nickerson and P. Zodhiates (eds.), *Technology in education: Looking toward 2020*. Hillsdale, NJ: Lawrence Erlbaum.

Gardner, H. (1989a). Balancing specialized and comprehensive knowledge: The growing education challenge. In T. Sergiovanni (ed.), *Schooling for tomorrow: Directing reforms to issues that count*. Boston, MA: Allyn and Bacon.

Gardner, H. (1989b). *To open minds: Chinese clues to the dilemma of contemporary education*. New York: Basic Books.

Gardner, H. (1989c). Zero-based arts education. *Studies in Art Education: A Journal of Issues and Research*, 30(2).

Gardner, H. (1991a). Assessment in context: The alternative to standardized testing. In B.R. Gifford and M.C. O'Connor (eds.), *Changing assessments: Alternative views of aptitude, achievement, and instruction*. Boston, MA: Kluwer.

Gardner, H. (1991b). The school of the future. In J. Brockman (ed.), *Ways of knowing: The Reality Club 3*. Englewood Cliffs, NJ: Prentice Hall.

Gardner, H. (1991c). *The unschooled mind: How children think and how school should teach*. New York: Basic Books.

Gardner, H. (1993a). *Creating minds: An anatomy of creativity seen through the lives of Freud, Einstein, Picasso, Stravinsky, Eliot, Graham, and Gandhi*. New York: Basic Books.

Gardner, H. (1993b). Educating for understanding. *The American School Board Journal*, 80(7).

Gardner, H. (1993c). *Multiple intelligences: The theory in practice*. New York: Basic Books.

Gardner, H. (1993d). Progressivism in a new key. Paper delivered at the conference on education and democracy, Jerusalem, June.

Gardner, H. (1994). How extraordinary was Mozart? In J.M. Morris (ed.), *On Mozart*, Washington, DC: Woodrow Wilson Center Press.

Gardner, H. (1995a). *Leading minds: An anatomy of leadership*. New York: Basic Books.

Gardner, H. (1995b). Reflections on multiple intelligences: Myths and realities. *Kappan*, 77(3).

Gardner, H. (1997). *Extraordinary minds*. New York: Basic Books.

Gardner, H. (1999). *Intelligence reframed: Multiple intelligences for the 21st century*. New York: Basic Books.

Gardner, H. (2000). *The disciplined mind: Beyond facts and standardized tests. K-12 education that every child deserves*. New York: Penguin Putnam.

Gardner, H. (in press). A blessing of influences. In *Gardner under fire*.

Gardner, H. (n.d.). In his own words. Available at <http://www.howardgardner.com/bio/bio.html>.

Gardner, H. and Boix-Mansilla, V. (1994a). Teaching for understanding in the disciplines – and beyond. *Teachers College Record*, 96(2).

Gardner, H. and Boix-Mansilla, V. (1994b). Teaching for understanding within and across the disciplines. *Educational Leadership*, 51(5).

Gardner, H. and Gardner, J. (1970). Development trends in sensitivity to painting style and subject matter. *Studies in Art Education*, 12.

Gardner, H. and Gardner, J. (1973). Developmental trends in sensitivity to form and subject matter in paintings. *Studies in Art Education*, 14.

Gardner, H. and Nemirovsky, R. (1991). From private intuitions to public symbol systems: An examination of creative process in Georg Cantor and Sigmund Freud. *Creativity Research Journal*, 4(1).

Gardner, H. and Perkins, D. (1989). *Art, mind, and education*. Urbana, IL: University of Illinois Press. Originally published as an issue of *Journal of Aesthetic Education*, 21(1), spring 1988.

Gardner, H. and Perkins, D. (1994). The mark of Zero: Project Zero's identity revealed. *Harvard Graduate School of Education Alumni Bulletin*, 39(1).

Gardner, H. and Winner, E. (1981). Artistry and aphasia. In M.T. Sarno (ed.), *Acquired Aphasia*. New York: Academic Press.

Gardner, H. and Winner, E. (1982). First intimations of artistry. In S. Strauss (ed.), *U-shaped behavioral growth*. New York: Academic Press.

Gardner, H. and Wolf, C. (1988). The fruits of asynchrony: A psychological examination of creativity. *Adolescent Psychiatry*, 15.

Gardner, H. and Wolf, D.P. (1983). Waves and streams of symbolization. In D.P. Rogers and J.A. Sloboda (eds.), *The acquisition of symbolic skills*. London: Plenum Press.

Gardner, H., Csikszentmihalyi, M., and Damon, W. (2001). *Good work: When excellence and ethics meet*. New York: Basic Books.

Gardner, H., Feldman, D.H., and Krechevsky, M. (eds.) (1998). *Project Zero frameworks for early childhood education*, Vols. 1–3. New York: Teachers College Press.

Gardner, H., Howard, V., and Perkins, D. (1974). Symbol systems: A philosophical, psychological, and educational investigation. In D. Olson (ed.), *Media and symbols: The forms of expression, communication, and education*. Chicago, IL: University of Chicago Press.

Gardner, H., Wolf, D., and Smith, A. (1975). Artistic symbols in early childhood. *New York Education Quarterly*, 6.

Gardner, H., Kircher, M., Winner, E., and Perkins, D. (1975). Children's metaphoric productions mad preferences. *Journal of Child Language*, 2.

Gardner, H., Winner, E., Bechhofer, R. and Wolf, D. (1978). The development of figurative language. In K. Nelson (ed.), *Children's language*. New York: Gardner Press.

Gardner, H., Silverman, J., Denes, G., Semenza, C. and Rosenstiel, A. (1977). Sensitivity to musical denotation and connotation in organic patients. *Cortex*, 13.

Geertz, C. (1983). *Local knowledge*. New York: Basic Books.

Gelman, R. (1969). Conservation acquisition: A problem of learning to attend to relevant attributes. *Journal of Experimental Child Psychology*, 7.

Gelman, R. (1972). The nature and development of early number concepts. In H.W. Reese (ed.), *Advances in child development and behaviour*, Vol. VII. New York: Academic Press.

Gelman, R. (1991). Epigenetic foundations of knowledge structures: Initial and transcendent constructions. In S. Carey and R. Gelman (eds.), *The epigenesis of mind*. Hillsdale, NJ: Lawrence Erlbaum.

Geschwind, N. and Galaburda, A. (1987). *Cerebral lateralization*. Cambridge, MA: Harvard University Press.

Giddens, A. (2000). *Runaway world: How globalization is reshaping our lives*. New York: Routledge.

Goldhagen, D. (1996). *Hitler's willing executioners*. New York: Knopf.

Goleman, D. (1995). *Emotional intelligence: Why it can matter more than IQ*. New York: Bantam Books.

Golomb, C. (1973). Children's representation of the human figure: The effects of models, media, and instruction. *General Psychology Monograph*, 87.

Gombrich, E.H. (1960). *Art and illusion*. Princeton, NJ: Princeton University Press.

Goodman, N. (1968). *Languages of art: An approach to a theory of symbols*. Indianapolis, IN: Bobbs-Merrill. Republished in 1976. Indianapolis, IN: Hackett.

Goodman, N. (1988). Aims and claims. *Journal of Aesthetic Education*, 21(1).

Goodman, N., Perkins, D., and Gardner, H. (1972). Basic abilities required for understanding and creation in the arts. Final Report for the U.S. Office of Education. Cambridge, MA: Harvard University Press.

Goodnow, J. (1972). Rules and repertoires, rituals and tricks of the trade: Social and informational aspects to cognitive representational development. In S. Farnham-Diggory (ed.), *Information processing in children*. New York: Academic Press.

Gould, S.J. (1981). *The mismeasure of man*. New York: W.W. Norton.

Gould, S.J. (1993). *Wonderful life*. New York: Norton.

Graham, P. (1967). *Progressive education: From arcady to academe*. New York: Teachers College Press.

Grant, D. (1978). *On competence*. San Francisco, CA: Jossey-Bass.

Gregg, M. and Leinhardt, G. (1994). Mapping out geography: An example of epistemology and education. *Review of Educational Leadership*, 64(2).

Gruber, H. (1981). *Darwin on man*. Chicago, IL: University of Chicago Press.

Gunnar, M. and Maratsos, M. (eds.) (1992). *Modularity and constraints in language and cognition. The Minnesota Symposia on Child Psychology*, Vol. XXV. Hillsdale, NJ: L. Erlbaum.

Halberstam, D. (1972). *The best and the brightest*. New York: Random House.

Haley, M.H. (2004). Language-centered instruction and the theory of multiple intelligences with second language learners. *Teachers College Record*, 106(1).

Harris, L. (1981). Sex related variations in spatial skill. In L. Liben, A. Patterson, and N. Newcombe (eds.), *Spatial representation and behavior across the lifespan*. New York: Academic Press.

Hauser, M., Chomsky, N., and Fitch, T. (2002). The faculty of language: What is it, who has it, and how did it evolve? *Science*, 298.

Head, H. (1926). *Aphasia and kindred disorders of speech*. London: Cambridge University Press.

Heath, S.B. (1983). *Ways with words*. New York: Cambridge University Press.

Herrnstein, R. and Murray, C. (1994). *The bell curve*. New York: Free Press.

Hewes, D. (1982). Pre-school geography. *Journal of Geography*, 81.

Hirsch, E.D. (1987). *Cultural literacy*. Boston, MA: Houghton Mifflin.

Hirsch, E.D. (1996). *The schools we need and why we don't have them*. New York: Doubleday.

Hirst, P. (1972). *Education and the development of reason*. London: Routledge & Kegan Paul.

Hirst, P. (1975). Education and reason. In R.F. Dearden, P.H. Hirst, and R.S. Peters (eds.), *Education and the development of reason*. Boston, MA: Routledge & Kegan Paul.

Holton, G. (1988). *Thematic origins of scientific thought*. Cambridge, MA: Harvard University Press.

Horgan, J. (1996). *The end of science*. Reading, MA: Addison-Wesley.

Howard, V. (1971). Harvard Project Zero: A fresh look at art education. *Journal of Aesthetic Education*, 5(1).

Huttenlocher, J. and Higgins, E.T. (1978). Issues in the study of symbolic development. Unpublished paper, University of Chicago.

Jackson, J.H. (1932). *Selected writing of John Hughlings-Jackson*. London: Hodder & Stoughton.

Jacobs, H. (1989). *Interdisciplinary curriculum: Design and implementation*. Alexandria, VA: Association for Supervision and Curriculum Development.

Jenkins, H. (2003). Pop cosmopolitanism: Mapping cultural flows in an age of media convergences. In M. Suarez-Orozco and D. Qin-Hilliard (eds.),

Globalization: Culture and education in the new millennium. Berkeley, CA: University of California Press.

Jervis, K. and Tobier, A. (1988). *Education for democracy.* Weston, MA: The Cambridge School.

Judd, T., Gardner, H., and Geschwind, N. (1983). Alexia without agraphia in a composer. *Brain*, 106.

Kagan, J. (1993). *Galen's prophecy: Temperament and human nature.* New York: Basic Books.

Kagan, J., Kearsley, R., and Zelazo, R. (1978). *Infancy. Its place in human development.* Cambridge, MA: Harvard University Press.

Kaplan, E. (1968). Gestural representation of implement usage: An organismic-developmental study. Unpublished doctoral dissertation, Clark University, MA.

Kaplan, E. (1983). Process and achievement revisited. In S. Wapner and B. Kaplan (eds.), *Toward a holistic developmental psychology.* Hillsdale, NJ: Lawrence Erlbaum.

Kaplan, J. and Gardner, H. (1989). Artistry after unilateral brain disease. In F. Boller and J. Grafman (eds.), *Handbook of neuropsychology.* Amsterdam: Elsevier Science Publishers.

Karmiloff-Smith, A. (1992). *Beyond modularity.* Cambridge, MA: MIT Press.

Kendler, H.H and Kendler, T.S. (1962). Vertical and horizontal processes in problem-solving. *Psychological Review*, 69.

Kessen, W., Levine, J. and Peindich, K. (1978). The imitation of pitch in infants. *Infant Behavior and Development*, 2.

Kinsbourne, M. (1973). *The control of attention by interaction between the cerebral hemispheres in attention and performance.* New York: Academic Press.

Knox, R. (1995). Brainchild. *Boston Globe Magazine*, November 5.

Kohlberg, L. (1969). Stage and sequence: The cognitive-developmental approach to socialization. In D. Goslin (ed.), *Handbook of socialization theory and research.* New York: Rand McNally.

Kohnstamm, G. (1963). An evaluation of part of Piaget's theory. *Aeta Psychologica*, 2.

Kornhaber, M. (1999). MI theory in practice. In J. Block, S.T. Everson, and T.R. Guskey (eds.), *Comprehensive school improvement programs.* Dubuque, IA: Kendall/Hunt.

Kornhaber, M., Fierros, E., and Veenema, S. (2004). *Multiple intelligences: Best ideas from research and practice.* Needham Heights, MA: Allyn & Bacon.

Krechevsky, M. and Gardner, H. (1990). Approaching school intelligently: An infusion approach. In D. Kuhn (ed.), *Developmental perspectives on teaching and learning thinking skills.* Basel: S. Karger.

Krumhansl, C. (1990). *Cognitive foundations of musical pitch.* New York: Oxford.

Kuhn, T.S. (1970). *The structure of scientific revolutions.* Chicago, IL: University of Chicago Press.

Laboratory of Comparative Human Cognition (1982). Culture and intelligence. In R.J. Sternberg (ed.), *Handbook of human intelligence.* New York: Cambridge University Press.

Landau, B. (1988). The construction and use of spatial knowledge in blind and sighted children. In J. Stiles-Davis, U. Bellugi, and M. Kritchevsky (eds.), *Spatial cognition: Brain bases and development.* Hillsdale, NJ: Lawrence Erlbaum.

Landau, B., Spelke, E., and Gleitman, H. (1984). Spatial knowledge in a young blind child. *Cognition*, 16.

Langer, S. (1942). *Philosophy in a new key*. Cambridge, MA: Harvard University Press.

Lave, J. (1980). What's special about experiments as contexts for thinking? *Quarterly Newsletter of the Laboratory of Comparative Human Cognition*, 2.

Levy, M. (1968). *The family revolution in modern China*. New York: Atheneum.

Li, J. and Gardner, H. (1993). How domains constrain creativity: The case of traditional Chinese and Western painting. *American behavioral scientist*, 37(11).

Liben, L. and Downs, R. (1991). The role of graphic representations in understanding the world. In R. Downs, L. Liben, and D. Palermo (eds.), *Visions of aesthetics, the environment, and development*. Hillsdale, NJ: Lawrence Erlbaum.

Lippmann, W. (1976). Readings from the Lippmann–Terman debate (original work published in 1922–3). In N. Block and G. Dworkin (eds.), *The IQ controversy: Critical readings*. New York: Pantheon.

Lorenz, K. (1977). *Behind the mirror*. New York: Harcourt, Brace, Jovanovich.

Lowenfeld, V. (1947). *Creative and mental growth*. New York: Macmillian.

Luria, A. and Yudovich, F. (1971). *Speech and the development of mental processes in the child*. London: Penguin Books.

McFarland, H. and Fortin, D. (1982). Amusia due to right temporoparietal infarct. *Archives of Neurology*, 39.

McLuhan, M. (1964). *Understanding media*. New York: McGraw Hill.

Maira, S. (2003). Imperial feelings: Youth culture, citizenship, and globalization. In M. Suarez-Orozco and D. Qin-Hilliard (eds.), *Globalization: Culture and education in the new millennium*. Berkeley, CA: University of California Press.

Mandler, J. (1983). Representation. In P. Mussen (ed.), *Handbook of child psychology*, Vol. III. New York: Wiley.

Margules, J. and Gallistel, C. (1988). Heading in the rat: Determination by environmental shape. *Animal Learning and Behavior*, 10.

Marzolf, D. and DeLoache, J. (1994). Transfer in young children's understanding of spatial representations. *Child Development*, 65.

Mead, G.H. (1934). *Mind, self, and society*. Chicago, IL: University of Chicago Press.

Mead, M. (1964). *Continuities in cultural evolution*. New Haven, CT: Yale University Press.

Meringoff, L. (1978). The influence of the medium on children's apprehension of stories. Unpublished doctoral dissertation, Harvard University, MA.

Messick, S. (1988). Validity. In R. Linn (ed.), *Educational measurement* (third edition). New York: Macmillan.

Mithen, S. (1996). *The prehistory of the mind*. London: Thames & Hudson.

Moran, S. and Gardner, H. (in press). The development of extraordinary achievements. In W. Damon (ed.), *Handbook of child psychology* (sixth edition), Vol. II: *Cognition, Perception and Language*. New York: Wiley.

Murnane, R. and Levy, F. (1996). *Teaching the new basic skill: Principles for educating children to thrive in a changing economy*. New York: Free Press.

Neisser, U. (1998). *The rising curve*. Washington, DC: The American Psychological Association.

Newell, A. (1980). Physical symbol systems. *Cognitive Science*, 4.

Ogden, C.K. and Richards, I.A. (1929). *The meaning of meaning*. London: Kegan Paul.

Olson, D. (1970). *Cognitive development*. New York: Academic Press.

Olson, D. (1994). *The world on paper*. New York: Cambridge University Press.

Pascual-Leone, J. (1970). A mathematical model for the transition rule in Piaget's developmental stages. *Acta Psychologica*, 63.

Peirce, C.S. (1933). *Collected papers*. C. Hartshorne and P. Weiss, (eds.). Cambridge, MA: Harvard University Press.

Pepper, S. (1942). *World hypotheses*. Berkeley, CA: University of California Press.

Perkins, D. (1981). *The mind's best work*. Cambridge, MA: Harvard University Press.

Perkins, D. (1992). *Smart schools*. New York: Free Press.

Perkins, D. and Leondar, B. (1977). *The arts and cognition*. Baltimore, MD: Johns Hopkins University Press.

Phenix, P. (1964). *Realms of meaning*. New York: McGraw-Hill.

Piaget, J. (1929). *The child's conception of the world*. New York: Harcourt Brace.

Piaget, J. (1962). *Play, dreams, and imitation*. New York: Norton.

Piaget, J. (1983). Piaget's theory. In P. Mussen (ed.), *Handbook of child psychology*, Vol. I. New York: John Wiley.

Piechowski, M. (1993)."Origins" without origins. *Creativity Research Journal*, 6(4).

Polanyi, M. (1958). *Personal knowledge*. Chicago, IL: University of Chicago Press.

Posner, M.I. (2004). Neural systems and individual differences. *Teachers College Record*, 106(1).

Pylyshyn, Z. (1973). What the mind's eye tells the mind's brain: A critique of mental imagery. *Psychological Bulletin*, 80.

Ravitch, D. and Finn, C. (1987). *What do our seventeen year olds know?* New York: Harper & Row.

Resnick, L. (1987). *Education and learning to think*. Washington, DC: National Academy Press.

Resnick, L. (ed.) (1989). *Knowing, learning and instruction: Essays in honor of Robert Glaser*. Hillsdale, NJ: Lawrence Erlbaum.

Rheingold, H. and Cook, K. (1975). The content of boys' and girls' rooms as an index of parents' behavior. *Child Development*, 46.

Richards, I.A. (1929). *Practical criticism*. New York: Harcourt Brace. Republished in 1956.

Rock, I. (1974). *Orientation and form*. New York: Academic Press.

Rogoff, B. (1982). Integrating context and cognitive development. In M. Lamb and A. Brown (eds.), *Advances in developmental psychology*, Vol. II. Hillsdale, NJ: Lawrence Erlbaum.

Rogoff, B. (1990). *Apprenticeship in thinking*. New York: Oxford University Press.

Rosnow, R., Skedler, A., Jaeger, M., and Rin, B. (1994). Intelligence and the epistemics of interpersonal acumen: Testing some implications of Gardner's theory. *Intelligence*, 19.

Rumelhart, D. and McClelland, J. (1986). *Parallel distributed systems*. Cambridge, MA: MIT Press.

Salomon, G. (1978). The "languages" of media and the cultivation of mental skills. Paper presented at the American Educational Research Association, Toronto.

Salovey, P. and Mayer, J. (1990). Emotional intelligence. *Imagination, Cognition and Personality*, 9.

Scarr, S. (1985). An author's frame of mind: Review of *Frames of mind* by Howard Gardner. *New Ideas in Psychology*, 3(1).

Schwab, J. (1978). *Science curriculum and liberal education*. Chicago, IL: University of Chicago Press.

Scribner, S. (1986). Thinking in action: Some characteristics of practical thought. In R. Sternberg and R. Wagner (eds.), *Practical intelligence*. New York: Cambridge University Press.

Scribner, S. and Cole, M. (1973). Cognitive consequences of formal and informal education. *Science*, 182.

Selman, R.L. (1974). *The development of conceptions of interpersonal relations*. Boston, MA: Harvard Judge Baker Social Reasoning Project.

Sergent, J. (1993). Music, the brain and Ravel. *Trends in Neurosciences*, 16(5).

Shotwell, J., Wolf, D., and Gardner, H. (1979). Exploring early symbolization: Styles of achievement. In B. Sutton-Smith (ed.), *Playing and Learning*. New York: Gardner Press.

Sizer, T. (1984). *Horace's compromise*. Boston, MA: Houghton Mifflin.

Sizer, T. (1992). *Horace's school*. Boston, MA: Houghton Mifflin.

Skinner, B.F (1938). *The behavior of organisms*. New York: Appleton Century Crofts.

Sloboda, J. (1994). Musical performance: Expression and the development of excellence. In R. Aiello and J. Sloboda (eds.), *Musical perceptions*. New York: Oxford University Press.

Smolensky, P. (1989). On the proper treatment of connectionism. *The Behavioral and Brain Sciences*, 11(1).

Spearman, C. (1904). General intelligence, objectively determined and measured. *American Journal of Psychology*, 15.

Squire, L. (1986). Mechanisms of memory. *Science*, 232.

Sternberg, R. (1985). *Beyond IQ: A triarchic theory of human intelligence*. New York: Cambridge University Press.

Stevens, A. and Coupe, P. (1978). Distortions in judged spatial relations. *Cognitive Psychology*, 10.

Stiles-Davis, J. (1988). Spatial dysfunctions in young children with right cerebral hemisphere injury. In J. Stiles-Davis, U. Bellugi, and M. Kritchevsky (eds.), *Spatial cognition: Brain bases and development*. Hillsdale, NJ: Lawrence Erlbaum.

Suarez-Orozco, C. (2003). Formulating identity in a globalized world. In M. Suarez-Orozco and D. Qin-Hilliard (eds.), *Globalization: Culture and education in the new millennium*. Berkeley, CA: University of California Press.

Suarez-Orozco, M. and Qin-Hilliard, D. (2003). Globalization: Culture and education in the new millennium. In M. Suarez-Orozco and D. Qin-Hilliard (eds.), *Globalization: Culture and education in the new millennium*. Berkeley, CA: University of California Press.

Swanwick, K. and Tillman, J. (1986). The sequence of musical development: A study of children's composition. *British Journal of Music Education*, 3.

Terman, L. (1916). *The measurement of intelligence*. Boston, MA: Houghton Mifflin.

Thurstone, L.L. (1938). *Primary mental abilities*. Chicago, IL: University of Chicago Press.

Tomasello, M. (2000). *The cultural origins of cognition*. Cambridge, MA: Harvard University Press.

Tompkins, S. (1963). *Affect, imagery and consciousness*, 2 vols. New York: Springer.

Tooby, J. and Cosmides, L. (1991). The psychological foundations of culture. In J. Barkow, L. Cosmides, and J. Tooby (eds.), *The adapted mind*. New York: Oxford University Press.

Torff, B. and Winner, E. (1994). Don't throw out the baby with the bathwater: On the role of innate factors in musical accomplishment. *The Psychologist*, August.

Traub, J. (1998). Multiple intelligence disorder. *New Republic*, October 26.

Turkle, S. (1997). *Life on the screen: Identity in the age of the Internet*. New York: Touchstone.

Tversky, B. (1981). Distortions in memory for maps. *Cognitive Psychology*, 13.

Viscott, D. (1970). A musical *idiot savant*. *Psychiatry*, 33.

Vygotsky, L. (1978). *Mind in society*. Cambridge, MA: Harvard University Press.

Walker, G. (2002a). Reflections on the International Baccalaureate. Paper presented at the Retreat on Education and Globalization, Tarrytown, NY, April 2002.

Walker, G. (2002b). *To educate the nations*. Suffolk, NY: John Cart Educational Limited.

Walters, J. and Gardner, H. (1986). The crystallizing experience: Discovery of an intellectual gift. In R. Sternberg and J. Davidson (eds.), *Conceptions of giftedness*. New York: Cambridge University Press.

Wapner, W. and Gardner, H. (1978). *Symbol use in organic patients*. Chicago, IL: Academy of Aphasia.

Watson, J. (2003). Globalization in Asia: Anthropological perspectives. In M. Suarez-Orozco and D. Qin-Hilliard (eds.), *Globalization: Culture and education in the new millennium*. Berkeley, CA: University of California Press.

Watson, J.S. (1968). Conservation: An S-R analysis. In I. Sigel and F. Hooper (eds.), *Logical thinking in children*. New York: Holt, Rinehart & Winston.

Werner, H. (1948). *Comparative psychology of mental development*. New York: Harper & Row.

Werner, H. and Kaplan, B. (1963). *Symbol formation*. New York: Wiley.

Wexler-Sherman, C., Gardner, H. and Feldman, D. (1988). A pluralistic view of early assessment: The Project Spectrum approach. *Theory into Practice*, 27.

White, J. with Rumsey, S. (1993). Teaching for understanding in a third-grade geography lesson. In J. Brophy (ed.), *Advances in research on teaching*, Vol. IV. Greenwich, CT: JAI Press.

White, S. (1976). Quotation from *Spencer Foundation Annual Report*. Chicago, IL: Spencer Foundation.

Whitehead, A.N. (1929). *The aims of education*. New York: Free Press.

Willats, J. (1977). How children learn to represent three-dimensional space in drawings. In G. Butterworth (ed.), *The child's representation of the world*. New York: Plenum Press.

Williams, W., Blythe, T., White, N., Li, J., Sternberg, R., and Gardner, H. (eds.) (1996). *Practical intelligence for children*. New York: Harper Collins.

Winner, E. (1982). *Invented worlds*. Cambridge, MA: Harvard University Press.

Winner, E. (ed.) (1992). *Arts PROPEL handbooks*. Cambridge, MA: Harvard Project Zero.

Winner, E. (n.d.). The history of Howard Gardner. Available at <http://www. howardgardner.com/bio/bio.html>.

Winner, E., Rosenblatt, E., Windmueller, G., Davidson, L., and Gardner, H. (1986). Children's perception of "esthetic" properties of the arts: Domain-specific or pan-artistic? *British Journal of Developmental Psychology*, 4.

Wiske, M.S. (1998). *Teaching for understanding*. San Francisco, CA: Jossey-Bass.

Witelson, S. and Swallow, J. (1988). Neuropsychological study of the development of spatial cognition. In J. Stiles-Davis, U. Bellugi, and M. Kritchevsky (eds.), *Spatial cognition: Brain bases and development*. Hillsdale, NJ: Lawrence Erlbaum.

Witkin, H., Dyk, R.B., Faterson, H.D., Goodenough, D.R., and Karp, S. (1962). *Psychological diffentiation*. New York: Wiley.

Wolf, D. (1986). All the pieces that go into it: The multiple stances of arts education. In A. Hurwitz (ed.), *Aesthetics in education: The missing dimension*. Mattituck, MD: Amercon House.

Wolf, D. (1988a). Opening up assessment. *Educational Leadership*, 45 (4).

Wolf, D. (1988b). Artistic learning: What and where is it? *Journal of Aesthetic Education*, 22(1).

Wolf, D. and Gardner, H. (1979). Style and sequence in early symbolic play. In N.R. Smith and M.B. Franklin (eds.), *Symbolic functioning in children*. Hillsdale, NJ: Lawrence Erlbaum.

Wolf, D. and Gardner, H. (1980). Beyond playing or polishing: The development of artistry. In J. Hausman (ed.), *The arts and the schools*. New York: McGraw Hill.

Wolf, D. and Gardner, H. (1981). On the structure of early symbolization. In R. Schiefelbush and D. Bricker (eds.), *Early language: Acquisition and intervention*. Baltimore, MD: University Park Press.

Wolf, D and Gardner, H. (eds.) (1988). *The making of meanings*. Harvard Project Zero Technical Report.

Wolf, D., Davidson, L., Davis, M., Walters, J., Hodges, M., and Scripp, L. (1988). Beyond A, B, and C: A broader and deeper view of literacy. In A. Pelligrini (ed.), *Psychological bases of early education*. Chichester: Wiley.

Woo, E. (1995). Teaching that goes beyond IQ. *Los Angeles Times*, January 20, pp. A1 and A22.

INDEX

education 222; and responsibility 240; suitability for formal testing 173; in survey of cognitive strengths 180

science of learning 227–8

scientific advances 236–7; influence on education 208, 214, 216–17, 219; restraints preventing abuse of 237–8, 238

scientific theories 227–8

Scripp, L. 203

scripts/stereotypes 211; on difficulties in arts and humanities 138, 141

Second World War: Bruner's work 19; Goodman's work as psychologist 24

Selman, R.L. 43

semiotics: symbol systems 199

sensory and motor systems 42

September 11 2001 events 224

sexual intelligence 91

Shady Hill School, Cambridge: Massachusetts 2

Sharpsburg *see Antietam/Sharpsburg* (CD-ROM)

The Shattered Mind (Gardner) 87

Silicon Valley 223

Simon, Herbert 30

Simon, Théodore 133

Sizer, Theodore 25, 28, 148, 209

skills: acquisition of 210; assessment in apprenticeship 171; for education in global society 223–5; increasing importance of expertise 195–6; needed for inter-disciplinary work 221; relations with symbol systems 42; training 49; *see also* basic skills

Skinner, B.F. 1, 15, 16, 19, 75, 216–17, 217; view of child 2–3, 125, 194

Smalley, George W 79

social intelligence: in survey of cognitive strengths 180

societal activities 91–2

society: professionals' ethical responsibility to 238, 239

Socrates 12, 120

Soviet Union 20, 25

spatial cognition 200, 204–6; education and achievement 206–8

spatial intelligence 49, 55, 85, 91;

mobilization through symbolic products 100; testing 176

Spearman, Charles 64, 217–18

Sperry, Roger 30

spiritual intelligence 58, 91

Sputnik satellite 20, 25

Stalin, Joseph 70

standards: in judgment of work 197; lack of for inter-disciplinary work 221

Star Wars 'script' 139

Steel, Claude 65

stereotypes *see* scripts/stereotypes

Sternberg, Robert 66–7, 89

stories *see* narrative/stories

Stork, Janet 89

Stravinsky, Igor 121

student projects 165

student-curriculum broker 51, 187–8

students: aiding through new approach to assessment 178; author's examples on understanding 134–5, 136, 137–8, 139; 'crystallizing experiences' 188–9; experience of alienation 234; in findings from education for understanding 157; lack of understanding of disciplines 146; observation of 143; scenario of formal testing 171; use of information technologies 230

Sturgis, Katharine 24

subject matters 147–8; distinction with disciplines 219–20; *see also* topics

symbol systems 38–42; approach in music education 200–4; approach in spatial domain 204–8; approach to human development 195, 197–200, 212; in the arts 25, 98; author's work at Project Zero (Harvard) 9, 10, 98; Piaget's disregard for 37, 40–2; relation to other lines of inquiry 42–3; two distinct meanings 199

symbolic development 43–4

symbolic products 99–100

Szilard, Leo 237

talents 58

'teacher's fallacy' 148, 157

teachers: Chinese 123; establishment of